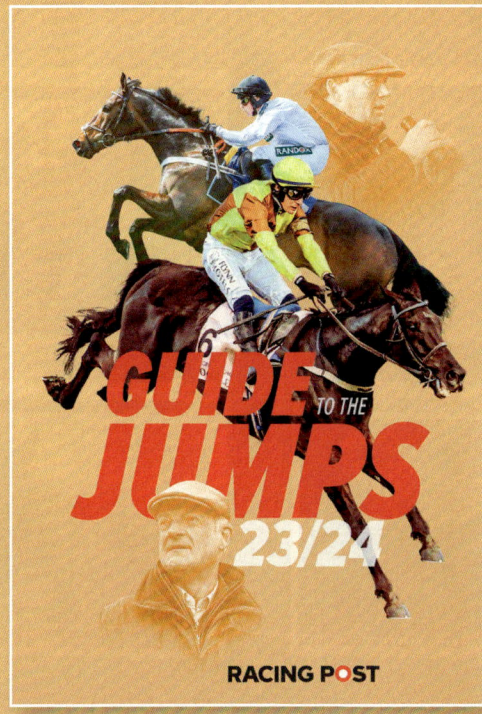

Edited and designed by David Dew

Contributors

Richard Birch
James Burn
Ian Greensill
Dylan Hill
Lawrie Kelsey

Graeme Rodway
Craig Thake
Nick Watts
Robbie Wilders

Cover artwork by Duncan Olner

Inside artwork by Stefan Searle

Published in 2023 by Pitch Publishing on behalf of Racing Post, A2 Yeoman Gate, Yeoman Way, Worthing, Sussex, BN13 3QZ.

Copyright © Pitch Publishing and Racing Post, 2023. Every effort has been made to trace the copyright holders. Any oversight will be rectified in future editions at the earliest opportunity by the publisher.

All rights reserved. No part of this book may be reproduced, sold or utilised in any form or transmitted in any form or by any means, electronic or mechanical, including photocopying, recording or by any information storage and retrieval system, without prior permission in writing from the publisher. Pitch Publishing specifies that post-press changes may occur to any information given in this publication. A catalogue record for this book is available from the British Library.

ISBN: 978-1839501302

Printed by Pureprint

RACING POST

GUIDE TO THE JUMPS **2023-24**

LOWDOWN FROM THE TRAINERS

Harry Derham Upper Farm Stables, Boxford, Berkshire	4-11
Harry Fry Higher Crockermoor, Corscombe, Dorset	14-21
Nicky Henderson Seven Barrows, Upper Lambourn, Berkshire	22-29
Anthony Honeyball Potwell Farm Stables, Beaminster, Dorset	30-36
Emma Lavelle Bonita Racing Stables, Marlborough, Wiltshire	38-45
Charlie Longsdon Hull Farm Stables, Chipping Norton, Oxfordshire	46-55
Neil Mulholland Conkwell Lodge Stables, Limpley Stoke, Bath	56-63
Paul Nicholls Manor Farm Stables, Ditcheat, Somerset	64-70
Jamie Snowden Folly House, Upper Lambourn, Berkshire	72-80
Evan Williams Fingerpost Farm, Llancarfan, Vale of Glamorgan	82-87

RACING POST EXPERTS

Graeme Rodway Festival fancies	89-97
Nick Watts Ante-post analysis	98-100
Richard Birch My ten for the season	102-105
Robbie Wilders Below the radar	106-108

THIS SEASON'S KEY HORSES

Key horses who can make a mark this season	110-203
Key horses listed by trainer	204-205
Index of horses	206-208

RACING POST

HARRY DERHAM

Start of a new era

THERE can't be many better feelings for a trainer than watching a careful plan succeed, which is precisely what Harry Derham achieved on Boxing Day last year.

His first runner as a new trainer had been laid out for a race at Huntingdon, and the plan came together in perfect style.

Six years' experience of being assistant to his uncle and champion trainer Paul Nicholls was poured into preparing **Seelotmorebusiness** for the modest

GUIDE TO THE JUMPS **2023-24**

WINNERS LAST SEASON 14

Harry Derham: made the perfect start to his training career when his first runner was a winner

"I was very pleased indeed with my first season. You hope your first four months will go like they did"

Harry Derham's string works up the Peter Walwyn gallop in Upper Lambourn

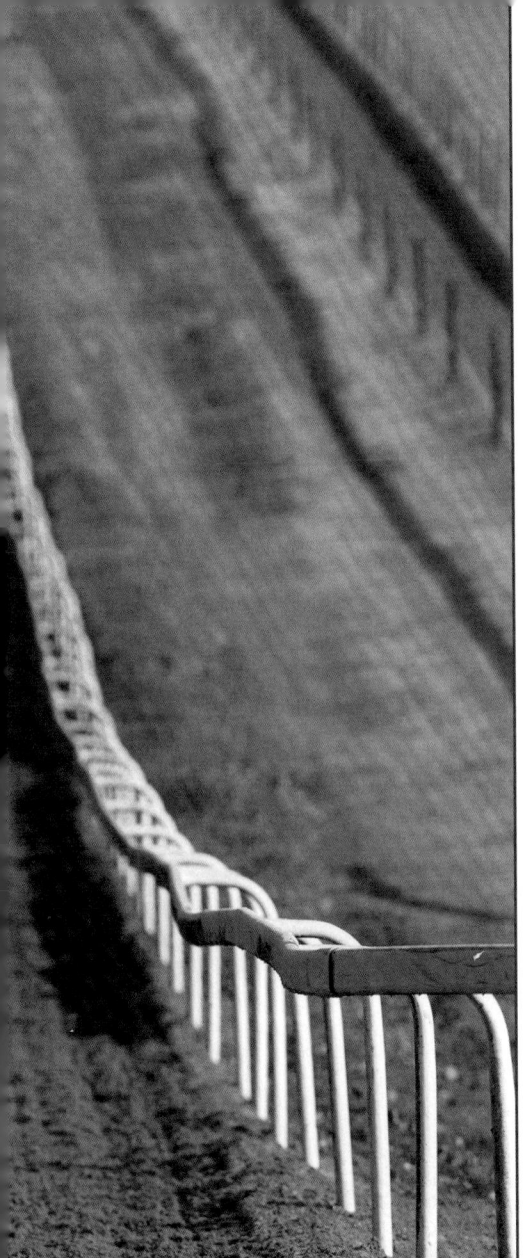

GUIDE TO THE JUMPS 2023-24

Huntingdon hurdle, but the prize was at the opposite end of the pleasure scale compared with it being his first winner from his first runner – and owned by his mother Julie.

"This is a feeling I cannot describe," he wrote in a subsequent blog on his website, which is as good a description of watching a plan blossom as any trainer has written, and is well worth a read.

"It was amazing. I absolutely loved it. It was one of those days you never ever think you'll be lucky enough to have. It was just surreal," remembers Derham.

"We were excited to run him and we thought he'd win. But you only get one chance with your first runner. He won by twelve lengths but he could have won by a hundred lengths and I couldn't have cared less. I would never ever change that day. It was extraordinary."

Derham ended his first season with 14 winners from a string of 20 at an impressive strike-rate of 25 per cent, although eight-year-old "Sid", as everyone in the yard calls him, failed to add to his 12-length Huntingdon romp in two further outings after his rating rose 11lb.

"I was very pleased indeed with my first season. You hope your first four months will go like they did. My horses were healthy and they ran well, but it comes back to having good support from good people and if you've got good horses, then you've got a chance."

This season Derham's 51 boxes are "full to the brim" at his purpose-built Upper Farm Stables in Boxford, five miles north-east of Newbury, just under 20 of which came from Lambourn trainer Oliver Sherwood, who retired this summer after almost 40 years with a licence.

Sherwood, who won the 2015 Grand National with Many Clouds, joined his horses by becoming assistant trainer to Derham, who described the new relationship as "a big positive".

He adds: "I'm very much looking forward to the new season. You just hope the horses

7

stay healthy and from then on you just hope you have a bit of luck."

The eight-year-old **Dargiannini** did well last season, winning at Uttoxeter and Newbury, although he subsequently finished down the field at Aintree and then perhaps found three miles and half a furlong at Haydock too far in May.

"He's probably not that well handicapped this season," admits Derham. "He'll start at Newbury's Coral Gold Cup meeting over two and a half miles and then go on from there."

Brentford Hope, who won three times and reached a rating of 107 at one point on the Flat for Richard Hughes, joined Derham in the spring and won his first two outings over hurdles comfortably at Wincanton and Huntingdon before finishing sixth in the Swinton Hurdle at Haydock.

"The ground went a bit quick for him in the Swinton and he never really got going," says the trainer, who plans to start the six-year-old this season in the Gerry Feilden at Newbury.

The four-year-old filly **Bella Civena** made an impressive racecourse debut over hurdles in soft ground at Market Rasen in late March against a couple of rivals with winning form, and on that performance looks to have a bright future.

"She won well for me and she's a nice filly," says Derham, who aims to start her in a mares' novice hurdle in November when she's likely to get her ground.

The Two Harrys, owned by Harry Redknapp, is described by Derham as "a lovely horse" after the four-year-old finished third in a Wincanton bumper in April.

"He ran well but the ground went a little bit quick for him on the day and we probably ran him at the wrong track. I imagine he'll

Dargiannini: could struggle from his current mark, warns Derham

GUIDE TO THE JUMPS **2023-24**

A level £1 stake on all of Harry Derham's runners during his first season returned a profit of £29.77

probably have another run in a bumper before he goes novice hurdling," says Derham.

The six-year-old gelding **Any Biscuits** was a winner at Market Rasen and Exeter for the yard in the spring and could have more to offer this season.

"He was great last season. He's been tricky and was very keen on his first few starts, so we've just been trying to get him settled," says Derham.

"I should think he can improve again. Although he's not obviously well handicapped now, he's a very willing horse and is genuine, and I hope he can improve to win again."

The four-year-old **Salvatore** had some decent form on the Flat in France last year, winning twice in the provinces, and is being lined up for a first season over hurdles.

"He's had plenty of time and will be ready to go novice hurdling at the start of November and, as long as the ground isn't quick, he'll be fine," says Derham.

Queens Gamble is a talented mare who won two bumpers at Cheltenham for Sherwood in 2022, including a Listed race, and was a creditable 12th in the Champion Bumper at the festival meeting.

Unsurprisingly, she was long odds-on to land her first start over hurdles at Warwick in May, duly obliging by almost five lengths.

"Hopefully, she can turn into a Listed mare," says Derham, perhaps with the Mares' Novices' Hurdle at the festival in mind as an end-of-season target.

Monviel has moved to Derham from Philip Hobbs's Somerset yard for whom the six-year-old won an Ascot handicap hurdle last season, and was then a solid fifth in both the Betfair Hurdle and the Imperial Cup, two highly competitive Grade 3s.

He looks a useful recruit over fences and could pay his way when the rain arrives.

"He looks a nice horse to go novice chasing. He'll be out in October somewhere and, as long as the ground isn't quick, he'll be fine."

Another who could make the transition from hurdles to fences and should be followed is **Picks Lad**, a novice handicap hurdle winner for Kim Bailey's yard in April and who was bought by Derham for £25,000 at Goffs horses-in-training sale. "He looks potentially well treated to go novice chasing," says the trainer.

Make a note of **Mojo Ego**, who has arrived from France where he finished fifth in a Group 3 on the Flat last year after winning a seven-furlong maiden for Jean-Claude Rouget.

"He's come to me to go three-year-old hurdling and looks like he could be a good fun juvenile hurdler. He'll be out at the end of October," says Derham.

Ascending Lark is a "nice mare" who was placed in two of her three Irish bumpers and will go novice hurdling. I think she'll do quite nicely but she won't run until the end of November."

Another ex-Sherwood horse to watch closely is the five-year-old **Scrum Diddly**, who won two handicap hurdles in runaway fashion and finished second in a third race over a 15-day period in May.

Not surprisingly, Derham hopes the gelding can transfer his hurdling prowess to fences. "He looks a nice horse to go chasing," says the trainer.

Siroco Jo was bought privately out of Paul Nicholls' yard where he won twice over hurdles. "He'll be a horse to go novice handicap chasing this season and should be a fun horse."

Derham's pick from all his horses to follow is the former Irish pointer **Il Va De Soi**, who marked himself out after a promising debut in a Kempton bumper when beaten in a photo finish. He then finished fourth in a Taunton bumper behind the well-regarded **Geezer Rockstar**.

"He'll be a nice novice hurdler. He looks a much more mature horse this season, jumps well and I'm hopeful for him. He'll be out in early November."

Interview by Lawrie Kelsey

GUIDE TO THE JUMPS **2023-24**

HARRY DERHAM
BOXFORD, BERKSHIRE

RECORD AROUND THE COURSES

	Total W-R	Per cent	Non-hcp Hdle	Non-hcp Chase	Hcp Hdle	Hcp Chase	N.H. Flat	£1 level stake
Wincanton	3-11	27.3	1-3	0-0	1-5	1-2	0-1	+2.17
Huntingdon	2-3	66.7	1-2	0-0	1-1	0-0	0-0	+11.10
Market Rasen	2-3	66.7	1-1	0-0	1-1	0-1	0-0	+8.50
Southwell	1-1	100.0	0-0	0-0	0-0	1-1	0-0	+1.25
Doncaster	1-2	50.0	1-1	0-0	0-0	0-1	0-0	+3.00
Exeter	1-2	50.0	0-1	0-0	1-1	0-0	0-0	+2.50
Newbury	1-2	50.0	0-1	0-0	1-1	0-0	0-0	+1.00
Wetherby	1-3	33.3	1-2	0-0	0-1	0-0	0-0	+23.00
Uttoxeter	1-3	33.3	0-0	0-0	1-2	0-1	0-0	+3.50
Haydock	1-3	33.3	1-1	0-0	0-2	0-0	0-0	-1.20
Kempton	1-3	33.3	1-2	0-0	0-0	0-0	0-1	-1.80
Ludlow	0-1	0.0	0-1	0-0	0-0	0-0	0-0	-1.00
Hereford	0-1	0.0	0-1	0-0	0-0	0-0	0-0	-1.00
Catterick	0-1	0.0	0-1	0-0	0-0	0-0	0-0	-1.00
Lingfield	0-1	0.0	0-1	0-0	0-0	0 0	0-0	-1.00
Worcester	0-1	0.0	0-1	0-0	0-0	0-0	0-0	-1.00
Ascot	0-1	0.0	0-0	0-0	0-1	0-0	0-0	-1.00
Plumpton	0-1	0.0	0-0	0-0	0-1	0-0	0-0	-1.00
Aintree	0-2	0.0	0-1	0-0	0-1	0-0	0-0	-2.00
Chepstow	0-2	0.0	0-1	0-0	0-1	0-0	0-0	-2.00
Cheltenham	0-2	0.0	0-0	0-1	0-1	0-0	0-0	-2.00
Fontwell	0-2	0.0	0-0	0-0	0-2	0-0	0-0	-2.00
Ffos Las	0-2	0.0	0-1	0-0	0-0	0-1	0-0	-2.00
Musselburgh	0-2	0.0	0-1	0-0	0-0	0-1	0-0	-2.00
Newton Abbot	0-3	0.0	0-3	0-0	0-0	0-0	0-0	-3.00
Taunton	0-7	0.0	0-2	0-1	0-2	0-1	0-1	-7.00

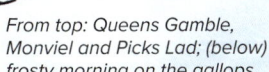

From top: Queens Gamble, Monviel and Picks Lad; (below) frosty morning on the gallops

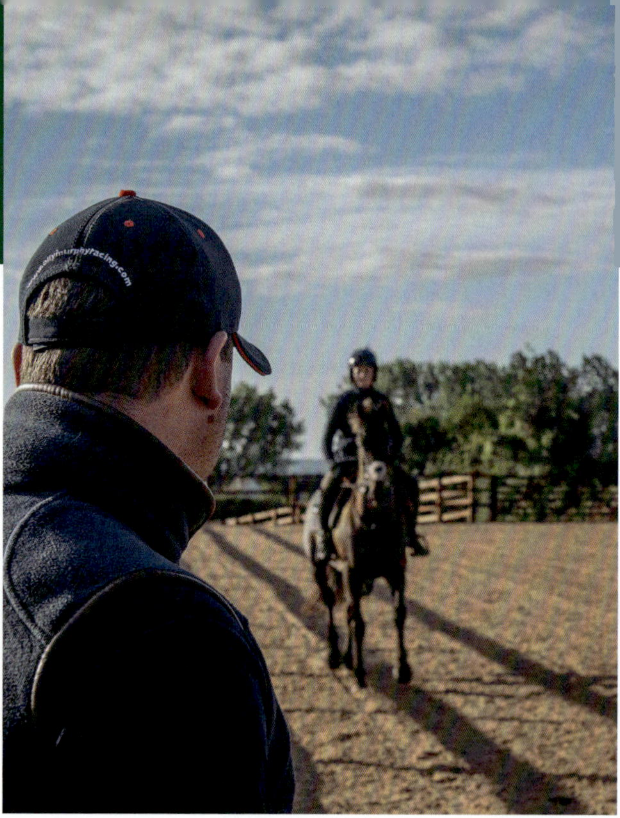

Offering quality and consistency, our high-performance surfaces have been designed to support the movements of horses, allowing them to work deeper in the surface, meaning riders can work confidently and with peace of mind.

THE CUSHION TRACK SURFACE RANGE IS BROUGHT TO YOU BY EQUESTRIAN SURFACES LTD.

CUSHION TRACK
RACING

We're proud to have supplied our Cushion Track surfaces to some of the industry's most respected trainers, including **Nicky Henderson**, **Charlie Longsdon**, **Olly Murphy**, **Warren Greatrex**, **Ed Walker** and **Richard Hughes**.

HARRY FRY

It must be Love

LOVE ENVOI, who was a gallant second to Honeysuckle in the Mares' Hurdle at the Cheltenham Festival in March, will return for another crack at winning it.

First, however, the seven-year-old must satisfy connections she is back to her best after recovering from a leg fracture sustained on her last outing at the Punchestown festival.

"Our sole focus will be on trying to go one better

GUIDE TO THE JUMPS **2023-24**

WINNERS IN LAST FIVE SEASONS 39, 38, 31, 30, 47

Love Envoi: flagbearer for the Fry stable

■ Fry has a strike-rate of 24% in bumpers, which translates to a level-stake profit of £61.80

> Boothill (right) is still lightly raced and I'd like to think he could win another valuable prize. There are races at Ascot in November and Kempton over Christmas, such as the Desert Orchid

this time around," says Fry. "She can be forgiven her run at Punchestown because she came back with a stress fracture of her left fore, which explained why she was hanging left.

"We were quite fortunate really. The vet told us after a scan it wouldn't have taken much for it to go completely."

Owned by the Noel Fehily syndicate, Love Envoi – known around Fry's purpose-built yard at Higher Crockermoor Farm in Dorset as Polly, "which solves any debate about Envoy or Envoi" – has been recovering at Fehily's pre-training facilities at Hagg Hill Farm, a few miles over the county border in Wiltshire.

"She's fully recovered and is in work but she won't realistically be seen out before Christmas time at the earliest," says Fry.

"Her whole campaign will be geared towards the Mares' Hurdle and trying to go one better in March, so she'll follow a similar route to last season, all being well. The races pick themselves – those good mares' races – taking in the Sandown race she won in January. If we can get her there in the same sort of form as last season, you'd like to think we'd have a very good chance.

"I can't think of any other British mares rated higher than her and there won't be any Honeysuckle, but there will be plenty

GUIDE TO THE JUMPS **2023-24**

of other mares to worry about."

Gin Coco is another stable favourite who is expected to pay his way again. Runner-up in the Grade 3 Greatwood at Cheltenham, the seven-year-old returned to the track in March but was unplaced in the County Hurdle.

"We kept him for a spring campaign but he came back from the County Hurdle with a pelvic stress fracture, which explained his below-par performance," says Fry.

"He's back after making a full recovery and we feel there's a decent handicap hurdle in him. There are a number of options. There's the two-mile handicap at Ascot in their first fixture in November or we could wait for the Greatwood at Cheltenham the same month.

"Then, on the back of that, we'll decide whether we go novice chasing or not, although we might stick to hurdling; there are plenty of valuable handicaps to be won."

Might I might have been expected to win last season after being placed in Grade 1 and Grade 2 races the season before, but things "didn't work out" with fourth in the Martin Pipe at Cheltenham the best he could manage.

"We'll send him novice chasing this season over two, two and a half miles and see how

17

he progresses. Hopefully, he'll make up into a chaser. I'd like to think he'll be out in the second half of October."

In the same Brian and Sandy Lambert ownership as Might I is **Boothill**, the yard's joint-highest-rated horse on 153 with Love Envoi, and leading prize-money winner with just over £137,000.

He was a model of consistency in his last six races, winning three, finishing second twice and third once.

"He had a very fruitful campaign, including finishing runner-up to Jonbon in the Grade 1 Henry VIII at Sandown and winning the Grade 2 Wayward Lad at Kempton," says Fry.

"We tried him over two and a half in the Pendil at Kempton but his preference is for a strongly run two.

"He's still lightly raced and I'd like to think he could win another valuable prize. There are races at Ascot in November and Kempton over Christmas, such as the Desert Orchid.

"He runs off 149 and if he were to win one of those he could be running in level-weights conditions races. The Grand Annual could be on the agenda but we'll see where we are at the turn of the year first."

The supremely versatile dual-purpose **Metier** is a yard favourite having top and tailed his season with victory in the November Handicap over a mile and a half in heavy ground at Doncaster, and the 2m2½f Chester Cup on soft ground in May.

"He'll be campaigned again on the Flat in the Prix Royal-Oak [1m7½f] at Longchamp in October if the conditions are right. You'd like to think he'd get his conditions at that time of year," says Fry, who has opted not to run him on Ascot Champions Day or in the Cesarewitch.

"His handicap hurdle rating is down to 139, the mark of his last victory at Lingfield in heavy ground, so I think it'll be too tempting not to have another go, probably up in trip to two and a half and maybe further. But we'll wait to see how he does on the Flat first."

Monjules was joint-top leading horse in the yard numerically with three victories and was slightly unlucky not to win a fourth when clouting the last flight at Fontwell, then hanging right on the run-in.

"He's a versatile horse," says Fry. "He was second on the Flat at Salisbury and could run again on the Flat, but he jumps well, so we could look sooner rather than later at putting him over fences. He did well for us last season and there's more to come this season."

That group of six forms the nucleus of Fry's first team but it will definitely pay to take note of "some lovely young horses coming through" as the Higher Crockermoor demographic of its 60-strong string changes

Metier (left): versatile performer with big wins over hurdles and on the Flat

after older inmates have been retired or sold.

One of the main hopes is **Credrojava**, a promising five-year-old who is unbeaten in three mares' races, including a Listed novice hurdle at Taunton in December.

"She's done nothing wrong. Unfortunately, she picked up a tendon injury which ruled her out for the rest of the campaign. So, all being well, she'll be out for the second half of the season.

"Stamina won her the race at Taunton and a step up in trip is definitely on the cards. Whether she's progressed enough to think about the Mares' Hurdle at Cheltenham, we'll have to wait and see.

"She's a mare we're looking forward to jumping a fence, but because she'll only have half the season, it's not the time to go chasing."

Gidleigh Park is another five-year-old for whom big things are hoped for, if not expected, after winning a Chepstow bumper in March in runaway style on his only start.

"He's another one who will jump a fence in time," says Fry. "He couldn't have been much more impressive on his racecourse debut and the form has worked out well. The runner-up has won since and others have been placed.

"He's a lovely, big, rangy horse who we hope can take high rank in novice hurdles over two and a half miles this year.

"We'll start him off on a galloping track and get some experience into him before we raise his sights and up him in grade."

Altobelli is yet another of Fry's five-year-olds expected to fill the Crockermoor coffers. He won twice last season, including over two and a half miles at Carlisle by a wide margin.

He had a break and reappeared in the Grade 1 Top Novices' Hurdle at Aintree in April but failed to fire and finished down the field.

"It wasn't ideal sending a young horse that far but we needed to get a run into him. Unfortunately, the Carlisle race left its mark; the long journey and the race took too much

out of him. We had to take a chance at Aintree but you can forget that result.

"But what it means is we have a fairly unexposed, second-season hurdler. We'll get a run into him in early November to give him more experience with a view to targeting a valuable two-mile handicap hurdle at Ascot just before Christmas.

"He loves soft ground and will be very competitive in other two-mile handicaps and we're really looking forward to him."

Hymac ran only twice last season, finishing third at Ffos Las and second at Chepstow on Welsh Grand National day when caught in the final stride.

"I still don't know how he lost out in the photo-finish at Chepstow," muses Fry. "He's always been a chaser in the making and we're looking forward to running over two and a half on soft ground. It's just a case of getting a bit more experience into him and taking it from there."

Beat The Bat won his bumper at Chepstow, but found a Grade 2 bumper too hot at Aintree.

"He's a lovely young horse but he got lit up and ran with the choke out," says Fry, who will start him off in novice hurdles. "Whether he makes a Graded horse or a handicapper by next spring we'll have to wait and see."

Geezer Rockstar is another debut-making bumper winner to follow. The four-year-old gelding by Getaway is from a chasing family but had the speed to be a comfortable winner on the Flat at Taunton in the spring.

"He's not really a bumper type, so that was a bonus winning like that on debut," says Fry. "That was a good sign, nonetheless, so I'm really looking forward to seeing him in novice hurdles this season."

Silver Jet is a new recruit who fetched £125,000 after finishing a close second on his only start in an Irish point-to-point in March.

"He's a tall, striking son of Getaway who looked an out-and-out galloper that day. He's another for the novice hurdle division and we'll start him out over two and a half at a galloping track."

Great Snow was bought at the Dai Walters dispersal sale at Goffs in May for £100,000. The six-year-old mare did well for Neil Mulholland last year, winning once and was placed five times in her last six races, and could be aimed at a mares' handicap hurdle at Wincanton in November.

"It's a race we've won several times," says Fry, who then plans to send Great Snow novice chasing. "We're obviously getting to know her, but so far, so good. She's a two-and-a-half-plus mare, definitely."

Goodtimecrew is a five-year-old mare who is a graduate of Colin Bowe's County Wexford point-to-point academy. She was runner-up in her point at Ballyknock, was sold for £135,000 at Tattersalls' Cheltenham sale last year and won her bumper on debut at Wincanton in February.

"She then got stuck in the mud in a Listed mares' bumper at Sandown, a race won by the horse who finished second to her at Wincanton.

"She'll go novice hurdling and could go for the Listed mares' race at Taunton we won with Credrojava last year. Then we'll see whether she's good enough to go for the Mares' Novice Hurdle at the Cheltenham Festival."

From the same talented team of five-year-old mares' bumper winners who should be followed in novice hurdles is **Queen Annie**. Her victory came at Chepstow in March.

"The ground can't be soft enough for her; she's a real mudlark," says Fry. "She jumps well, as she showed in two Irish point-to-points. We'll start her off over two and a half miles on soft ground, which will be right up her street."

Anno Power is an unraced four-year-old filly by Affinisea, who will start out in a bumper at Uttoxeter or Aintree with a view to running her in the Listed mares' bumper at Cheltenham's November meeting.

"She came to us in the spring from Colin Bowe and does everything nicely at home. We're looking forward to her," says Fry.

GUIDE TO THE JUMPS 2023-24

HARRY FRY
CORSCOMBE, DEVON

From top: Credrojava, Monjules and Hymac

RECORD AROUND THE COURSES

	Total W-R	Per cent	Non-hcp Hdle	Non-hcp Chase	Hcp Hdle	Hcp Chase	N.H. Flat	£1 level stake
Exeter	45-153	29.4	23-64	8-19	5-36	5-17	4-17	+55.02
Taunton	34-159	21.4	15-64	1-4	8-56	3-14	7-21	-37.78
Wincanton	30-167	18.0	5-55	2-6	10-53	3-24	10-29	-26.32
Uttoxeter	29-120	24.2	6-22	1-10	7-34	11-38	4-16	+16.19
Newton Abbot	24-93	25.8	10-24	1-5	7-44	3-8	3-12	-10.76
Fontwell	22-84	26.2	8-29	1-4	10-33	3-7	0-11	-10.32
Ascot	22-98	22.4	12-25	1-7	4-27	5-29	0-10	-5.67
Kempton	21-102	20.6	7-28	2-8	8-28	3-25	1-13	-23.70
Newbury	16-103	15.5	5-26	1-7	2-31	4-24	4-15	-33.76
Cheltenham	15-134	11.2	7-34	0-11	3-46	3-33	2-10	-54.24
Plumpton	13-37	35.1	2-6	1-4	6-17	1-4	3-6	+1.07
Sandown	12-73	16.4	9-19	0-5	2-26	0-17	1-6	-22.48
Warwick	12-74	16.2	5-26	3-11	2-11	1-7	1-19	-15.94
Market Rasen	11-46	23.9	5-12	1-3	1-15	1-10	3-6	-4.27
Ffos Las	11-56	19.6	2-19	3-7	2-10	2-8	2-12	-7.57
Bangor	10-38	26.3	4-22	1-3	1-4	0-3	4-6	+7.76
Southwell	10-38	26.3	3-13	0-0	2-8	3-11	2-6	+5.89
Ludlow	10-52	19.2	3-13	1-3	2-11	2-15	2-10	-18.96
Chepstow	10-72	13.9	3-26	0-2	1-12	3-19	3-13	-37.93
Aintree	10-78	12.8	2-22	1-5	3-20	2-18	2-13	-21.40
Doncaster	9-34	26.5	0-8	6-10	0-6	1-5	2-5	-4.08
Huntingdon	7-43	16.3	1-10	2-8	2-10	0-3	2-12	-19.48
Stratford	6-35	17.1	2-6	3-5	1-15	0-6	0-3	-19.20
Worcester	6-46	13.0	3-21	1-4	1-9	1-6	0-6	-26.68
Kempton (AW)	5-9	55.6	0-0	0-0	0-0	0-0	5-9	+55.25
Lingfield	5-15	33.3	3-6	0-0	1-5	1-4	0-0	+5.17
Hereford	5-29	17.2	2-9	2-6	0-7	1-6	0-1	-3.35
Leicester	4-12	33.3	2-6	1-1	0-2	1-3	0-0	+4.08
Wetherby	4-18	22.2	2-8	1-2	0-3	0-2	1-3	-5.75
Haydock	4-28	14.3	1-4	0-0	3-17	0-7	0-0	-2.20
Towcester	3-5	60.0	0-1	0-0	1-1	0-0	2-3	+4.75
Sedgefield	2-3	66.7	0-1	0-0	2-2	0-0	0-0	+6.50
Carlisle	2-3	66.7	1-1	1-2	0-0	0-0	0-0	+3.67
Fakenham	1-2	50.0	0-0	0-0	0-0	1-2	0-0	+0.25
Newcastle	1-2	50.0	1-2	0-0	0-0	0-0	0-0	-0.60
Kelso	1-6	16.7	0-2	0-1	1-3	0-0	0-0	-0.50
Catterick	0-1	0.0	0-0	0-0	0-1	0-0	0-0	-1.00
Musselburgh	0-2	0.0	0-0	0-0	0-2	0-0	0-0	-2.00
Perth	0-3	0.0	0-1	0-1	0-1	0-0	0-0	-3.00
Ayr	0-4	0.0	0-0	0-0	0-2	0-2	0-0	-4.00
Lingfield (AW)	0-4	0.0	0-0	0-0	0-0	0-4	0-0	-4.00

Finally, **How Will I Know** should be added to the list. The Irish point runner-up won his maiden hurdle readily at Exeter on New Year's Day after finishing third in a similar race at the track a month earlier, a race which is working out well.

"He had a setback but he's made a good recovery and I hope to see him out from January onwards. He's lightly raced and unexposed and looks as though he could make a useful two-and-a-half mile handicap hurdler."

Fry's youngsters combined with his established stars give him plenty of optimism this season's team can improve on last term.

He was pleased with last season's 39 winners, the yard's best total since moving in three years ago, but several near-misses rankled.

"We hit the crossbar a few too many times for my liking," he says. "If one or two of those runner-up spots go your way they can make a big difference.

"We're definitely looking to the younger, unexposed horses to come through the ranks. In fact, I think our novice hurdling division has the potential to be as strong as any we've had for a number of seasons. They're exciting."

Interview by Lawrie Kelsey

RACING POST

NICKY HENDERSON

Constitution the brightest star among huge array of firepower

ALL eyes will be on Constitution Hill's every move this season to see if he can repeat last term's stupendous performances.

Racing is going through tough times and needs a champion more than ever, and in Nicky Henderson's hurdler it has one almost as iconic as Red Rum, Dawn Run, Kauto Star, Desert Orchid or Frankel.

If he lands a second successive

Nicky Henderson and the superb Constitution Hill

GUIDE TO THE JUMPS **2023-24**

WINNERS IN LAST FIVE SEASONS 90, 120, 103, 118, 141

On the schooling ground at Seven Barrows, where Nicky Henderson is preparing his powerful squad

Champion Hurdle in March, and in equally decisive fashion as last spring, there'll be no holding back the flood of hyperbole, and his iconic status will be confirmed.

Henderson has already described his hurdler's headline-grabbing impact on the racing public as "ridiculous" but the thrilling way the six-year-old thrashed his rivals last season demanded high acclaim.

"He shouldn't dominate the season, but he will, I can't help it," says Henderson, who revealed in mid-September what most people had confidently predicted, that Constitution Hill would not go chasing this season.

"It's bound to happen, people talking him up, and it's not me doing it, he's doing it for himself.

"As Michael [Buckley, owner] has said, he's no longer his horse, he's public property; but we don't really mind that.

"He's the one the public wants to know about and it's almost every day you get asked about him.

"He's got to this level in seven runs, which is ridiculous if you think Sprinter [Sacre] perhaps got to his heyday, when he came back from his heart problem, after five or so seasons."

The first opportunity the public will have of seeing "their" horse will be at Newcastle in the Betfair Fighting Fifth Hurdle on December 2.

The next outing in his programme will be the Ladbrokes Christmas Hurdle at Kempton on Boxing Day, followed by the Unibet International Hurdle at Cheltenham on January 27, and finally the race which will be the highlight of the Cheltenham Festival for many racing fans, the Champion Hurdle on March 12 on the opening day.

"We've won nine Champion Hurdles and ten would be very nice," says Henderson,

GUIDE TO THE JUMPS **2023-24**

■ Henderson has a strike-rate of 37% in graduation chases – and a level-stake profit of £19.66

"but he's a young horse, so he can hopefully continue on that route for a few more years."

Although Constitution Hill is unquestionably the ace of trumps in Henderson's pack of hurdlers, the master trainer is optimistic that **Champ**, who runs well when fresh, can do well in three-mile hurdles, while **On The Blind Side**, **Call Me Lord**, **Mill Green** and **King Alexander** are also expected to pay their way.

The Seven Barrows senior chasers are led by the talented duo, Shishkin and Jonbon.

Successful in the Ascot Chase and Aintree's Bowl, **Shishkin** is around 5-1 to win the Ladbrokes King George VI Chase on Boxing Day and 14-1 with William Hill for the Boodles Cheltenham Gold Cup, while Jonbon will start in the Betfair Tingle Creek before going down the Betway Queen Mother Champion Chase path.

"The foremost aim for Shishkin is the King George, although I don't know by which route yet," Henderson says. "If that happened to go right, it's pretty obvious what we'd do.

"I would like to get a run into him before Kempton and the options are the Charlie Hall and Betfair Chase. He's been away doing some dressage with Zara Tindall.

"She liked him and I just wanted a different way to build him up as he's a character, and I think sometimes he can get bored. He had a month there instead of just trotting around here.

"He looks very well, quite straight actually, and everything finished the right way when he won at Aintree, and the more we moved him up in trip, the better things got."

Jonbon, who is 7-1 for the Champion Chase with bet365, could be seen as Britain's best two-mile chaser and his only defeat over fences came behind El Fabiolo in the Arkle.

"You can go for the Shloer at Cheltenham in November, but it's close to the Tingle Creek. Let's just see how he's going, but he's very, very well," says Henderson.

"Paddy [Murphy], who rides him every day, is thrilled with him. He's much more relaxed than he used to be. There were times we'd take him to the racecourse just to lead him around the paddock but, unless you change the routine dramatically, he's better now and thoroughly enjoys what he's doing.

"He's moving beautifully and looks great in his skin. He never had a clip all last winter, which is very rare. I've seen horses do it before, but he had a summer coat – the most wonderful one – all winter."

Jonbon's victories last season included three at the top level in the Henry VIII, Maghull and Celebration Chase.

"I wanted to run him over two and a half miles at Aintree, but the two-mile novice chase was blatantly easier and I don't think you saw Jonbon at his best at Cheltenham, which was the second year running, although don't forget the year before it was Constitution Hill beating him.

"The whole point of Sandown and the Celebration Chase was to see where he fitted in with the older two-milers and the second, third and fourth from the Champion Chase were in the race, so he proved himself.

"I don't know what the Irish boys will do in the next few months, but our plan is straightforward.

"He didn't jump with his normal fluency in the Arkle and I don't think that's anything to do with the course. Take nothing away from El Fabiolo, but there was nothing between them over hurdles and there was a big gap in the Arkle, which we've got to close.

"He's very good and I hope he's up to that Sprinter Sacre-Altior level. He and Shishkin are top class, as good a chaser as we've had for a while."

The Grand National is the biggest race missing from Henderson's roll of big-race victories, although when **Mister Coffey** led between the second-last and final fences in last season's race after making much of the running, he thought momentarily that omission was about to be put right.

The eight-year-old weakened to finish eighth but will return for another crack this season as part of an interesting team which includes **Dusart**, **Chantry House** and **City Chief**.

Bold Endeavour should continue to perform well in top handicap chases over shorter trips, and **Emir Sacree** is a name to note for cross-country races.

Among Henderson's novice chasers, the Coolmore team could strike it rich with **Walking On Air**, who has always had a tall reputation.

He runs in the black and white silks of Michael Tabor's wife Doreen and Henderson says: "He could be good. He was very unlucky when spot on for the Pertemps Final, but got no run coming down the hill.

"I don't know what happened to him at Punchestown as he travelled and jumped beautifully but then emptied. I'm really looking forward to him going chasing though."

Henderson anticipates **Wiseguy** developing into a proficient staying novice chaser and that also applies to **Amrons Sage** and **The Carpenter**.

"I like **Russian Ruler**, **Boom Boom** and **Persian Time** for fences too and we might give **Captain Morgs** another spin over them.

"**Blairgowrie** is worth noting for novice handicap chases and **Doddiethegreat**, who is undefeated, is back too. He had a horrible injury, but was ready to go in the spring only for the ground to get too quick. His owner Kenny Alexander will continue to donate any prize-money he wins to Doddie Weir's motor neurone disease charity."

That squad could be joined by some other exciting sorts.

"There are a few we've said to the owners we'll school and see," the trainer says. "They

GUIDE TO THE JUMPS 2023-24

NICKY HENDERSON
UPPER LAMBOURN, BERKSHIRE

RECORD AROUND THE COURSES

	Total W-R	Per cent	Non-hcp Hdle	Non-hcp Chase	Hcp Hdle	Hcp Chase	N.H. Flat	£1 level stake
Kempton	116-468	24.8	46-162	25-60	22-120	12-71	11-55	-45.22
Newbury	102-428	23.8	57-159	8-18	19-113	7-88	11-50	+13.92
Cheltenham	81-662	12.2	35-206	22-101	17-211	4-121	3-23	-180.38
Sandown	65-281	23.1	26-77	17-47	16-98	3-51	3-8	-32.94
Ascot	59-287	20.6	26-99	13-40	10-82	7-46	3-20	-37.10
Doncaster	58-184	31.5	34-86	9-23	9-35	4-26	2-14	+19.49
Warwick	55-205	26.8	21-78	6-12	12-47	6-16	10-52	+4.13
Ludlow	53-213	24.9	28-92	3-13	3-33	6-33	13-42	-65.34
Huntingdon	50-197	25.4	27-82	10-22	5-42	4-15	4-36	-67.10
Worcester	47-172	27.3	19-47	5-18	9-53	3-16	11-38	+26.73
Aintree	45-263	17.1	20-83	9-33	8-65	6-60	2-22	-52.04
Uttoxeter	42-176	23.9	17-56	6-17	8-56	5-32	6-15	-44.19
Southwell	39-135	28.9	13-45	1-7	3-30	3-13	19-40	-28.39
Market Rasen	38-148	25.7	17-44	3-11	6-48	4-22	8-23	-14.42
Ffos Las	28-77	36.4	15-35	2-5	6-20	1-6	4-11	+14.71
Bangor-On-Dee	21-101	20.8	9-31	2-9	5-24	2-15	3-22	-33.73
Towcester	20-49	40.8	10-20	3-6	4-5	0-0	3-18	+4.24
Fakenham	20-64	31.2	11-32	2-8	2-11	1-4	4-9	-19.91
Newton Abbot	20-67	29.9	8-19	2-8	6-26	2-8	2-6	+8.68
Stratford	19-90	21.1	2-15	3-8	8-36	3-16	3-15	-22.85
Plumpton	18-61	29.5	5-20	4-8	7-24	2-4	0-5	+20.71
Exeter	18-67	26.9	9-25	1-8	4-16	2-8	2-10	-7.68
Haydock	18-89	20.2	8-25	3-13	3-40	3-8	1-3	-28.41
Taunton	17-72	23.6	9-32	1-3	4-24	1-8	2-5	-18.53
Fontwell	17-77	22.1	8-28	4-8	4-20	0-5	1-16	-22.34
Chepstow	17-95	17.9	9-35	2-7	2-23	1-18	3-12	-25.07
Wincanton	16-91	17.6	7-36	3-6	4-26	1-12	1-11	-31.44
Wetherby	15-37	40.5	6-11	6-9	1-8	0-5	2-4	+7.00
Newcastle	13-19	68.4	11-14	0-0	0-0	1-4	1-1	+4.40
Musselburgh	11-32	34.4	8-16	1-3	2-11	0-1	0-1	-5.85
Hereford	11-37	29.7	7-20	1-4	2-9	1-2	0-2	-13.79
Ayr	10-67	14.9	1-6	1-5	2-30	4-21	2-5	-32.99
Kelso	9-16	56.2	3-3	2-2	1-4	1-2	2-5	+7.18
Leicester	9-37	24.3	4-16	2-4	0-3	3-14	0-0	-1.77
Lingfield (AW)	9-40	22.5	0-0	0-0	0-0	0-0	9-40	-5.66
Kempton (AW)	7-15	46.7	0-0	0-0	0-0	0-0	7-15	+12.44
Hexham	6-15	40.0	1-2	1-2	1-6	1-2	2-3	+1.98
Perth	5-26	19.2	2-8	0-1	0-4	3-11	0-2	-14.35
Lingfield	4-15	26.7	3-12	1-2	0-0	0-1	0-0	-9.25
Catterick	3-11	27.3	0-3	3-5	0-1	0-1	0-1	-2.27
Sedgefield	2-2	100.0	2-2	0-0	0-0	0-0	0-0	+0.71
Carlisle	2-3	66.7	1-1	0-0	0-1	1-1	0-0	+4.41
Cartmel	1-4	25.0	0-1	1-1	0-1	0-1	0-0	-1.80
Wolverhampton (AW)	0-3	0.0	0-0	0-0	0-0	0-0	0-3	-3.00

From top: Chantry House, Jonbon and Walking On Air

could include **First Street**, who won the Gerry Feilden last year, but is in no man's land over hurdles, while **No Ordinary Joe**, second in the Martin Pipe, might also be in that bracket.

"**Jet Powered**, **Impose Toi** and **Iberico Lord** have very little experience, but big futures, although we've not decided what they'll do just yet.

"**Attacca** was a good novice hurdler last season, but missed the backend with a rare joint problem that affects his pastern, so he's still on the easy list. Otherwise, he'd probably have been top of this list."

Recent victories with Altior, Shishkin and Constitution Hill in the Supreme Novices' Hurdle mean Henderson is often a good starting point for the race.

An outstanding prospect has yet to emerge for this season, but the trainer is keeping his fingers crossed.

"I hope there's a Supreme or Ballymore contender here, but anyone's guess is as good as mine at the moment," he says, "and I

27

Inside Seven Barrows as the Henderson string is prepared

would have said the same two years ago when Constitution Hill was relatively unknown from the pointing sphere."

He mentions the likes of **Kintail** and **Ideal Des Bordes** – first and third in a Warwick bumper in May – especially as the second, the Dan Skelton-trained Rock House, rocked up next time out at Worcester in mid-September by 13 lengths.

Henderson says: "You'd hope that form's solid after seeing what Dan's horse did and our two horses are really nice.

"That also applies to **Immortal**. I love him, he's beautiful. He hasn't won over hurdles yet, but can put that right soon, as can **Issuing Authority** and **Iolaos Du Mou**, whom we call Pablo. He ought to have won his last race but was a bit weak. I like him and he could be early, while **Park Hill Dancer** will be useful over two and a half miles on easy ground."

Of the other bumper horses going novice hurdling, Henderson adds: "**Southoftheborder** won at Ffos Las and is a strapping, future chaser, while **Montecam** is obviously interesting being a half-brother to Altior, and he's shaped up a lot over the summer.

"**East India Express** is also interesting and was sick after his Kempton win, but could be anything and jumps superbly. **Choccabloc**, **Johnny Blue** and **Fierce Warrior** will definitely be all right.

"I've got plenty of time for **Lucky Place** and my assistant George Daly thinks he's as hard as nails – he's got a great mind – and I'd like to think **Strutter**, **Scandisk Park**, Hurricane Fly's half-brother, and **Gentleman's Relish** are much better than they showed in bumpers, when they had genuine excuses."

Shanagh Bob, **De Tellers Fortune** and **Jingko Blue** all fetched six figures at the sales after each won an Irish point-to-point and have yet to run under rules, but they have been educated before their holidays at Seven Barrows.

Interview by James Burn

RACING POST

ANTHONY HONEYBALL

Eyeing more big wins and looking to reach new levels

ANTHONY HONEYBALL is looking to climb a few rungs up the ladder of success that is the trainers' statistical list by the end of this latest season.

He has reached as high as 24th, although for the last three seasons his name has been hovering in the 30s, but it is the top 20 where he hopes to be next April.

If that happens it will almost certainly mean he has bettered last season's record haul of 40 winners and £489,000 prize-money from his Potwell Farm stables in Dorset.

"Considering we had a blip mid-season with what was probably a low-grade virus, when the horses weren't running well, that wasn't bad," says Honeyball.

"We've had a good start to this season, although we don't normally run them in the summer. We have a good string of about 60 who look a strong set of horses, and

GUIDE TO THE JUMPS 2023-24

WINNERS IN LAST FIVE SEASONS 40, 35, 27, 36, 15

Crest Of Glory: impressive bumper winner at Newbury who looks to be a bright prospect

we'll be pushing for 50 winners and hoping to move up the trainers' ladder a bit more.

"We're managing to find a horse to win us a big race each season and we obviously want to do more of that."

Leading the march to Honeyball's half-century target is runaway bumper winner **Crest Of Glory**, who impressed everyone with his 15-length win in a £100,000 Newbury sales race on soft ground in March, handsomely paying off connections' £48,000 outlay on his first racecourse appearance.

"We went to great lengths to have him prepared for the Newbury race and it was brilliant to win a hundred-grand race on debut," he says.

"The ground came right for him – he definitely acts on soft ground – but I was surprised how well he did. His dam was fourth in a Newbury maiden on the Flat, so there's a good bit of sharpness on that side of the pedigree.

"If it's softish ground we'll look at a Listed bumper at Cheltenham in November and see where we go after that. We can either look at a maiden hurdle in December or put him away. We'll have to wait and see.

"It's not entirely straightforward because he's only four, but he's got to be big enough and strong enough to jump hurdles and may take a bit of time.

"However, I won't run him in the Cheltenham bumper if the ground's not soft enough and may be forced into running him over hurdles. We did lots of schooling with him last year and he's definitely an exciting horse."

Into notebooks should also go his stablemate **Dartmoor Pirate**, who was seventh in the same Newbury race on his debut too after the pair had been prepared together by Honeyball.

"He was only beaten a handful of lengths by the placed horses," says the trainer. "He'll run in a bumper in November and he's definitely one to follow. If he wins it well, we'll probably go for a Listed bumper at Ascot in December. If he won in average style or was placed in average style, he'd go novice hurdling. He's got a definite aptitude for jumping."

The veteran **Sam Brown** is 11 but stays in training with Honeyball in the hope he has better fortune than last season.

"He was unlucky not to win a valuable handicap at Punchestown at the end of last season after falling two out when leading. That followed a spin in the Grand National when he fell at the Chair. We had a blip mid-season with him when the wheels seemed to fall off.

"The Grand National won't be on his agenda this season but other big handicaps will be. He'll start out in the Charlie Hall at Wetherby again – he was third to Bravemansgame last year – and we'll see where we go from there. But he's rated 155, so he'd struggle to win a handicap, and he can't run in veterans' qualifiers because they're 0-150, so he's got to run in the Graded races."

Kilbeg King won a valuable Punchestown hurdle – the third season in succession Honeyball had landed a big race at the festival.

"Where I want to be with him is the Kauto Star Novices' Chase at Kempton on Boxing Day, and I want two chase runs into him before then," says Honeyball.

"You'd like to think that if I had ambitions like that he'd be winning a novice chase off 137. If he can do that sometime in November, we can find another race in December before going for the Kauto.

"If things don't go to plan, we'll just educate him for a decent novice handicap chase somewhere and prepare him for a hundred-grand novice chase at Punchestown.

"We hope he's going to shape into a top chaser. Now, we may be getting ahead of ourselves, but if he could be running in Listed or Graded chases this season we'd be delighted – and if we end up in the Kauto

Honeyball has saddled 80 winners of bumpers – a strike-rate of 21% and a profit of £57.49

Kilbeg King (right): smart hurdler will be tackling fences this season

Star, I'd be even more pleased."

Forward Plan proved something of a revelation last season, winning three times, finishing second twice and third once in six outings.

"He progressed really well, which surprised us, to be honest. He won a run-of-the-mill chase at Southwell, then a 20-grand chase at the same track. He was third at Kelso when the ground was probably a bit too soft, then ran a cracker at Ayr in a 50-grand race.

"The Badger Beers Chase at Wincanton in November is the plan. A flat track, decent ground and a half-decent weight – it would be a nice place to start him off. He doesn't want boggy ground, so we'll get a couple of runs into him, then we might have to give him time off until the spring."

Somespring Special is a five-year-old mare who won her last two races over hurdles and will be aimed at the same Wincanton meeting as Forward Plan. Her target will be a £35,000 mares' handicap hurdle.

"She ran well over course and distance last season and races off 114. She's just had a minor breathing op, is a hardy mare with a bit of toe and just has to go there.

"She jumps well at home and we're looking forward to going chasing, but she'll have this one hurdle race first."

Coquelicot is a versatile seven-year-old mare who is worth following having won three races over hurdles, three bumpers and one on the Flat.

"The plan is clear. She'll run on the Flat in a two-mile handicap at Newmarket in November, then on to Ascot for a mares' handicap hurdle and a return to Kempton for a 20-grand race in which she was second last year," says Honeyball.

"We'd be then looking at a 100-grand handicap at Sandown in which she was second in February. She's still progressing over hurdles and whether she's up to the level of the Pertemps Final at Cheltenham, I don't know. She's off 127 and will run in mares' races but we'd love her to compete in some of the conditions races rather than just the handicaps."

Brookie is a six-year-old gelding who arrived from Irish trainer Tony Martin after running a close fourth in a handicap hurdle at the Punchestown festival and fourth at Cork in August.

"He's a lovely horse with a lovely pedigree and is coming on well," reports Honeyball. "He's a half-brother to Captain Guinness, who was second in the Champion Chase to Energumene. He looks on a nice mark and will be running from mid-October onwards.

ANTHONY HONEYBALL
MOSTERTON, DORSET

RECORD AROUND THE COURSES

	Total W-R	Per cent	Non-hcp Hdle	Non-hcp Chase	Hcp Hdle	Hcp Chase	N.H. Flat	£1 level stake
Fontwell	65-193	33.7	15-48	1-8	22-65	12-39	15-33	+52.56
Plumpton	29-128	22.7	7-28	1-3	9-47	6-34	6-16	-32.26
Exeter	26-113	23.0	8-40	2-7	9-34	5-25	2-7	+20.09
Uttoxeter	21-115	18.3	3-21	2-6	10-47	1-25	5-16	-15.71
Taunton	18-95	18.9	1-34	0-0	11-31	3-19	3-11	+22.42
Ffos Las	18-116	15.5	5-28	1-4	3-29	4-29	5-26	-43.72
Wincanton	16-140	11.4	4-57	1-4	3-30	5-31	3-18	-25.57
Worcester	13-79	16.5	5-27	0-2	5-23	3-19	0-8	-38.59
Chepstow	13-89	14.6	5-34	0-1	4-16	2-20	2-18	-18.36
Newton Abbot	10-40	25.0	1-11	1-2	4-13	3-10	1-4	-0.76
Warwick	8-37	21.6	1-8	1-2	0-4	5-15	1-8	-7.25
Ascot	7-43	16.3	0-1	0-2	2-5	5-28	0-7	+30.58
Ludlow	6-16	37.5	1-4	0-2	1-3	1-3	3-4	+45.00
Lingfield	6-31	19.4	0-5	1-1	3-8	2-17	0-0	-3.60
Newbury	6-51	11.8	0-9	1-5	1-9	1-13	3-15	-14.75
Hereford	5-23	21.7	1-6	0-0	3-9	0-7	1-1	+1.28
Southwell	5-28	17.9	0-4	1-2	0-11	3-6	1-5	-5.55
Market Rasen	4-17	23.5	0-2	0-1	2-6	2-6	0-2	-3.38
Aintree	4-28	14.3	0-1	0-3	1-6	2-8	1-10	+22.00
Cheltenham	4-46	8.7	0-3	0-1	1-5	2-16	1-21	-23.50
Stratford	3-12	25.0	1-1	0-0	2-4	0-4	0-3	-2.09
Kempton	3-17	17.6	0-2	0-2	1-4	1-7	1-2	-9.47
Sandown	3-24	12.5	1-6	0-0	1-6	1-6	0-6	-8.00
Carlisle	2-7	28.6	0-1	0-2	0-0	2-4	0-0	+1.75
Huntingdon	2-14	14.3	0-4	0-0	0-1	0-1	2-8	-5.25
Bangor	2-19	10.5	1-3	0-0	0-3	1-12	0-1	-12.50
Cartmel	1-2	50.0	0-0	1-1	0-1	0-0	0-0	+0.75
Catterick	1-6	16.7	0-1	0-0	0-1	1-3	0-1	-4.64
Wetherby	1-7	14.3	0-2	0-1	0-0	0-3	1-1	-2.67
Leicester	1-10	10.0	0-3	0-2	0-2	1-3	0-0	-5.00
Doncaster	1-18	5.6	0-3	0-1	0-8	1-3	0-3	-11.50
Haydock	1-22	4.5	0-2	1-1	0-6	0-13	0-0	-18.75
Newcastle	0-1	0.0	0-0	0-0	0-0	0-1	0-0	-1.00
Musselburgh	0-1	0.0	0-0	0-0	0-0	0-1	0-0	-1.00
Ayr	0-2	0.0	0-1	0-0	0-0	0-1	0-0	-2.00
Kelso	0-2	0.0	0-0	0-0	0-0	0-1	0-1	-2.00
Lingfield (AW)	0-2	0.0	0-0	0-0	0-0	0-0	0-0	-2.00
Hexham	0-12	0.0	0-6	0-0	0-3	0-0	0-3	-12.00

From top: Sam Brown; Coquelicot; (left) Blackjack Magic

"We'll start in something like a 0-120 or 0-125 decent-value handicap hurdle, then we might look at a 30-, 40-, 50-grand handicap somewhere; there are any number of them. He's got talent and hopefully he can adapt to our routine."

Blackjack Magic won twice over fences last season on soft ground at Exeter and Uttoxeter, and is predicted to be "an interesting horse when the mud is really flying". His optimum distance is two and a half miles, although he does stay three miles.

Credo is "an admirable mare" who won twice and was runner-up three times in her first season over fences.

"She's one we might try in a valuable handicap off a lightish weight, something like the Rehearsal Chase at Newcastle over three miles in December. We'll also be looking at mares' chase options."

Fortuna Ligna is rated another decent mare. She was third in a Listed bumper at Cheltenham in November, fourth in a mares' Grade 2 handicap hurdle at Newbury in March, then managed to get off the mark in a mares' maiden hurdle at Chepstow in April.

"She stays very well, copes with any ground and could be aimed at the 20-grand race Coquelicot won at Sandown. Options could be big mares' handicaps at Cheltenham in mid-December or Kempton in late December.

"I think she has leeway off her mark of 108. The better the race we put her in, the better she runs. She's got lots of stamina and finds it more difficult to win smaller races where they go a bit steadier. She's better with a stronger pace."

Baby Shally has come across from Ireland where she won a mares' maiden point-to-point impressively. "She'll quickly switch to novice hurdling but we'll start her off in a mares' bumper," says her trainer. "If she goes and wins that, there's a Listed mares' bumper at Huntingdon in December she could go for. She jumps very well, has plenty of ability and will go novice hurdling later."

Another Irish pointer Honeyball bought and who he hopes can turn into a useful recruit, is **Ask Lileen**.

The reason for his optimism is the mare he beat by six lengths at Bandon in February last year was Apple Away, who joined Lucinda Russell and ended last season by winning the Grade 1 Sefton Novices' Hurdle at Aintree.

"We were nine days away from running her last season but she got an injury and we couldn't run her, but she's A1 now," he says. "She jumps very well and we'll be looking at a mares' hurdle in November. She's not fast, she's more of a strong stayer with a good fighting mentality. We don't have any targets. We'll see how the maiden goes, and get excited after that!"

Crest Of Fortune is a three-year-old gelding bought by the same owners of Crest Of Glory. He's by Doyen, the same sire as Kilbeg King, and his dam was placed in a Listed mares' hurdle and fourth in a mares' Listed bumper. His half-brother won a bumper and was fifth in a Grade 2 bumper at Aintree.

"His number one plan," says Honeyball, "is the sales bumper in March at Newbury which Crest Of Glory won. He's definitely one we're looking forward to."

He adds: "One who is shaping really nicely and one I really like is **Park Princess**, whose dam won three for Willie Mullins. She's by Walk In The Park and is a sister to four winners. I like the way she's progressing. She's qualified for the sales bumper at Punchestown, so that will be a target we keep in mind for her."

Interview by Lawrie Kelsey

PREMIER EQUINE
ENGLAND

Turnout Rugs

Stable Rugs

Cooler Rugs

Horse Boots

Saddle pads

Saddles

Therapy

PROUD SUPPLIERS TO THE RACING COMMUNITY

To apply for a trainer's trade account, please contact:
sales@premierequine.co.uk | Order Line 01469 532279
www.premierequine.co.uk

EMMA LAVELLE

Emma Lavelle and husband Barry Fenton in the tack room at Bonita Racing Stables

GUIDE TO THE JUMPS **2023-24**

WINNERS IN LAST FIVE SEASONS 32, 42, 32, 29, 35

Paisley Park back to fly the flag again

PAISLEY PARK has become a treasured friend for thousands of racing fans and the good news from his Wiltshire home is he's not ready for retirement.

At the age of 11, Andrew Gemmell's old boy returns for his eighth season of a career that has brought 11 victories and a few quid over £678,000.

And, just as in the previous four or five years, his programme is already mapped out: Long Distance Hurdle at Newbury in November, Long Walk at Ascot in December, Cheltenham's Cleeve

Hurdle in January and the Stayers' Hurdle at the festival in March.

His record reads: Long Distance Hurdle won in 2019; Long Walk 2018/20/22; Cleeve Hurdle 2019/20/22; Stayers' Hurdle 2019.

"There's no getting away from the fact we didn't have the most straightforward of seasons last season. They weren't all 100 per cent and there's no reason to think Paisley was any different to that," says Lavelle.

"That's why I really won't go, 'Oh yeah, his last run in the Stayers' Hurdle wasn't good, let's call it quits'. Two runs before that he'd won a Grade 1 [Long Walk Hurdle at Kempton] on a track he should never have been able to win a Grade 1 on.

"So, it may be that he is not far off ready for retirement but, if he is, let him tell us, rather than us tell him."

Paisley Park has returned from his summer break and is pleasing Lavelle's team at Bonita Racing Stables near Marlborough.

"He's back in training, is very fresh and well, in great shape and loving life," says Lavelle. "At this stage we're very happy with him and, all things being equal, we'll start back at Newbury for the Long Distance Hurdle in November. We know his programme pretty well by now, but we'll take one race at a time and see how it goes."

Lavelle's reference to the health of her string last season was the reason the yard had "only" 32 winners when hopes were on breaking the record-equalling 42 of the previous season, although prize-money was a healthy £525,000.

"If you look at the bare statistics you'd say it wasn't a bad season, but with the ammunition we had it wasn't what we hoped for," says Lavelle.

"That's why it was so disappointing. I just think if we can get a clear run at it this season, we should have an excellent year.

"This is always the time of year when they all look like swans, but there are a few that have actually shown it and that gives us a bit more confidence.

"We have a lovely cover of bumper horses, novice and handicap hurdlers, and novice and handicap chasers. So we have plenty of variety in the team as well as quality horses that have had a year on their backs and laid down the foundation to go and show what they're really made of. We're excited."

One of the major reasons for the bubbling excitement at Bonita is that the poor showing of some horses last season means they start this term with competitive ratings.

"I think one of the advantages with having had a difficult season healthwise," she says, "is that you do hope you're going into the new season with horses that are pretty well handicapped and that hopefully gives us an advantage going into it this year."

One such horse is **My Silver Lining**. "She has come back in really good form with herself. I was really pleased with her win at Cheltenham in April but I don't think she was really 100 per cent last year, so hopefully we've got room for manoeuvre with her handicap mark," says Lavelle.

"She's as hard as nails and doesn't care what the ground is, going left-handed or right-handed, and the more fences she gets to jump the happier she is.

"She's a horse who could step up from where we've got to, but the ultimate aim is the race she won at Cheltenham in April, although there should be some nice races on the way. She's rated 113 and to have won a couple, one of them a 50-grand race, I'm pretty happy with that.

"Some of it is on how the horses were last season, and she was a little bit hit and miss as well, but from looking at her and from what I see at home I think she is very well handicapped."

Another mare expected to be ahead of her mark is the 107-rated six-year-old **Porter In The Park**.

"She won over hurdles and should have won more races than she did," says Lavelle. "She was unlucky not to win at Newbury [beaten a head]. She's so gutsy, as hard as nails, and will go novice handicap chasing –

GUIDE TO THE JUMPS 2023-24

EMMA LAVELLE
MARLBOROUGH, WILTSHIRE

RECORD AROUND THE COURSES

	Total W-R	Per cent	Non-hcp Hdle	Non-hcp Chase	Hcp Hdle	Hcp Chase	N.H. Flat	£1 level stake
Wincanton	26-146	17.8	4-36	2-5	9-42	7-44	4-19	+19.16
Worcester	25-122	20.5	6-25	2-6	5-34	12-46	0-11	+16.60
Kempton	22-141	15.6	4-45	1-5	4-33	10-47	3-11	+84.77
Stratford	19-91	20.9	4-19	0-4	6-24	7-31	2-13	+0.15
Newton Abbot	18-70	25.7	5-17	2-6	5-26	4-17	2-4	+63.40
Exeter	18-119	15.1	3-36	0-3	5-30	9-40	1-10	-14.25
Doncaster	17-81	21.0	5-24	0-2	5-17	4-24	3-14	-11.11
Market Rasen	15-83	18.1	3-8	1-2	5-29	5-35	1-9	+4.95
Chepstow	15-115	13.0	8-43	1-4	3-18	1-32	2-18	-39.26
Fontwell	14-103	13.6	3-28	0-2	7-35	3-30	1-8	-30.55
Uttoxeter	13-106	12.3	3-21	2-7	2-36	4-30	2-12	-48.64
Taunton	11-74	14.9	1-18	0-1	6-23	4-25	0-7	-22.60
Warwick	10-109	9.2	2-28	0-4	2-29	6-29	0-19	-30.34
Southwell	9-57	15.8	2-13	0-0	3-19	2-15	2-10	-0.70
Plumpton	8-52	15.4	3-14	0-0	0-16	5-19	0-3	-25.48
Huntingdon	8-73	11.0	3-18	1-3	3-20	0-17	1-15	-27.92
Cheltenham	8-92	8.7	5-18	1-11	0-21	2-38	0-4	-48.13
Ludlow	7-52	13.5	1-15	0-0	3-14	3-20	0-3	-21.70
Newbury	7-111	6.3	1-28	0-3	2-32	3-35	1-13	-63.47
Haydock	6-38	15.8	1-5	0-4	4-20	1-8	0-1	+8.50
Hereford	6-42	14.3	2-10	1-1	1-14	2-10	0-7	-14.38
Sandown	6-57	10.5	2-6	0-3	0-24	3-21	1-3	-27.83
Ascot	6-68	8.8	3-11	1-3	1-18	1-27	0-9	-42.25
Leicester	5-22	22.7	3-9	0-0	0-1	2-12	0-0	-8.37
Lingfield	5-30	16.7	3-12	0-1	0-1	2-16	0-0	+3.00
Ffos Las	5-36	13.9	3-15	0-1	1-11	1-6	0-3	-20.59
Bangor	4-26	15.4	0-3	0-1	1-3	2-14	1-5	-5.75
Fakenham	3-12	25.0	2-3	0-0	0-2	1-6	0-1	-0.38
Lingfield (AW)	2-12	16.7	0-0	0-0	0-0	0-0	2-12	+4.50
Aintree	2-40	5.0	0-7	0-2	2-9	0-19	0-3	-25.50
Cartmel	1-3	33.3	0-0	0-0	1-1	0-2	0-0	+0.50
Kempton (AW)	1-8	12.5	0-0	0-0	0-0	0-0	1-8	+9.00
Musselburgh	0-1	0.0	0-0	0-0	0-1	0-0	0-0	-1.00
Sedgefield	0-1	0.0	0-0	0-0	0-0	0-1	0-0	-1.00
Kelso	0-4	0.0	0-1	0-0	0-0	0-3	0-0	-4.00
Ayr	0-4	0.0	0-0	0-1	0-0	0-3	0-0	-4.00
Newcastle	0-4	0.0	0-0	0-0	0-0	0-4	0-0	-4.00
Wetherby	0-6	0.0	0-3	0-0	0-1	0-2	0-0	-6.00

From top: My Silver Lining, De Rasher Counter and Tightenourbelts

and will be winning her races over fences. She wasn't right all last season and I think she's well ahead of her handicap mark."

Joining Lavelle's list of well-handicapped inmates is **Tarahumara**, who was another horse who had health problems.

"It hasn't been straightforward with him. When things have been right, he's been right and he's won.

"He's an enormous horse. We sent him over fences at Uttoxeter and he couldn't have been right because he didn't jump the way we knew he could and he ended up bursting a blood vessel. It took a long time to get him right again.

"He went to Southwell over hurdles and won really easily. We're going to keep him over hurdles for the moment. He doesn't want the ground to be too soft. He's in good shape and is a horse with a big engine as long as everything is pulling in the right direction. He should be very well handicapped off a mark of 112."

Much is expected over hurdles this season of **Classic King**, who is "the most beautiful-looking horse", according to Lavelle.

"He ran really creditably in his three bumpers last season, and his last run was a lovely race [second at Wincanton]," says his trainer. "He'll go novice hurdling. He's schooled really nicely, although he probably doesn't want the ground to be too soft. He

41

looks a horse with that bit of quality. He's a big horse, so I can only hope he's going to get stronger and better.

"He should be ready to go by October and I'd like to think he could be one of the smart novices later in the season, but we'll start small and build up."

Tightenourbelts was second in a couple of decent novice hurdles, then went to Ludlow, his last run of the season, and bolted up by 18 lengths.

"He was always a smashing jumper over hurdles, a strong traveller with a natural skill over fences, so he'll go novice handicap chasing and will be one of our exciting chasers this season," predicts Lavelle.

"I'm very happy about him and really looking forward to getting him started. He'll be out in mid-October and we'll get the first couple of races under our belts, then see where we go."

Doughmore Bay looked on his way to winning his only Irish point-to-point last November until falling two out. He was bought by Lavelle and proved such a willing homeworker that he was given a run over hurdles in May at Worcester, where he won really well.

"He then had his summer holiday, he's back in and we'll keep him over hurdles," says Lavelle. "He's going to be a staying hurdler and ultimately a staying chaser. He's one of those that whenever you ask him, he delivers and could be one of those that becomes a really nice horse. He's not a flamboyant work horse but he delivers on the track and is a horse who will win races."

Hardy Fella "had a liking for finishing second last year" but came out and won impressively in his final race at Ludlow.

"He'll go novice handicap chasing and I'm hoping he'll be a natural over fences and should make his mark handicapping."

General Medrano was very keen in his races early last season and Lavelle's team took time out to teach him to settle.

"Once he learned to settle he started to show he was a nice horse," Lavelle says. "He won well at Fontwell and was second in a decent race at Exeter. Then he was fourth in a 100-grand race at Sandown at the end of the season.

"He's a big horse and will go chasing. He's also been a good jumper and I'm looking forward to seeing him in novice handicap chases. He's pretty versatile as to ground."

Manorbank *(below)* arrived at Bonita stables having had various issues but won his last two races really impressively. "He's a big

RACING POST

> As long as Red Rookie has got straight heavy ground, he'll be there or thereabouts and when he has, he usually wins. Two miles, go a good gallop, and he can be very impressive

■ James Best has ridden three winners for the yard from just 11 runners – a profit of £14.25

horse who has loads of pace at home and looks very exciting."

There are several Lavelle horses with "exciting" profiles and **Call To Duty** is probably near the top of that list.

"He's only four and it's very unusual for us to run four-year-olds in the spring," says Lavelle, "but he was just doing everything so easily, so we finished up running him in a bumper at Taunton at the back end of last season.

"He finished fourth after getting into all sorts of trouble and didn't get a clear run, but I think he's very smart. He'll probably have another run in a bumper just for education and, with a fair wind and unless there's a superstar in it, I'd expect him to go and win it. Then he'll go novice hurdling.

"He has something just a little bit special about him. If he went and won his bumper really easily, we may keep him in bumpers for all of this season and look at some of the Graded bumpers. If it doesn't go that way, then we'll go novice hurdling. But from what he's showing us, you'd like to think he'd be running in those better bumpers or novice hurdles further into the season."

Big Fish was just beaten in his first bumper

Red Rookie is well handicapped and thought capable of winning a valuable contest

If it's a wet autumn Red Rookie could be contesting the valuable two-mile handicaps.

"He hasn't got many miles on the clock and he's a horse with a big pot in him, but because of his rating and the ground he wants, there are only certain races available to us and we are absolutely dictated to by the ground. He's on a good mark, so I don't want to waste it."

Baltray finished third in a bumper in Ireland and looked in poor condition when he arrived, but he has done "physically fantastically" through the summer.

"He's been working nicely and will go novice hurdling and looks like a horse who should be winning his races and giving people lots of fun."

Silver Thorn hasn't run yet but has been showing up well on the gallops and is expected to prove a decent bumper horse. He'll be out in October.

De Rasher Counter is 11 and will be campaigned in veterans' chases in which he is expected to be "very competitive".

"He looks great in himself, squealing every morning and loving his work. He has competed at the top level and done well and still has life in him," says Lavelle.

Hang In There, who mixes chasing and hurdling with aplomb, has been "a little star" for the Lavelle team.

"He's won ten races for us and I think there's still room for manoeuvre off his handicap mark.

"We'll have a look at the Old Roan Chase at Aintree or the Prelude Hurdle at Market Rasen, then we'll put him away for his winter break. He's a proper, good-ground horse, but all credit to him, he ran a cracker to finish third in the Summer Plate at Market Rasen where the ground was bottomless."

Monks Meadow is an ex-Irish pointer who will go novice hurdling. "With the work he's been showing he's a horse we definitely like at this stage. We'll start him in a two-and-a-half novice hurdle and see how we go."

Interview by Lawrie Kelsey

at Exeter when he was too green. Then he ran at Ffos Las but was "full of mucus" and finished fifth.

"He's twice the horse this time around and is a smashing individual. He was unlucky he got so sick, but he's filled out and probably it wasn't the worst thing for him. He's in great order and is very sharp at the moment," says Lavelle, who will send him novice hurdling.

Red Rookie is very easy to predict, says Lavelle. "As long as he's got straight heavy ground, he'll be there or thereabouts and when he has, he usually wins. Two miles, go a good gallop, and he can be very impressive."

RACING POST
CHARLIE LONGSDON

Looking for the next flagbearer – and there is no shortage of candidates

THERE'S a vacancy for a flagbearer at Charlie Longsdon's Hull Farm stables in North Oxfordshire after the retirement of Snow Leopardess.

The eyecatching grey grabbed the attention of the public in the 2021-22 season after she won the Becher Chase and she was made one-time favourite for the 2022 Grand National.

She failed to win any of her six races last season, despite some

GUIDE TO THE JUMPS **2023-24**

WINNERS IN LAST FIVE SEASONS 46, 47, 31, 29, 36

honourable efforts, and now Hull Farm is searching for a replacement for their icon as they begin the journey to beating last season's total of 46 winners.

"We had no flagship money-earner last season apart from Snow Leopardess, who was retired, yet we still went and won the best part of 50 races from 55 horses, which isn't a bad shout, and we had a lot of novice-hurdle winners," says Longsdon.

Charlie Longsdon keeps a watchful eye on his string

47

Rare Edition: smart hurdler heads over fences this season

"So I'd like to hope that shows plenty of promise going forward and that some of those novice hurdlers can go on and be better handicappers.

"It's potentially an exciting season with so many good novice hurdlers coming through."

One of those hurdlers could be the flagbearer Hull Farm is searching for. After rattling off three victories by an aggregate of almost 28 lengths and finishing second in the Listed Sidney Banks Hurdle at Huntingdon last season, **Rare Edition** was considered good enough to tackle the Supreme Novices' Hurdle at the Cheltenham Festival with his trainer sounding rather bullish at the time.

"It's not my style to talk up a horse but he's certainly at this stage of his career as good a novice as we've had – no doubt," said Longsdon in January.

"My only worry is that he jumps his hurdles well but not as quick as some of them, so everything might happen too quick."

That latter comment was prescient because Rare Edition folded after leading the field to

GUIDE TO THE JUMPS 2023-24

> "I should never have sent him to Cheltenham or Aintree because it blew his head massively. He's not quick but he's got a relentlessly big stride. He shows it at home every day"

the third-last flight and was pulled up before the last when tailed off.

It was a similar story in Aintree's Grade 1 Top Novices' Hurdle, so after Longsdon had said the gelding's future lay over fences, Rare Edition's last two outings confirmed it.

"I was disappointed after the Sidney Banks, but giving him [Marble Sands] weight I probably shouldn't have been disappointed because the horse that beat him was the best of the British horses in the Ballymore at Cheltenham.

"I should never have sent him to Cheltenham or Aintree because it blew his head massively. He's not quick but he's got a relentlessly big stride. He shows it at home every day."

Longsdon plans to have Rare Edition ready to run in a novice chase in October. "We'll start him over two with a view to stepping him up in trip later. There are some lovely races for novices but we have nothing in mind for him.

"At one stage last season he was seen as the best of the English novice hurdlers, so if he maintains that form we can look at something

RACING POST

Parramount: won three times last season and showed "huge promise"

more fancy, but we'll stay very grounded."

If Rare Edition fails to fill the Snow Leopardess role, perhaps **Parramount** can step up. The seven-year-old had a busy season, running seven times, winning three, and being placed in two others.

"He showed huge promise," says Longsdon. "The only times he was well beaten were at Aintree and Haydock. I fancied him for both those races but the ground was too soft at Aintree, and he was just suffering the effects of a long season in the Swinton at Haydock.

"If we take these two blips away, he has a very exciting future, both over hurdles and fences, and could be able to take over the mantle from his half-sister Snow Leopardess. I think he's far more talented than her, although he's probably not as hardy.

"I think he may stay hurdling one more season and we'll try to pick up a nice handicap somewhere. We'll start him over two sometime in November but step him up to two and a half pretty sharpish. His sister wanted soft ground but I think he wants better ground."

Described by Longsdon as "a revelation", **Tea For Free** was a money-spinner for the yard last season, winning four chases as his handicap mark rose from 105 to 139.

He was joint favourite for the £100,000 Sky Bet Handicap Chase at Doncaster in January, but fell at the second-last fence when upsides the winner.

"He picked up an odd injury that day, which our vet had never seen before. He pulled a ligament in a hind leg, which is an injury more associated with old ponies. He's in pre-training now but you won't see him until Christmas time at the earliest. The

GUIDE TO THE JUMPS 2023-24

CHARLIE LONGSDON
CHIPPING NORTON, OXFORDSHIRE

RECORD AROUND THE COURSES

	Total W-R	Per cent	Non-hcp Hdle	Non-hcp Chase	Hcp Hdle	Hcp Chase	N.H. Flat	£1 level stake
Uttoxeter	43-227	18.9	11-53	4-10	12-60	16-93	0-11	-18.84
Worcester	33-220	15.0	6-42	1-12	13-69	9-76	4-21	+4.06
Market Rasen	31-204	15.2	8-32	1-5	10-68	10-77	2-22	-91.32
Huntingdon	31-220	14.1	8-53	2-8	9-79	10-62	2-18	-53.42
Southwell	30-175	17.1	9-40	2-6	9-61	6-48	4-20	+14.43
Fontwell	28-132	21.2	9-24	0-2	6-44	10-47	3-15	-15.35
Warwick	25-193	13.0	7-57	0-6	5-56	10-52	3-22	-63.21
Stratford	23-133	17.3	3-28	2-5	11-42	5-50	2-8	-1.89
Doncaster	20-167	12.0	7-51	0-6	3-40	8-59	2-11	-46.23
Bangor-On-Dee	19-100	19.0	5-26	2-5	2-22	7-37	3-10	-8.92
Wetherby	18-97	18.6	5-24	2-8	1-22	8-35	2-8	-18.41
Ludlow	18-134	13.4	7-40	0-2	2-34	8-46	1-12	-34.93
Kempton	13-115	11.3	3-19	1-5	2-34	7-52	0-5	-29.55
Towcester	11-66	16.7	1-20	4-9	2-16	3-15	1-6	-27.69
Carlisle	10-47	21.3	5-10	2-5	0-7	2-20	1-5	-26.58
Plumpton	10-78	12.8	4-29	0-1	2-17	4-28	0-3	-36.42
Sandown	9-92	9.8	1-5	1-5	0-23	7-57	0-2	+4.25
Hereford	8-50	16.0	4-16	0-0	2-13	2-19	0-2	-22.77
Musselburgh	7-25	28.0	5-8	0-0	0-5	2-12	0-0	+9.87
Ascot	7-75	9.3	0-14	0-7	2-23	3-23	2-8	+1.50
Chepstow	7-86	8.1	2-18	0-1	1-26	4-38	0-3	-51.27
Newcastle	6-19	31.6	2-5	0-0	2-3	1-9	1-2	-1.51
Exeter	6-36	16.7	0-4	2-3	2-13	2-15	0-1	+0.87
Haydock	6-56	10.7	1-5	1-2	2-20	1-25	1-4	-2.50
Sedgefield	5-20	25.0	0-4	1-2	1-3	3-9	0-2	-4.81
Hexham	5-21	23.8	2-8	2-3	1-3	0-5	0-2	-9.28
Newton Abbot	5-35	14.3	1-2	1-3	1-14	2-15	0-1	-18.55
Wincanton	5-50	10.0	0-6	1-2	1-19	3-22	0-1	-7.50
Aintree	5-90	5.6	1-19	0-2	2-22	2-35	0-12	-64.47
Newbury	5-99	5.1	0-18	0-6	2-19	3-46	0-10	-59.50
Cheltenham	5-138	3.6	1-17	0-9	3-40	1-60	0-12	-99.00
Cartmel	4-12	33.3	0-0	0-0	1-5	3-7	0-0	+12.00
Lingfield	4-28	14.3	1-9	1-2	1-6	1-11	0-0	+4.92
Leicester	4-44	9.1	0-16	2-2	0-4	2-22	0-0	-32.40
Perth	3-8	37.5	0-0	1-2	0-2	2-4	0-0	+6.73
Fakenham	3-24	12.5	0-7	0-1	1-7	2-9	0-0	-13.40
Kelso	2-19	10.5	0-2	0-0	0-3	2-14	0-0	-9.25
Ffos Las	2-22	9.1	0-3	0-1	2-8	0-8	0-2	-7.50
Catterick	2-25	8.0	1-8	0-0	0-8	1-8	0-1	-18.46
Southwell (AW)	1-1	100.0	0-0	0-0	0-0	0-0	1-1	+3.00
Ayr	1-15	6.7	1-2	0-2	0-5	0-6	0-0	-13.90
Taunton	1-28	3.6	0-4	0-0	1-14	0-10	0-0	-23.00
Lingfield (AW)	0-1	0.0	0-0	0-0	0-0	0-0	0-1	-1.00
Kempton (AW)	0-8	0.0	0-0	0-0	0-0	0-0	0-8	-8.00

■ Following runners from the stable during August has returned a profit every year since 2019, totalling £23.13

prognosis is good; we just need to give him time.

"I think there's still room for improvement and he'll be aimed at the big staying handicaps next spring and, on the form he has shown so far, he will be winning a nice prize."

Guetapan Collonges is an improved chaser over the last two seasons, winning four times and rising from a lowly mark of 108 to 130.

Longsdon "threw him in at the deep end" in the Classic Chase at Warwick and the Midlands National at Uttoxeter, but he managed to more than stay afloat by finishing fourth on both occasions.

"I think there's a big chase in this horse this season. He was probably still a bit weak to be winning one of those chases, but when he was dropped into a normal grade he won both times," says the trainer.

"He's bigger and stronger this year and those better races are the ones he's made for this season with another year under his belt."

51

Castle Robin is another staying chaser to note. He landed a big-money chase at Sandown in February, confirming the promise his trainer had seen, and is fancied to add to his tally this season.

"I always said there was a decent chase in him and I was disappointed when he got struck into at Cheltenham as I thought he would have won that day," says Longsdon. "I think he's well able to win another big chase off his current handicap mark of 136 and I think he'll be better on slow ground. They were going a bit too quick for him at Aintree on good ground when he fell."

Glimpse Of Gala is the mare who keeps on giving, says Longsdon. "She's as tough as tough can be. At the beginning of last season, I wasn't sure there would be much improvement with her then handicap mark of 123, however she won two ITV races at Kempton and Warwick and ended up running at both Cheltenham and Aintree.

"She's only small, but she's hard as nails. That's why she's such a good mare. There are plenty of opportunities for mares to run in valuable chases and these are the races she will be aimed at."

Hector Javilex gave the stable a great day out at Cheltenham on New Year's Day when winning a good handicap hurdle. He couldn't quite win again last season but continued to run well in good company.

Good as he was over hurdles, the excitement is expected to come this season when he goes chasing.

"He jumps his hurdles like fences and I think he'll be a far better horse chasing than hurdling. I'm looking forward to him running in a novice chase," says Longsdon.

"He'll be out in mid-October, probably over two and a half miles. He'll go on most ground, although he wouldn't want it bottomless."

Of the Hull Farm hurdlers, it should pay to follow Irish point runner-up **Realisation**, who went some way to justifying her £130,000 price tag when thrashing £240,000 buy **Peaky Boy** by almost ten lengths in a Bangor bumper.

The latter won his bumper next time out and, with another dual winner appearing from the Bangor race, as well as plenty of horses who were placed, the form looks strong.

"She may have had only one appearance for us, but she was very impressive," says Longsdon. "She had a little niggling pelvis injury in the spring, so she hasn't run again. She could have run in May but I didn't bother because I thought she needed slower ground.

Hector Javilex: got the Longsdon stable off to the perfect start in 2023 with victory on New Year's Day

"I think she'll want two and a half miles but we'll start her over two, probably at the end of October at Worcester.

"If she goes and does that nicely, we'll step her into stronger company as the season goes on. I have nothing particular in mind. I'd just like her to stay sound and be right for this year. We have a lot to look forward to."

Realisation's owners, Merriebelle Irish Farm Ltd, who sponsor Longsdon's yard, also have another promising mare in **Jayapura**.

"She won an Irish point at Dromahane in the spring very comfortably and from what she's shown so far she looks a very nice mare.

"We'll look for a bumper in the middle of October and if she can win that, you'd like to think she could go and get some black type."

Alien Storm won his novice hurdle last season and was second to a nice horse of Nicky Henderson's in Russian Ruler.

"I wanted to run him in the Swinton at Haydock in May but he was balloted out by one. I think he's nicely handicapped and can go and win a decent handicap this season before he goes chasing."

Gaelic Park wasn't quite right for most of last season, says Longsdon, despite finishing a close second in a couple of novice hurdles, but he ended it in runaway style, landing a maiden hurdle at Warwick by 30 lengths.

"To go novice chasing and off a mark of 119 I do think he could be well handicapped," says Longsdon. "He'll be out in mid-October and there's a race for him at Huntingdon. He likes slower ground."

There's plenty of optimism around **Mint Condition**, who arrived from Jennie Candlish's yard after finishing fifth in the Kim Muir at the 2022 Cheltenham Festival.

"That was quite a performance. He's had a leg injury and been off for 18 months. He'll turn ten in January, therefore we'll have a good look at some of those veterans' races. There are a few fun things that could fit him. He wants slow ground and three miles."

Miss Applejack, a half-sister to Glimpse Of Gala, just held on to win a mares' bumper at Ludlow in May.

"She's a homebred from a hardy, tough family, which is good because she can go and do her bit. If she can win another bumper with a penalty, she could go on and win some black type. She'll then go on and win her hurdles as well."

Mint Condition: could be one to follow in veterans' races

Another Irish point winner for whom expectations are high is **New Order**. The brother to Gordon Elliott's 145-rated chaser The Goffer won his point at Castlelands easily in March with a bold front-running display before being bought for £95,000 at the Cheltenham spring sale.

"He's not the most straightforward horse to ride but he can only improve," says Longsdon. "We'll start him off in a maiden hurdle in October before hopefully running in better novice hurdles later in the season. I think he's a nice horse.

"He is another exciting addition to the team and looks to have a bright future."

Western Zephyr ran six times last season, winning three novice hurdles. "He's quite quirky," says Longsdon. "In a couple of races he'd run his race before he got to the start. But there's no doubt he's got an engine and could be good in novice chases.

"He'll step up to two and a half miles because he won his races being slow in my eyes. Jumping is his forte. If we can keep him sane before the flag goes up, then he'll have a chance."

Well Dick is a big horse who loves soft ground. "He's a proper mudlark, a proper stayer," says Longsdon. "He'll go novice chasing but I can see him being a Welsh National type next season because he loves soft ground."

Book Of Tales is a double Flat winner who won on his debut over hurdles at Fontwell in August and could develop into a useful juvenile hurdler. "I think he's a little better than an average juvenile. He has the right attitude and jumps well."

Gentleman Jacques showed enough in a Newbury bumper in March, when second a furlong out before tiring to finish ninth of 19 in very soft ground behind a runaway winner, for Longsdon to predict a bumper triumph this season followed by victory in his novice hurdle.

"He's grown this year and has had a summer on his back and looks a nice horse."

Interview by Lawrie Kelsey

RACING POST

NEIL MULHOLLAND

Stars of the future and old favourites

NEIL MULHOLLAND has made some shrewd purchases from the Irish point-to-pointing fraternity down the years and he is poised to launch another highly promising recruit this season.

From an exciting group of young horses starting the new season among a string of around 80 at Mulholland's Conkwell Lodge yard, near Bath, he has singled out a handful to follow.

Top of the list is **Hawaii Du**

GUIDE TO THE JUMPS **2023-24**

WINNERS IN LAST FIVE SEASONS 61, 62, 62, 50, 49

Lord Accord: the leading prize-money earner for Neil Mulholland (inset) last season and could be suited by targets early in the season

Milkwood: will bid to go one better than last season's second in the Welsh Champion Hurdle

Mestivel, bought for £100,000 after finishing third, beaten only two lengths, at Corbeagh House in December 2021.

The winner was Kalanisi Star, who won a bumper, a maiden hurdle and subsequently ran in two Grade 1 novice hurdles. Runner-up was Rare Edition, who joined Charlie Longsdon and was at one time Britain's leading novice hurdler last season after three successive victories.

Not surprisingly, Mulholland is keen to discover whether Hawaii Du Mestivel can follow their example after missing last season through injury.

"He's a nice horse who we've always liked," he says. "He had a setback and, if he stays in one piece, we're really looking forward to him. He'll go novice hurdling but we'll start him off in a bumper first.

"We'll take him away for a gallop and see how that goes before deciding. We like this lad. I suppose you could call him a dark horse – and we could do with a few more like him."

The five-year-old **Moonset** is another promising ex-Irish pointer for whom hopes are high after he finished fourth and third in two starts, beaten only six lengths each time.

"He's a nice horse who will start in a bumper, then go novice hurdling and

GUIDE TO THE JUMPS 2023-24

NEIL MULHOLLAND
LIMPLEY STOKE, BATH

RECORD AROUND THE COURSES

	Total W-R	Per cent	Non-hcp Hdle	Non-hcp Chase	Hcp Hdle	Hcp Chase	N.H. Flat	£1 level stake
Fontwell	66-350	18.9	11-69	5-15	29-152	14-84	7-30	+14.82
Worcester	59-381	15.5	12-71	4-12	29-174	14-98	0-26	+59.06
Uttoxeter	33-265	12.5	4-48	0-1	18-138	10-69	1-9	-58.66
Sedgefield	25-66	37.9	6-18	1-1	8-26	9-19	1-2	+8.96
Newton Abbot	25-213	11.7	6-38	0-9	9-109	10-50	0-7	-55.44
Plumpton	24-184	13.0	2-47	0-3	12-84	8-38	2-12	-56.37
Wincanton	24-317	7.6	2-107	0-6	14-112	7-73	1-19	-130.05
Taunton	23-212	10.8	3-55	0-2	13-106	7-35	0-14	-36.20
Stratford	22-147	15.0	5-40	1-4	11-59	4-38	1-6	+49.19
Chepstow	22-184	12.0	2-63	1-5	10-54	7-49	2-13	-28.47
Ffos Las	21-185	11.4	3-38	1-3	8-71	6-55	3-18	-17.01
Southwell	21-192	10.9	2-20	2-5	9-100	7-54	1-13	-60.21
Fakenham	20-84	23.8	3-16	0-0	14-45	3-21	0-2	-1.75
Wetherby	17-83	20.5	3-13	2-5	6-30	5-29	1-6	-0.19
Huntingdon	16-118	13.6	3-22	2-3	4-48	7-36	0-9	-45.60
Perth	15-76	19.7	3-8	0-0	7-29	4-37	1-2	-0.12
Doncaster	15-86	17.4	4-22	1-3	5-33	2-21	3-7	-7.00
Cheltenham	15-146	10.3	2-25	3-13	2-46	8-60	0-2	-35.10
Warwick	14-102	13.7	2-20	3-7	4-39	4-28	1-8	-34.68
Market Rasen	14-111	12.6	2-12	1-3	5-45	4-44	2-7	-48.84
Hereford	13-71	18.3	2-10	0-0	8-37	1-16	2-8	-3.44
Ludlow	12-67	17.9	3-17	0-0	6-27	3-15	0-8	-2.50
Bangor	12-94	12.8	3-21	1-4	5-37	3-27	0-5	-41.24
Exeter	11-133	8.3	3-57	1-3	5-50	1-18	1-5	-82.38
Newbury	8-82	9.8	0-16	0-0	4-23	3-39	1-4	-1.88
Newcastle	7-32	21.9	0-3	0-0	4-11	2-17	1-1	-6.75
Cartmel	7-43	16.3	2-8	1-2	3-18	1-15	0-0	-14.06
Sandown	7-58	12.1	0-5	0-1	2-19	5-33	0-0	-14.00
Kempton	7-82	8.5	1-12	0-3	1-33	5-33	0-1	+10.00
Catterick	6-23	26.1	4-7	0-3	1-4	1-7	0-2	+1.95
Aintree	4-35	11.4	0-3	0-2	2-11	2-14	0-5	-5.50
Lingfield	4-42	9.5	1-13	0-0	2-15	1-14	0-0	+13.50
Ascot	3-33	9.1	0-5	0-0	1-12	2-14	0-2	-18.75
Hexham	2-7	28.6	0-1	0-0	1-4	0-1	1-1	-2.00
Kelso	2-14	14.3	0-2	0-0	0-2	2-9	0-1	-9.20
Haydock	2-40	5.0	0-3	0-1	0-20	2-16	0-0	-26.75
Lingfield (AW)	1-7	14.3	0-0	0-0	0-0	0-0	1-7	-3.75
Musselburgh	1-14	7.1	0-3	0-0	1-7	0-3	0-1	-10.00
Ayr	1-17	5.9	0-0	0-0	1-7	0-10	0-0	-13.00
Carlisle	1-17	5.9	1-6	0-2	0-1	0-4	0-4	-15.75
Leicester	1-20	5.0	0-7	0-0	1-7	0-6	0-0	-7.00
Kempton (AW)	0-4	0.0	0-0	0-0	0-0	0-0	0-4	-4.00

■ Conditional rider Joe Anderson has a 26% strike-rate for the stable and a level-stake profit of £10.50

hopefully be one of the nice horses coming through."

The four-year-old **Double Powerful** is yet another Mulholland hopes can translate his third-place finish in an Irish point-to-point in February, a race in which the fourth came out and won, into winning British form.

"The form stacks up well," he says. "We'll start him out in a bumper and see how that goes before deciding whether to send him novice hurdling. He'll be out in October/November time."

The five-year-old mare **Lahinch Wave** is another recruit from the Irish pointing field. She finished third, beaten a length and a quarter, on her only start. "She's had a summer break and is another one we're looking forward to. She'll want nice ground."

The French-bred **Inoui Machin** is a half-brother to five winners and looks yet another promising sort among the Conkwell tyros destined for better things. He won two bumpers early this year since when he's been schooled over hurdles for a novice campaign.

"He's taken well to them, has had a good summer break and looks well," says

Mulholland. "He's an honest, genuine horse with a will to win. We like him and he'll be one of our nicer horses.

"He's unbeaten so far and I'm sure he'll be going for some of the nicer hurdle races later in the season, but I'll be happy for him to win his novice hurdle and let him do the talking. It's a bit early to be hyping him up."

Of the older horses, make a note of **Lord Accord**, the yard's leading money-earner last season with £50,000.

He finished ninth in the Scottish Grand National at Ayr where he found the four miles a little too taxing, pulled up in the Kim Muir at the Cheltenham Festival, and was ninth in the Coral Gold Cup.

But earlier in the season he had won at Cheltenham in October and was second in the Badger Beer at Wincanton, two races which will kick off this season, and maybe he will take in the Coral Gold Cup as well.

"He's in good order and hopefully can give a good account of himself again this season," says Mulholland, who might try to give him a run over hurdles before his Cheltenham race.

The nine-year-old **Milkwood** has been a good servant for the yard and, all being well, his seasonal opener will be the Welsh Champion Hurdle at Ffos Las in October.

"He finished second last year and seems in good order. I'm very happy with him. We might step him up in trip after that."

Ragamuffin is a very consistent horse, winning over fences and hurdles. From eight chase starts last season, he won three and was second five times.

"He hasn't got any big dates in the diary because there are races for him every day of the week. We'll probably stick to hurdles at the moment. Good ground and two miles four is what he wants, and going left-handed."

Sainte Doctor won her last two chases in April but has had a minor setback and will be saved for a spring campaign. "She's a good, solid, consistent mare but she wouldn't want

the ground too testing," says Mulholland.

Ike Sport comes into the same "solid and consistent" category after winning once and finishing a close runner-up twice in handicap hurdles this season.

Six-year-old handicap hurdler **Abbeyhill** has finished fourth in his last two runs but is "going the right way", according to Mulholland, and off a moderate rating of 70 could be worth following.

"He's had a good summer break. He's not going to go for any big races at the moment because he has a low rating, but he's a horse who will be competitive and hopefully has a good season ahead of him. He'll be out in October."

Any News is a handicap chaser who won at Worcester in September after five successive placed efforts. "He's a grand horse

GUIDE TO THE JUMPS 2023-24

Ragamuffin (noseband front): proven and consistent performer who can continue to pay his way

who is always there or thereabouts. He's won £42,000 and is a solid, consistent horse. He wants three miles and nice ground. It took a bit of time to get his confidence over fences but he jumps them well, so we'll stick to chasing now.

"The ground was too soft for him at Worcester on his last run. There's a handicap at Chepstow in October we could run him in or a three-mile novice handicap at Wetherby."

The six-year-old handicap hurdler **Broomfields Cave** has done little wrong this season and his form is rock solid.

"He won in June at Southwell, was upsides the winner when falling at the last at Uttoxeter, and was second, giving a stone to the winner, last time out at Southwell.

"He should be up to winning a couple of races throughout the season and is one who is worth following," says Mulholland.

Celtic Fortune is a six-year-old who has found his feet now he's running in handicaps. "He's had a nice summer break and should be competitive off his mark of 93 and hopefully could win a few nice races."

Shuil Ceoil might not be rated particularly highly after three moderate runs over hurdles, but Mulholland expects him to be competitive off his 97 rating.

"He had a few setbacks throughout last season but we've had a nice run with him and he seems in good order and so, fingers crossed, he's a bit stronger and can be competitive again."

The seven-year-old handicap hurdler **Watergrange Jack** has risen a stone in the ratings this season to 125 after winning his last three races. His future lies over fences but this season his targets will be over hurdles.

"He's been a very consistent horse who has won four and been second three times and third once in 16 outings for us," says the trainer.

"We could step him up into some better races this season at the nicer meetings, including Cheltenham, but whatever he does over hurdles is a bonus because he's a big chaser in the making."

Brief Times is rated 137 over fences and has won six times for Mulholland, including two of his last three outings, and has finished second four times and third twice.

"He's a solid horse, wants nice ground and is better going left-handed. There's a race for him at Cheltenham in October, possibly the same race as for Lord Accord, or the three-mile Native River Chase at Chepstow."

Garincha is a soft-ground specialist who won three of his six races last season and is expected to be equally effective this season once the rains arrive.

"He's taken to chasing and goes well on heavy ground. I'm really happy with him. He won first time out at Bangor last year and we're just waiting for soft ground, then he'll be out," says Mulholland.

The final appearance for three-mile chaser **Excelerator Express** last season came in the Galway Plate in July for which he'd been carefully prepped. But the plan ended at the third fence where Sam Twiston-Davies was unseated when his mount unavoidably collided with a faller.

"He was very unlucky because he was fairly tuned for the race. He was just cantering away nicely in behind but unfortunately that's jump racing. They were still a long way from home but the jockey was very happy with him.

"He's back in and cantering away and will be ready around Christmas time for some of the nicer races in the spring, like those at the festival and Aintree.

"He goes on good and good-to-soft ground, but he wouldn't want it too soft. He's a good solid horse and you wouldn't mind having a yard [full of horses] like him."

Five-time winning chaser **Court Master** has reached the veteran stage at the age of ten and will be aimed at those types of races.

He ran creditably in the bet365 Gold Cup at Sandown in April before being pulled up before the last fence, and joined Mulholland at the start of this season, since when he's been placed three times in four outings.

"He was second in a Class 2 race at Uttoxeter, only beaten a length and a half, and the winner has come out and won again. He was going well at Bangor last time out when he unseated the rider.

"We'll be looking at veterans' races, starting at Chepstow's two-day meeting, and see how he goes."

Interview by Lawrie Kelsey

Court Master: five times a winner over fences and will have veterans' chases on his agenda

GUIDE TO THE JUMPS **2023-24**

> "We could step him up into some better races this season at the nicer meetings, including Cheltenham, but whatever he does over hurdles is a bonus because he's a big chaser in the making"

RACING POST

PAUL NICHOLLS

Bravemansgame could be key to a 15th trainers' title

GUIDE TO THE JUMPS 2023-24

WINNERS IN LAST FIVE SEASONS 163, 143, 176, 96, 135

MISSING at Manor Farm Stables this season will be the towering presence of its former owner Paul Barber, but the much-lamented father figure of West Country jump racing, who died in June, would have been proud of the exciting team Paul Nicholls has assembled as he sets out in pursuit of a record-equalling 15th trainers' title.

In **Bravemansgame** the yard houses the top staying chaser in Britain, but for Nicholls there remains some unfinished business and he is already relishing another crack at his Gold Cup conqueror, Galopin Des Champs, next March.

"I know we have seven lengths to make up on Willie Mullins' horse," he says, "but we might ride ours a bit different next time and take our time with him a bit more." The rematch is an intriguing prospect, but ask the trainer to nominate his stable star's No. 1 objective this winter and he replies: "Without a doubt, the King George. All roads lead to Kempton on Boxing Day and we could start off in the Charlie Hall, going permitting, like he did last year."

The stats speak in favour of a successful title defence, as four of Nicholls' five previous King George winners managed to double up when returning to Kempton a year later.

After Christmas don't be surprised if Bravemansgame is off the track until the spring, as Nicholls will want him as fresh as possible for an assault on Grade 1 targets at Cheltenham, Aintree and Punchestown.

Another likely King George entry is **Pic D'Orhy**, who broke his Grade 1 duck in the Marsh (formerly Melling) Chase at Aintree over two and a half miles. "We think he'll get three miles when we want him to," says Nicholls, "but we're likely to stick to the shorter trip for now." As the owner loves having runners at Ascot, the 1965 Chase in November is an ideal starting point.

No chaser at Ditcheat has a bigger following than **Frodon**, but retirement beckons for the ever-popular veteran who turns 12 in January. However, the multiple Graded winner has been in such fine form on the gallops this autumn that his trainer argues: "How can we possibly think about retiring him when he's in such mad form?" The plan is to have Frodon spot-on for Wincanton in early November when he will attempt to repeat last year's victory under 12st in the Badger Beer Chase. Don't be surprised, however, if he is rerouted to the Charlie Hall Chase should the ground come up too quick for Bravemansgame.

If he lines up at Wincanton, Frodon might struggle this time to concede 11lb to stable companion **Threeunderthrufive**. The eight-year-old was largely disappointing last season, when he was poorly handicapped and rarely got the good ground he likes, but he could bounce back rejuvenated by corrective wind surgery over the summer, and his close fourth in the Scottish National in April suggests there's a big staying handicap to be won with him.

There were broad smiles, and relief, on Nicholls' face when **Stage Star** held the Irish at bay to land the Grade 1 Turners at the Festival. But the trainer is under no illusion the seven-year-old will face some tough tasks in open Grade 1 company this winter.

"The balance of his form suggests he'll have to improve to mix it with the best, and he may not be the easiest to place, but I hope come the spring he'll be worth his place in the Ryanair."

As Stage Star needs to go left-handed and won twice at Cheltenham last season, he is a possible for the Paddy Power Gold Cup, and could warm up for that task in the intermediate chase at Newton Abbot the yard has captured recently with Pic D'Orhy and Bravemansgame.

The trainer feels his smart two-miler **Greaneteen** has probably achieved as much as he's going to over the minimum trip, so he could be stepped up in distance. He'll start off in the Haldon Gold Cup, which he won last year, or the Shloer Chase at Cheltenham. If Exeter is chosen he could have his work cut out conceding 17lb to stablemate **Solo**, whose victory in the Grade 2 Pendil suggested there could be more to come at Graded level.

Nicholls likes to lay one out for the Coral Gold Cup and **Complete Unknown** could line up strongly fancied this November. He did nothing but improve as a novice and can show he's still going the right way in the Colin Parker Chase at Carlisle in October. One word of warning, though, as the trainer

GUIDE TO THE JUMPS **2023-24**

PAUL NICHOLLS
DITCHEAT, SOMERSET

RECORD AROUND THE COURSES

	Total W-R	Per cent	Non-hcp Hdle	Non-hcp Chase	Hcp Hdle	Hcp Chase	N.H. Flat	£1 level stake
Wincanton	171-559	30.6	81-190	15-39	29-139	30-129	16-62	-43.86
Taunton	118-393	30.0	68-170	6-14	21-109	16-65	7-35	-30.21
Newton Abbot	92-330	27.9	37-89	29-67	8-73	17-87	1-14	-105.11
Chepstow	88-376	23.4	41-146	4-22	15-64	9-94	19-50	-73.36
Kempton	88-431	20.4	27-116	33-100	10-76	13-106	5-33	-76.48
Exeter	75-265	28.3	38-120	18-38	5-32	8-48	6-27	-52.02
Newbury	69-343	20.1	20-55	13-53	12-98	21-116	3-21	+8.85
Cheltenham	67-631	10.6	12-130	22-142	12-151	17-188	4-20	-115.64
Ascot	65-350	18.6	11-62	19-65	12-86	16-114	7-23	+26.39
Sandown	64-363	17.6	12-51	19-89	17-105	14-106	2-12	+5.47
Fontwell	60-158	38.0	14-50	29-48	5-19	11-34	1-7	+1.00
Worcester	33-107	30.8	10-31	11-25	2-18	5-27	5-6	-1.17
Aintree	32-264	12.1	8-54	12-66	2-35	7-93	3-16	-79.90
Doncaster	31-141	22.0	9-39	10-31	4-23	7-40	1-8	-38.57
Haydock	29-119	24.4	9-31	16-32	1-36	2-17	1-3	-27.02
Ludlow	27-113	23.9	8-34	5-14	4-16	9-43	1-6	-36.79
Musselburgh	24-72	33.3	6-20	5-13	8-23	5-15	0-1	+5.44
Warwick	24-98	24.5	2-26	12-28	4-14	3-22	3-8	-28.43
Plumpton	21-65	32.3	7-26	2-7	5-13	4-16	3-3	+11.14
Stratford	19-69	27.5	7-22	4-20	1-5	5-18	2-4	-11.27
Ayr	18-83	21.7	5-7	2-7	7-35	3-31	1-3	+24.20
Hereford	16-58	27.6	8-24	0-6	4-8	2-11	2-9	-8.78
Ffos Las	14-45	31.1	4-11	3-7	3-10	3-9	1-8	+11.03
Fakenham	14-45	31.1	5-18	6-17	1-4	2-6	0-0	-6.96
Huntingdon	14-46	30.4	2-8	5-16	3-12	1-5	3-5	+7.64
Southwell	13-35	37.1	5-14	4-5	1-4	3-9	0-3	-0.27
Kelso	12-38	31.6	3-9	5-14	2-6	2-8	0-1	-7.90
Wetherby	12-39	30.8	5-16	3-10	0-0	2-10	2-3	-2.06
Market Rasen	11-55	20.0	5-9	2-9	1-6	3-30	0-1	-12.00
Leicester	8-17	47.1	1-3	4-10	0-0	3-4	0-0	-0.44
Perth	8-22	36.4	2-6	1-3	0-2	5-11	0-0	+9.53
Bangor	8-27	29.6	1-6	5-14	0-3	2-4	0-0	-5.17
Uttoxeter	7-57	12.3	0-9	1-4	2-15	3-28	1-1	-23.16
Carlisle	6-11	54.5	1-1	4-7	0-0	1-3	0-0	+4.72
Lingfield	6-21	28.6	3-7	2-5	1-5	0-4	0-0	+6.68
Hexham	4-4	100.0	1-1	3-3	0-0	0-0	0-0	+4.60
Newcastle	4-12	33.3	4-8	0-0	0-0	0-3	0-1	+1.70
Catterick	3-7	42.9	1-3	2-3	0-0	0-0	0-1	-2.00
Kempton (AW)	2-23	8.7	0-0	0-0	0-0	0-0	2-23	-7.00
Southwell (AW)	1-2	50.0	0-0	0-0	0-0	0-0	1-2	+2.00
Wolverhampton (AW)	1-3	33.3	0-0	0-0	0-0	0-0	1-3	-1.27
Sedgefield	1-4	25.0	0-2	1-2	0-0	0-0	0-0	-2.82
Lingfield (AW)	1-8	12.5	0-0	0-0	0-0	0-0	1-8	-1.00
Cartmel	0-7	0.0	0-0	0-0	0-1	0-6	0-0	-7.00

*From top:
Complete Unknown,
Threeunderthrufive
and Hitman*

added: "The key to this horse is the going, as he's done all his winning on soft or heavy ground."

In the staying handicap chase department there could be a decent prize in **Flash Collonges**, who was in the process of running a good race in the Scottish National when falling. He is unexposed over marathon trips, and with his preference for decent ground a return trip to Ayr next spring might prove fruitful.

Hitman was beaten a head in the Old Roan 12 months ago and will try to go one better in the Aintree Grade 2. His win record over fences of 1-10 is off-putting, but that percentage may improve now the trainer has stopped trying to turn him into a three-mile chaser.

As he is only six, further improvement is expected from **Il Ridoto**. He's been plying his trade in big-field Cheltenham handicaps and may be weighted up to his best now, so might be one to try in conditions chases.

There is an exceptionally strong-looking

Stay Away Fay: the Cheltenham Festival winner could be a major force in staying novice chases

GUIDE TO THE JUMPS 2023-24

■ Conditional rider Ben Bromley has a 50% strike-rate for the stable (8-16) and a level-stake profit of £5.62

squad of novice chasers. **Knappers Hill** is the highest-rated hurdler switching to fences. He ended up a good jumper of hurdles so can be a potent force if translating his Grade 2-winning form to the bigger obstacles. He could debut in a usually informative novice chase at Chepstow's big October meeting that Nicholls likes to target, and if all goes well he'll step up in class in the Grade 2 Rising Stars at Wincanton.

Stay Away Fay (Albert Bartlett), Hermes Allen (Challow) and Tahmuras (Tolworth) were Grade 1 winners over hurdles last season and whose chasing debuts will be keenly anticipated. **Stay Away Fay** should develop into an out-and-out stayer; the physically imposing **Tahmuras** has the look of a promising two-miler and he arguably has more scope than **Hermes Allen**, who is not an obvious chaser on looks. But the last-named amazed his trainer last season when proving size isn't everything, so having turned out to be a surprise package over hurdles, maybe he can now do the same over fences.

Five hurdlers who are destined for fences will first be given a run in a decent handicap hurdle; success there might result in chasing being put on hold for 12 months. **Rubaud** should become a lovely two-mile chaser, be it this season or next, but to start with will head to Kempton in mid-October for a Listed hurdle, before stepping up in grade in the Elite Hurdle at Wincanton.

Hugos New Horse showed progressive form as a novice hurdler and this strong finisher may have further improvement in him. A run in the Grade 2 staying hurdle at Wetherby or Haydock's £100,000-plus long distance hurdle in November will tell connections where they stand. Either way, this likeable sort is destined for further success; he is admirably versatile regards trip and ground.

Chepstow's Silver Trophy is a possible target for Sonigino, Beau Balko and Lallygag. Of the trio, **Sonigino** has the potential to be a very good novice chaser when the time comes.

Henri The Second, **Makin'yourmindup** and **Knowsley Road** should all do well in staying novice events. **Henri The Second** didn't reach the heights expected of him as a novice hurdler, but a summer breathing operation, plus a step up to three miles, could spark improvement. He'll always need some cut in the ground.

Nicholls seems especially sweet on the chasing prospects of Imperial Cup winner **Iceo** and **Outlaw Peter**. Iceo is best with some cut but Outlaw Peter is versatile ground-wise.

The ex-French pair Golden Son and Jetronic look interesting. Some heat in a leg prevented **Golden Son** running for Nicholls last winter but he boasted high-class form over hurdles and fences in France. He's taking a lot of getting fit after his absence. **Jetronic** had just the two runs in France but looked highly promising on each occasion. His novice status over fences runs out on December 1, so should he be out before then, the hint should be taken.

Afadil and Blueking D'Oroux look the pair to follow in this category. **Afadil** is a big, strong sort and the type to improve in his second season; the Greatwood at Cheltenham might suit. **Blueking D'Oroux** has already shown the benefit of a winter breathing operation and his trainer believes he'll continue to progress. Ascot's valuable handicap hurdle the Saturday before Christmas looks a likely target.

Lower down the ratings, Rare Middleton and Lime Avenue are considered well handicapped. Provided **Rare Middleton** sharpens up his jumping he can take advantage of an attractive mark, while **Lime Avenue** could make a mockery of her mark granted decent ground. Nicholls says: "She looks an ideal sort for the Richard Barber memorial race at Wincanton in early November."

The lightly raced **Matterhorn** *(below)* needs to settle better to fulfil his undoubted potential; the Grade 2 Persian War has been mooted before his novice status runs out, so the five-year-old is clearly highly regarded.

An impressive victory at Ayr in April pushed **Sabrina**'s handicap mark to a level that makes conditions races now a viable option. The trainer notes there's a lovely programme nowadays for mares like her.

It augurs well for this season and beyond that Paul Nicholls had 18 individual winners of 20 bumper races last season. They will now be plying their trade in novice hurdles this season and there are some lovely prospects among them, none more so than **Captain Teague** who looks a future star. Considering he suffered on and off from sore shins last season and wasn't a sharp bumper type, his Champion Bumper third was an amazing run. He has proved a natural over hurdles this autumn and big things are expected of him. His trainer is even thinking of letting him debut in the Grade 2 Persian War, and that tells you how highly regarded he is.

Inthewaterside was the other star from last season. Being a giant of a horse – he's the tallest in the yard – he wasn't a natural bumper sort in appearance and it was raw talent and guts that got him home on his debut. He made it 2-2 at Sandown and is another for whom the sky's the limit.

Third to Inthewaterside at Sandown and now expected to win his share of staying novice hurdles is **Wrappedupinmay**. He may have found the ground a bit too lively when losing his unbeaten record and is still seen as a lovely prospect.

Forget **Fire Flyer**'s defeat at Newbury in February; the ground was way too quick and Nicholls regrets running. He had overcome greenness when making an impressive winning debut in the autumn and is expected to show his class now he goes hurdling.

Farland has come over from Ireland with a big reputation. The trainer says: "Everyone seemed to fancy him when he made his debut in a valuable bumper at the Punchestown festival, where he ran an eye-catcher in fourth."

Another very interesting recruit, this one from Germany, is **Panjari**. In a lightly raced career on the Flat he has scored twice in Listed company at up to a mile and a half and Nicholls says: "I'm a big fan of his sire Camelot. This one's profile reminds me of Irving, who came from Germany and won two Fighting Fifths for us."

Among the lightly raced novices boasting a 1-1 record in bumpers or point-to-points, the well-related **Farnoge**, another Camelot offspring, can benefit from a softly-softly approach so far; **Byorderofthecourt** missed last season with heat in a front leg but can make up for lost time; **Thames Water** would have gone on to further success last season but for getting jarred up when making a winning debut at Ascot; and **Tarras Wood** *(right)* was backward last season but it didn't stop him making a winning debut at Wetherby. The trainer rates him quite highly.

There are fewer novices than usual who have come from France via Auteuil, the reason being most of the potentially good ones cost a small fortune and make their way to Willie Mullins. One promising sort now at Ditcheat is **Irandando Has**, who cost a packet following his second place in the Listed Prix Finot last September, a race that is often chock-full of future talent. Connections have been very patient with him and he's probably one of the best lookers in the yard. Time will tell if he has the ability to match.

Beny Nahar Road was no great shakes on the Flat but looks the type to make a jumper and has been working well this autumn. And there's more to come from dual bumper winner **Meatloaf**, a Doctor Dino half-brother to the smart but ill-fated Thyme White.

A backward pair who are expected to leave last season's placed efforts well behind now they are going hurdling are **Tinklers Hill**, who improved bundles from his first run to his second, and **Pentire Head**, who comes from an excellent family and ran into a machine of Jonjo O'Neill's on his final start.

Four mares who are each expected to do well in mares' novice hurdles are **Country Lady**, a half-sister to Frodon who was babyish last season; the ex-Irish **Florencethemachine**, whose name gives her a lot to live up to; Sandown bumper winner **Larchmont Lass**, who can be a bit keen but has a lot of ability; and **Seeyouinmydreams**, who has also been too keen, both at home and when she ran at Aintree. But she created a huge impression at Newbury and can progress provided she learns to relax.

The standout on looks among a small team of juveniles is **Liari**. A winner once from three starts on the Flat in France for the Aga Khan, he has proved a natural hurdler in home schools and could take high rank.

One of the early three-year-olds to appear should be **Kabral Du Mathan**, who transferred to Ditcheat after making a winning hurdling debut for Arnaud Chaille-Chaille at Clairefontaine in Deauville in mid-July.

Interview by Ben Newton

JAMIE SNOWDEN

You Wear It Well the star turn as excitement builds for new season

AFTER a record haul of prize-money last season Jamie Snowden is "excited" about repeating the feat with his team at Folly House stables in Upper Lambourn.

"We had a phenomenal year last season with six big wins, from Pisgah Pike in the Summer Hurdle through to Gino [Datsalrightgino] winning the Grade 2 at Ayr in April," says Snowden.

"It would be nice if we could do it again.

GUIDE TO THE JUMPS **2023-24**

WINNERS IN LAST FIVE SEASONS 44, 49, 23, 46, 31

You Wear It Well at home with Jamie Snowden

RACING POST

Datsalrightgino: big improver last season and will start his latest campaign at Aintree in October

We have a team of around 65, from established stars to a nice batch of newcomers. There's a lot of hope and enthusiasm in the team, so hopefully we can progress and be competing on the top stage. It's exciting."

Heading the team is **You Wear It Well**, winner of the Mares' Novices' Hurdle at the Cheltenham Festival.

"She won a bumper in the previous season and we were conscious not to overdo her because we thought she was going to be a smart horse over hurdles as a novice. And so it proved.

"She had a fabulous season. She won at Worcester and Hexham, was second in the Challow at Newbury, then came out and won the Grade 2 Jane Seymour at Sandown before winning at the festival.

"She was probably over the top when we ran her at Aintree in the Grade 1 Merseyside Novices' Hurdle.

"We were contemplating going chasing with her this season. We've schooled her over fences and she jumps beautifully, but the programme over hurdles is enticing, so we'll work back from the mares' race at the festival.

GUIDE TO THE JUMPS **2023-24**

JAMIE SNOWDEN
LAMBOURN, BERKSHIRE

RECORD AROUND THE COURSES

	Total W-R	Per cent	Non-hcp Hdle	Non-hcp Chase	Hcp Hdle	Hcp Chase	N.H. Flat	£1 level stake
Fontwell	32-174	18.4	10-50	2-3	8-48	7-39	5-34	-25.21
Stratford	17-79	21.5	6-23	1-4	4-17	4-27	2-8	-15.35
Uttoxeter	17-121	14.0	6-30	0-6	3-38	7-36	1-11	-21.85
Worcester	17-123	13.8	3-36	2-6	2-34	9-38	1-9	-35.43
Ffos Las	16-69	23.2	6-19	0-2	5-23	4-17	1-8	-5.41
Newton Abbot	15-98	15.3	5-32	1-7	4-31	5-21	0-7	-43.23
Catterick	13-27	48.1	4-9	2-2	0-5	5-8	2-3	+3.09
Southwell	12-85	14.1	4-25	0-0	5-24	3-21	0-15	-10.93
Market Rasen	11-85	12.9	3-29	1-4	1-20	4-21	2-11	-5.73
Exeter	10-53	18.9	3-18	0-5	2-14	4-13	1-3	+0.83
Wincanton	10-75	13.3	4-25	1-5	1-22	3-19	1-4	-33.85
Haydock	9-30	30.0	1-5	2-4	2-7	4-11	0-3	+9.20
Hexham	9-33	27.3	5-12	1-4	0-7	1-7	2-3	-12.01
Wetherby	9-54	16.7	4-17	2-5	2-8	0-11	1-13	-9.51
Chepstow	9-60	15.0	2-19	0-0	2-17	4-15	1-9	-4.64
Ludlow	9-60	15.0	3-17	2-3	1-17	1-9	2-14	-17.30
Sedgefield	8-38	21.1	5-16	0-0	0-6	1-8	2-8	+7.52
Cheltenham	8-76	10.5	2-18	1-6	1-21	4-22	0-9	+6.50
Huntingdon	8-90	8.9	3-35	0-5	1-21	2-19	2-10	-58.58
Taunton	7-51	13.7	4-19	1-1	1-16	0-7	1-8	-2.33
Bangor	7-56	12.5	2-12	0-4	1-16	2-18	2-6	-17.87
Plumpton	7-81	8.6	3-28	1-4	1-19	1-21	1-9	-49.09
Carlisle	6-22	27.3	2-5	1-3	1-5	0-4	2-5	+4.69
Lingfield	6-35	17.1	5-20	0-0	0-3	1-12	0-0	-9.96
Fakenham	6-36	16.7	1-10	0-2	2-6	3-14	0-4	-7.40
Hereford	6-40	15.0	1-12	0-2	1-12	4-9	0-5	-7.00
Kempton	4-26	15.4	1-5	0-4	1-9	2-8	0-0	-12.75
Sandown	4-38	10.5	3-10	0-9	1-12	0-5	0-2	-7.42
Newcastle	3-8	37.5	3-4	0-0	0-2	0-1	0-1	-3.55
Kelso	3-10	30.0	2-4	0-1	1-1	0-4	0-0	-2.08
Doncaster	3-32	9.4	1-12	0-1	1-12	0-4	1-3	-16.00
Newbury	3-46	6.5	0-15	0-1	1-13	1-9	1-8	-22.00
Warwick	3-47	6.4	1-9	0-2	0-14	0-13	2-9	-27.47
Ayr	2-9	22.2	0-1	1-3	1-2	0-1	0-0	+17.00
Leicester	2-20	10.0	0-3	0-3	2-6	0-8	0-0	-10.00
Musselburgh	1-2	50.0	0-0	1-1	0-1	0-0	0-0	+1.25
Perth	1-3	33.3	1-2	0-0	0-0	0-1	0-0	-1.39
Ascot	1-16	6.2	0-5	0-2	1-4	0-2	0-3	-10.50
Cartmel	1-16	6.2	0-3	0-1	0-4	1-8	0-0	-12.00
Aintree	1-35	2.9	0-7	0-3	0-7	1-15	0-3	-18.00
Southwell (AW)	0-1	0.0	0-0	0-0	0-0	0-0	0-1	-1.00
Kempton (AW)	0-2	0.0	0-0	0-0	0-0	0-0	0-2	-2.00
Lingfield (AW)	0-6	0.0	0-0	0-0	0-0	0-0	0-6	-6.00

"We'll probably start her in a Listed mares' race at Wetherby [October 28], then Listed mares' races at Sandown in January and Warwick in February.

"She's pleased me since last season. She's a belter of a mare now."

The seven-year-old chaser **Datsalrightgino** improved 20lb last season in eight outings, his season culminating in a Grade 2 victory at Ayr in April.

"He was disappointing in the Plate at the festival but the rain came and made it soft, which didn't suit him.

"He's a big, strong horse and has pleased me since last season. We'll start him off in the Old Roan at Aintree [October 29] and he'll definitely have an entry in the Paddy Power at Cheltenham [November 18].

"At some point I'm sure he'll go up to three miles; we've just got to figure out when and where, and the Ultima [3m1f] at the Cheltenham Festival is the race I'm sure we'll end up going for."

Ga Law had "a phenomenal season", winning the Paddy Power Gold Cup and would have gone close to landing the Sky Bet

RACING POST

Chase at Doncaster at the end of January had he not fallen at the last fence upsides eventual winner Cooper's Cross.

"He was unlucky not to win but that put us on the back foot a little bit for the rest of the season," says Snowden, "although he ran a career-best fifth in the Ryanair at the festival, only beaten ten lengths.

"He progressed throughout the season and was probably over the top when pulled up at Aintree.

"He'll start off in the West Yorkshire Hurdle at Wetherby [October 29] with a view to going on to the Coral Gold Cup Chase at Newbury [December 2]. We'll cross those bridges before thinking about Cheltenham."

Git Maker is the epitome of consistency, having finished outside the first three only once in eight races under rules, when he was fourth, and four runs in Irish point-to-points.

"The Git has a phenomenal strike-rate and has won five times in eight starts, his last two

Sean Bowen has ridden two winners from six rides for the stable (33%), returning a profit of £15

Ga Law: winner of last season's Paddy Power Gold Cup

SO MUCH MORE THAN A MUSEUM!

NHRM occupies a 5-acre site in the heart of Newmarket and provides a wonderful day out for all ages.

Using the latest interactive and audio-visual displays you can find out about the history of horseracing, enjoy some of the country's best examples of sporting art, meet former racehorses, have a go on the racehorse simulator and watch the sparks fly as a farrier works in the forge.

EXPLORE GREAT EXHIBITIONS, BROWSE OUR GIFT SHOP & BOOKSTORE.

DISCOVER THE RESTAURANT AND BAKERY AT NHRM

National Horseracing Museum   Palace Street, Newmarket, Suffolk, CB8 8EP

@NHRMuseum

Book Online: www.nhrm.co.uk

RACING POST

> Git Maker (right) has a phenomenal strike-rate and has won five times in eight starts. We'll look at the Midlands Grand National this season at Uttoxeter in March

wins over 3m1f. He now runs off 128 and is one for those big staying handicap chases. We'll look at the Midlands Grand National this season at Uttoxeter in March.

"He's only a young horse and is lightly raced, but there's every chance he could develop into a Grand National type. He has to keep improving though to get in."

Reach For The Moon, owned by the King and Queen, is an interesting recruit from the Flat. Trained by John and Thady Gosden in Newmarket, the four-year-old former Classic hope won the Group 3 Solario Stakes two years ago, as well as being beaten in a photo finish for the Group 2 Champagne Stakes. Last season he was runner-up in the Group 3 Hampton Court Stakes at Royal Ascot.

"He slightly lost his form this year but he's been down to Henrietta Knight's for some jumping tuition and then on to Sandringham for a bit of a holiday. He's taken to hurdles very well and he'll start out novice hurdling."

Super Survivor is a "lovely individual" who has won three of his six starts, including one at Chepstow, and is rated 132.

"He's one I'm hoping can go down the Welsh National route this year," says Snowden. "He'll have a prep run and see if we can get into it. He's obviously got to keep improving, but he loves soft ground, stays very well and if we can get some soft

ground for his prep race and he wins that, we can go down the Welsh National route."

Colonel Harry had a decent hurdling campaign, winning two races and finishing runner-up twice, including a Grade 2 at Kelso, and was fourth in the Grade 1 Tolworth at Sandown.

"He jumps fences really well and is tailor-made for two miles on soft ground. I'm hoping he can really step forward again this season and become a Graded novice chaser."

Obsessedwithyou won twice last season and finished third in a Listed juvenile hurdle at Aintree and a close fourth in a Grade 3 juvenile hurdle at Cheltenham in April.

"She has a handicap mark of 107, which I hope can be exploitable. Hopefully, she can head towards the Grade 2 EBF final at Newbury in March."

Passing Well won twice last season and was fourth in the Grade 1 Challow Hurdle behind You Wear It Well in second.

"He jumps his hurdles like fences and jumps fences hugely. He should progress over fences this year. He should be ready by October time when there's a bit of rain. He definitely needs a bit of cut."

Park This One is a dual novice hurdle winner who was also fourth in two Graded races.

"He'll go novice chasing," says Snowden. "He's a winning English point-to-pointer

Park This One: twice a winner over hurdles last season and set to go novice chasing this time

who has schooled well and will be out this autumn. He and Passing Well could be two who could really progress well over fences in a similar way to what Datsalrightgino did."

Roger Pol is a brother to Minella Crooner, who was placed in a Grade 1, and a half-brother to Adrrastos, who won seven races for Snowden between 2017 and 2019. He has already shown bags of promise by landing two bumpers last season and Snowden is keen to send him novice hurdling. "He jumps great and will be out in the autumn."

A newcomer to Folly House whom Snowden feels is worth following this season is **Torneo**, a Toronado colt who fetched €110,000 at the Arqana July sales after twice finishing runner-up in French provincial races over 1m3f.

"He's rated 84 and unexposed on the Flat and looks the type to jump hurdles well. He should like soft ground and should be a decent novice hurdler this year," says Snowden.

Another newcomer Snowden feels could have a bright future is the six-year-old **Ballydesmond**, a dual winner between the flags in Ireland this spring.

"He won a hunter chase at Down Royal on the first of May, which means he's still a novice this season."

The four-year-old filly **Bellas Bridge** won her sole point-to-point in Ireland this spring with the front two 18 lengths clear of the third. Unsurprisingly, she fetched €155,000 at the Goffs sale.

"She's by Telescope out of a Listed French winner and is a big filly who could be quite smart. She should be ready by autumn."

Another ex-Irish point to make the grade over here was **Idy Wood**, who won his bumper at Newbury in February and is expected to do well as a novice hurdler.

Kitesurfer, winner of a French juvenile hurdle race, came from Harry Whittington's yard where he had one outing over hurdles, finishing fourth at Kempton. "He wasn't quite wound up for that, but he goes well and could be well handicapped off 115," says Snowden.

Finally, take note of two ex-Irish pointers who finished first and third in the same race at Monksgrange in March, **San Frandisco** and **Wendigo**, the latter stepping up to win at Taylorstown in May.

"We bought them both and they're both nice horses. They'll start in bumpers and then go novice hurdling fairly soon."

Interview by Lawrie Kelsey

ANDREWS BOWEN Ltd.
www.andrewsbowen.co.uk
WORLD LEADERS IN SURFACE TECHNOLOGY

Delivering Excellence When Performance Is Paramount

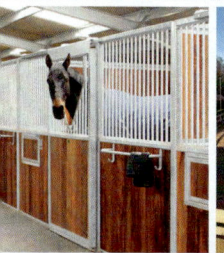

World-leading solutions for all of your surface, facility and stabling requirements.

Providing a fully comprehensive development service for professional racing and equestrian facilities alongside international competition venues in all climates.

Finance Options Now Available

E: sales@andrewsbowen.co.uk   T: +44 (0)1995 672103

RACING POST

EVAN WILLIAMS

Looking to the future

THERE has been a changing of the guard at Evan Williams' Fingerpost Farm stables in the Vale of Glamorgan after a modest haul by his standards last season.

Out have gone established horses and underperformers, retired or sold, and in has come a batch of newcomers.

"We have to be realistic. There's no point being jam-packed with horses who aren't winning," says Williams pragmatically.

Not since the 2004-05 season had Williams sent out so few winners as last term, when his total of 41 was only eight more than his previous lowest. Nor was his prize-money total of £525,270 much better. It was the lowest haul since 2007-08 when his runners earned £428,236.

"We've retired a lot of horses this year and we have a lot of young, unraced horses who could be good, bad or indifferent," says the Welshman, unwilling to try to offer a forecast of how the new season will unfold.

"It's very much a changing of the guard. Some very good horses have gone and a lot of young horses have come in.

"We always try to have 80 horses

GUIDE TO THE JUMPS **2023-24**

WINNERS IN LAST FIVE SEASONS 41, 53, 44, 49, 53

Secret Reprieve (left): the 2020 Welsh Grand National winner returns to the track this season but the stable's emphasis has switched to finding stars of the future

looking over the stable doors but it will be a difficult year. It was a tough year last year because we lost a few of those really good boys who won us big prizes.

"It was a moderate year and 100 per cent down to losing the established horses and having young ones in their place. We ground out a few winners but it was tough."

Uncovering top-flight horses is the ambition of every yard and the Fingerpost team is no different. They have their fingers crossed that **L'Astroboy** turns into one of those horses the yard seems to produce every couple of seasons, such as State Of Play, Silver Streak, Esprit Du Large, Court Minstrel and Secret Reprieve.

After winning a Ffos Las bumper at 25-1 on his racecourse debut, L'Astroboy returned to the track last November to justify favouritism impressively over hurdles.

Williams then stepped him straight into Grade 1 company in the Tolworth Hurdle at Sandown where he didn't let the side down, despite finishing second to Tahmuras, whom he'd beaten by a neck in the bumper.

It left Williams with the knowledge he had a potential top-notcher in the yard, even after being caught on the run-in two months later at Chepstow when a 2-9 shot, suggesting he didn't stay the 2m3½f.

In retrospect, Williams also felt the Tolworth Hurdle had left its mark. "He took to hurdling very nicely and ran a very good race at Sandown. I thought it was a very good performance," says Williams.

"But he's a very strong horse and put a lot into it that day, and it took a good deal out of him. Then he got beaten at Chepstow with a penalty over a couple of furlongs further than the Sandown race.

"He's fine after a break and has summered well. Now we have a lot of options. He could stick over hurdles, if we thought that was the right thing to do, but he lacks a bit of experience and I think there's a strong likelihood he'll go chasing.

"We'll school him when we get a drop of rain and I think novice chasing will be the way we go with him. If the weather isn't kind to us though, and time is running out, we could always stick to hurdling.

"We have no targets whatsoever with him. He was second in a Grade 1 over hurdles and you just hope he can build on that. We'll educate him – he needs education – and he's got very low miles on the clock. He'll also need cut in the ground."

Secret Reprieve has already forged a reputation after landing the rescheduled 2020 Welsh Grand National in January 2021. He was a big fancy for the 2022 Grand National but missed the cut by two and failed to make last season's line-up because his official rating was too low.

The public was as disappointed as the trainer when Secret Reprieve was denied his chance to make an entrance on the Aintree stage, but Williams was philosophical, pointing out he had won a Welsh Grand National with him, which had been a lifelong ambition.

Now there is little chance of the horse's rating rising enough to get into the National, Williams is forced to consider other avenues.

"He had a bit of a setback after the Midlands Grand National at Uttoxeter where he had a fair old bump. He whacked a leg and was pulled up," says Williams.

"We were worried for a bit but thankfully everything seems all right now. He's had a nice summer break but we won't see him until after Christmas."

Attempts to qualify him for the Grand National, however, will probably be too difficult.

"I think that ship has sailed and the days of thinking of him as a National horse are behind him," says Williams, "but there are other options for him, plenty of those big handicaps. The most important thing, though, is to get him fit, in one piece, fresh and ready to go again."

Six-year-old **Balkardy** improved for a switch from hurdles to fences and ended last

GUIDE TO THE JUMPS 2023-24

EVAN WILLIAMS
LLANCARFAN, VALE OF GLAMORGAN

From top: Walkinthewoods, L'Astroboy and Kym Eyre

RECORD AROUND THE COURSES

	Total W-R	Per cent	Non-hcp Hdle	Non-hcp Chase	Hcp Hdle	Hcp Chase	N.H. Flat	£1 level stake
Ffos Las	86-695	12.4	19-153	0-14	33-240	26-241	8-47	-153.00
Chepstow	62-453	13.7	21-111	1-4	17-146	22-161	1-31	+56.96
Ludlow	54-409	13.2	12-105	3-11	13-100	22-167	4-26	-143.96
Newton Abbot	32-223	14.3	5-41	3-15	10-81	14-82	0-4	-56.31
Exeter	27-156	17.3	3-36	5-20	13-50	6-45	0-5	+17.37
Taunton	24-226	10.6	3-61	0-0	13-85	8-74	0-6	-87.54
Uttoxeter	23-216	10.6	6-45	1-6	8-89	7-67	1-9	-22.55
Sedgefield	19-82	23.2	3-9	0-0	4-26	11-45	1-2	+14.03
Worcester	17-147	11.6	4-34	1-3	6-51	5-56	1-3	-38.31
Stratford	14-122	11.5	4-22	0-2	2-28	8-60	0-10	-49.63
Warwick	13-96	13.5	3-23	1-5	4-33	5-26	0-9	-11.92
Fontwell	13-104	12.5	1-18	0-0	4-42	8-39	0-5	-28.44
Hereford	13-173	7.5	1-37	3-5	3-61	5-65	1-5	-94.53
Haydock	12-118	10.2	1-18	0-7	10-46	1-45	0-2	+14.25
Cheltenham	11-152	7.2	1-25	1-8	2-52	7-65	0-2	-14.00
Bangor	10-123	8.1	1-32	0-4	3-37	6-41	0-9	-50.73
Southwell	10-134	7.5	6-36	0-4	1-55	1-31	2-8	-81.40
Carlisle	9-31	29.0	2-5	2-6	1-7	4-11	0-2	-1.22
Leicester	8-43	18.6	0-11	1-2	1-10	6-20	0-0	-4.17
Wincanton	8-70	11.4	1-18	1-1	3-21	2-22	1-8	-13.26
Fakenham	7-47	14.9	2-7	0-2	1-13	4-24	0-1	-23.34
Market Rasen	7-54	13.0	0-5	0-4	4-26	3-18	0-1	-13.67
Catterick	6-22	27.3	1-5	0-2	1-7	3-7	1-1	+8.24
Aintree	6-67	9.0	2-13	0-1	1-19	3-29	0-5	-20.50
Ascot	5-64	7.8	0-10	1-4	1-24	3-24	0-2	-27.25
Sandown	5-82	6.1	1-13	1-5	1-30	2-33	0-1	-25.75
Ayr	4-10	40.0	2-2	0-0	0-2	2-6	0-0	+16.96
Lingfield	4-28	14.3	0-8	0-0	1-8	3-12	0-0	-10.00
Huntingdon	4-32	12.5	2-7	0-2	0-8	1-12	1-3	-14.84
Kempton	4-47	8.5	3-13	0-3	0-11	1-19	0-1	-26.25
Newbury	4-76	5.3	2-12	0-0	2-27	0-24	0-13	-40.01
Doncaster	3-20	15.0	1-5	0-2	1-4	1-8	0-1	-4.25
Cartmel	3-27	11.1	0-0	0-2	1-12	2-13	0-0	-4.50
Perth	2-12	16.7	1-1	0-1	1-3	0-7	0-0	-1.00
Wetherby	2-18	11.1	1-5	0-2	0-3	1-8	0-0	-6.33
Plumpton	2-34	5.9	0-2	0-0	0-15	2-14	0-3	-25.63
Musselburgh	1-1	100.0	0-0	0-0	1-1	0-0	0-0	+3.50
Kelso	1-5	20.0	0-2	0-1	0-1	1-1	0-0	+0.00
Newcastle	1-12	8.3	0-4	0-1	0-3	1-4	0-0	-1.00
Lingfield (AW)	0-3	0.0	0-0	0-0	0-0	0-0	0-3	-3.00
Hexham	0-4	0.0	0-2	0-0	0-1	0-1	0-0	-4.00

season winning three chases from 2m3½f to 2m5½f on good ground in April and May, and was placed in his other three races over fences.

"He's a nice little horse who has improved over fences," says the trainer. "I can see him being a bit of fun around the likes of Ludlow and Hereford and places like that.

"There are plenty of those very good prize-money handicaps at those lesser tracks. He's not a big horse but he's a good jumper who'll be a great sport in those better races off a light weight."

Can You Call is a versatile type who has won over hurdles and fences and was considered good enough to take in the Grade 2 Ballymore Novices' Hurdle at Cheltenham in January, although he finished down the field.

"He's a grand fella. When he's right he runs very well, but the handicapper has been harsh with him and left him in no man's land. I imagine he'll mix chasing and hurdling this year. He's a good jumper but he can miss a fence at times. He's a big old unit and not as nimble as you'd like to see."

Can You Call prefers plenty of cut and will run in winter when the ground softens,

85

conditions which suit the majority of Williams' runners, as he readily admits.

"I'm a waste of time to any man when the sun is shining," he laughs.

Walkinthewoods is the type of horse every trainer yearns for – consistently good. In his last 11 races since February 2022, the six-year-old hurdler has finished out of the first four only once, when he was fifth. In that time he has won twice and finished runner-up three times.

"He had a smashing season last year. He runs regularly from two miles to three miles. He's not a big horse but he jumps a fence around the lesser tracks. He's a great fun horse who will continue to pay his way wherever he goes. He'll win races and is the perfect horse for his racing club owners."

Another consistent type is **Kym Eyre**, described by her trainer as "a thoroughly genuine, tough mare".

"She's the sort who runs regularly and is a good, honest mare who always gives her running. She's very adaptable and could win over extreme distances or two and a half if the ground is soft. She's the type who could end up in one of those regional Nationals off a featherweight."

Doyen Star won his only Irish point-to-point and has proved a shrewd purchase, winning both his starts over hurdles last season over two miles at Chepstow.

"We've just been mooching around with him until we put a fence in front of him, which I imagine is the route we'll go down because he's an out-and-out chaser. We'll stay low key, give him experience and see where we end up."

Quoi De Neuf is another who can switch between hurdles and fences having won over both last season.

"He's a smashing little fella on his day. He can blow hot and cold a bit but when he's hot he's very good. He's a great bit of sport around the likes of Ludlow, Taunton and Fakenham, places like that, so that's where he'll stay.

"I think he prefers the ground on the quicker side, I don't think he'll be running in the winter. He's a genuine little horse and he'll continue to be so."

The six-year-old mare **Pageant Material** comes into the same category, consistent and genuine, having won twice over hurdles and once over fences, all at Ffos Las.

"If you could fill your yard with the likes of her, you'd always be winning races. She loves cut in the ground and comes alive in those conditions, particularly Ffos Las, where she saves her best for. She's definitely a winter mare and is adaptable to distance."

Libberty Hunter won his maiden hurdle at Chepstow at the third attempt after two placed efforts and, although he has little experience over hurdles, Williams feels it's time to send him chasing.

■ James Bowen has a 27% strike-rate for the stable – and level-stake backers are £12.75 to the good

"He strikes me as a horse who will be suited by a fence, so we won't mess around with him, he'll go straight chasing. He's a very athletic horse, so he'll probably start sooner than the winter horses. I can see him being ready in October."

The syndicate-owned **Henry Box Brown** is described as a "fun horse" by his trainer, who finds it difficult to pin down what the six-year-old's optimum distance is or which ground he prefers, having run from two miles to two miles five furlongs on heavy to good conditions.

"He won his little race over hurdles [two miles at Uttoxeter] when there was plenty of cut in the ground and I tried him over fences, which wasn't a success.

"He's one of them, you know. It's difficult to know what he wants," admits Williams disarmingly. "But we'll mooch away with him and he'll end up winning in a strange place on a strange day, but he's great sport for his owners."

Of the newcomers to Fingerpost Farm, Williams likes the look of winning Irish pointers **Everyonesacritic**, said to be "shaping up nicely," **Followango** who "could be anything", **Minella Blueway** and **Minella Missile**.

Hurricane Highway is another ex-Irish pointer who won a novice hurdle at Ffos Las and "could be a very nice horse who could make up into a chaser", as is **Out Of Office**, who landed a big-field Chepstow novice hurdle impressively as favourite and looks to have a bright future.

Also make a note of a couple of oddities – fallers in bumpers at Chepstow last winter. The well-backed **Three Cliffs Bay** had every chance of winning when holding a narrow lead but stumbled and fell close home, and **Duc Du Rene** fell inside the last furlong when in second place.

"They were both in the process of running good races and have shown they have a semblance of ability, so could do well over hurdles," says Williams.

He finishes by stressing readers should add the four-year-old filly **Tour Ovalie** to their horses-to-follow lists. She showed plenty of potential to finish fourth and second in bumpers.

"She could just come alive with a hurdle in front of her," stresses Williams. "She's shown enough in bumpers to say she's got ability and has a bit about her, but she'll need a bit of cut in the ground."

Interview by Lawrie Kelsey

Out Of Office: impressive Chepstow winner

FESTIVAL FANCIES GRAEME RODWAY

Constitution Hill leads ten for the big festivals

CONSTITUTION HILL

Any list of horses that can make it to the spring festivals wouldn't be worthy of the name if Constitution Hill wasn't among them. He is the outstanding hurdler of his generation and has the potential to be the best of all time if he can continue last season's complete dominance.

He has won all seven races under rules and only twice has he failed to do it by a double-digit margin. Those two runs did come on his last two starts of the season, but he could have won the Champion Hurdle at Cheltenham by double the nine-length margin had he been asked.

It was harder work when he beat Sharjah in the Aintree Hurdle by only three lengths, but he never really looked in any danger and might have been feeling his Cheltenham exertions.

He has done it on all types of tracks and varying ground, so it's hard to find any chinks in his armour. Provided he stays fully fit another Champion Hurdle win is a foregone conclusion.

GALOPIN DES CHAMPS

Any list wouldn't be complete without the Gold Cup winner and last year's was an exceptional one. Galopin Des Champs thrashed King George winner Bravemansgame by seven lengths at Cheltenham and his subsequent defeat at Punchestown should be forgiven.

Maybe he was still feeling the effects of a hard race that day and this six-time Grade 1 winner will probably take the same route as he did last season before attempting to retain his crown.

With a Racing Post Rating of 184, he was the best horse in Britain and Ireland by 5lb last season and is just seven. Who's to say he won't be even better with another year behind him?

Provided all goes smoothly it's hard to see him being anything other than favourite come Gold Cup day and it's going to take something special to stop him justifying that position.

GOOD LAND

Marine Nationale wasn't the only star novice hurdler in the Connell stable last season because Good Land was the impressive winner of a Grade 1 at the Dublin Racing Festival.

Good Land isn't as quick as his stablemate, but he jumps and stays well and it was a lack of an instant turn of foot that cost him when he finished fourth behind Impaire Et Passe in the Ballymore at Cheltenham. Connell also felt that the ground was softer than he would prefer.

Chasing is going to be on Good Land's agenda this season and he has loads of scope to jump fences, so could go all the way to the top in the novice ranks. Connell doesn't think he is slow and will campaign him at intermediate trips, but staying could be his game come the spring.

If there is one novice chaser who can go right to the top on this list, it's probably Good Land.

HANSARD

When putting together a list like this it's always tempting to stick to the top yards, but don't forget about Gary Moore. He is an outstanding trainer and should be trusted to coax the best from Hansard, who was a smart novice hurdler last season and has a lot more left in the tank.

Hansard won his first two starts after joining Moore from Charles O'Brien in Ireland last year and went off favourite for the Dovecote at Kempton on the back of those wins. He disappointed when finishing fifth, but showed his class after a short break at Aintree in April.

Moore pitched Hansard into the Grade 1 Top Novices' Hurdle and he cantered through the race like a top-class horse. It briefly looked like he would spring a 40-1 surprise and he was backed to a low of 3.35 in running on Betfair, but he just didn't get home and finished fourth.

Nevertheless, the way he went through that race was eyecatching and there is more to come.

IMPAIRE ET PASSE

What would this list be without the highest-rated novice hurdler of last season, so step forward Impaire Et Passe, who went unbeaten in four and won by a long way each time.

His most impressive win came in the Ballymore at Cheltenham and he supplemented that with an equally magnificent performance in the Champion Novice Hurdle at Punchestown.

We just don't know how good Impaire Et Passe could be and that's what makes him so exciting. What will he find if he goes eyeball to eyeball with the great Constitution Hill?

Impaire Et Passe: unbeaten in four novice hurdles last season

RACING POST

If there is a horse in training who can threaten the Champion Hurdle winner it will be Impaire Et Passe, but he ended his novice hurdle campaign with a BHA rating of 160 and that is 10lb lower than the 170 that Constitution Hill had achieved at the same stage of his career. When you consider that Constitution Hill is now rated 175, Impaire Et Passe has a long way to go.

IRISH POINT

Gordon Elliott is another trainer who cannot be ignored when it comes to the spring festivals and his most exciting horse for the coming season is the Aintree Grade 1 winner Irish Point.

He maintained a high level of form throughout the season, but looked better than ever on his last two starts when following his win in a Grade 3 at Naas with that success at Aintree. He powered through the line there to give Gordon Elliott a second consecutive win in the race.

Elliott had won it with his most exciting prospect the year before, the ill-fated Three Stripe Life, so it's evidently a race that the trainer targets and Irish Point is held in high regard.

The way he improved suddenly in the spring bodes well for further progress that he should have made this summer and he looks likely to be even better with another year on his back.

Irish Point: Aintree winner and not hard to see him making further progress

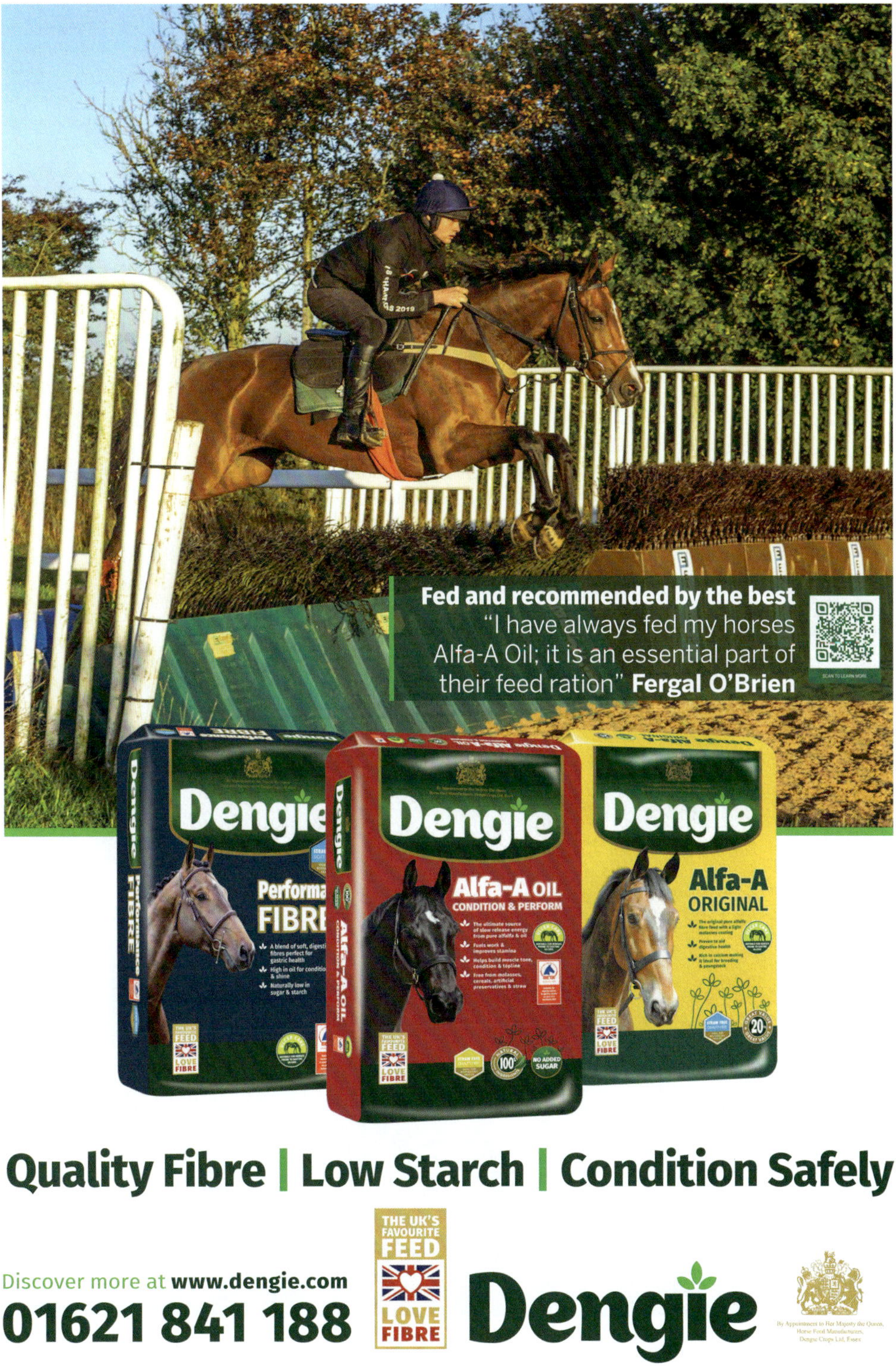
Fed and recommended by the best
"I have always fed my horses Alfa-A Oil; it is an essential part of their feed ration" Fergal O'Brien
Dengie
Performance FIBRE
Dengie
Alfa-A OIL
CONDITION & PERFORM
Dengie
Alfa-A
ORIGINAL
NO ADDED SUGAR
Quality Fibre | Low Starch | Condition Safely
Discover more at www.dengie.com
01621 841 188
THE UK'S FAVOURITE FEED
LOVE FIBRE
Dengie
By Appointment to Her Majesty the Queen, Horse Feed Manufacturers, Dengie Crops Ltd, Essex

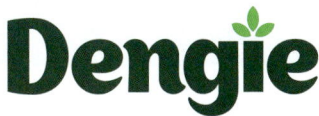

MARINE NATIONALE

The other outstanding novice hurdler last season was Marine Nationale and he is rated just 2lb behind Impaire Et Passe. However, chasing rather than hurdling is likely to be his game.

Marine Nationale landed what looks like one of the strongest runnings of the Supreme Novices' Hurdle in recent years and that is quite a statement given it's always a hot race.

He had subsequent Grade 1 winners Facile Vega and Inthepocket behind in second and fourth and the well-held 11th, Fennor Cross, came out to win a handicap head-in-chest at Aintree.

Marine Nationale recorded a 1lb higher Topspeed figure than Impaire Et Passe did at Cheltenham, so the time is good, and speed is his primary asset. Trainer Barry Connell reckons he is a Group 1 horse on the Flat, so it will take a good one to beat him in the Arkle.

GUIDE TO THE JUMPS **2023-24**

" Marine Nationale landed what looks like one of the strongest runnings of the Supreme Novices' Hurdle in recent years and that is quite a statement given it's always a hot race "

RACING POST

PAWAPURI

There are so many races for mares at the spring festivals nowadays that any list wouldn't be complete without a female who can sweep all before them and Pawapuri is under the radar.

Mares' races at the big festivals have been dominated by the Mullins and Henderson yards and it caught my eye that Henderson pitched Pawapuri into a Grade 2 and then a Grade 1 over hurdles last season. She was well beaten in both, but twice shaped with lots of promise.

That was particularly true on her hurdles debut in the Adonis at Kempton in February when she was matched at a low of 4 in running from an SP of 10-1, before fading to finish fourth.

She is only four and Henderson probably gave her those runs with one eye on preserving her novice status for this season when I expect she will be able to rack up a sequence of victories.

PEMBROKE

It would be remiss not to include at least one of Dan Skelton's up-and-comers and Pembroke is the horse who has the most scope to improve with another season behind him.

He went off a relatively short-priced favourite (9-2) for a race as competitive as the County Hurdle at Cheltenham and finished well beaten. But there was more to like about his next run.

Skelton added a tongue-strap when Pembroke contested the Grade 1 Top Novices' Hurdle at Aintree in April and he was in contention at the second-last flight before fading to finish fifth.

The appearance of the tongue-strap makes me wonder whether he has had breathing problems, but that is nothing Skelton can't rectify with surgery and Pembroke appeared to stay two and a half miles at Cheltenham in January. So maybe his future lies at that trip, too.

STAY AWAY FAY

Willie Mullins might dominate Cheltenham every year but there still isn't a better trainer of staying chasers than Paul Nicholls and Stay Away Fay could be his next superstar.

Stay Away Fay became the first horse from the Nicholls stable to win the Albert Bartlett at the Cheltenham Festival and that's

probably because the champion trainer rarely overfaces his horses at such an early stage of their careers. He prefers to bring his chasers along slowly.

He adopted the same approach with Stay Away Fay last season. He went into Cheltenham with only two races behind him and it says a huge amount about his natural ability that he was able to land a Grade 1 given his relative inexperience. There will be loads more to come.

Maybe a hard race at Cheltenham took the edge off him when he was beaten into fourth at Aintree on his final start of the campaign, but he still only gave way on the run-in there and fences will be the making of him. Nicholls has said himself: "He will be an awesome chaser."

RACING POST

ANTE-POST ANALYSIS NICK WATTS

Impaire the alternative to mighty Constitution

CHAMPION HURDLE

Thank goodness for Willie Mullins. Without him the Champion Hurdle would be as good as a walkover for Constitution Hill. It still might be, but at least by taking the decision to keep Impaire Et Passe and State Man over hurdles we have some credible rivals to the odds-on favourite.

In State Man's case he needs to find nine lengths with Constitution Hill from their running in last season's Champion Hurdle. That's an awful lot, even if there was a suspicion he was a bit flat that day.

That leaves us with **Impaire Et Passe**. He is unbeaten in four starts for Mullins, and has thrashed everything in his path – his smallest winning margin has been six and a half lengths.

His big spring wins, at Cheltenham and Punchestown, were both achieved over longer trips, but he did win the Moscow Flyer prior to that over two miles and he has never appeared to lack pace.

Officially he has 15lb to find with Constitution Hill, but if you really want to have a bet in this market he is realistically the only option, and he is still an each-way price at 6-1 with bet365 and Paddy Power.

CHAMPION CHASE

The roles are reversed in the Champion Chase with Nicky Henderson providing the only real resistance to a Mullins-dominated picture.

Energumene is on a hat-trick in this race after convincing wins in the previous two seasons. However, he isn't even likely to start favourite for the 2024 running, with stablemate El Fabiolo having launched himself on to the scene following a stellar novice chase campaign.

He won three Grade 1s in succession and slammed Jonbon in the Arkle, albeit I don't feel we saw the best of the latter that day. Rated 170, El Fabiolo looks the most likely winner but it might be worth chancing **Jonbon** at 7-1.

Below par in the Arkle, he was flawless otherwise and ended his season with a pair of convincing Grade 1 wins at Aintree and Sandown. The better the ground the better he seems to be and he is a marvellous jumper when in full flow.

The Tingle Creek is probably the race for him in the early part of the season and, if he wins that well, the probability is a few points will be shaved off his current price.

While he is 0-2 at Cheltenham, that doesn't really tell the story as he has still finished second in a Supreme and Arkle. It doesn't add up to a dislike of the track just yet and he looks the best of the British, with Edwardstone on a bit of a retrieval mission following a mystifyingly poor run at the festival last season.

GUIDE TO THE JUMPS **2023-24**

STAYERS' HURDLE

The Stayers' Hurdle has been difficult to predict of late, with 12-1, 33-1 and 50-1 shots obliging in three of the last four years.

Sire Du Berlais became the first horse to triumph as an 11-year-old since Crimson Embers in 1986 when winning for Gordon Elliott last season, but surely he can't do it again as a 12-year-old?

He will almost certainly try, but younger, fresher legs are sure to be snapping at his heels including **Gaelic Warrior**, who will be six next year.

Impaire Et Passe was the only horse to get the better of him last season in five starts, and he looked monstrous when upped to three miles on his final start of the campaign at Punchestown, thrashing Affordale Fury by ten lengths.

Jonbon: has a good record in defeat at Cheltenham but this could be his year to shine

The feeling after that was he would go chasing, but that appears to have been shelved and he now finds himself market leader for the Stayers' at a top price of 5-1 with Sky Bet. That might not be a bad price either when you look at what is behind him in the market.

Impaire Et Passe is next best and he will be going for the Champion Hurdle. Then there is Teahupoo, third in the race last season but then beaten at Punchestown too. Following that there is Marie's Rock, Klassical Dream and the reigning champ Sire Du Berlais.

They're all solid types but not ones that would strike fear into you either. In Gaelic Warrior you have an exposed type at the trip, who is lightly raced and has huge potential for further improvement.

A lot has been made of his tendency to jump a bit right-handed, but he's run well at the previous two festivals and has won a big handicap at Leopardstown too so it's not that much of a problem.

CHELTENHAM GOLD CUP

The Gold Cup might be 2-1 the field, with Galopin Des Champs rightfully at the top, but I think it might be more open than the betting suggests and there are several angles to consider.

Gerri Colombe is second favourite and is a horse certain to relish the Gold Cup trip. He was eating up the ground in the Brown Advisory, only just failing to reel in The Real Whacker, and then went to Aintree and spreadeagled his opponents. If it's an attritional year, look no further.

Shishkin is turning into an enigma, but did relish three miles at Aintree in April when getting the better of Ahoy Senor. That proves he still has plenty of class but his age is off-putting.

He turns ten on New Year's Day and the last horse to win this race at that age was Cool Dawn way back in 1998.

L'Homme Presse is still young enough to make his mark if he is over the injury which kept him out of the second half of last season. He was running well in the King George when last seen on a track that wouldn't have suited.

However, the one to be one has to be **Fastorslow**, trained by Martin Brassil – one of the best target men on either side of the Irish Sea.

Numerically he doesn't have a big string, but he sure knows how to campaign them, and his recent win in the Kerry National proves that point.

Fastorslow put up a great effort to run Corach Rambler to a head in the Ultima at Cheltenham, giving the National winner 4lb. He then went to Punchestown for a Grade 1 and took the biggest scalp of the lot – that of Gold Cup winner, Galopin Des Champs. There didn't seem to be any fluke about that, with the third, Bravemansgame, helping to underline the value of the form.

Form at the end of April is usually best taken with a pinch of salt, and Galopin Des Champs may well show in time that it was a mere blip.

However, the fact Brassil ran him in that race shows the esteem he holds him in, and this lightly raced seven-year-old must have room for more improvement. At a generally available 16-1 he makes plenty of appeal.

GRAND NATIONAL

It's early to think about the National, but one horse who must have a chance if pointed that way is Christian Williams' **Kitty's Light**.

Big-field handicaps over marathon trips are perfect fodder for Kitty's Light - he won three of them in a row last season, taking the Eider, followed by the Scottish National before rounding off with the bet365 Gold Cup.

A mark of 147 ought to get him into a National, and if the ground is decent there will be nothing finishing better if he is anywhere near contention after the last. He is 25-1 for this and it's hard to think of a horse who will be better suited to a modern-day National.

RACING POST

MY TEN FOR THE SEASON RICHARD BIRCH

Names to note from Azof to Well Vicky

AZOF DES MOTTES

I will be astounded if strong-travelling six-year-old Azof Des Mottes doesn't prove a massive money-spinner for punters this season.

The son of Sinndar possesses a notably high cruising speed for a horse of his rating, and made a huge impression when landing a Kelso 2m5f handicap chase in April by half a length from The Jad Factor.

A big horse with considerable scope, Azof Des Mottes jumps wonderfully fast and low, and starts the autumn on a mark of just 89.

He will be even better when dropped to 2m or 2m2f where the faster pace should play to his strengths.

BAVINGTON BOB

In hindsight, perhaps it wasn't surprising that Bavington Bob *(left)* drew a blank last term following a prolific 2021-22 campaign which resulted in five wins.

He started the season off a mark of 139 and it proved beyond him. However, seven straight defeats means he is able to resume off 12lb lower.

Bavington Bob's principal attribute is stamina, and he remains largely untried over marathon trips.

It would be no surprise if connections have the Eider as his big target, and the underfoot conditions which usually exist at Newcastle in late February suit him well.

BLENKINSOP

Blenkinsop made such rapid progress over hurdles last winter that he improved his official rating from 104 to 131 during the space of just two lucrative months.

Winner of four handicaps in that period,

Blenkinsop: particularly caught the eye when winning in the mud at Newbury

Blenkinsop was particularly impressive at Newbury over 2m4f when ploughing through deep mud to slam Moulins Clermont by four and three-quarter lengths.

He boasts an eyecatching blend of pace and stamina, and is likely to make further progress when upped to 3m+ this season.

His astute trainer has been quoted as saying Blenkinsop is "still well treated on 131", and he seems sure to win a valuable staying handicap this term.

BRETNEY

Bretney is related to 4m winner Captain Cattistock, so it was no surprise that he took a significant step forward in terms of form when upped to 3m5f at Bangor in February.

Always going well in first-time blinkers, Bretney bolted up by three and a half lengths from rock-solid yardstick No Cruise Yet.

You can put a line through his subsequent Cheltenham defeat. He travelled strongly for much of the way before stopping quickly. Perhaps it was one race too many after a busy campaign?

Marathon handicap chases open up exciting new avenues for the eight-year-old, who is best on left-handed tracks. Lingfield's stamina-sapping Surrey National could prove an ideal target.

RACING POST

BUBBLE DUBI

While most eve-of-Cheltenham punters were focusing on day one of the Festival, backers of Bubble Dubi enjoyed a great start to the biggest week in jump racing when landing a Stratford gamble.

Backed from 6-1 to 7-4 favourite, the suspicion he had been underestimated by the handicapper proved spot-on when he moved through a 2m handicap hurdle like a horse with a stone in hand of 112.

Bubble Dubi merely needed to be shaken up to beat Word Has It by three lengths, and there should be plenty more to come during the 2023-24 season.

COLONIAL EMPIRE

Colonial Empire made giant strides over hurdles last winter, winning three of his last four starts in the manner of a horse who has some way to go before he reaches his ceiling.

The third of those wins was particularly impressive. Stepped up markedly in grade to Class 2 company at Taunton, the 108-rated Colonial Empire unleashed a smart turn of foot to settle matters between the final two flights, and romped home by four and a half lengths from Boombawn.

His best form is at 2m, but there seems no reason why he won't stay further and progress into a 120+ performer this term.

HIPOP DES ONGRAIS

Hipop Des Ongrais didn't win again over fences after making a deep impression at Fontwell in December.

He looked a young chaser of some promise that day, jumping fluently and breezing 11 lengths clear of Forward Plan.

Robert Walford is renowned for his patience, and the fact six-year-old Hipop Des Ongrais was given only three further outings last season seems sure to prove beneficial in the long run.

The 103-rated grey ran excellent races in

Santos Blue: won three on the bounce last season and rates one to follow

defeat in two of those starts at Taunton and Ludlow, and is a 3m chaser going places at the minor to middling tracks this season.

SANTOS BLUE

Santos Blue's bid for a magnificent four-timer in handicap hurdles was thwarted at Cheltenham in April when he went down by three-quarters of a length and a nose to Broadway Boy and Hurricane Harvey.

He lost nothing in defeat, having been given plenty to do, and may just have been feeling the effects of a tough campaign in the closing stages.

Fluent successes at Wetherby, Chepstow

and Kelso stamped Santos Blue as one to follow. He should stay 3m well this term.

TESTFLIGHT

The best is yet to come from well-handicapped staying hurdler Testflight. Gambled on at both Stratford and Newton Abbot during the summer, this unexposed six-year-old is likely to prove infinitely better than a mark of 72 in due course.

He travelled powerfully in those two races prior to finding much less than looked likely off the bridle.

It's possible Testflight is still weak and needs time to strengthen. It's also possible he will prove best at trips just short of 3m while he matures. There is no doubt he possesses a big engine.

WELL VICKY

This progressive mare may have been 'over the top' when failing to live up to expectations at Cheltenham in April.

Previous wins at Hereford, Bangor and Plumpton were all achieved in a style which suggests Well Vicky could develop into a 120 performer this term.

She starts off on 101, and her high cruising speed and sharp turn of foot make her of interest in 2m4f handicap hurdles.

RACING POST

BELOW THE RADAR ROBBIE WILDERS

Ten smart performers whose talent might have been underestimated

ETALON

The EBF Final at Sandown in March is always a race to note and the form of Etalon's fourth-placed effort there, when he didn't quite get home over the 2m4f trip on heavy ground, is working out tremendously. The second, third, fifth, sixth and eighth scored in the six weeks that followed, as did three who were pulled up. This six-year-old has only raced four times over hurdles and needs respecting off his mark of 120 wherever he goes for top connections.

FIDELIO VALLIS

Harry Derham has made an exceptional start to his training career, operating at a strike-rate similar to the likes of his former boss Paul Nicholls and Nicky Henderson in his first season, and Fidelio Vallis could be a flag-bearer for the yard. The eight-year-old lost his way for Nicholls and almost landed a touch on his first start for new connections at Musselburgh in February, just giving best to the well-treated Pay The Piper. He was rated in the high 140s two years ago, so is expected to exploit a mark of 141 at some point this term.

FONTANA ELLISSI

The Sam Drinkwater-trained seven-year-old deserves a change of fortunes this campaign. He filled the runner-up position in two ultra-competitive handicap hurdles at Cheltenham's October and November meetings, pulling ten lengths clear of the third in the first of those when second to subsequent easy festival scorer Seddon. Fontana Ellissi's season ended prematurely as we haven't seen him since last November, but he has time on his side to rate much higher than a mark of 120 if Drinkwater can bring him back.

GIOVINCO

Lucinda Russell might have a star staying novice chaser to go to war with this season and that is Giovinco, who ran out a wide-margin winner of his three novice hurdles in March and April. He recorded a Racing Post Rating of 146 when storming home in a Listed race at Perth to round off an excellent spring, relishing the step up to 3m, and that figure suggests he is Grade 2 class at least. Proven on ground ranging from good to heavy, this lightly raced type can enjoy a fruitful campaign.

ICEO MADRIK

Perhaps the 2023-24 season is where David Pipe will get the best out of Iceo Madrik, who was purchased by top owner Caroline Tisdall after placing in a Grade 1 chase in France last year. Horses can often struggle in

Fontana Ellissi: could be open to significant improvement from a handicap mark of 120

GUIDE TO THE JUMPS **2023-24**

their five-year-old season and Iceo Madrik was thrown into the deep end on his first run for this team, pulling up in the Ultima at the Cheltenham Festival. He was again pulled up at Newton Abbot a few weeks later, but crucially his mark has dropped 10lb to 130, so he is looking exceptionally well treated.

LEAVE OF ABSENCE

The Grade 2 bumper at the Aintree festival often produces a really smart horse and Leave Of Absence ran a big race when third in the 2022 running. He translated that useful bumper form to hurdles when a smooth front-running winner at Ascot on his debut in that discipline in October, but, in keeping with his name, missed the remainder of the campaign. At the age of six there is still plenty of time for Leave Of Absence to build on the promise he has already shown for Chris Gordon.

MR FREEDOM

Irish-trained horses often dominate the Boodles at the Cheltenham Festival and Mr Freedom fared best of the British runners in fifth last term. Plenty went wrong that day too. He was bumped by a rival, his saddle slipped, his rider briefly lost an iron and he was struck into on his left hind. The fact he is just 1lb higher over hurdles now makes him of immediate interest, as do his recent Flat exploits. He has climbed 16lb in the ratings in that code after winning three times and can notch another win or two in this discipline for Sheena West.

NEMEAN LION

Kerry Lee is an excellent placer of her horses, and Nemean Lion *(above)* is a likely leading light for the yard this term. Third in the Grade 1 Tolworth in January, he followed that with a convincing success over Colonel Harry and Feronily at Kelso. Those horses have landed top races since and a mark of 135 undersells Nemean Lion's ability. Given he stayed 1m7f on the Flat (second in the Group 2 Prix Chaudenay on Arc weekend in 2020), stretching out in distance over hurdles could be the making of him.

PETIT TONNERRE

Petit Tonnerre was a regular fixture in some of the top handicap hurdles for Jonjo O'Neill last season and, with the exception of Kempton's Lanzarote when he was pulled up through no fault of his own after being badly hampered, he always emerged with credit. He is versatile regarding trip and ground conditions and is open to significant progression as a five-year-old. I'm sure a big prize will fall the way of this strong-travelling sort.

SALSADA

This daughter of Mukhadram is rated 91 on the Flat and gives the impression she could break through her 126 jumps mark. Salsada entered the notebook when an excellent second to serial Group 1 winner Epatante in the Grade 2 Yorkshire Rose Mares' Hurdle at Doncaster in January, and ran okay when fifth in the Scottish Champion Hurdle behind several vastly more experienced hurdlers to round off her season. She can thrive in two-mile handicap hurdles when the ground is on the quicker side.

Newly Designed

Equilume Stable Light
Maximising Fertility, Performance and Well-Being.

Scientifically developed and specifically designed for horses, the Equilume Stable Light is a fully automated lighting system that replicates the benefits of sunlight for the stabled horse by providing biologically effective levels of blue-enriched light by day and restful red light at night.

Experience benefits including:

- Optimised breeding performance for mares and stallions
- Enhanced coat condition
- Promoted muscle development
- Positively influenced mood & behaviour
- Permitted rest & enhanced recovery
- Reduced bacteria in stables

Scan to find out more about Equilume!

www.equilume.com   •   conor@equilume.com   •   +353 87 097 8083

RACING POST

THIS SEASON'S KEY HORSES

By Dylan Hill

A Dream To Share (Ire)
5 b g Muhaarar - Hikari (Galileo)
John Kiely (Ire) — John P McManus
PLACINGS: 11111-   RPR **140+b**

Starts	1st	2nd	3rd	4th	Win & Pl
5	5	-	-	-	£161,140
4/23	Punc	2m½f Gd1 NHF 4-7yo yield			£52,212
3/23	Chel	2m½f Cls1 Gd1 NHF 4-6yo yield			£45,560
2/23	Leop	2m Gd2 NHF 4-7yo yield			£52,212
6/22	Rosc	2m NHF 4yo good			£5,454
5/22	Tipp	2m NHF good			£5,702

Last season's outstanding bumper performer, winning all five races including a Grade 1 double; coped well with soft ground when scoring at Cheltenham and stepped up on that form when grinding out victory over Tullyhill at Punchestown; likely Supreme type.

A Plus Tard (Fr)
9 b g Kapgarde - Turboka (Kahyasi)
Henry De Bromhead (Ire) — Cheveley Park Stud
PLACINGS: 21/3213/212/121/PP3-   RPR **159c**

Starts	1st	2nd	3rd	4th	Win & Pl
22	8	8	4	-	£955,575
3/22	Chel	3m2½f Cls1 Gd1 Ch gd-sft			£351,688
11/21	Hayd	3m1½f Cls1 Gd1 Ch gd-sft			£114,865
12/20	Leop	3m Gd1 Ch yield			£75,000
12/19	Leop	2m1f Gd1 Ch soft			£66,441
144 3/19	Chel	2m4f Cls1 Nov List 138-145 Ch Hcap soft			£39,389
12/18	Naas	2m3f Ch yield			£7,904
0 4/18	Autl	2m2f List Hdl 4yo Hcap heavy			£39,823
10/17	Sbri	2m2f Hdl 3yo gd-sft			£6,974

Sensational 15-length winner of the Cheltenham Gold Cup in 2022, improving on second place in the race 12 months earlier; nowhere near that level last season when pulled up on first two runs before a distant third in the Aintree Bowl.

Absolute Notions (Ire)
5 b g Milan - Colleen Donnoige (Beneficial)
Gordon Elliott (Ire) — Robcour
PLACINGS: 1132P-   RPR **142+h**

Starts	1st	2nd	3rd	4th	Win & Pl
5	2	1	1	-	£83,511
11/22	Punc	2m3½f Mdn Hdl 4yo yield			£5,950
4/22	Punc	2m½f NHF 4-5yo gd-yld			£49,580

Fine chasing type who showed promise over hurdles last season without quite living up to €370,000 price tag; produced best run when second in a 2m6f Grade 1 at Leopardstown; beaten favourite twice either side of that.

Afadil (Fr)
4 b g Camelot - Afsheen (Invincible Spirit)
Paul Nicholls — P J Vogt
PLACINGS: 116821-   RPR **121+h**

Starts	1st	2nd	3rd	4th	Win & Pl
6	3	1	-	-	£46,918
122 4/23	Ayr	2m Cls3 101-127 Hdl Hcap gd-sft			£9,506
2/23	Muss	1m7½f Cls1 List Hdl 4yo good			£22,780
1/23	Tntn	2m½f Cls4 Mdn Hdl soft			£4,792

Useful and progressive juvenile hurdler last season; won first two races over hurdles before doing well when switched to handicaps in the spring; finished well when eighth in the Fred Winter and was a good second at Ascot before beating older horses at Ayr.

Affordale Fury (Ire)
5 b g Affinisea - No Greater Fury (Choisir)
Noel Meade (Ire) — P L Polly
PLACINGS: 1/11F622-   RPR **150h**

Starts	1st	2nd	3rd	4th	Win & Pl
6	2	2	-	-	£61,678
10/22	Gway	2m6f Mdn Hdl soft			£6,197
10/22	Gway	2m½f NHF 4yo soft			£4,958

Belied 150-1 odds when second behind Stay Away Fay in last season's Albert Bartlett at Cheltenham, relishing step up to 3m; sixth on previous run at Grade 1 level but went some way to backing up the form when second again at Punchestown, albeit no match for Gaelic Warrior.

Ahoy Senor (Ire)
8 b g Dylan Thomas - Dara Supreme (Darazari)
Lucinda Russell — Mrs C Wymer & PJS Russell
PLACINGS: /1211/U12121/5351F2-   RPR **174+c**

Starts	1st	2nd	3rd	4th	Win & Pl
15	6	4	1	-	£373,160
1/23	Chel	3m1½f Cls1 Gd2 Ch soft			£67,843
4/22	Aint	3m1f Cls1 Nov Gd1 Ch gd-sft			£67,524
2/22	Weth	3m Cls1 Nov Gd2 Ch good			£25,628
11/21	Newb	2m7½f Cls1 Nov Gd2 Ch gd-sft			£28,475
4/21	Aint	3m1½f Cls1 Nov Gd1 Hdl gd-sft			£42,328
3/21	Ayr	2m4½f Cls4 Mdn Hdl soft			£3,769

Dual Grade 1 novice winner (both at Aintree) who has been a work in progress over fences but thrived in the second half of last season; won the Cotswold Chase and going well in front when falling six out in the Cheltenham Gold Cup; collared late by Shishkin in the Aintree Bowl.

Ain't That A Shame (Ire)
9 b g Jeremy - Castletown Girl (Bob Back)
Henry De Bromhead (Ire) — Robcour
PLACINGS: 2/531/3220/2410-9   RPR **150+c**

Starts	1st	2nd	3rd	4th	Win & Pl
12	2	3	2	1	£41,663
3/23	Gowr	2m4f Ch sft-hvy			£6,788
2/21	Thur	2m7½f Mdn Hdl heavy			£6,848

Very lightly raced for his age and continued to progress last season until disappointing when just 10-1 for the Grand National; beaten a head in the Munster National and finished a close fourth in the Paddy Power Chase; below par on return this season in the Kerry National.

Al Dancer (Fr)
10 gr g Al Namix - Steel Dancer (Kaldounevees)
Sam Thomas — Walters Plant Hire

PLACINGS: 12425/139P/04532/10- RPR **152+**c

Starts	1st	2nd	3rd	4th	Win & Pl
25	8	4	3	3	£200,049

144	11/22	Aint	2m5f Cls2 133-159 Ch Hcap gd-sft £51,440
	10/20	NAbb	2m5f Cls2 Ch gd-sft £14,076
	10/19	Chel	2m Cls2 Nov Ch gd-sft £15,640
141	2/19	Asct	1m7½f Cls1 Gd3 125-145 Hdl Hcap gd-sft £47,830
129	12/18	Chel	2m1f Cls3 116-137 Hdl Hcap good £9,747
	11/18	Ffos	2m Cls4 Nov Hdl soft £4,159
	10/18	Carl	2m1f Cls4 Nov Hdl gd-sft £4,549
	3/18	Bang	2m½f Cls5 Mdn NHF 4-6yo soft £2,395

Veteran of top handicap chases who has been lightly raced in recent seasons but showed he remains a force when winning last season's Grand Sefton Chase; ran only once more when tenth in the Topham; third in the 2020 Paddy Power Gold Cup off peak mark and still 6lb lower.

Allaho (Fr)
9 b g No Risk At All - Idaho Falls (Turgeon)
Willie Mullins (Ire) — Cheveley Park Stud

PLACINGS: 13/2213/6411/2111/1- RPR **180**c

Starts	1st	2nd	3rd	4th	Win & Pl
17	8	4	2	2	£719,269

	4/22	Punc	3m Gd1 Ch gd-sft £136,345
	3/22	Chel	2m4½f Cls1 Gd1 Ch soft £211,425
	1/22	Thur	2m4½f Gd2 Ch gd-yld £18,097
	12/21	Punc	2m4½f Cls1 Gd1 Ch yld-sft £42,143
	3/21	Chel	2m4½f Cls1 Gd1 Ch gd-sft £150,350
	1/21	Thur	2m4f Gd2 Ch yld-hvy £18,438
	1/20	Fair	2m5½f Ch yld-sft £7,012
	2/19	Clon	3m Nov Gd3 Hdl gd-yld £21,261

Missed last season through injury but had looked the best chaser around prior to his layoff; wide-margin winner of the Ryanair Chase for the second year in a row in 2022 before a similar demolition job over 3m at Punchestown (first run over the trip since 2020).

Allegorie De Vassy (Fr)
6 b m No Risk At All - Autignac (Solon)
Willie Mullins (Ire) — Mrs S Ricci

PLACINGS: P52/311/11223- RPR **159+**c

Starts	1st	2nd	3rd	4th	Win & Pl
11	4	3	2	-	£122,490

	1/23	Thur	2m4½f Nov Gd2 Ch yield £26,106
	12/22	Limk	2m6½f Nov Gd2 Ch heavy £20,328
	1/22	Fair	2m2½f Nov Gd3 Hdl gd-yld £14,378
	1/22	Fair	2m2½f Hdl yield £6,693

Highly talented mare who won her first four races for Willie Mullins before bubble burst last spring; ran a fine race in defeat when second behind Impervious in the Mares' Chase at Cheltenham but increasingly flat when beaten at Fairyhouse and Punchestown.

Altobelli (Ire)
5 b g Maxios - Atiana (Samum)
Harry Fry — Charlie Walker And Jonny Craib

PLACINGS: 1/119- RPR **142+**h

Starts	1st	2nd	3rd	4th	Win & Pl
4	3	-	-	-	£10,075

	2/23	Carl	2m3½f Cls4 Nov Hdl gd-sft £4,629
	12/27	Ffos	2m Cls4 Mdn Hdl soft £3,540
	2/22	Extr	2m½f Cls5 NHF 4-6yo soft £1,906

Shaped with huge promise during a quiet novice hurdle campaign last season; won first two races to add to sole bumper victory, defying a penalty by 25 lengths at Carlisle; found out by sharp rise in class when losing unbeaten record in ninth in a Grade 1 at Aintree.

Altobelli: has won all but one of his races

Amarillo Sky (Ire)

7 b g Westerner - Bag Of Tricks (Flemensfirth)
Joe Tizzard J P Romans

PLACINGS: 44710/16412F156/114-				RPR **161c**
Starts	1st	2nd	3rd	4th	Win & Pl
17	6	1	-	4	£91,598

144	11/22	Newb	2m¹/₂f Cls2 123-144 Ch Hcap good	£21,260
140	11/22	Chel	2m Cls2 130-145 Ch Hcap good	£26,015
135	2/22	Newb	2m¹/₂f Cls2 Nov 116-137 Ch Hcap soft	£10,892
128	11/21	Winc	1m7¹/₂f Cls3 Nov 125-134 Ch Hcap good	£8,169
125	5/21	NAbb	2m1f Cls3 116-126 Hdl Hcap good	£5,146
115	3/21	Extr	2m1f Cls4 100-120 Hdl Hcap gd-sft	£3,769

Progressive chaser who won handicaps at Cheltenham and Newbury early last season, building on a promising novice campaign that had seen him sent off 5-1 when fifth in the Grand Annual; nine-length fourth in the Clarence House Chase when found to have finished lame.

American Mike (Ire)

6 b g Mahler - American Jennie (Lord Americo)
Gordon Elliott (Ire) Bective Stud

PLACINGS: 1/112/312474-				RPR **139h**
Starts	1st	2nd	3rd	4th	Win & Pl
9	3	2	1	2	£56,055

11/22	DRoy	2m6¹/₂f Mdn Hdl soft	£6,445
12/21	Navn	2m List NHF 4-7yo gd-yld	£11,853
10/21	DRoy	2m1f NHF 4-7yo soft	£5,268

Held in very high regard as a bumper horse and went some way to justifying the hype when second behind Facile Vega in the 2022 Champion Bumper; steadily lost his lustre during a disappointing novice hurdle campaign last term, failing to add to debut win.

Amirite (Ire)

7 b g Sholokhov - Belle Again (Shantou)
Henry De Bromhead (Ire) Patrick Hale

PLACINGS: 1451/13U3P-				RPR **140c**
Starts	1st	2nd	3rd	4th	Win & Pl
8	2	-	2	1	£17,752

| 10/22 | Fair | 2m5f Ch good | £6,941 |
| 4/22 | Kbgn | 2m3f Mdn Hdl gd-yld | £4,958 |

Potentially smart stayer who was sent off favourite for last season's Irish National only to be pulled up; had made a winning chase debut at Fairyhouse and then shown useful form in defeat, twice finishing third in Graded races.

An Epic Song (Fr)

6 b g Authorized - Morning Sun (Law Society)
Martin Brassil (Ire) Sean & Bernardine Mulryan

PLACINGS: 71/481/0029-				RPR **142h**
Starts	1st	2nd	3rd	4th	Win & Pl
9	2	1	-	1	£36,932

| 124 | 12/21 | Punc | 2m3f 104-121 Hdl Hcap heavy | £8,429 |
| | 3/21 | Gowr | 2m Mdn Hdl 4yo heavy | £6,321 |

Lightly raced hurdler who showed little last season other than a huge run when a head

GUIDE TO THE JUMPS 2023-24

second in the Coral Cup at Cheltenham; better clearly expected that day, going off at 16-1 having been 80-1 and 50-1 on previous runs; disappointed when ninth at Punchestown next time.

Andy Dufresne (Ire)

9 b g Doyen - Daytona Lily (Beneficial)
Gordon Elliott (Ire) John P McManus

PLACINGS: 13/113P/22/F3788U-U5				RPR **152c**
Starts	1st	2nd	3rd	4th	Win & Pl
19	5	3	3	-	£113,646

12/20	Navn	2m1f Nov Gd3 Ch soft	£17,500
10/20	Wxfd	2m Ch soft	£5,500
1/20	Punc	2m¹/₂f Nov Gd2 Hdl soft	£22,250
11/19	Navn	2m4f Mdn Hdl sft-hvy	£7,188
1/19	DRoy	2m NHF 5-7yo yield	£5,550

Very highly rated in younger days and landed six of first eight runs under rules but hasn't won since 2020; ran a big race when second in the 2022 Grand Annual on handicap debut but eighth when again well fancied for that race last term and becoming disappointing again.

Angels Dawn (Ire)

8 b m Yeats - Angels Guard Thee (Dylan Thomas)
Sam Curling (Ire) Alfred Sweetnam

PLACINGS: 322/336315/B8421U16-				RPR **143+c**
Starts	1st	2nd	3rd	4th	Win & Pl
23	3	5	5	3	£76,851

131	3/23	Chel	3m2f Cls2 119-145 Am Ch Hcap soft	£36,668
122	1/23	DRoy	3m 103-123 Ch Hcap soft	£7,571
	3/22	Limk	3m Mdn Hdl sft-hvy	£6,197

Progressive staying novice chaser last season who flourished in good staying handicaps; gained biggest win in the Kim Muir at Cheltenham having been travelling well when unseating two out in Punchestown's Grand National Trial; didn't jump well when sixth in the Irish National.

Annsam

8 b g Black Sam Bellamy - Bathwick Annie (Sula Bula)
Evan Williams Wayne Clifford

PLACINGS: /F21P/431P31/861710-				RPR **155+c**
Starts	1st	2nd	3rd	4th	Win & Pl
23	8	1	3	1	£113,654

142	4/23	Ludl	3m Cls5 114-142 Ch Hcap gd-sft	£9,506
135	1/23	Kemp	3m Cls2 126-143 Ch Hcap soft	£13,082
130	4/22	Newb	3m Cls2 124-141 Hdl Hcap gd-sft	£8,169
134	12/21	Asct	3m Cls1 List 130-150 Ch Hcap gd-sft	£39,865
	12/20	Ludl	2m4f Cls3 Ch soft	£7,389
118	1/20	Catt	2m3¹/₂f Cls3 115-130 Hdl Hcap soft	£6,563
113	12/19	Tntn	2m3f Cls3 109-129 Hdl Hcap soft	£8,382
	5/19	Winc	1m7¹/₂f Cls5 Mdn Hdl gd-fm	£3,249

Useful staying handicap chaser who won at Kempton and Ludlow last season, the latter under 12st 2lb; seems best off big weights in lesser company and struggled in bigger handicaps, finishing no better than sixth in five Class 1 races since winning the Silver Cup at Ascot in 2021.

113

RACING POST

Any Second Now (Ire)
11 b g Oscar - Pretty Neat (Topanoora)

Ted Walsh (Ire) — John P McManus

PLACINGS: U31/99P13/9612/241P- — RPR **158+**c

Starts	1st	2nd	3rd	4th	Win & Pl
33	7	7	5	1	£491,274

3/23	Navn	2m4½f Gd2 Ch heavy £19,058
2/22	Fair	3m1½f Gd3 Ch soft £14,130
3/21	Navn	2m Gd2 Ch heavy £18,438
2/20	Naas	2m Gd3 Ch heavy £23,250
143 3/19	Chel	3m2f Cls2 133-144 Am Ch Hcap gd-sft £41,510
1/17	Punc	2m Nov Hdl soft £22,440
12/16	Navn	2m Mdn Hdl 4yo yld-sft £5,426

Top staying chaser who has become synonymous with the Grand National; placed in 2021 and 2022 but was pulled up last season after being badly hampered; has won his Aintree prep run in each of the last three seasons having been quietly campaigned prior to the weights lunch.

Apple Away (Ire)
6 b m Arctic Cosmos - Dr A Day (Dr Massini)

Lucinda Russell — Old Gold Racing

PLACINGS: 241/1632111- — RPR **143+**h

Starts	1st	2nd	3rd	4th	Win & Pl
7	4	1	1		£85,956

4/23	Aint	3m½f Cls1 Nov Gd1 Hdl soft £56,270
3/23	Donc	3m½f Cls1 Nov List Hdl good £17,085
113 2/23	Ayr	3m½f Cls4 92-113 Hdl Hcap gd-sft £4,753
9/22	Bang	2m3½f Cls4 Nov Hdl good £3,812

Thorough stayer who was massively progressive once stepped up to 3m last season, ending up a Grade 1 winner at Aintree; second off 111 on handicap debut at Ayr but then rose through the ranks in winning her next three, culminating in the Sefton; likely to go novice chasing.

Appreciate It (Ire)
9 b g Jeremy - Sainte Baronne (Saint Des Saints)

Willie Mullins (Ire) — Miss M A Masterson

PLACINGS: /3112/1111/6/113432- — RPR **156**c

Starts	1st	2nd	3rd	4th	Win & Pl
15	8	2	2	1	£311,873

1/23	Naas	2m Nov Ch soft £10,442
12/22	Punc	2m Ch soft £6,445
3/21	Chel	2m½f Cls1 Nov Gd1 Hdl soft £52,799
2/21	Leop	2m Nov Gd1 Hdl sft-hvy £65,848
12/20	Leop	2m Nov Gd1 Hdl soft £40,000
11/20	Cork	2m Mdn Hdl heavy £7,000
2/20	Leop	2m Gd2 NHF 4-7yo yield £50,000
12/19	Leop	2m4f NHF 4-7yo soft £6,389

Wide-margin winner of the Supreme Novices' Hurdle in 2021 but then missed a year through injury and hasn't recaptured those heights; won twice over fences last season but came up short in Grade 1 novice company, though did go close on first run over 3m at Punchestown.

Ascending (Ire)
4 b g Awtaad - Midnight Martini (Night Shift)

Henry De Bromhead (Ire) — C Jones

PLACINGS: 245- — RPR **135**h

Starts	1st	2nd	3rd	4th	Win & Pl
3	-	1	-	1	£11,407

Very highly tried in juvenile hurdles last season, running only in Grade 1 company after a half-length defeat on debut; finished fourth at Leopardstown and probably did even better when fifth in the Triumph Hurdle; won't be many novice hurdlers rated higher.

Apple Away: proved a revelation over 3m last season

GUIDE TO THE JUMPS **2023-24**

Ashdale Bob (Ire)
8 b g Shantou - Ceol Rua (Bob Back)
Jessica Harrington (Ire)   Diarmuid Horgan
PLACINGS: F91/2U37323/2342P5-5   RPR **158**h

Starts	1st	2nd	3rd	4th	Win & Pl
22	3	4	5	2	£170,511

	4/21	Fair	2m4f Nov Gd2 Hdl yield	£18,438
	12/20	Navn	2m4f Nov Gd2 Hdl sft-hvy	£17,500
	11/20	Navn	2m4f Mdn Hdl soft	£7,500

Hasn't won since a Grade 2 novice hurdle in 2021 but has been knocking on the door in top staying hurdles following an aborted chase career; finished second at Grade 1 level for the third time in last year's Christmas Hurdle behind Home By The Lee; pulled up in the Stayers' Hurdle.

Ashroe Diamond (Ire)
6 b m Walk In The Park - Saine D'Esprit (Dom Alco)
Willie Mullins (Ire)   Blue Blood Racing Club
PLACINGS: 1241/13211-   RPR **139+**h

Starts	1st	2nd	3rd	4th	Win & Pl
9	5	1	2	1	£126,869

	4/23	Fair	2m4½f Nov Gd1 Hdl yield	£52,212
	1/23	Fair	2m2½f Nov Gd3 Hdl sft	£15,142
	11/22	Naas	2m Mdn Hdl yld-sft	£6,197
	4/22	Aint	2m1f Cls1 Gd2 NHF 4-6yo gd-sft	£28,135
	5/21	Wxfd	2m NHF 4-7yo sft-hvy	£5,795

Smart mare who won a Grade 1 mares' novice hurdle at Fairyhouse last season to make amends for missing the Cheltenham Festival with injury, still looking a work in progress; had also twice finished third against the boys in the top grade.

Ashtown Lad (Ire)
9 b g Flemensfirth - Blossom Trix (Saddlers' Hall)
Dan Skelton   Darren & Annaley Yates
PLACINGS: /2115P4/14235/3123P-   RPR **147+**c

Starts	1st	2nd	3rd	4th	Win & Pl
17	4	3	3	3	£139,927

138	12/22	Aint	3m2f Cls1 Gd3 121-147 Ch Hcap gd-sft	£84,195
	10/21	Weth	3m Cls3 Nov Ch gd-sft	£7,080
123	11/20	Uttx	2m7½f Cls3 119-133 Hdl Hcap soft	£5,913
	10/20	Weth	2m3½f Cls4 Hdl soft	£5,198

Lightly raced chaser who defied inexperience to win the Becher Chase last season in just his sixth chase; ran well over hurdles subsequently before switching back to fences at Aintree but went for the Topham rather than the Grand National and pulled up as favourite.

Aspire Tower (Ire)
7 b g Born To Sea - Red Planet (Pivotal)
Henry De Bromhead (Ire)   Robcour
PLACINGS: 11F2/124/8/   RPR **160**h

Starts	1st	2nd	3rd	4th	Win & Pl
8	3	2	-	1	£125,180

	10/20	DRoy	2m½f Gd2 Hdl yld-sft	£30,000
	12/19	Leop	2m Gd2 Hdl 3yo sft	£26,577
	11/19	Punc	2m½f Mdn Hdl 3yo soft	£6,922

Hasn't run since April 2021 but was a high-class hurdler when last seen; has won all three races over hurdles below Grade 1 level but yet to strike in five attempts at the top level; came closest when second to Sharjah at Leopardstown in 2020 and was fourth in the 2021 Champion Hurdle.

Asterion Forlonge (Fr)
9 gr g Coastal Path - Belle Du Brizais (Turgeon)
Willie Mullins (Ire)   Mrs J Donnelly
PLACINGS: 4/1FF433/1UF47/212-0   RPR **159**h

Starts	1st	2nd	3rd	4th	Win & Pl
19	6	2	2	3	£264,709

152	4/23	Fair	2m4f Gd2 Hdl yld-sft	£31,327
	4/21	Punc	2m5f Nov 131-152 Ch Hcap yield	£42,143
	11/20	Punc	2m3½f Ch sft-hvy	£6,250
	2/20	Leop	2m Nov Gd1 Hdl yield	£75,000
	1/20	Naas	2m Mdn Hdl gd-yld	£7,986
	11/19	Thur	2m NHF 5-7yo soft	£5,591

Seems destined never to fulfil potential over fences due to jumping issues (has fallen or unseated four times in 11 races) but did well reverting to hurdles last spring after a long layoff; won a Grade 2 at Fairyhouse before finishing second to Klassical Dream at Punchestown.

Attacca (Ire)
5 b g Mahler - Listening (King's Theatre)
Nicky Henderson   Mrs Patricia Pugh
PLACINGS: 2/113-   RPR **129**h

Starts	1st	2nd	3rd	4th	Win & Pl
4	2	1	1		£16,154

	12/22	Chel	2m1f Cls3 Nov Hdl 4-6yo good	£7,804
	11/22	Kemp	2m Cls4 Nov Hdl gd-sft	£4,357

Showed plenty of promise in a light novice hurdle campaign last season; won first two races over 2m at Kempton and Cheltenham; missed the Challow through injury and lost unbeaten record when a fair third at Ascot up in trip; type to keep progressing with age.

Aucunrisque (Fr)
7 b g No Risk At All - Saintheze (Saint Des Saints)
Chris Gordon   Goodwin Racing
PLACINGS: 2/143211141/122103-0   RPR **152**c

Starts	1st	2nd	3rd	4th	Win & Pl
17	7	4	2	2	£203,719

138	2/23	Newb	2m½f Cls1 Gd3 124-148 Hdl Hcap good	£87,219
	10/22	Uttx	2m Cls3 Nov Ch gd-sft	£8,714
133	4/22	Plum	2m Cls2 120-133 Hdl Hcap good	£26,164
	2/22	Kemp	2m Cls1 Nov Gd2 Hdl gd-sft	£34,170
117	1/22	Winc	1m7f Cls3 Nov 117-123 Hdl Hcap good	£6,154
	1/22	Plum	2m Cls4 Nov Hdl soft	£4,357
	10/21	Strf	2m½f Cls4 NHF 4-6yo gd-sft	£2,723

Earned a huge payday when exploiting lower hurdles mark to win last season's Betfair Hurdle at Newbury, although less effective after 9lb rise subsequently; had done well in three runs over fences, winning at Uttoxeter and finishing second in a Grade 2 novice chase at Kempton.

115

RACING POST

Aurora Vega (Ire)

5 b m Walk In The Park - Quevega (Robin Des Champs)
Willie Mullins (Ire)   Hammer & Trowel Syndicate

PLACINGS: 11					RPR **124+**b
Starts	1st	2nd	3rd	4th	Win & Pl
2	2	-	-	-	£11,747

| 8/23 | Klny | 2m½f NHF yld-sft............................. £6,004 |
| 6/23 | Slig | 2m2f NHF good................................ £5,743 |

Full-sister to Facile Vega out of superstar hurdler Quevega who hasn't had to come out of second gear to register two wide-margin bumper victories; hacked up by 12 lengths on debut at Sligo and even better when scoring by ten lengths at Killarney.

Authorised Speed (Fr)

6 b g Authorized - Tangaspeed (Vertical Speed)
Gary Moore   Gallagher Bloodstock

PLACINGS: 22145/11518-					RPR **138+**h
Starts	1st	2nd	3rd	4th	Win & Pl
10	4	2	-	1	£30,849

3/23	Sand	2m Cls4 Nov Hdl soft.......................... £5,446
12/22	Sand	2m Cls2 Nov Hdl soft.......................... £7,805
11/22	Ling	2m3½f Cls4 Mdn Hdl soft..................... £4,901
1/22	Newb	2m½f Cls5 NHF 4-6yo gd-sft................ £1,906

Best of the British in the 2022 Champion Bumper and looked top of the tree in novice hurdles last season until well beaten at 5-4 in the Tolworth; scoped dirty after that and got back on track in calmer waters at Sandown only to disappoint again in Grade 1 company at Aintree.

GUIDE TO THE JUMPS 2023-24

Authorized Art (Fr)
8 b g Authorized - Rock Art (Rock Of Gibraltar)
Willie Mullins (Ire)   Nicholas Peacock

PLACINGS: 4/337P5/121114456-24   RPR **150**c

Starts	1st	2nd	3rd	4th	Win & Pl
20	5	3	2	4	£114,243

10/22	Tipp	2m3½f Nov Gd3 Ch gd-yld	£14,874
8/22	Klny	2m4f Nov Ch gd-yld	£6,445
7/22	Limk	2m3½f Ch good	£6,445
5/22	Wxfd	2m1f Hdl good	£8,429
5/19	Punc	2m1½f Mdn Hdl good	£7,214

Ran a huge race on handicap chase debut when second in the Galway Plate this summer; had also flourished at the same time of year in 2022, winning three of first four chases, but was below par during the winter in stronger company and on softer ground.

Aye Right (Ire)
10 b g Yeats - Gaybric (Presenting)
Harriet Graham & Gary Rutherford   Geoff & Elspeth Adam

PLACINGS: 15/232230/5139/2P44-   RPR **158**c

Starts	1st	2nd	3rd	4th	Win & Pl
31	8	9	4	3	£220,485

151	11/21	Newc	2m7½f Cls1 List 132-151 Ch Hcap gd-sft	£39,865
	1/20	Newc	2m7½f Cls4 Nov Ch soft	£4,289
136	9/19	Kels	2m5f Cls2 124-136 Hdl Hcap good	£11,696
130	4/19	Ayr	3m½f Cls3 Nov 111-135 Hdl Hcap good	£10,007
122	1/19	Ayr	2m5½f Cls3 120-136 Hdl Hcap soft	£9,357
	10/18	Kels	2m5f Cls4 Nov Hdl good	£4,549
	9/18	Kels	2m5f Cls4 Nov Hdl gd-fm	£4,224
	11/17	Carl	2m1f Cls5 NHF 4-6yo soft	£2,274

Smart staying chaser who has run well in numerous big handicaps in recent years and gained an overdue win in the Rehearsal Chase in 2021; close third in the Cotswold Chase and ninth in the Gold Cup that season but form tailed off last term, albeit in just four runs.

Balco Coastal (Fr)
7 b g Coastal Path - Fliugika (Roi De Rome)
Nicky Henderson   Mark Blandford

PLACINGS: 27/112P3/5127P-   RPR **156**c

Starts	1st	2nd	3rd	4th	Win & Pl
11	3	2	1	-	£61,752

133	12/22	Kemp	2m4½f Cls3 Nov 122-142 Ch Hcap soft	£13,615
	12/21	Ludl	2m Cls4 Nov Hdl gd-sft	£4,901
	12/21	Kemp	2m Cls4 Nov Hdl good	£5,010
	2/21	Kemp	2m Cls5 NHF 4-6yo std-slw	£2,274

Very useful novice chaser last season; hacked up in a novice handicap at Kempton before chasing home Gerri Colombe in a Grade 1 at Sandown; disappointed in the spring when last of seven in the Turners at Cheltenham and pulled up when favourite for a Grade 2 at Ayr.

Ballyburn (Ire)
5 b g Flemensfirth - Old Moon (Old Vic)
Willie Mullins (Ire)   R A Bartlett & David Manasseh

PLACINGS: 111-   RPR **134**+b

Starts	1st	2nd	3rd	4th	Win & Pl
2	2	-	-	-	£14,358

4/23	Punc	2m NHF 4-7yo gd-yld	£9,137
2/23	Punc	2m NHF yield	£5,221

Looked an exciting prospect in bumpers last season despite being kept to ordinary company; won twice to add to sole point-to-point win, powering home by six lengths on final run at Punchestown having raced keenly; potential star over hurdles.

Ballygrifincottage (Ire)
8 b g Stowaway - Long Long Time (Dr Massini)
Dan Skelton   Friends From Insurance

PLACINGS: U/111314/1PP-   RPR **147**+c

Starts	1st	2nd	3rd	4th	Win & Pl
6	2	-	1	1	£39,495

11/22	Hayd	2m5½f Cls2 Nov Ch soft	£10,892
1/22	Ling	2m7f Cls2 Nov Hdl heavy	£15,843

Looked a potential star early last season but campaign unravelled subsequently; fine fourth in the 2022 Albert Bartlett and then won well on chase debut last term; bled from the nose when odds-on for a weak Grade 2 at Wetherby and then pulled up again back over hurdles.

Banbridge (Ire)
7 ch g Doyen - Old Carton Lass (Presenting)
Joseph O'Brien (Ire)   R A Bartlett

PLACINGS: /328/11147110/11321-   RPR **159**+c

Starts	1st	2nd	3rd	4th	Win & Pl
14	8	1	1	1	£202,812

	4/23	Aint	2m4f Cls1 Nov Gd1 Ch gd-sft	£67,524
	11/22	Chel	2m Cls1 Nov Gd2 Ch good	£29,753
	10/22	Gowr	2m4f Ch gd-yld	£6,197
137	3/22	Chel	2m4½f Cls2 132-144 Cond Hdl Hcap gd-sft	£39,023
	1/22	Navn	2m Nov Hdl yield	£7,933
	7/21	Rosc	2m5f Nov Hdl soft	£8,429
	5/21	Punc	2m½f Mdn Hdl soft	£6,321
	5/21	Klny	2m1f NHF 5-8yo gd-yld	£5,268

Won a 2m4f Grade 1 novice chase at Aintree last term to crown a fine first season over fences; sole disappointment came on soft ground in the Drinmore and connections avoided similar conditions at Cheltenham; lacked speed to live with El Fabiolo over 2m and could even want 3m in time.

Authorised Speed: talented hurdler who was a winner three times last season

117

RACING POST

Beauport (Ire)
7 b g Califet - Byerley Beauty (Brian Boru)
Nigel Twiston-Davies — Bryan & Philippa Burrough

PLACINGS: 43131/22214/1249F- — RPR **144**c

Starts	1st	2nd	3rd	4th	Win & Pl
15	4	4	2	3	£116,740

	10/22	Carl	2m4f Cls1 List Ch soft.................................. £17,085
	3/22	Uttx	2m4f Cls2 121-142 Hdl Hcap soft................... £25,720
142	3/22	Uttx	
122	3/21	Sand	2m4f Cls1 Nov Gd3 117-132 Hdl 4-7yo Hcap soft.. £28,230
	1/21	Font	2m5½f Cls4 Nov Hdl soft............................. £3,769

Former EBF Final winner who didn't quite build on rich promise of chase debut win at Carlisle last season; better expected when stepped up in trip in handicaps in the spring and unlucky not to make more impact (lost a shoe in the Kim Muir and fell when going well at Aintree).

Better Days Ahead (Ire)
5 b g Milan - Bonnie And Bright (Topanoora)
Gordon Elliott (Ire) — Bective Stud

PLACINGS: 1/210- — RPR **119**+b

Starts	1st	2nd	3rd	4th	Win & Pl
3	1	1	-	-	£6,873

| | 12/22 | Fair | 2m NHF 4yo soft... £4,958 |

Bought for £350,000 after winning sole point-to-point in 2022 and made a promising start in bumpers last season, winning notably well at Fairyhouse; went off Gordon Elliott's number one for the Champion Bumper at Cheltenham but could never land a blow from the rear.

Bialystok (Ire)
5 b g Zoffany - Deauville Shower (High Chaparral)
Willie Mullins (Ire) — Mrs S Ricci

PLACINGS: 3411-73 — RPR **143**+h

Starts	1st	2nd	3rd	4th	Win & Pl
6	2	-	2	1	£35,420

| 130 | 4/23 | Punc | 2m½f 119-145 Hdl Hcap yld-sft.................. £26,106 |
| | 2/23 | Naas | 1m7½f Mdn Hdl yield................................ £6,527 |

Recruited off the Flat in France and made rapid progress following the turn of the year last season; got off the mark at Naas and sprang a 14-1 surprise on handicap debut at Punchestown; not beaten far when seventh in the Galway Hurdle this summer.

Bill Baxter (Ire)
7 gr g Milan - Blossom Rose (Roselier)
Warren Greatrex — Glassex Holdings

PLACINGS: 214/21524/811F11- — RPR **146**+c

Starts	1st	2nd	3rd	4th	Win & Pl
13	6	2	-	2	£128,462

133	4/23	Aint	2m5f Cls1 Gd3 131-157 Ch Hcap soft............ £84,195
128	3/23	Kels	2m5½f Cls3 Nov 116-136 Ch Hcap gd-sft...... £10,562
120	12/22	Kels	2m6½f Cls3 Nov 110-120 Ch Hcap heavy £7,951
115	11/22	Ling	2m4f Cls4 Nov 106-118 Ch Hcap soft............ £12,358
	11/21	Ayr	2m4f Cls4 Mdn Hdl gd-sft....................... £4,085
	1/21	Fknm	2m Cls5 NHF 4-6yo soft............................ £2,774

Hugely progressive chaser who won his last four completed races last season; won three novice handicaps either side of a fall when going well at Hereford; stepped out of novice company for

Bill Baxter (right): scores over the National fences

For all former racehorses to enjoy a good life

RoR is British Horseracing's official charity for the welfare of horses that have retired from racing.

It is our mission to safeguard the wellbeing of all former racehorses and we have made a real difference to the lives of thousands of them through our education programme for new owners, our provision of promotional activity to highlight the versatility and adaptability of the thoroughbred together with a nationwide safety net for horses in need of charitable support.

DONATE

To donate £5, text ROR2 to 70970
To donate £10, text ROR2 to 70191

None of the vital work we do would be possible without our generous supporters. Your contribution today will make a significant difference to the wellbeing of former racehorses.

Fundraising, payments and donations will be processed and administered by the National Funding Scheme (Charity No: 1149800), operating as DONATE. Texts will be charged at your standard network rate. For Terms & Conditions, see www.easydonate.org

T: 01488 648998 **DONATE** **W: ror.org.uk**

the first time and maintained winning streak in the Topham at Aintree; raised another 8lb.

Blazing Khal (Ire)
7 b g Kalanisi - Blazing Sonnet (Oscar)
Charles Byrnes (Ire) — Byrnes Bloodstock/F McCarthy

PLACINGS: 52/541/111/16-   RPR **164+h**

Starts	1st	2nd	3rd	4th	Win & Pl
10	5	-	-	1	£93,743
	2/23	Navn	2m5f Gd2 Hdl gd-yld		£19,058
	12/21	Chel	3m Cls1 Nov Gd2 Hdl gd-sft		£28,475
	11/21	Chel	2m5f Cls1 Nov Gd2 Hdl good		£28,230
	10/21	Gway	2m3f Mdn Hdl soft		£6,321
	12/20	Limk	2m NHF 4-7yo heavy		£4,500

Exciting, lightly raced stayer who returned from a 14-month layoff with an impressive win in last season's Boyne Hurdle; had won all three novice hurdles in 2021, including twice at Cheltenham, but lost unbeaten record back there when sixth in the Stayers' Hurdle.

Blizzard Of Oz (Ire)
5 b g Arctic Cosmos - Definite Jt (Definite Article)
Willie Mullins (Ire) — Simon Munir & Isaac Souede

PLACINGS: 2/3212-   RPR **122b**

Starts	1st	2nd	3rd	4th	Win & Pl
5	1	3	1	-	£27,676
	3/23	Cork	2m NHF heavy		£7,832

Held in very high regard and was sent off favourite for all four bumpers last season, including a Grade 2 at Aintree, despite winning only once; got off the mark at Cork and finished a good second after travelling notably well at Aintree; from a staying family.

Blood Destiny (Fr)
4 ch g No Risk At All - High Blood (High Yield)
Willie Mullins (Ire) — Roaringwater Syndicate

PLACINGS: 2/1192-   RPR **145+h**

Starts	1st	2nd	3rd	4th	Win & Pl
5	2	2	-	-	£33,069
	1/23	Fair	2m Hdl 4yo sft-hvy		£9,659
	12/22	Cork	2m1f Mdn Hdl 3yo yld-sft		£6,197

Last season's highest-rated juvenile hurdler on Racing Post Ratings but didn't quite live up to that billing in the spring; hacked up by 18 lengths at Fairyhouse in January; below-par ninth in the Triumph Hurdle and then beaten at odds-on by smart filly Enjoy The Dream.

Blow Your Wad (Ire)
5 b g Walk In The Park - Molly's Mate (Goldmark)
Tom Lacey — Jerry Hinds & Ashley Head

PLACINGS: 224/21619-   RPR **134+h**

Starts	1st	2nd	3rd	4th	Win & Pl
8	2	3	-	1	£24,663
	125	3/23	Newb	2m3f Cls3 Nov 112-128 Hdl Hcap soft	£10,905
		11/22	Kemp	2m Cls4 Nov Hdl 4-6yo gd-sft	£4,901

Useful novice hurdler last season; had wind surgery after a poor run in the Tolworth and most impressive when stepped up to 2m3f to win a novice handicap at Newbury on first run back; not disgraced at Aintree when returned to Grade 1 company; likely to go novice chasing.

Blue Lord (Fr)
8 b g Blue Bresil - Lorette (Cachet Noir)
Willie Mullins (Ire) — Simon Munir & Isaac Souede

PLACINGS: 123F/31113/111283-   RPR **169+c**

Starts	1st	2nd	3rd	4th	Win & Pl
15	7	2	4	-	£351,948
	12/22	Leop	2m1f Gd1 Ch yield		£61,975
	11/22	Clun	2m4½f Gd2 Ch sft-hvy		£29,748
	4/22	Punc	2m Nov Gd1 Ch gd-yld		£61,975
	2/22	Leop	2m1f Nov Gd1 Ch yield		£4,370
	1/22	Naas	2m Nov Ch soft		£9,668
	12/21	Fair	2m Ch yld-sft		£6,848
	11/20	Punc	2m½f Mdn Hdl soft		£6,000

Three-time Grade 1 winner, adding an impressive victory over subsequent Champion Chase runner-up Captain Guinness at Leopardstown last Christmas to two top-flight novice wins; disappointing subsequently, including a 1-4 defeat behind Gentleman De Mee.

Blueking D'Oroux (Fr)
4 b g Jeu St Eloi - Belle Du Bresil (Blue Bresil)
Paul Nicholls — Mrs Johnny De La Hey

PLACINGS: 12/4P912-   RPR **132+h**

Starts	1st	2nd	3rd	4th	Win & Pl
7	2	2	-	1	£58,515
	127	4/23	Asct	1m7½f Cls2 106-127 Hdl 4yo Hcap gd-sft	£20,812
		3/22	Fntb	1m7f Hdl 3yo v soft	£9,000

French recruit who bounced back last spring after a false start to his British career, winning an Ascot handicap at 50-1 and finishing a fine second at Aintree; had been rated highly enough to go off 6-4 in a Grade 2 on British debut but needed wind surgery to produce best form.

Blow Your Wad (right): could do well as a novice chaser this season

Bo Zenith (Fr)

4 b g Zarak - Boreale Du Berlais (Presenting)

Gary Moore   O S Harris

PLACINGS: 1/3112-   RPR **135+**h

Starts	1st	2nd	3rd	4th	Win & Pl
5	3	1	1	-	£64,790
3/23	Strf	2m2½f Cls3 Hdl 4yo gd-sft................£5,446
2/23	Hayd	1m7½f Cls2 Hdl 4yo gd-sft..............£13,615
4/22	Autl	1m7f Hdl 3yo v soft......................£20,975

Highest-rated juvenile hurdler in Britain last season on the strength of a near miss behind Zenta in a Grade 1 at Aintree; had won previous two runs in ordinary company at Haydock and Stratford to add to French debut win; has won over 2m2f and sure to get further.

Bob Olinger (Ire)

8 b g Sholokhov - Zenaide (Zaffaran)

Henry De Bromhead (Ire)   Robcour

PLACINGS: 11/2111/111/P253-   RPR **157+**h

Starts	1st	2nd	3rd	4th	Win & Pl
12	7	2	1	-	£245,851
3/22	Chel	2m4f Cls1 Nov Gd1 Ch soft............£101,564
1/22	Punc	2m4f Nov Gd3 Ch soft..................£17,353
11/21	Gowr	2m4f Ch soft..............................£8,165
3/21	Chel	2m5f Cls1 Nov Gd1 Hdl gd-sft..........£52,753
1/21	Naas	2m4f Nov Gd1 Hdl heavy................£42,143
12/20	Navn	2m4f Mdn Hdl sft-hvy...................£6,000
3/20	Gowr	2m2f NHF 4-7yo sft-hvy.................£5,000

Once seen as racing's next superstar but bubble well and truly burst last season; hasn't won since being gifted a second Cheltenham Festival win in 2022 by Galopin Des Champs's final-fence exit; reverted to hurdles last term but regressed after promising second at Navan.

Bold Endeavour

7 b g Fame And Glory - Araucaria (Accordion)

Nicky Henderson   Countrywide Park Homes

PLACINGS: 1/1113P/P11252-2   RPR **151+**c

Starts	1st	2nd	3rd	4th	Win & Pl
12	5	3	1	-	£67,428
1/23	Donc	2m4½f Cls3 Nov 120-139 Ch Hcap gd-sft.......£11,142
12/22	Leic	2m4f Cls3 118-132 Ch Hcap gd-fm..............£7,407
1/22	Weth	2m3½f Cls4 Nov Hdl soft......................£5,827
11/21	Sedg	2m4f Cls4 Mdn Hdl good......................£4,085
5/21	Sedg	2m1f Cls5 NHF 4-6yo good...................£1,906

Impressed in winning first two runs over fences last season but didn't quite build on that; well beaten in second when odds-on for a three-runner Reynoldstown at Ascot and then reverted to hurdles, finishing a solid second in handicaps at Cheltenham and Haydock.

Boothill (Ire)

8 b/br g Presenting - Oyster Pipit (Accordion)

Harry Fry   Brian & Sandy Lambert

PLACINGS: 221/1/3492/P112123-   RPR **153+**c

Starts	1st	2nd	3rd	4th	Win & Pl
13	5	3	2	1	£161,775
12/22	Kemp	2m Cls1 Nov Gd2 Ch soft.....................£30,538
11/22	Asct	2m1f Cls2 135-151 Ch Hcap good...............£65,038
10/22	NAbb	2m½f Cls3 Nov 127-136 Ch Hcap good..........£7,013
12/20	Tntn	2m½f Cls4 Nov Hdl gd-sft.....................£3,769
2/20	Kemp	2m Cls5 NHF 4-6yo gd-sft....................£3,119

Very useful novice chaser last season despite not

quite progressing as expected; won a valuable handicap at Ascot in just his third chase and later added a Grade 2 at Kempton; twice a beaten favourite at that level subsequently, including when failing to stay 2m4f.

Botox Has (Fr)

7 b g Dream Well - Bournie (Kahyasi)
Gary Moore   John & Yvonne Stone
PLACINGS: 21/1406P/F8231/2174-   RPR **152**+h

Starts	1st	2nd	3rd	4th	Win & Pl
18	5	4	1	2	£202,442
144	11/22 Hayd	3m¹/₂f Cls1 Gd3 126-147 Hdl Hcap soft...£71,188
	2/22 Font	2m3f Cls1 Gd2 Hdl gd-sft...£51,496
	10/20 Chel	2m¹/₂f Cls2 Hdl 4yo good...£20,019
	12/19 Chel	2m1f Cls2 Hdl 3yo soft...£15,640
*	10/19 Font	2m1¹/₂f Cls4 Hdl 3yo good...£3,861

Deservedly landed a big staying handicap hurdle at Haydock last season, defying a big weight having been placed in three similar races at Cheltenham in the previous 12 months; has won at Grade 2 level but twice came up short back at that level, though still a fair fourth in the Cleeve.

Brandy Love (Ire)

7 b m Jet Away - Bambootcha (Saddlers' Hall)
Willie Mullins (Ire)   Mrs J Donnelly
PLACINGS: 1/13/121/355-   RPR **150**+h

Starts	1st	2nd	3rd	4th	Win & Pl
8	3	1	2	-	£81,494
	4/22 Fair	2m4f Nov Gd1 Hdl yield...£49,580
	12/21 Naas	2m Mdn Hdl yield...£6,321
	12/20 Fair	2m NHF 4yo sft-hvy...£5,000

High-class novice hurdler two seasons ago, beating Love Envoi by eight lengths in a Grade 1 at Fairyhouse, but failed to run up to that form last season; didn't return until February, when looking rusty in third, and then only fifth at Cheltenham and Punchestown.

Brave Seasca (Fr)

8 bl g Brave Mansonnien - Miss Laveron (Laveron)
Venetia Williams   Brooks & Taylor Families
PLACINGS: 9/4/41/61113F/10PP-   RPR **159**+c

Starts	1st	2nd	3rd	4th	Win & Pl
14	5		1	2	£59,566
146	12/22 Aint	2m4f Cls2 119-146 Ch Hcap gd-sft...£20,576
137	1/22 Wwck	2m Cls2 133-157 Ch Hcap soft...£16,338
128	12/21 Asct	2m1f Cls3 Nov 125-136 Ch Hcap gd-sft...£8,169
121	12/21 Wwck	2m Cls4 Nov 105-121 Ch Hcap soft...£4,357
	2/21 Hntg	2m Cls4 Nov Hdl soft...£3,769

Scored first time out at Aintree last season to make it four wins in first seven races over fences but badly lost his way after that; twice flopped in big handicaps at Cheltenham and pulled up for the second time in a row at Kempton on final run; quickly tumbled back down the weights.

Bravemansgame (Fr)

8 b g Brave Mansonnien - Genifique (Nickname)
Paul Nicholls   Bryan Drew
PLACINGS: 6/211132/11114/1123-   RPR **177**+c

Starts	1st	2nd	3rd	4th	Win & Pl
17	9	3	3	1	£532,429
	12/22 Kemp	3m Cls1 Ch soft...£142,375
	10/22 Weth	3m Cls1 Gd2 Ch gd-sft...£56,950
159	2/22 Newb	2m7¹/₂f Cls3 Nov 140-159 Ch Hcap gd-sft...£10,519
	12/21 Kemp	3m Cls1 Nov Gd1 Ch soft...£56,950
	11/21 Hayd	2m5¹/₂f Cls2 Ch gd-sft...£26,015
	10/21 NAbb	2m5f Cls2 Ch gd-sft...£12,155
	12/20 Newb	2m4¹/₂f Cls1 Nov Gd1 Hdl soft...£23,848
	11/20 Newb	2m4¹/₂f Cls3 Nov Hdl good...£6,498
	11/20 Extr	2m1f Cls3 Nov Hdl good...£5,913

Top-class staying chaser who won last season's King George (left clear at the last but was getting the better of L'Homme Presse); fine second in the Cheltenham Gold Cup behind Galopin Des Champs but failed to cash in on that one's below-par display at Punchestown.

Brewin'Upastorm (Ire)

10 b g Milan - Daraheen Diamond (Husyan)
Olly Murphy   Mrs Barbara Hester
PLACINGS: U/65115/1F12P/U2518-   RPR **154**+h

Starts	1st	2nd	3rd	4th	Win & Pl
25	9	3	-	3	£262,118
	2/23 Font	2m3f Cls1 Gd2 Hdl good...£45,560
	1/22 Ling	2m3¹/₂f Cls2 Hdl heavy...£52,030
	11/21 Aint	2m4f Cls2 Hdl gd-sft...£20,812
	2/21 Font	2m3f Cls1 Gd2 Hdl gd-sft...£28,609
148	1/21 Tntn	2m3f Cls2 122-148 Hdl Hcap soft...£9,495
	11/19 Tntn	2m2f Cls Nov Ch good...£6,590
	10/19 Carl	2m Cls3 Ch gd-sft...£7,473
	12/18 Hntg	2m Cls4 Nov Hdl gd-sft...£5,523
	1/18 Hrfd	2m Cls5 Am NHF 4-6yo soft...£2,599

Smart but fragile veteran hurdler who benefited from a fourth wind operation last season to win the National Spirit Hurdle at Fontwell last term; had won that race in 2021 and beaten a head in 2022; form has become increasingly patchy.

Brighterdaysahead (Fr)

4 b f Kapgarde - Matnie (Laveron)
Gordon Elliott (Ire)   Gigginstown House Stud
PLACINGS: 11-   RPR **120**+b

Starts	1st	2nd	3rd	4th	Win & Pl
2	2	-	-	-	£57,955
	4/23 Fair	2m NHF 4-5yo yield...£52,212
	2/23 Gowr	2m1f NHF sft-hvy...£5,743

Half-sister to Grade 1 winner Mighty Potter who cost €310,000 as an unraced three-year-old before winning both bumpers last season; hacked up on debut at Gowran before following up in a sales bumper at Fairyhouse; fine prospect for novice hurdles.

Brewin'Upastorm: talented performer who landed a Grade 2 hurdle last season

GUIDE TO THE JUMPS 2023-24

Broadway Boy (Ire)
5 b g Malinas - Broadway Theatre (King's Theatre)
Nigel Twiston-Davies — D M Proos
PLACINGS: 2214U11- — RPR **131**+h

Starts	1st	2nd	3rd	4th	Win & Pl
7	3	2	-	1	£30,472

126	4/23	Chel	3m Cls2 120-141 Hdl Hcap good £13,050
119	3/23	MRas	2m7f Cls4 112-119 Hdl Hcap gd-sft £6,601
112	12/22	Aint	3m¹/₂f Cls4 Nov 103-112 Hdl Hcap gd-sft £5,991

Useful and progressive novice hurdler last season; beaten favourite twice after getting off the mark at Aintree but got back on track by winning twice more in the spring, most notably in a 3m handicap at Cheltenham; fine prospect for staying novice chases.

Bronn (Ire)
6 b g Notnowcato - Cluain Easa (Accordion)
Willie Mullins (Ire) — Simon Munir & Isaac Souede
PLACINGS: 1/1521/42133- — RPR **159**c

Starts	1st	2nd	3rd	4th	Win & Pl
10	4	2	2	1	£82,642

1/23	Fair	2m5¹/₂f Ch soft £6,788
4/22	Fair	2m4f Nov Gd2 Hdl yield £19,832
1/22	Naas	2m Mdn Hdl soft £6,941
4/21	Baln	2m1¹/₂f NHF 4yo yld-sft £5,268

Yet to win in four attempts at Grade 1 level but did produce his best effort when third at 50-1 in the Brown Advisory at last season's Cheltenham Festival; didn't quite build on that when beaten further in filling the same spot behind Gerri Colombe at Aintree.

123

RACING POST

Broomfield Present (Ire)
7 b g Presenting - Diklers Oscar (Oscar)
Kim Bailey   Turf 2022 & K C Bailey
PLACINGS: 3/P/41/121-   RPR **130+**h

Starts	1st	2nd	3rd	4th	Win & Pl
3	2	1	-	-	£13,245
122	3/23	Hayd	3m½f Cls4 110-122 Hdl Hcap soft................		£6,337
	11/22	Ffos	2m4f Cls4 Mdn Hdl soft..............................		£4,901

Lightly raced and progressive novice hurdler last season; made the most of point-to-point experience (won at fourth attempt) to get off the mark first time out at Ffos Las and took a big step forward when making a winning handicap debut at Haydock; likely to go novice chasing.

Buddy One (Ire)
6 b g Sans Frontieres - May's Magic (Bob's Return)
Paul John Gilligan (Ire)   E Lynch & T C Quinn & John J McGrath
PLACINGS: 70612232-43   RPR **142**h

Starts	1st	2nd	3rd	4th	Win & Pl
10	1	3	2	1	£42,611
	1/23	Fair	2m4½f Mdn Hdl soft....................................		£6,265

Hugely progressive novice hurdler despite winning only once; beaten a short head in a Grade 3 at Thurles and then improved again in two big handicaps, finishing third in the Martin Pipe and second at Aintree's Grand National meeting; more to come over further.

Busselton (Fr)

6 b g Mastercraftsman - Blessed Luck (Rock Of Gibraltar)
Joseph O'Brien (Ire)   Michael Hilary Burke
PLACINGS: 4/221311242/22154P-5   RPR **148**c

Starts	1st	2nd	3rd	4th	Win & Pl
21	5	7	2	3	£252,318
142	9/22	List	3m 137-163 Ch Hcap good		£99,160
	11/21	Punc	2m3½f Nov Ch gd-yld		£8,429
	10/21	Cork	2m4f Nov Ch good		£9,746
	9/21	List	2m6f Ch good		£6,585
	5/20	Autl	1m7f Hdl 3yo v soft		£19,241

Flourished when sent chasing as just a four-year-old in 2021 and completed a remarkably busy and productive spell when winning the following year's Kerry National; fifth in the Coral Gold Cup next time but hasn't fired since, albeit from limited opportunities.

Calico (Ger)

7 b g Soldier Hollow - Casanga (Rainbow Quest)
Dan Skelton   John J Reilly
PLACINGS: 1214/842306/224121F-   RPR **149**c

Starts	1st	2nd	3rd	4th	Win & Pl
17	4	5	1	3	£76,395
137	3/23	Donc	2m½f Cls2 128-142 Ch Hcap good		£20,812
129	1/23	Sthl	2m Cls3 115-129 Ch Hcap good		£9,348
	3/21	Wwck	2m Cls4 Nov Hdl soft		£3,769
	1/21	Ludl	2m Cls4 Nov Hdl heavy		£3,899

Useful and progressive novice chaser last season who won handicaps at Southwell and Doncaster; did better according to Racing Post Ratings in two runs behind Jonbon (set to finish second in a Grade 1 at Aintree when falling at the last) but left alone by the handicapper.

Camprond (Fr)

7 b g Lope De Vega - Bernieres (Montjeu)
Philip Hobbs & Johnson White   John P McManus
PLACINGS: 2/31421144/1U4B0830-   RPR **145**+h

Starts	1st	2nd	3rd	4th	Win & Pl
20	5	3	3	4	£151,193
137	4/22	Punc	2m3f 119-145 Hdl Hcap good		£49,580
	10/21	Chel	2m4f Cls2 Nov Hdl good		£10,406
	10/21	Chep	2m3½f Cls1 Nov Gd2 Hdl good		£34,170
	6/21	MRas	2m½f Cls4 Nov Hdl good		£3,159
	3/21	Tntn	2m½f Cls4 Mdn Hdl good		£3,769

Classy handicap hurdler who has made the frame in the last two runnings of the Coral Cup at Cheltenham and looked unlucky not to win last season (bad mistake at the last); had shown little otherwise as handicap mark plummeted; didn't jump well when tried over fences.

Capodanno (Fr)

7 ch g Manduro - Day Gets Up (Muhtathir)
Willie Mullins (Ire)   John P McManus
PLACINGS: 2/3134/112U4/13P-   RPR **164**+c

Starts	1st	2nd	3rd	4th	Win & Pl
13	4	2	3	2	£132,314
	4/22	Punc	3m½f Nov Gd1 Ch gd-yld		£61,975
	12/21	Naas	2m3f Ch yield		£6,585
132	4/21	Punc	3m 125-140 Hdl Hcap yield		£26,339
	1/21	Clon	2m Mdn Hdl heavy		£5,268

Progressive novice chaser two seasons ago and won a Grade 1 at Punchestown after finishing fourth in the Brown Advisory; solid third over an inadequate 2m4f on belated reappearance last term but pulled up on only subsequent run in the Grand National.

Captain Cody (Ire)

5 b g Arctic Cosmos - Fromthecloudsabove (Cloudings)
Willie Mullins (Ire)   Vincent Caldwell, Angela Shamoon & Mrs A Shamoon
PLACINGS: F/42160-   RPR **130**b

Starts	1st	2nd	3rd	4th	Win & Pl
4	1	1	-	-	£11,298
	1/23	Limk	2m NHF soft		£7,832

Useful bumper performer last season; turned over Grade 2 runner-up Blizzard Of Oz to win at Limerick and did best of those to force the pace when sixth in the Champion Bumper at Cheltenham; trapped wide and raced keenly when below par at Aintree.

Captain Guinness (Ire)

8 b g Arakan - Presenting D'Azy (Presenting)
Henry De Bromhead (Ire)   Declan Landy
PLACINGS: /P12F3/U13316/41222-   RPR **165**c

Starts	1st	2nd	3rd	4th	Win & Pl
19	5	7	3	1	£266,064
	11/22	Navn	2m Gd2 Ch yield		£18,097
	2/22	Naas	2m Gd3 Ch soft		£14,130
	11/21	Naas	2m Gd3 Ch gd-yld		£14,487
	12/20	Punc	2m Ch heavy		£6,250
	12/19	Navn	2m Mdn Hdl soft		£7,986

High-class two-mile chaser who has won all three races below Grade 1 level in the last two seasons and has been getting closer in the top grade; best of the rest behind Energumene in last season's Champion Chase and second again to Jonbon in the Celebration Chase.

Broomfield Present: won two out of three over hurdles last season and could prove a handy recruit to the novice chase ranks

RACING POST

Captain Teague (Ire)
5 ch g Doyen - Dancingwithbubbles (Supreme Leader)
Paul Nicholls   Mrs Johnny De La Hey
PLACINGS: 1/13-   RPR **134**+b

Starts	1st	2nd	3rd	4th	Win & Pl
2	1	-	1	-	£11,282
	12/22	Plum	2m1½f Cls5 NHF 4-6yo soft.................£2,722

By far the best of the British runners (only one in top 11) when a terrific third in last season's Champion Bumper at Cheltenham; had won only previous bumper at Plumpton to add to sole point-to-point win; fine prospect for novice hurdles.

Champ (Ire)
11 b g King's Theatre - China Sky (Definite Article)
Nicky Henderson   John P McManus
PLACINGS: 21/11F1/2P/1243/135-   RPR **162**h

Starts	1st	2nd	3rd	4th	Win & Pl
22	11	5	2	1	£454,196
	11/22	Newb	3m Cls2 Gd2 Hdl good.................£34,572
	12/21	Asct	3m1½f Cls1 Gd1 Hdl gd-sft.................£59,798
	3/20	Chel	3m1½f Cls1 Nov Gd1 Ch soft.................£98,764
	11/19	Newb	2m4f Cls1 Nov Gd2 Ch gd-sft.................£22,887
	11/19	Newb	2m6½f Cls3 Ch gd-sft.................£7,018
	4/19	Aint	3m½f Cls1 Nov Gd1 Hdl soft.................£56,130
139	12/18	Newb	2m4½f Cls1 Nov Gd1 Hdl gd-sft.................£25,628
	12/18	Newb	2m4½f Cls2 120-145 Hdl Hcap soft.................£25,992
	5/18	Wwck	2m5f Cls4 Nov Hdl gd-sft.................£4,549
	5/18	Prth	2m4f Cls4 Mdn Hdl good.................£4,224
	1/17	Sthl	1m7½f Cls6 Mdn NHF 4-6yo soft.................£2,053

Talented stayer who lost confidence over fences after winning the RSA Chase in 2020 but has thrived over hurdles in the last two seasons; won last year's Long Distance Hurdle at Newbury to add to the 2021 Long Walk; only third when defending that crown and then fifth at Aintree.

GUIDE TO THE JUMPS **2023-24**

Champ Kiely (Ire)
7 b g Ocovango - Cregg So (Moscow Society)
Willie Mullins (Ire)   Miss M A Masterson
PLACINGS: U/1/114133-   RPR **151**h

Starts	1st	2nd	3rd	4th	Win & Pl
7	4	-	2	1	£107,175

1/23	Naas	2m4f Nov Gd1 Hdl soft	£52,212
10/22	Tipp	2m Nov Gd3 Hdl gd-yld	£14,130
7/22	Gway	2m5f Mdn Hdl good	£8,429
5/21	Limk	2m NHF yld-sft	£5,268

Talented but frustrating gelding who enjoyed a fruitful novice campaign last term despite looking very awkward on occasions; won a Grade 1 at Naas and did well to finish third behind Impaire Et Passe at Cheltenham (hung right-handed) and Punchestown (jumped left and poorly).

Chasing Fire
6 b g Maxios - Kahara (Sadler's Wells)
Olly Murphy   Mrs Diana L Whateley
PLACINGS: 11/11103-   RPR **135+**h

Starts	1st	2nd	3rd	4th	Win & Pl
6	4	-	-	-	£18,663

2/23	Sand	2m Cls3 Nov Hdl gd-sft	£5,809
12/22	MRas	2m½f Cls4 Nov Hdl gd-sft	£3,812
11/22	MRas	2m½f Cls4 Mdn Hdl gd-sft	£3,812
3/22	Weth	2m Cls5 NHF 4-6yo gd-sft	£2,722

Very useful novice hurdler last season, winning first three races by wide margins to add to point-to-point and bumper victories; couldn't quite build on that in two runs at Cheltenham, finishing third in April after struggling in the Supreme; likely to go novice chasing.

Cheddleton
8 br g Shirocco - Over Sixty (Overbury)
Jennie Candlish   P & Mrs G A Clarke
PLACINGS: /2113/4113/32243/32-   RPR **154**c

Starts	1st	2nd	3rd	4th	Win & Pl
16	5	4	5	2	£74,189

12/20	Hayd	2m½f Cls3 Nov Ch heavy	£6,882
11/20	Carl	2m Cls3 Ch soft	£7,018
1/20	Kels	2m Cls4 Nov Hdl heavy	£4,224
12/19	Bang	2m½f Cls4 Nov Hdl heavy	£4,094
3/19	Hayd	1m7½f Cls4 NHF 4-6yo soft	£3,899

Had a good strike-rate in novice company in younger days but hasn't quite got the job done in good 2m handicap chases since then despite continuing to progress; never beaten far in seven runs across last two seasons and has finished second at Cheltenham and Wetherby (twice).

Cheddleton: consistent performer and should continue to pay his way in 2m handicap chases this season

Chemical Energy (Ire)
7 ch g Well Chosen - Meadstown Miss (Flemensfirth)
Gordon Elliott (Ire)   Caldwell Construction
PLACINGS: 1140/12185/1142P-6   RPR **154**c

Starts	1st	2nd	3rd	4th	Win & Pl
15	6	2	-	2	£89,103

10/22	Chel	3m½f Cls2 Nov Ch good	£13,008
9/22	List	2m1f Nov Ch good	£8,676
11/21	Fair	2m4f Nov Hdl good	£7,638
9/21	Navn	2m4f Mdn Hdl good	£6,321
10/20	DRoy	2m1½f NHF 4-7yo yld-sft	£5,750
9/20	Rosc	2m NHF 4yo good	£4,500

Very useful staying novice chaser last season; finished second in the National Hunt Chase at Cheltenham having won well at the course on his third chase run in October; pulled up in the Irish National on handicap chase debut but ran well for a long way in the Kerry National.

Churchstonewarrior (Ire)
8 br g Mahler - Western Approaches (Westerner)
Jonathan Sweeney (Ire)   T A Hegarty
PLACINGS: 2/6312/112432/2221-   RPR **151+**c

Starts	1st	2nd	3rd	4th	Win & Pl
14	4	6	2	1	£78,278

2/23	Navn	3m Nov Gd2 Ch gd-yld	£19,058
11/21	Thur	2m7f Nov Hdl good	£7,112
10/21	Slig	3m1½f Mdn Hdl yield	£6,848
1/21	Thur	2m3½f NHF 5-7yo sft-hvy	£5,268

Very useful stayer who deservedly won a 3m Grade 2 at Navan on final run last season, beating Mahler Mission; had been second four times in a row, including in a Grade 1 novice chase and Grade 2 novice hurdle; well fancied for the Irish National only to miss out through injury.

City Chief (Ire)
6 b g Soldier Of Fortune - Galant Ferns (Bob Back)
Nicky Henderson   Mrs J Donnelly
PLACINGS: 12211/52113-   RPR **149+**c

Starts	1st	2nd	3rd	4th	Win & Pl
9	4	3	1	-	£65,243

2/23	Weth	3m Cls1 Nov Gd2 Ch gd-sft	£23,491
134	Hrfd	3m1f Cls3 Nov 126-134 Ch Hcap soft	£9,823
127	4/22	Ayr	3m½f Cls3 Nov 105-127 Hdl Hcap gd-sft	£7,897
3/22	Hrfd	3m1½f Cls4 Mdn Hdl soft	£5,446

Lightly raced gelding who won twice over fences last season to add to two hurdling wins the previous spring; landed a weak 3m Grade 2 at Wetherby but came up short under top weight in a valuable novice handicap at Ayr.

Classic Getaway (Ire)
7 br g Getaway - Classic Magic (Classic Cliche)
Willie Mullins (Ire)   Cheveley Park Stud
PLACINGS: 1/121P/2d14-   RPR **151+**c

Starts	1st	2nd	3rd	4th	Win & Pl
7	3	1	1	1	£26,675

11/22	Gowr	2m4f Ch heavy	£7,685
1/22	Punc	2m4½f Mdn Hdl good	£5,950
5/21	Tipp	2m4f NHF 4-7yo soft	£5,268

£570,000 purchase who finally looked worthy

127

of the price tag when a runaway winner on chase debut last season only to miss five months through injury; didn't jump fluently enough to get involved when fourth in a 3m Grade 1 at Punchestown on only subsequent run.

Cloudy Glen (Ire)
10 b g Cloudings - Ribble (Supreme Leader)
Venetia Williams   Exors Of The Late Trevor Hemmings
PLACINGS: 02F6/150U2P/1P9/3PU-   RPR **147**c

Starts	1st	2nd	3rd	4th	Win & Pl
30	6	4	2	1	£214,950

140	11/21	Newb	3m2f Cls1 Gd3 135-158 Ch Hcap gd-sft	£142,375
134	11/20	Font	3m3½f Cls3 118-137 Ch Hcap heavy	£10,222
	12/19	Hayd	2m4f Cls3 Ch soft	£9,747
	3/19	Carl	2m3½f Cls3 Nov Hdl heavy	£6,498
115	1/19	Chep	2m3½f Cls4 94-118 Hdl Hcap gd-sft	£4,094
115	12/18	Hayd	2m3f Cls4 99-119 Cond Hdl Hcap soft	£6,498

Best known for shock 33-1 victory in the Coral Gold Cup at Newbury in 2021; hasn't come close to that level since then, albeit in just five runs, failing to complete three times, though had been a notoriously inconsistent performer even before his biggest win.

Coeur Sublime (Ire)
8 b g Elusive Pimpernel - Love Knot (Lomitas)
Henry De Bromhead (Ire)   C Jones
PLACINGS: /130/47/2317/2F420P-   RPR **153**c

Starts	1st	2nd	3rd	4th	Win & Pl
21	3	5	3	3	£133,046

1/22	Gowr	2m Ch soft	£6,445
11/19	DRoy	2m½f Gd2 Hdl yld-sft	£26,577
11/18	DRoy	2m½f Hdl 3yo gd-yld	£8,177

Very useful chaser on his day (pushed Blue Lord to a head in a Grade 1 novice at Punchestown in 2022) but struggled last term; might well have won a Grade 3 at Naas but for falling at the last but then beaten at 1-2 at that track and twice below par back in handicap company.

Coko Beach (Fr)
8 gr g Cokoriko - Solana Beach (Take Risks)
Gordon Elliott (Ire)   Gigginstown House Stud
PLACINGS: 23117/46P6448/9441P-   RPR **154+**c

Starts	1st	2nd	3rd	4th	Win & Pl
29	5	4	2	6	£202,928

146	2/23	Punc	3m4f 123-149 Ch Hcap yield	£46,991
	2/21	Navn	3m Nov Gd2 Ch heavy	£18,438
138	1/21	Gowr	3m1f 135-156 Ch Hcap heavy	£52,679
	10/19	Punc	2m2½f Hdl gd-yld	£10,649
	10/18	Nant	2m1½f Hdl 3yo v soft	£6,796

Standing dish in top Irish staying handicaps ever since winning the Thyestes as a novice in 2021 and finally landed another big one in last season's Grand National Trial at Punchestown; made the frame in the Troytown and Thyestes but pulled up in the Grand National.

Collectors Item (Ire)
6 b g Flemensfirth - Leading Lady (Fraam)
Jonjo O'Neill   Jackdaws Antiques
PLACINGS: 22/15123-   RPR **133**h

Starts	1st	2nd	3rd	4th	Win & Pl
6	2	2	1	-	£30,489

| 1/23 | Kemp | 3m1½f Cls3 Nov Hdl soft | £7,026 |
| 10/22 | Chep | 2m Cls4 Nov Hdl good | £4,520 |

Useful staying novice hurdler last season; won twice, most notably from Makin'yourmindup at Kempton, before running the same rival to a short head in a 3m Grade 2 at Haydock; stayed on too late when third on handicap debut at Uttoxeter; likely to go novice chasing.

Colonel Harry (Ire)
6 ch g Shirocco - Stateable Case (Be My Native)
Jamie Snowden   The GD Partnership
PLACINGS: F1/21412-   RPR **136**h

Starts	1st	2nd	3rd	4th	Win & Pl
5	2	2	-	1	£27,021

| 1/23 | Newc | 2m1f Cls4 Nov Hdl soft | £4,901 |
| 11/22 | Sand | 2m Cls4 Mdn Hdl heavy | £5,446 |

Very useful novice hurdler last season; won twice and ran well in stronger company when second in a Grade 2 at Kelso and fourth in the Tolworth; point-to-point winner and likely to go novice chasing.

Colonel Mustard (Fr)
8 ch g Makfi - Waldblume (Halling)
Lorna Fowler (Ire)   Mrs A Frost & P G Davies & R H Fowler
PLACINGS: 21243/212337/42223-   RPR **150**h

Starts	1st	2nd	3rd	4th	Win & Pl
16	2	7	4	2	£133,602

| 10/21 | Gway | 2m1½f Mdn Hdl soft | £6,321 |
| 9/20 | Punc | 2m1½f NHF 4-7yo soft | £4,500 |

Didn't quite cut it in two runs over fences last season but resumed progress when reverting to hurdles; had been third in the 2022 County Hurdle and came second in two more valuable 2m handicaps before finishing third in a Grade 1 at Punchestown behind State Man.

Comfort Zone (Ire)
4 b g Churchill - Iveagh Gardens (Mastercraftsman)
Joseph O'Brien (Ire)   John P McManus
PLACINGS: 1311-   RPR **130+**h

Starts	1st	2nd	3rd	4th	Win & Pl
4	3	-	1	-	£83,557

1/23	Chel	2m1f Cls1 Gd2 Hdl 4yo soft	£45,540
12/22	Chep	2m Cls1 Gd2 Hdl 3yo soft	£29,720
11/22	Navn	2m Mdn Hdl 3yo soft	£6,197

Very useful juvenile hurdler last season, winning three out of four races; no match for

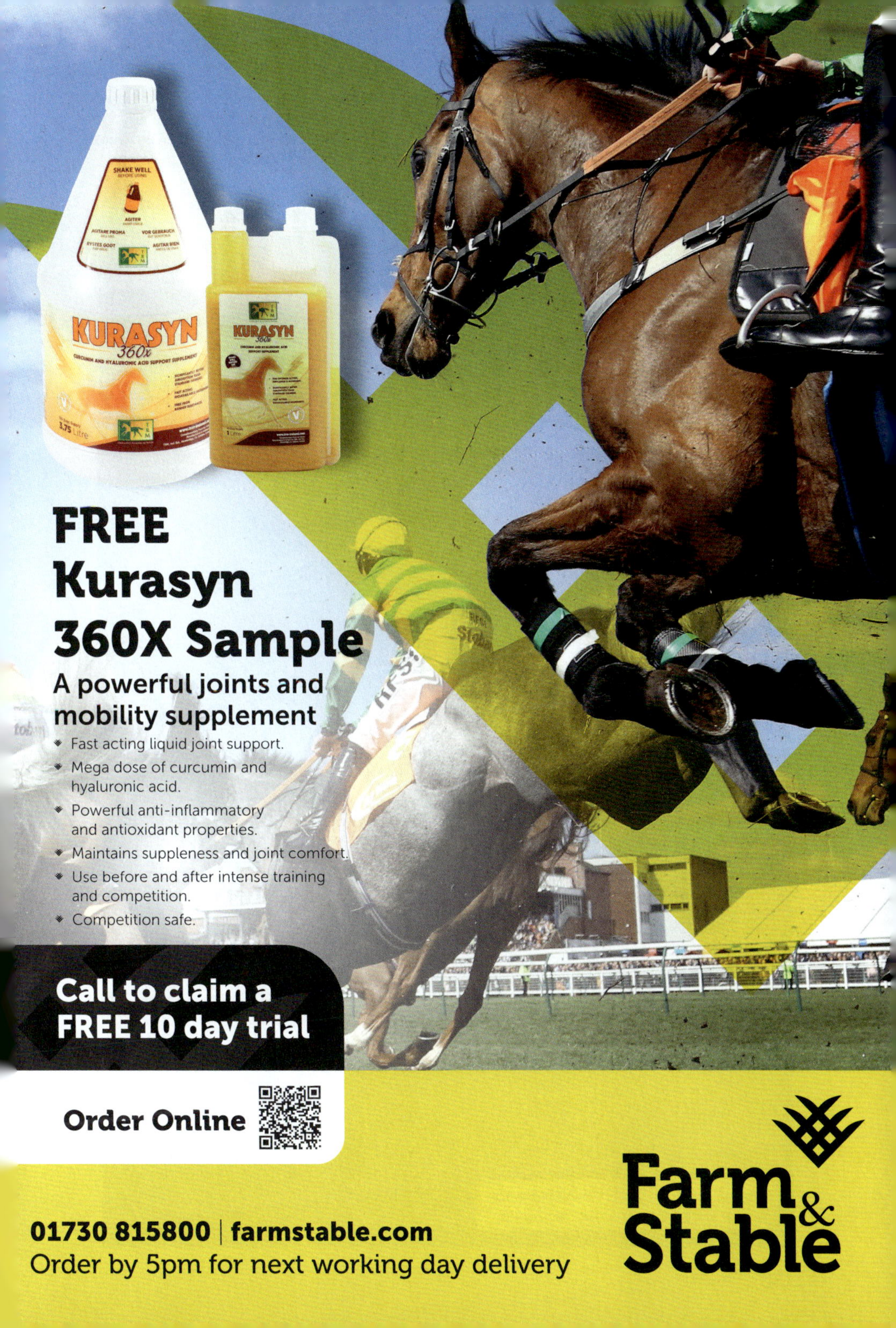

FREE Kurasyn 360X Sample

A powerful joints and mobility supplement

- Fast acting liquid joint support.
- Mega dose of curcumin and hyaluronic acid.
- Powerful anti-inflammatory and antioxidant properties.
- Maintains suppleness and joint comfort.
- Use before and after intense training and competition.
- Competition safe.

Call to claim a FREE 10 day trial

Order Online

01730 815800 | **farmstable.com**

Order by 5pm for next working day delivery

RACING POST

Lossiemouth and Zarak The Brave when third at Fairyhouse but beat top British juveniles when winning Grade 2 juvenile hurdles at Chepstow and Cheltenham; missed big spring races.

Complete Unknown (Ire)
7 b g Dylan Thomas - Silver Stream (Milan)
Paul Nicholls   Jcg Chua & I Warwick
PLACINGS: U/1/323212/51212-   RPR **158**c

Starts	1st	2nd	3rd	4th	Win & Pl
12	4	5	2	-	£141,767
142	3/23	Kemp	2m4½f Cls2 128-152 Ch Hcap soft............£31,218
135	12/22	Ffos	2m5f Cls3 Nov 128-147 Ch Hcap soft........£7,452
126	3/22	Sand	2m4f Cls1 Nov Gd3 116-135 Hdl 4-7yo Hcap soft........ £45,016
	3/21	Thur	2m NHF 5-7yo heavy.............................£5,268

Hugely progressive chaser who has improved with virtually every run in the last two seasons;

won the EBF Final over hurdles in 2022 and again flourished in the spring last term; hacked up in a Kempton handicap and second behind Gerri Colombe when up in class and trip at Aintree.

Conflated (Ire)
9 b g Yeats - Saucy Present (Presenting)
Gordon Elliott (Ire)   Gigginstown House Stud
PLACINGS: /321314/U211F2/313P-   RPR **171**c

Starts	1st	2nd	3rd	4th	Win & Pl
27	7	4	6	4	£420,769
	12/22	Leop	3m Gd1 Ch soft.................................£86,765
	2/22	Leop	3m½f Gd1 Ch yield...........................£117,647
145	12/21	Navn	2m4f 119-145 Ch Hcap yield................£21,071
	3/21	Naas	2m4½f Nov Gd3 Ch sft-hvy...................£14,487
	12/20	Navn	2m4f Ch soft...................................£6,250
	11/19	Fair	2m Mdn Hdl soft..............................£6,922
	3/19	Clon	2m NHF 5-7yo good...........................£5,550

Has won 3m Grade 1 chases at Leopardstown in

Corach Rambler: 2023 Grand National winner will be aimed at Aintree repeat

each of the last two seasons; broke through by winning the Irish Gold Cup in 2022 and added the Savills Chase last term; followed up with a fine third in the Cheltenham Gold Cup but pulled up in the Aintree Bowl.

Constitution Hill
6 b g Blue Bresil - Queen Of The Stage (King's Theatre)
Nicky Henderson   Michael Buckley
PLACINGS: 2/111/1111-   RPR **177+**h

Starts	1st	2nd	3rd	4th	Win & Pl
7	7	-	-	-	£657,607
	4/23	Aint	2m4f Cls1 Gd1 Hdl gd-sft £140,325
	3/23	Chel	2m¹/₂f Cls1 Gd1 Hdl sft £253,215
	12/22	Kemp	2m Cls1 Gd1 Hdl soft..........................£74,906
	11/22	Newc	2m Cls1 Gd1 Hdl gd-sft.......................£64,711
	3/22	Chel	2m¹/₂f Cls1 Nov Gd1 Hdl gd-sft............£76,594
	1/22	Sand	2m Cls1 Nov Gd1 Hdl heavy.................£40,053
	12/21	Sand	2m Cls3 Nov Hdl gd-sft.........................£7,805

Outstanding hurdler of his generation and perhaps all time who has swept to a string of wide-margin victories; won the 2022 Supreme by 22 lengths and easily won all four starts at long odds-on last season, including a nine-length stroll in the Champion Hurdle.

Cool Survivor (Ire)
6 b g Westerner - Pale Face (High Chaparral)
Gordon Elliott (Ire)   Gigginstown House Stud
PLACINGS: 1/26/611240F-   RPR **140+**h

Starts	1st	2nd	3rd	4th	Win & Pl
9	2	2	-	1	£32,012
	11/22	Cork	3m Nov List Hdl heavy £13,634
	10/22	Punc	2m4¹/₂f Mdn Hdl good..........................£6,197

Very useful novice hurdler last season who shaped better than his bare form; won twice and finished a close fourth in a Grade I at Leopardstown; disappointed when favourite for the Martin Pipe at Cheltenham but was travelling strongly in a Grade I at Aintree until falling three out.

Corach Rambler (Ire)
9 b g Jeremy - Heart N Hope (Fourstars Allstar)
Lucinda Russell   The Ramblers
PLACINGS: 5/21161/3114U1/5411-   RPR **162+**c

Starts	1st	2nd	3rd	4th	Win & Pl
13	7	-	1	2	£686,240
	4/23	Aint	4m2¹/₂f Cls1 Gd3 143-167 Ch Hcap gd-sft....£500,000
	3/23	Chel	3m1f Cls1 Gd3 129-155 Ch Hcap soft............£70,538
	3/22	Chel	3m1f Cls1 Gd3 138-164 Ch Hcap gd-sft £70,538
	12/21	Chel	3m1¹/₂f Cls3 Nov 132-143 Ch Hcap good £8,169
	10/21	Aint	3m1f Cls3 Nov 123-134 Ch Hcap good............£8,714
	3/21	Carl	3m1f Cls4 Nov Hdl good.........................£3,769
	1/21	Ayr	2m¹/₂f Cls4 Nov Hdl heavy......................£3,769

Brilliant winner of last season's Grand National, bolstering a remarkable record in big staying handicaps having landed the last two runnings of the Ultima at the Cheltenham Festival; beat subsequent Grade I winner Fastorslow in that race last term and 13lb higher mark fully merited.

Corbetts Cross (Ire)
6 ch g Gamut - Annagh Hill Lady (Amilynx)
Emmet Mullins (Ire)   John P McManus
PLACINGS: F213/5121110-   RPR **150**h

Starts	1st	2nd	3rd	4th	Win & Pl
8	4	1	1	-	£41,885
130	2/23	Naas	1m7¹/₂f Nov Gd2 Hdl yield £18,274
	1/23	Fair	3m 104-130 Hdl Hcap sft-hvy £8,876
	12/22	Limk	2m5f Mdn Hdl sft-hvy............................£6,197
	10/22	Cork	2m3f NHF soft......................................£5,454

Exciting and progressive hurdler who was seeking a four-timer when running out at the last in the Albert Bartlett at Cheltenham last season; had already won a 3m handicap at Fairyhouse but produced best performance when running away with a 2m Grade 2 novice at Naas.

Crambo
6 b g Saddler Maker - Cardline (Martaline)
Fergal O'Brien   Sullivan Bloodstock & Chris Giles
PLACINGS: 11/1P117-   RPR **136+**h

Starts	1st	2nd	3rd	4th	Win & Pl
7	5	-	-	-	£61,498
123	3/23	Sand	2m4f Cls1 Nov Gd3 109-132 Hdl 4-7yo Hcap heavy.....£45,016
	2/23	Bang	2m¹/₂f Cls3 Nov Hdl 4-7yo gd-sft £5,203
	11/22	Asct	2m3¹/₂f Cls3 Mdn Hdl gd-sft....................£6,535
	3/22	Hntg	2m Cls5 NHF 4-6yo gd-sft £2,178
	12/21	Hntg	2m Cls5 NHF 4-6yo heavy £1,906

Useful novice hurdler last season, winning three times including the EBF Final at Sandown on heavy ground; suffered both defeats in Grade I company, doing better on the second occasion when seventh at Aintree; likely to go novice chasing.

Crebilly (Ire)
6 b g Soldier Of Fortune - Blueberry Bramble (Pistolet Bleu)
Jonjo O'Neill   John P McManus
PLACINGS: 33/12261-   RPR **136+**h

Starts	1st	2nd	3rd	4th	Win & Pl
6	2	2	1	-	£29,193
127	4/23	Sand	2m4f Cls2 124-143 Hdl Hcap gd-sft £18,211
	12/22	Newc	2m Cls4 Mdn Hdl gd-sft........................£4,901

Chasing type who progressed well in novice hurdles last season; twice finished second when a short-priced favourite for big-field novices at Chepstow; did better when stepped up to 2m4f, finishing sixth in the EBF Final before landing another handicap at Sandown on final run.

Crystal Glory
7 b g Fame And Glory - Nile Cristale (Northern Crystal)
Nicky Richards   Charlie Doocey & Cathal Doocey
PLACINGS: 11/11224/1P-   RPR **145+**c

Starts	1st	2nd	3rd	4th	Win & Pl
7	3	2	-	1	£34,529
	11/22	Hexm	3m Cls3 Nov Ch soft £7,080
	12/21	Newc	2m6f Cls4 Nov Ch gd-sft £4,085
	11/21	Hexm	2m4f Cls4 Nov Hdl gd-sft......................£4,193

Looked a fine chase prospect when winning by

RACING POST

20 lengths at Hexham first time out last season but was injured on only subsequent run; had been a useful novice hurdler in 2021-22, finishing fourth in the Sefton after a good second behind Hillcrest at Haydock.

Dancing On My Own (Ire)
9 b g Milan - Morning Supreme (Supreme Leader)
Henry de Bromhead (Ire) Sean & Bernardine Mulryan
PLACINGS: 234P/416/13F02/091-2 RPR **154+c**

Starts	1st	2nd	3rd	4th	Win & Pl
17	3	3	2	2	£102,693
144	4/23	Aint	2m Cls1 Gd3 130-148 Ch Hcap gd-sft		£56,270
	10/21	Klny	2m1f Ch yld-sft		£5,795
	10/19	Wxfd	2m½f Mdn Hdl heavy		£5,537

Won last season's Red Rum Chase at Aintree having finished second in the same race in 2022; yet to run close to the same level elsewhere and particularly disappointing in just two runs in between Aintree runs, though did better when second at Clonmel this summer.

Dashel Drasher
10 b g Passing Glance - So Long (Nomadic Way)
Jeremy Scott Mrs B Tully & R Lock
PLACINGS: U1/3111/312P/122226- PR **163c**

Starts	1st	2nd	3rd	4th	Win & Pl
27	11	6	4	1	£378,373
	11/22	Aint	2m4f Cls2 Hdl soft		£24,311
149	12/21	Newb	2m4½f Cls2 123-149 Hdl Hcap soft		£10,406
	2/21	Asct	2m5f Cls1 Gd1 Ch soft		£59,620
152	1/21	Asct	2m5f Cls2 132-154 Ch Hcap soft		£32,844
	12/20	Asct	2m5f Cls2 Ch heavy		£18,768
	12/19	Hayd	2m5½f Cls2 Nov Ch soft		£12,996
	4/19	Chel	2m1f Cls2 Nov Hdl good		£12,380
	3/19	Newb	2m4½f Cls3 Nov Hdl gd-sft		£6,238
	2/19	Asct	2m3½f Cls2 Nov Hdl gd-sft		£15,857
	1/19	Chep	2m3½f Cls4 Nov Hdl gd-sft		£4,094
	2/18	Winc	1m7½f Cls5 NHF 4-6yo heavy		£2,274

Enjoyed his finest hour over fences when winning the Ascot Chase in 2021 but was reinvented as

Dashel Drasher: fine chaser and proved equally adept back over hurdles last season

a very smart staying hurdler last season; relished a strong test of stamina when second in the Stayers' Hurdle behind Sire Du Berlais; best on soft ground.

Datsalrightgino (Ger)
7 b g It's Gino - Delightful Sofie (Grand Lodge)
Jamie Snowden   The GD Partnership
PLACINGS: 322/11PP4/213422P1-   RPR **153+**c

Starts	1st	2nd	3rd	4th	Win & Pl
16	4	5	2	2	£78,534
129	4/23	Ayr	2m4¹/₂f Cls1 Nov Gd2 Ch good		£26,283
	11/22	Chep	2m Cls3 Nov 121-140 Ch Hcap good		£10,892
	12/21	Chel	2m1f Cls3 Nov Hdl 4-6yo good		£7,805
	11/21	Font	2m1¹/₂f Cls4 Nov Hdl good		£4,085

Very useful and progressive novice chaser last season; did well in novice handicaps, often in defeat, including when second to Stage Star at Cheltenham; pulled up when favourite for the Plate back there but deservedly got his head in front in a Grade 2 at Ayr on final run.

Delta Work (Fr)
10 b g Network - Robbe (Video Rock)
Gordon Elliott (Ire)   Gigginstown House Stud
PLACINGS: 115/5U3/46613/1361U-   RPR **169+**c

Starts	1st	2nd	3rd	4th	Win & Pl
32	11	3	7	4	£731,435
	3/23	Chel	3m6f Cls2 Ch soft		£39,023
	11/22	Punc	3m1f Ch yield		£8,676
	3/22	Chel	3m6f Cls2 Ch heavy		£39,023
	2/20	Leop	3m Gd1 Ch yield		£118,856
	12/19	Leop	3m Gd1 Ch yield		£93,018
	4/19	Punc	3m¹/₂f Nov Gd1 Ch yld-sft		£53,153
	12/18	Leop	3m Nov Gd1 Ch good		£52,212
	12/18	Fair	2m4f Nov Gd1 Ch good		£46,991
	11/18	DRoy	2m3¹/₂f Ch good		£8,177
139	3/18	Chel	3m Cls1 Gd3 135-155 Hdl Hcap soft		£56,950
	5/17	Punc	2m¹/₂f Mdn Hdl good		£6,844

One-time top-class staying chaser (five-time Grade 1 winner from 2018 to 2020) who has been reinvented as a cross-country specialist; won at the Cheltenham Festival for the second successive season in March; unseated in the Grand National having been third in 2022.

Dinoblue (Fr)
6 ch m Doctor Dino - Blue Aster (Astarabad)
Willie Mullins (Ire)   John P McManus
PLACINGS: 194/4122211-   RPR **158+**c

Starts	1st	2nd	3rd	4th	Win & Pl
10	4	3	-	2	£104,103
147	4/23	Punc	2m 124-150 Ch Hcap gd-yld		£26,106
140	4/23	Fair	2m¹/₂f Nov 117-128 Ch Hcap yld-sft		£23,496
	11/22	Cork	2m¹/₂f Ch soft		£7,685
	1/22	Clon	2m¹/₂f Mdn Hdl heavy		£4,958

Long held in very high regard and finally delivered last spring when switched to handicaps; beaten favourite for fifth time in seven races (and second time at the Cheltenham Festival) when second in the Grand Annual but then won easily at Fairyhouse and Punchestown.

Do Your Job (Ire)
9 b g Fame And Glory - Full Of Birds (Epervier Bleu)
Lucinda Russell   Mark Dunphy
PLACINGS: 2/112422/1F2211/655-   RPR **139**c

Starts	1st	2nd	3rd	4th	Win & Pl
17	5	6	-	1	£107,081
	4/22	Ayr	2m4¹/₂f Cls1 Nov Gd2 Ch gd-sft		£26,283
140	2/22	Newc	2m4f Cls3 117-140 Ch Hcap gd-sft		£6,535
	11/21	Wwck	2m Cls3 Nov Ch gd-sft		£9,516
	10/20	Ayr	2m Cls4 Nov Hdl 4-6yo soft		£3,769
	10/20	Ffos	2m Cls4 Nov Hdl 4-6yo heavy		£3,769

Smart and progressive novice chaser in 2021-22, finishing with a Grade 2 win at Ayr, but didn't get close to that level in three runs last term; only sixth when favourite for the Old Roan first time out and did little better subsequently, finishing fifth in the Peterborough Chase on final run.

Doctor Bravo (Fr)
6 gr g Doctor Dino - Bright Tango (Chichicastenango)
Gordon Elliott (Ire)   Caldwell Construction
PLACINGS: 12138P-   RPR **146**h

Starts	1st	2nd	3rd	4th	Win & Pl
6	2	1	1	-	£15,670
	1/23	DRoy	2m1f Mdn Hdl soft		£5,221
	12/22	Fair	2m NHF gd-yld		£5,206

Useful novice hurdler last season, though failed to build on initial promise in the spring; won twice before a good third against senior hurdlers at Gowran; couldn't land a blow when eighth in the Supreme and pulled up when stepped up to 2m4f at Fairyhouse.

Doctor Ken (Fr)
7 b g Doctor Dino - Kendoretta (Kendor)
Olly Murphy   Mrs Diana L Whateley
PLACINGS: 241/31542/121-   RPR **144+**c

Starts	1st	2nd	3rd	4th	Win & Pl
11	4	3	1	2	£34,588
130	3/23	Tntn	2m7f Cls3 120-130 Ch Hcap gd-sft		£8,714
123	11/22	Aint	2m4f Cls3 Nov 117-128 Ch Hcap gd-sft		£8,496
	11/21	Asct	2m3¹/₂f Cls3 Mdn Hdl good		£6,481
	3/21	MRas	2m¹/₂f Cls5 Mdn NHF 4-6yo gd-sft		£2,274

Big improver when sent chasing last season, winning twice from just three races; particularly impressive when stepped up in trip on final run at Taunton, winning by five lengths under 12st over 2m7f; likely type for better staying handicaps.

Doddiethegreat (Ire)
7 b g Fame And Glory - Asturienne (Sleeping Car)
Nicky Henderson   Kenneth Alexander
PLACINGS: 11/1/   RPR **137**h

Starts	1st	2nd	3rd	4th	Win & Pl
3	3	-	-	-	£8,958
	11/21	Kemp	2m5f Cls4 Nov Hdl good		£4,085
	3/21	Hntg	2m Cls5 NHF 4-6yo gd-sft		£2,274
	11/20	Ludl	2m Cls5 NHF 3-5yo good		£2,599

Unbeaten gelding who looked a hugely exciting prospect two seasons ago but hasn't run since through injury; hacked up by 22 lengths on hurdles debut at Kempton in November 2021 when stepping up to 2m5f after two bumper wins the previous season.

Does He Know

8 b g Alkaased - Diavoleria (Slip Anchor)
Kim Bailey   Yes He Does Syndicate
PLACINGS: 22/111085/11210/F13-   RPR **162**c

Starts	1st	2nd	3rd	4th	Win & Pl
16	7	3	1	-	£148,735
152	11/22	Chel	3m3½f Cls1 Gd3 127-152 Ch Hcap good		£42,513
	2/22	Asct	3m Cls1 Nov Gd2 Ch soft		£29,753
	10/21	Chel	3m½f Cls2 Nov Ch good		£13,008
	10/21	Chep	2m7½f Cls2 Nov Ch good		£10,892
	11/20	Chel	2m5f Cls1 Nov Gd2 Hdl gd-sft		£14,807
	10/20	Chel	2m5f Cls2 Nov Hdl good		£10,047
	10/20	Ludl	2m5f Cls4 Nov Hdl gd-fm		£3,899

Lightly raced staying chaser who produced a tremendous performance to win a big 3m3f handicap chase at Cheltenham last season under 12st; fair third in the Denman Chase on only subsequent run but ideally suited by a more thorough test of stamina.

Douglas Talking (Ire)

7 b g Dylan Thomas - Look Who's Talking (King's Theatre)
Lucinda Russell   The Bristol Boys & Russell
PLACINGS: F/1953411F1/571122-   RPR **144**+c

Starts	1st	2nd	3rd	4th	Win & Pl
15	6	2	1	1	£73,646
124	3/23	Sand	1m7½f Cls3 122-124 Ch Hcap gd-sft		£8,104
118	2/23	Ayr	2m½f Cls4 116-120 Ch Hcap gd-sft		£4,753
118	4/22	Ayr	2m½f Cls3 Nov 118-135 Ch Hcap soft		£10,819
111	2/22	Sand	1m7½f Cls3 111-133 Ch Hcap soft		£8,169
104	2/22	Muss	2m4½f Cls4 Nov 103-117 Ch Hcap gd-sft		£4,684
	5/21	Tipp	2m2f NHF 4-7yo good		£5,268

Progressive chaser who won three times as a novice in 2021-22 and got back on track in second half of last season after wind surgery;

won 2m handicaps at Ayr and Sandown before two big runs up in class when second at Aintree and Punchestown.

Down Memory Lane (Ire)
5 b g Walk In The Park - Credo Star (Presenting)
Gordon Elliott (Ire) — John P McManus
PLACINGS: 11- — RPR **125+b**

Starts	1st	2nd	3rd	4th	Win & Pl
1	1	-	-	-	£5,221
	2/23 Fair	2m¹/₂f NHF yield			£5,221

Easy winner of sole point-to-point last October and followed up at odds-on in a strong bumper at Fairyhouse (both placed horses won next time); looks a useful prospect for novice hurdles.

Dunvegan (Fr)
10 gr g Le Havre - Or Des Joncs (Turgeon)
Pat Fahy (Ire) — George Turner & Clipper Logistics Group
PLACINGS: 132/4PP36/39112/524- — RPR **157c**

Starts	1st	2nd	3rd	4th	Win & Pl
26	6	6	4	2	£172,594
146	1/22 Fair	2m1f 130-158 Ch Hcap soft			£42,143
139	11/21 Fair	2m¹/₂f 122-148 Ch Hcap good			£21,071
	12/19 Punc	2m Ch soft			£7,454
	12/18 Punc	2m4f Mdn Hdl gd-yld			£6,269
	4/18 Punc	2m NHF 4-7yo yld-sft			£9,540
	1/18 Leic	2m NHF 5-7yo heavy			£5,451

Big improver two seasons ago when winning back-to-back handicap chases at Fairyhouse and second at Grade 1 level at Leopardstown; failed to build on that last term when unable to land a blow in two Grade 1 races but better when second back in handicap company at Fairyhouse.

Dusart (Ire)
8 b g Flemensfirth - Dusty Too (Terimon)
Nicky Henderson — R A Bartlett
PLACINGS: 13/1151/6PB- — RPR **140h**

Starts	1st	2nd	3rd	4th	Win & Pl
9	4	-	1	-	£58,691
147	4/22 Ayr	3m Cls2 Nov 126-147 Ch Hcap gd-sft			£26,015
	2/22 Extr	3m Cls3 Nov Ch gd-sft			£7,951
	1/22 Leic	2m6¹/₂f Cls5 Nov Ch gd-sft			£7,895
	11/20 Newb	2m Cls4 Nov Hdl good			£3,769

Won three times as a novice chaser in 2021-22 and was long-time favourite for last season's Coral Gold Cup only to miss the race; ended up running just twice over fences last term when pulled up in the Cotswold Chase and brought down (going well) in the Scottish National.

Dysart Dynamo (Ire)
7 b g Westerner - Dysart Dancer (Accordion)
Willie Mullins (Ire) — Ms Eleanor Manning
PLACINGS: 1/111F/514F2- — RPR **158+c**

Starts	1st	2nd	3rd	4th	Win & Pl
10	5	1	-	1	£72,585
	12/22 Leop	2m1f Ch yield			£8,676
	1/22 Punc	2m Nov Gd2 Hdl soft			£18,097
	12/21 Cork	2m Mdn Hdl soft			£6,321
	4/21 Punc	2m NHF 4-7yo yield			£5,795
	3/21 Clon	2m2¹/₂f NHF 5-7yo soft			£5,268

Headstrong front-runner who has won all five runs below Grade 1 level by wide margins but come unstuck every time in the top grade; set to finish third when falling at the last in the Arkle at Cheltenham and ran to a similar level when second behind El Fabiolo at Punchestown.

Dysart Enos (Ire)
5 b m Malinas - Graces Benefit (Beneficial)
Fergal O'Brien — The Good Stock Syndicate
PLACINGS: 2/111- — RPR **127+b**

Starts	1st	2nd	3rd	4th	Win & Pl
3	3	-	-	-	£43,609
	4/23 Aint	2m1f Cls1 Gd2 NHF 4-6yo gd-sft			£28,135
	2/23 MRas	2m¹/₂f Cls1 List NHF 4-6yo gd-sft			£11,390
	11/22 Ludl	2m Cls4 NHF 4-6yo gd-sft			£4,085

Exciting mare who won all three runs in bumpers last season, most notably when hacking up in a Grade 2 at Aintree's Grand National meeting; had already claimed a notable scalp in Queens Gamble at Market Rasen but stepped up again with a stunning nine-length win.

Easy As That (Ire)
8 b g Sans Frontieres - Bell Storm (Glacial Storm)
Venetia Williams — Brooks & Taylor Families
PLACINGS: 11/241/2115- — RPR **147+c**

Starts	1st	2nd	3rd	4th	Win & Pl
9	5	2	-	1	£36,902
133	2/23 Newc	2m4f Cls2 122-135 Ch Hcap gd-sft			£13,008
126	12/22 Hayd	2m5¹/₂f Cls3 108-130 Ch Hcap gd-sft			£8,169
114	2/21 Chep	2m3¹/₂f Cls4 102-120 Hdl Hcap heavy			£3,769
	2/20 Muss	1m7¹/₂f Cls5 NHF 4-6yo gd-sft			£2,599
	12/19 Ffos	2m Cls5 NHF 3-5yo heavy			£2,274

Made rapid progress in a quiet novice chasing campaign last term, winning two of his last three races; raised 9lb for second win at Newcastle and sent off favourite for a premier novice handicap at Sandown only for jumping to fall apart (last of five).

Does He Know: smart chaser who is suited by a thorough test of stamina

RACING POST

Echoes In Rain (Fr)
7 b m Authorized - Amarantine (King's Best)
Willie Mullins (Ire) — Barnane Stud
PLACINGS: 5/1411/13435/2F141- — RPR **158+**h

Starts	1st	2nd	3rd	4th	Win & Pl
15	6	1	2	3	£281,051

4/23	Punc	2m3f Gd1 Hdl gd-yld	£65,265
1/23	Naas	2m7½f Gd3 Hdl soft	£14,881
4/21	Punc	2m½f Nov Gd1 Hdl yield	£52,679
4/21	Fair	2m Nov Gd2 Hdl yield	£18,438
2/21	Naas	1m7½f Nov Gd2 Hdl soft	£18,438
12/20	Naas	2m Mdn Hdl 4yo heavy	£6,000

Classy mare who has been very highly tried since her novice days and finally returned to the Grade 1 winner's circle in the Mares' Hurdle at Punchestown last season; had made the frame in five Grade 1 races since previous top-flight win, four times in open company.

Editeur Du Gite (Fr)
9 b g Saddex - Malaga De St Sulpice (Saint Cyrien)
Gary Moore — The Preston Family, Friends & T Jacobs
PLACINGS: /252P11/U114P/31144- — RPR **169**c

Starts	1st	2nd	3rd	4th	Win & Pl
20	7	2	1	3	£271,168

1/23	Chel	2m½f Cls1 Gd1 Ch soft	£52,280
12/22	Kemp	2m Cls1 Gd2 Ch soft	£57,218
147 12/21	Chel	2m½f Cls2 129-152 Ch Hcap gd-sft	£15,609
140 11/21	Chel	2m Cls2 132-152 Ch Hcap good	£23,234
132 4/21	Aint	2m Cls1 Gd3 123-149 Ch Hcap gd-sft	£42,203
125 3/21	Newb	2m½f Cls3 115-129 Ch Hcap good	£7,018
5/18	Comp	2m2f Hdl 4yo heavy	£19,115

Progressive chaser over the last two seasons and graduated from handicap to Grade 1 company last term; beat Edwardstone by a head in the Clarence House Chase to follow up wide-margin win in the Desert Orchid; below par at Cheltenham and Sandown in the spring.

Edwardstone
9 b g Kayf Tara - Nothingtoloose (Luso)
Alan King — Robert Abrey, Ian Thurtle
PLACINGS: 5U1353/B111112/1U25- — RPR **172+**c

Starts	1st	2nd	3rd	4th	Win & Pl
24	9	6	2	-	£429,266

12/22	Sand	1m7½f Cls1 Gd1 Ch gd-sft	£99,663
3/22	Chel	2m Cls1 Nov Gd1 Ch gd-sft	£102,482
2/22	Wwck	2m Cls1 Nov Gd2 Ch gd-sft	£29,614
12/21	Kemp	2m Nov Gd2 Ch soft	£29,614
12/21	Sand	1m7½f Cls1 Nov Gd1 Ch gd-sft	£42,914
11/21	Wwck	2m Cls3 Nov Ch gd-sft	£10,565
141 1/21	MRas	2m7½f Cls2 123-141 Hdl Hcap heavy	£9,384
12/19	Aint	2m1f Nov Hdl Cls3 gd-sft	£7,798
11/19	Winc	1m7½f Cls3 Nov Hdl 4-6yo good	£6,238

Won the Arkle in 2022 and added a brilliant victory in last season's Tingle Creek in first chase outside novice company; didn't quite build on that, just losing out to Editeur Du Gite in the Clarence House (travelled best) before a bitterly disappointing fifth in the Champion Chase.

Eklat De Rire (Fr)

9 b g Saddex - Rochdale (Video Rock)
Henry de Bromhead (Ire)   P Davies

PLACINGS: 121/11U/1P0/4-   RPR **120**h

Starts	1st	2nd	3rd	4th	Win & Pl
9	4	1	-	1	£42,408

10/21	Wxfd	2m7f List Ch heavy	£11,853
1/21	Naas	3m1f Nov Gd3 Ch heavy	£14,487
12/20	Punc	3m1½f Ch heavy	£6,250
3/20	Thur	2m7f Mdn Hdl sft-hvy	£7,000

Lightly raced for his age, especially after missing nearly all of last season; has looked set for big things at times and was just 3-1 for the 2021 Coral Gold Cup after beating Conflated first time out that season but was pulled up there and disappointed again when favourite for the Thyestes.

El Fabiolo (Fr)

6 b g Spanish Moon - Sainte Mante (Saint Des Saints)
Willie Mullins (Ire)   Simon Munir & Isaac Souede

PLACINGS: 3/12/11111-   RPR **173**+c

Starts	1st	2nd	3rd	4th	Win & Pl
8	6	1	1	-	£290,569

4/23	Punc	2m Nov Gd1 Ch gd-yld	£65,265
3/23	Chel	2m Cls1 Nov Gd1 Ch soft	£98,558
2/23	Leop	2m1f Nov Gd1 Ch yield	£78,319
12/22	Fair	2m Ch yld-sft	£6,445
4/22	Punc	2m Nov Hdl gd-yld	£9,916
1/22	Tram	2m Mdn Hdl heavy	£5,206

Last season's highest-rated novice chaser after a fabulous unbeaten campaign, winning four times over fences, three at Grade 1 level; had suffered sole defeat over hurdles behind Jonbon at Aintree but put that right with a comprehensive victory in the Arkle at Cheltenham.

Eldorado Allen (Fr)

9 gr g Khalkevi - Hesmeralda (Royal Charter)
Joe Tizzard   J P Romans & Terry Warner

PLACINGS: 4225/132137/2245754-   RPR **163**c

Starts	1st	2nd	3rd	4th	Win & Pl
26	6	7	4	3	£320,481

2/22	Newb	2m7½f Cls1 Gd2 Ch gd-sft	£34,572
151 11/21	Extr	2m1½f Cls1 Gd2 148-168 Ch Hcap gd-sft	£40,411
11/20	Chel	2m Cls1 Nov Gd2 Ch gd-sft	£17,387
10/20	NAbb	2m½f Cls3 Nov Ch gd-sft	£8,058
11/18	Sand	2m Cls4 Mdn Hdl heavy	£6,498

Failed to win last season and below best since finishing second in the Betfair Chase; had only run below Grade 2 level when fifth under top weight in a handicap on Grand National day; subsequently dropped to lowest mark since winning the Haldon Gold Cup in 2021.

Elixir De Nutz: bounced back to his best form last season and proved himself a smart chaser

---

GUIDE TO THE JUMPS 2023-24

Elixir De Nutz (Fr)

9 gr g Al Namix - Nutz (Turgeon)
Joe Tizzard   Terry Warner

PLACINGS: /77/2/4211PP/921292-   RPR **155**c

Starts	1st	2nd	3rd	4th	Win & Pl
22	7	6	-	1	£133,922

138 1/23	Winc	2m4f Cls2 129-143 Ch Hcap gd-sft	£15,843
135 2/22	Kemp	2m2f Cls3 Nov 123-135 Ch Hcap good	£8,169
1/22	Plum	2m3½f Cls3 Nov Ch soft	£7,407
1/19	Sand	2m Cls1 Nov Gd1 Hdl soft	£28,475
12/18	Chel	2m1f Cls3 Nov Hdl 4-6yo good	£9,285
11/18	Chel	2m½f Cls1 Nov Gd2 Hdl good	£18,006
10/17	Agtn	1m6f NHF 3yo gd-sft	£6,838

Developed into a classy and consistent 2m chaser last season, finally bouncing back to the form that saw him win the Tolworth in 2019 before suffering injury problems; unlucky not to win more than once, finishing second in the Game Spirit and a premier handicap at Ayr.

Elvis Mail (Fr)

9 gr g Great Pretender - Queenly Mail (Medaaly)
Nick Alexander   The Ladies Who

PLACINGS: 1422F/542244/1633U1-   RPR **150**+c

Starts	1st	2nd	3rd	4th	Win & Pl
28	7	5	4	7	£114,463

138 3/23	Kels	3m2f Cls2 121-147 Ch Hcap soft	£18,211
137 10/22	Ayr	2m4½f Cls3 113-137 Ch Hcap gd-sft	£7,624
137 11/20	Ayr	2m½f Cls3 Nov 124-137 Ch Hcap soft	£7,018
136 1/20	Kels	2m Cls2 118-142 Hdl Hcap heavy	£12,512
132 11/19	Ayr	2m Cls2 119-142 Hdl Hcap soft	£19,494
4/19	Kels	2m2f Cls4 Nov Hdl gd-sft	£4,549
12/18	Kels	2m Cls4 Nov Hdl good	£4,549

Flourished going up in trip last season; won at Ayr first time out when trying 2m4f for only the second time over fences and then finished third in the Sky Bet Chase on debut at 3m before winning when up in distance again over 3m2f at Kelso; still unexposed as a stayer.

Embassy Gardens

7 b g Shantou - Adriana Des Mottes (Network)
Willie Mullins (Ire)   Sean & Bernardine Mulryan

PLACINGS: 15/241P6-   RPR **149**+h

Starts	1st	2nd	3rd	4th	Win & Pl
7	2	1	-	1	£18,896

1/23	Thur	2m7f Nov Hdl yield	£7,049
12/21	Leop	2m4f NHF 4-7yo yld-sft	£6,321

Fine chasing type who showed real promise over hurdles last season despite failing to deliver in the spring; sent off just 8-1 for the Albert Bartlett after a stunning 35-length maiden win at Thurles but pulled up after racing too freely and did similar when sixth at Punchestown.

Energumene (Fr)

9 br g Denham Red - Olinight (April Night)
Willie Mullins (Ire)   Tony Bloom

PLACINGS: /311/111/1121/11311-   RPR **179**+c

Starts	1st	2nd	3rd	4th	Win & Pl
15	12	1	2	-	£1,031,687

4/23	Punc	2m Gd1 Ch yld-sft	£156,637
3/23	Chel	2m Cls1 Gd1 Ch soft	£226,672
12/22	Cork	2m¹/₂f Gd2 Ch yld-sft	£49,580
4/22	Punc	2m Gd1 Ch gd-yld	£136,345
3/22	Chel	2m Cls1 Gd1 Ch soft	£226,672
12/21	Cork	2m¹/₂f Gd2 Ch soft	£36,875
4/21	Punc	2m Nov Gd1 Ch yield	£60,580
2/21	Leop	2m1¹/₂f Nov Gd1 Ch soft	£65,848
1/21	Naas	2m Nov Ch heavy	£10,272
11/20	Gowr	2m4f Ch heavy	£7,750
3/20	Gowr	2m Nov Mdn Hdl sft-hvy	£6,750
1/20	Thur	2m NHF 4-7yo yield	£5,008

Wide-margin winner of the last two editions of the Champion Chase at Cheltenham and has doubled up at Punchestown both times, albeit narrowly last season; beaten just twice in three seasons over fences and still sets a clear standard in two-mile chase division.

Enjoy The Dream

4 b f Mastercraftsman - Enjoy The Life (Medicean)
Andrew McNamara (Ire)   Andrew Heffernan

PLACINGS: 315-7   RPR **139**+h

Starts	1st	2nd	3rd	4th	Win & Pl
4	1	-	1	-	£30,243

4/23	Fair	2m Gd2 Hdl 4yo yld-sft	£20,885

Dual Listed runner-up on the Flat who sprang a 33-1 surprise when winning a Grade 2 juvenile hurdle at Fairyhouse's Easter meeting last season; well beaten at Grade 1 level on next two runs, including when fifth behind Lossiemouth at Punchestown.

Envoi Allen (Fr)

9 b g Muhtathir - Reaction (Saint Des Saints)
Henry de Bromhead (Ire)   Cheveley Park Stud

PLACINGS: 11/111F/P1613/31714-   RPR **169**+c

Starts	1st	2nd	3rd	4th	Win & Pl
22	15	-	2	1	£795,800

3/23	Chel	2m4¹/₂f Cls1 Gd1 Ch soft	£211,013
11/22	DRoy	3m Gd1 Ch yield	£74,370
12/21	Leop	2m Gd1 Ch gd-yld	£65,848
10/21	DRoy	2m3¹/₂f Gd2 Ch soft	£26,339
1/21	Punc	2m4f Nov Gd3 Ch heavy	£18,438
11/20	Fair	2m4f Nov Gd1 Ch soft	£35,000
10/20	DRoy	2m3¹/₂f Ch soft	£5,500
3/20	Chel	2m5f Cls1 Nov Gd1 Hdl soft	£70,338
1/20	Naas	2m4f Nov Gd1 Hdl soft	£47,838
12/19	Fair	2m Nov Gd1 Hdl yld-sft	£47,838
11/19	DRoy	2m¹/₂f Mdn Hdl soft	£7,986
3/19	Chel	2m1¹/₂f Cls1 Gd1 NHF 4-6yo soft	£42,203
2/19	Leop	2m Gd2 NHF 4-7yo gd-yld	£46,509
12/18	Navn	2m List NHF 4-7yo yield	£14,967
12/18	Fair	2m NHF 4yo good	£5,451

Has never quite lived up to early hype but still enjoyed another fine campaign last season and took Grade 1 tally to eight when beating Shishkin in the Ryanair Chase; also proved himself at 3m at Down Royal but disappointed in the King George and Punchestown Gold Cup.

Erne River (Ire)

8 b g Califet - Lusty Beg (Old Vic)
Nick Kent   Crossed Fingers Partnership

PLACINGS: 321/31/111F3/22408-   RPR **152**c

Starts	1st	2nd	3rd	4th	Win & Pl
12	4	2	2	1	£53,757

	2/22	Weth	2m5¹/₂f Cls3 Nov Ch soft	£7,679
127	1/22	Donc	2m4¹/₂f Cls3 Nov 122-134 Ch Hcap gd-sft	£11,273
	5/21	Wwck	2m3f Cls4 Nov Hdl soft	£3,159
	3/21	Donc	2m3¹/₂f Cls4 Nov Hdl good	£3,769

Looked a potential star in 2021-22 and sent off 11-4 for a Grade 1 at Aintree only to fall; regressive since, albeit mainly over hurdles; still ran well when second in a handicap at Doncaster and fourth when favourite for the Rendlesham.

Espoir De Romay (Fr)

9 b g Kap Rock - Miss Du Seuil (Lavirco)
Kim Bailey   The Midgelets

PLACINGS: 3/1310/121F/33P/52-3   RPR **140**+h

Starts	1st	2nd	3rd	4th	Win & Pl
15	4	2	5	-	£47,412

140	3/21	Leic	2m4f Cls3 130-140 Ch Hcap heavy	£7,018
	11/20	Hntg	2m4f Cls3 Nov Ch good	£7,310
132	1/20	Winc	2m4f Cls3 112-132 Cond Am Hdl Hcap soft	£7,148
	11/19	Wwck	2m3f Cls4 Nov Hdl gd-sft	£4,549

Unlucky not to win a Grade 1 novice chase at Aintree in April 2021 (fell two out) but has struggled since, albeit in just six runs; missed much of last season and showed some promise over hurdles in the spring; has quickly dropped to a good mark if trainer can revitalise him.

Facile Vega (Ire)

6 b g Walk In The Park - Quevega (Robin Des Champs)
Willie Mullins (Ire)   Hammer & Trowel Syndicate

PLACINGS: 111/111521-   RPR **158**+h

Starts	1st	2nd	3rd	4th	Win & Pl
9	7	1	-	-	£302,057

4/23	Punc	2m¹/₂f Nov Gd1 Hdl yld-sft	£65,265
12/22	Leop	2m Nov Gd1 Hdl soft	£49,580
12/22	Fair	2m Mdn Hdl gd-yld	£5,950
4/22	Punc	2m¹/₂f Gd1 NHF 4-7yo gd-yld	£49,580
3/22	Chel	2m¹/₂f Cls1 Gd1 NHF 4-6yo heavy	£45,560
2/22	Leop	2m Gd2 NHF 4-7yo yield	£49,580
12/21	Leop	2m NHF 4yo soft	£5,268

Champion Bumper winner in 2022 who was a high-class novice hurdler last season without quite living up to sky-high expectations; bounced back from Leopardstown blip when second in the Supreme and added a fourth Grade 1 win in total at Punchestown; set to go chasing.

Fact To File (Fr)

6 b g Poliglote - Mitemps (Trempolino)
Willie Mullins (Ire)   John P McManus

PLACINGS: 1/122-   RPR **136**+b

Starts	1st	2nd	3rd	4th	Win & Pl
3	1	2	-	-	£39,859

12/22	Leop	2m4f NHF soft	£5,950

High-class bumper performer last season who

Did you know farriery is a registered profession?

It is illegal in Great Britain to practice farriery if unregistered

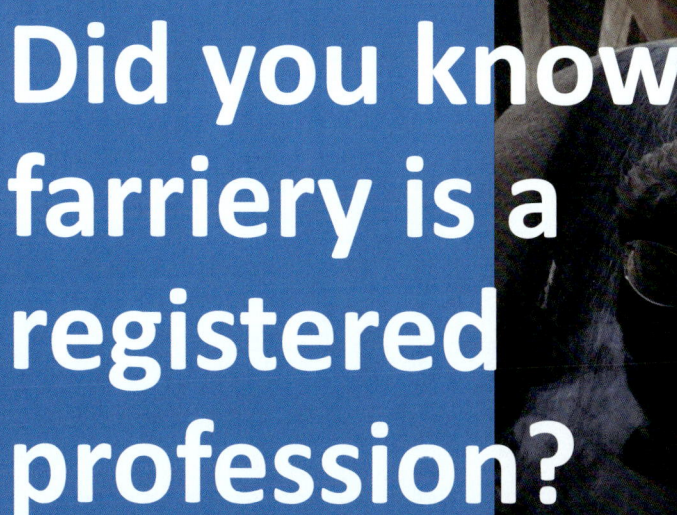

For the welfare of your horse or pony ask to see your farrier's registration card or check the Register at www.farrier-reg.gov.uk

frc@farrier-reg.gov.uk
01733 319911
Farriers Registration Council

twice finished second behind A Dream To Share; sent off favourite to reverse Leopardstown form at Cheltenham (favoured by stiffer track and softer ground) and ran a fine race to get closer; should stay well over hurdles.

Faivoir (Fr)
8 b g Coastal Path - Qape Noir (Subotica)
Dan Skelton — Mrs Suzanne Lawrence
PLACINGS: 11311/141223305/4P1-   RPR **141**h

Starts	1st	2nd	3rd	4th	Win & Pl
23	10	4	3	3	£170,174

134	3/23	Chel	2m1f Cls1 Gd3 133-155 Hdl Hcap soft	£56,270
144	11/21	Asct	2m3f Cls3 Nov 133-144 Ch Hcap good	£9,110
	10/21	Uttx	2m Cls3 Nov Ch gd-sft	£7,080
	4/21	Chel	2m4½f Cls2 Nov Hdl good	£7,805
	3/21	Newb	2m4½f Cls3 Nov Hdl gd-sft	£5,913
	1/21	Hayd	1m7½f Cls1 Nov Gd2 Hdl heavy	£12,814
	12/20	Ludl	2m Cls4 Nov Hdl soft	£3,899
	10/20	Chel	2m1½f Cls3 Mdn Hdl good	£7,221
	3/20	Hntg	2m Cls5 NHF 4-6yo gd-sft	£2,274
	2/20	Bang	2m1½f Cls5 NHF 4-6yo soft	£2,274

33-1 winner of last season's County Hurdle, exploiting handicapper's generosity after plummeting 9lb for previous three defeats; had been a five-time winner in 2020-21 but hadn't won since a novice handicap chase in November 2021; still below highest winning mark.

Fakir D'Oudairies (Fr)
8 b g Kapgarde - Niagaria Du Bois (Grand Tresor)
Joseph O'Brien (Ire) — John P McManus
PLACINGS: /2P221/314211/52132-   RPR **166**c

Starts	1st	2nd	3rd	4th	Win & Pl
30	9	11	2	4	£783,709

4/23	Thur	2m4½f Gd2 Ch yield	£19,058
4/22	Aint	2m4f Cls1 Gd1 Ch gd-sft	£140,561
2/22	Asct	2m5f Cls1 Gd1 Ch soft	£86,933
11/21	Clon	2m4½f Gd2 Ch soft	£26,339
4/21	Aint	2m4f Cls1 Gd1 Ch gd-sft	£104,963
12/19	Fair	2m4f Nov Gd1 Ch soft	£47,838
11/19	Navn	2m1f Ch sft-hvy	£9,051
1/19	Chel	2m1f Cls1 Gd2 Hdl 4yo gd-sft	£18,006
1/19	Cork	2m Mdn Hdl 4-5yo soft	£7,492

Classy and dependable Grade 1 performer over many seasons, winning four times and finishing second eight times at the top level; not quite at his best last term, with sole win coming on rare drop in grade; second to Pic D'Orhy when going for Marsh Chase hat-trick.

GUIDE TO THE JUMPS 2023-24

Famous Clermont (Fr)
8 b g Maresca Sorrento - Progest Des Mottes (April Night)
Chris Barber   Biddiscombe, Rousell, Collins & Rogers
PLACINGS: 30321/12111/P111161-   RPR **142+**c

Starts	1st	2nd	3rd	4th	Win & Pl
9	4	-	2	-	£37,698
4/23	Aint	2m5f Cls2 Am Hunt Ch gd-sft............£24,155
2/23	Hayd	2m6f Cls3 Am Hunt Ch gd-sft............£7,700
2/23	Winc	3m1f Cls6 Am Hunt Ch gd-sft............£2,139
3/22	Extr	3m Cls6 Nov Am Hunt Ch gd-sft........£2,053

Easy winner of the Foxhunters at Aintree's Grand National meeting last season; had been a patent non-stayer when sixth at Cheltenham but has otherwise won all four races under rules and four point-to-points since the start of 2022; has Aintree as his aim again.

Fanion D'Estruval (Fr)
8 b g Enrique - Urfe D'Estruval (Martaline)
Venetia Williams   David Wilson
PLACINGS: 15/2F445/41234/7340-   RPR **160**c

Starts	1st	2nd	3rd	4th	Win & Pl
21	6	2	2	5	£191,521
151	11/21	Newb	2m4f Cls2 131-151 Ch Hcap gd-sft........£26,015
137	11/19	Newb	2m¹/₂f Cls3 Nov 124-142 Ch Hcap soft.....£12,449
	7/19	Autl	2m1¹/₂f Ch 4yo v soft......£22,486
	6/19	Toul	2m1¹/₂f Ch 4yo gd-sft......£9,081
	5/19	Comp	2m2f Hdl 4yo v soft......£19,459
	4/19	Angl	2m3f Hdl 4-5yo gd-sft......£5,622

Below par last season (best run when third in the Rowland Meyrick) after a terrific 2021-22 campaign; finished first and second under big weights in handicaps at Newbury and Ascot before twice making the frame in Grade 1 races; dropped back to last winning mark.

Famous Clermont storms to success in the Foxhunters

RACING POST

Fantastic Lady (Fr)
8 b m Network - Latitude (Kadalko)
Nicky Henderson — Evan-Robert Hanbury

PLACINGS: 4F1/56113U/1023-   RPR **152**c

Starts	1st	2nd	3rd	4th	Win & Pl
13	4	2	2	1	£83,290

	11/22	MRas	3m Cls1 List Ch gd-sft...	£18,982
129	2/22	Bang	2m4½f Cls3 Nov 116-132 Ch Hcap soft...........	£5,882
120	1/22	Wwck	2m4f Cls4 Nov 108-120 Ch Hcap gd-sft..........	£5,582
	3/21	Donc	2m3½f Cls4 Nov Hdl good	£4,419

Smart mare who won a Listed chase at Market Rasen last season and stepped up again when placed in stronger races in the autumn; finished a fine second in the Topham at Aintree and then third behind Hewick in a Grade 2 at Sandown.

Fastorslow (Fr)
7 b g Saint Des Saints - Popova (Kahyasi)
Martin Brassil (Ire) — Sean & Bernardine Mulryan

PLACINGS: 121/2002/25571-   RPR **175**+c

Starts	1st	2nd	3rd	4th	Win & Pl
12	3	5	-	-	£266,182

	4/23	Punc	3m Gd1 Ch yield	£156,637
	9/19	Autl	2m1½f Ch 3yo v soft	£23,784
	6/19	Chat	2m1f Hdl 3yo v soft	£8,216

Very highly tried last season and justified bold campaigning by pulling off a huge upset to beat Galopin Des Champs and Bravemansgame at Punchestown; had been narrowly denied for the second successive Cheltenham Festival in the Ultima after two distant fifths in Grade 1s.

Favori De Champdou (Fr)
8 b g Saddler Maker - Pamella (Subotica)
Gordon Elliott (Ire) — Gigginstown House Stud

PLACINGS: 23/2421/2/111P4-   RPR **149**+h

Starts	1st	2nd	3rd	4th	Win & Pl
9	4	2	-	2	£44,683

	12/22	Limk	2m7f Nov Gd2 Hdl sft-hvy	£18,097
	11/22	Thur	2m7f Nov Hdl yld-sft	£6,693
	11/22	Thur	2m7½f Mdn Hdl yld-sft	£6,445
	2/20	Thur	2m NHF 5-7yo gd-yld	£5,000

Useful staying novice hurdler last season; won his first three races, including a 3m Grade 2 at Limerick; ran too freely and pulled up when 12-1 for the Albert Bartlett at Cheltenham; settled better at Punchestown but still came up short in fourth behind Gaelic Warrior.

Fennor Cross (Ire)
6 b g Elzaam - Persilian (Whipper)
John McConnell (Ire) — The Positivity Syndicate

PLACINGS: 31101-   RPR **142**+h

Starts	1st	2nd	3rd	4th	Win & Pl
5	3	-	1	-	£79,219

133	4/23	Aint	2m4f Cls1 Gd3 132-146 Hdl Hcap gd-sft.........	£42,203
	11/22	Chel	2m½f Cls1 Nov Gd2 Hdl good.............................	£28,230
	10/22	Chel	2m1½f Cls3 Mdn Hdl good	£7,804

Battle-hardened Flat campaigner who flourished when sent hurdling last season and won a big handicap at Aintree; also won twice at Cheltenham in the autumn but out of his depth in the Supreme after a winter break (also only run over hurdles on ground worse than good to soft).

Final Orders heads to his biggest victory so far at the Dublin Racing Festival in February

GUIDE TO THE JUMPS 2023-24

Ferns Lock
6 b g Telescope - Rattlin (Bollin Eric)
David Christie (Ire)   R Nicholas
PLACINGS: 1/111113-   RPR **155**+c

Starts	1st	2nd	3rd	4th	Win & Pl
4	3	-	1	-	£18,621
	3/23 Gowr	3m1f Hunt Ch sft-hvy			£7,049
	1/23 Thur	3m¹/₂f Hunt Ch yield			£5,221
	11/22 Fair	2m7¹/₂f Hunt Ch soft			£4,958

Exciting youngster who achieved by far the highest rating by a hunter chaser last season when beating Billaway by 20 lengths at Thurles; described as a "baby" by his trainer and duly skipped Cheltenham, instead following up at Gowran before a below-par run at Fairyhouse.

Ferny Hollow (Ire)
8 b/br g Westerner - Mirazur (Good Thyne)
Willie Mullins (Ire)   Cheveley Park Stud
PLACINGS: 1/2211/1/1/   RPR **169**c

Starts	1st	2nd	3rd	4th	Win & Pl
7	5	2	-	-	£117,251
	12/21 Leop	2m1f Nov Gd1 Ch soft			£52,679
	12/21 Punc	2m1f Ch yld-sft			£6,585
	11/20 Gowr	2m Mdn Hdl heavy			£7,000
	3/20 Chel	2m¹/₂f Cls1 Gd1 NHF 4-6yo soft			£42,203
	2/20 Fair	2m NHF 5-7yo heavy			£5,000

Immensely promising but fragile gelding who has won his last five races but has run just three times since landing the 2020 Champion Bumper; won a Grade 1 novice chase at Leopardstown in 2021 to become hot favourite for the Arkle but hasn't run since after successive setbacks.

Feronily (Ire)
6 b g Getaway - Vickeeto (Old Vic)
Emmet Mullins (Ire)   Paul Byrne
PLACINGS: 1234121-5   RPR **158**c

Starts	1st	2nd	3rd	4th	Win & Pl
7	2	2	1	1	£107,943
	4/23 Punc	3m¹/₂f Nov Gd1 Ch yld-sft			£65,265
	3/23 Limk	2m3f Mdn Hdl sft-hvy			£7,832

Astonishingly ended last season as a Grade 1 novice chase winner having still been in bumpers two months previously; improved immediately over fences and looked a natural jumper when beating Appreciate It at Punchestown in just his second chase; could be top-class.

Fil Dor (Fr)
5 gr g Doctor Dino - La Turbale (Ange Gabriel)
Gordon Elliott (Ire)   Caldwell Construction
PLACINGS: 11122/22135106-   RPR **152**+c

Starts	1st	2nd	3rd	4th	Win & Pl
13	5	4	1	-	£152,009
	2/23 Gowr	2m Gd3 Hdl sft-hvy			£15,664
	11/22 Navn	2m1f Ch soft			£8,181
	12/21 Leop	2m Gd2 Hdl 3yo soft			£23,705
	11/21 Fair	2m Gd3 Hdl 3yo good			£14,487
	10/21 DRoy	2m1f Hdl 3yo soft			£6,058

Three-time Grade 1 runner-up over hurdles but didn't live up to expectations over fences last season; sent off odds-on for a Grade 1 after fine win on chase debut but struggled in stronger company; won a Grade 3 at Gowran back over hurdles only to flop at Cheltenham and Fairyhouse.

Filey Bay (Ire)
7 b g Fame And Glory - You Should Know Me (Oscar)
Emmet Mullins (Ire)   John P McManus
PLACINGS: 556/5633/1123-50   RPR **147**+h

Starts	1st	2nd	3rd	4th	Win & Pl
13	2	1	3	-	£68,338
124	12/22 Winc	1m7f Cls3 104-124 Hdl Hcap gd-sft			£10,511
117	11/22 Donc	2m¹/₂f Cls3 117-129 Hdl Hcap good			£6,971

Remarkable improver following move to Emmet Mullins last season when transformed from a seven-race maiden to top handicap hurdler; won easily at Doncaster and Wincanton before improving again in defeat when second in the Betfair Hurdle and third in the County.

Fils D'Oudairies (Fr)
8 b g Saint Des Saints - Pythie D'Oudairies (Grand Tresor)
Gordon Elliott (Ire)   David L'Estrange
PLACINGS: F/FP22/25520145-F110   RPR **153**+h

Starts	1st	2nd	3rd	4th	Win & Pl
23	5	5	-	2	£139,343
	7/23 Tipp	2m Gd3 Hdl gd-yld			£36,549
	5/23 Baln	2m2¹/₂f Hdl good			£8,093
	3/23 Leop	2m2¹/₂f Hdl yield			£8,876
	12/20 Navn	2m4f Nov Ch heavy			£10,500
	11/19 Autl	2m1¹/₂f Hdl 4yo heavy			£19,459

Back on track this year, landing a third win of 2023 in a Grade 3 at Tipperary this summer having previously failed to win in 12 races since the end of 2020; had won a heavy-ground novice chase that day and now rated significantly lower over fences.

Final Orders
7 b g Camelot - Trapeze (Pivotal)
Gavin Cromwell (Ire)   C M D Syndicate
PLACINGS: 7552PP/212111115F-01   RPR **149**+c

Starts	1st	2nd	3rd	4th	Win & Pl
30	8	4	-	1	£113,674
102	8/23 Bell	2m4¹/₂f 83-102 Hdl Hcap good			£5,482
140	2/23 Leop	2m1f 123-144 Ch Hcap yield			£52,212
129	12/22 Leop	2m1f 116-141 Ch Hcap yield			£14,874
120	11/22 DRoy	3m 97-120 Ch Hcap yield			£7,189
	10/22 Cork	2m1¹/₂f Nov Ch soft			£5,454
	10/22 Klny	2m7f Ch good			£5,702
96	8/22 Bell	2m4f 84-102 Hdl Hcap good			£5,206
92	10/20 Wxfd	2m¹/₂f 85-105 Hdl Hcap soft			£5,500

Astonishing improver following move to Gavin Cromwell last summer, starting on a hurdles mark of 95 and finishing rated 150 over fences; won five chases in a row, culminating in a valuable 2m handicap at Leopardstown; solid fifth in the Grand Annual but fell in the Topham.

Firefox (Ire)

5 b g Walk In The Park - Cuteasafox (Vinnie Roe)
Gordon Elliott (Ire)   Bective Stud

PLACINGS: 4211-   RPR **131**+b

Starts	1st	2nd	3rd	4th	Win & Pl
4	2	1	-	1	£18,021
	4/23 Fair	2m NHF yld-sft			£10,442
	2/23 Navn	2m NHF gd-yld			£5,482

Developed into a very useful bumper performer last season after managing only fourth over hurdles first time out; hacked up by ten lengths at Navan and followed up in a much stronger race at Fairyhouse; should benefit from that experience back over hurdles.

First Flow (Ire)

11 b g Primary - Clonroche Wells (Pierre)
Kim Bailey   A N Solomons

PLACINGS: 132111/1116/613/3F2-   RPR **165**c

Starts	1st	2nd	3rd	4th	Win & Pl
25	11	4	3	2	£251,262
	12/21 Hntg	2m4f Cls1 Gd2 Ch good			£42,914
	1/21 Asct	2m1f Cls1 Gd1 Ch soft			£59,513
154	12/20 Weth	1m7f Cls2 133-154 Ch Hcap heavy			£12,021
148	11/20 Asct	2m1f Cls2 138-159 Ch Hcap soft			£15,640
	3/20 Carl	2m Cls3 Nov Ch heavy			£9,747
	2/20 Donc	$2m^{1}/_{2}f$ Cls4 Nov Ch heavy			£4,289
141	2/20 Leic	2m Cls3 Nov 125-141 Ch Hcap heavy			£6,498
	12/19 Hrfd	2m Cls3 Nov Ch soft			£8,769
	1/18 Hayd	$1m7^{1}/_{2}f$ Cls1 Nov Gd2 Hdl heavy			£17,085
	12/17 Newb	$2m^{1}/_{2}f$ Cls4 Hdl heavy			£4,549
	11/17 Ling	2m Cls4 Nov Hdl soft			£5,198

Very lightly raced for his age and has run just seven times since his finest hour in the Clarence House Chase in 2021; added the Peterborough Chase the following season; fair third in that race last term and did better when second behind Hewick in another Grade 2 at Sandown.

First Street

6 b g Golden Horn - Ladys First (Dutch Art)
Nicky Henderson   Lady Bamford & Alice Bamford

PLACINGS: 221151325/13308-   RPR **155**h

Starts	1st	2nd	3rd	4th	Win & Pl
14	4	3	3	-	£101,844
146	11/22 Newb	$2m^{1}/_{2}f$ Cls1 Gd3 121-146 Hdl Hcap good			£28,475
132	1/22 Kemp	2m Cls3 113-132 Hdl Hcap soft			£6,208
	9/21 Wwck	2m5f Cls4 Nov Hdl good			£4,085
	8/21 Bang	$2m3^{1}/_{2}f$ Cls4 Nov Hdl good			£4,085

Good winner of a handicap hurdle at Newbury first time out last season, maintaining progressive form in such races, but failed to go on from there; twice third in Grade 2 hurdles and disappointed in the County Hurdle and Scottish Champion; back to a realistic mark.

Flame Bearer (Ire)

8 b g Fame And Glory - Banba (Docksider)
Willie Mullins (Ire)   Linda Mulcahy & Mary Wolridge

PLACINGS: 2/11/53111/2317311-   RPR **158**+c

Starts	1st	2nd	3rd	4th	Win & Pl
14	8	1	2	-	£154,984
	4/23 Fair	2m4f Gd1 Ch yld-sft			£52,212
	3/23 Thur	2m2f Nov Gd3 Ch soft			£15,664
	1/23 Fair	2m1f Ch sft-hvy			£8,093
	4/22 Fair	2m Nov Gd2 Hdl yield			£19,832
	2/22 Naas	$1m7^{1}/_{2}f$ Nov Gd2 Hdl soft			£18,097
	1/22 Fair	2m Mdn Hdl gd-yld			£6,197
	3/21 Limk	2m NHF 5-7yo heavy			£5,268
	12/20 Thur	2m NHF 4-7yo soft			£4,500

Upset higher-profile stablemates when winning a Grade 1 chase at Fairyhouse last season; dual Grade 2 hurdles winner who took time to find his feet over fences but penny dropped in the spring with easy Grade 3 win before narrow defeat of Sir Gerhard.

Flanking Maneuver (Ire)
8 b g Beat Hollow - Corskeagh Shadow (Beneficial)
Noel Meade (Ire)   Gigginstown House Stud
PLACINGS: 4/45/1214/33-   RPR **149**c

Starts	1st	2nd	3rd	4th	Win & Pl
8	2	1	2	2	£24,902
	1/21 Fair	2m4f Mdn Hdl heavy			£6,321
	10/20 Dpat	2m3f NHF 4-7yo yield			£4,500

Ran just twice last season after two years off but showed he retains ability that had seen him come fourth at Grade 1 level in 2021; beaten just over a length behind Churchstonewarrior and Mahler Mission in a 3m Grade 3 at Navan; disappointed next time but retains novice status.

Flooring Porter (Ire)
8 b g Yeats - Lillymile (Revoque)
Gavin Cromwell (Ire)   Flooring Porter Syndicate
PLACINGS: /132111/PF212/4443-9   RPR **160**h

Starts	1st	2nd	3rd	4th	Win & Pl
25	7	4	2	4	£566,233
	3/22 Chel	3m Cls1 Gd1 Hdl soft			£182,878
	3/21 Chel	3m Cls1 Gd1 Hdl gd-sft			£135,048
	12/20 Leop	3m Gd1 Hdl soft			£50,000
136	12/20 Navn	3m½f 128-154 Hdl Hcap soft			£45,000
122	7/20 Gowr	3m½f 107-122 Hdl Hcap good			£7,250
105	10/19 Cork	3m 80-107 Hdl Hcap yield			£6,655
	8/19 Bell	2m½f Mdn Hdl good			£6,123

Dual winner of the Stayers' Hurdle in 2021 and 2022 but came fourth in pursuit of the hat-trick last season during a winless campaign; had been held up by a setback but then managed only third at Aintree before disappointing in France; hasn't won outside Cheltenham since 2020.

Florida Dreams (Ire)
5 b g Doyen - First Line (Big Shuffle)
Nicky Richards   J Fyffe
PLACINGS: 11-   RPR **124+**b

Starts	1st	2nd	3rd	4th	Win & Pl
2	2	-	-	-	£30,858
	4/23 Aint	2m1f Cls1 Gd2 NHF 4-6yo gd-sft			£28,135
	1/23 Muss	1m7½f Cls4 NHF 4-6yo soft			£2,723

Won both bumpers last season, including an 18-1 surprise in a Grade 2 at Aintree's Grand National meeting; also sent off in double figures when off the mark at Musselburgh; looked very strong at the finish in both races; good prospect for novice hurdles.

Found A Fifty (Ire)
6 b g Solskjaer - Fillmein (Gone Fishin)
Gordon Elliott (Ire)   Bective Stud
PLACINGS: 1/21284-   RPR **149**h

Starts	1st	2nd	3rd	4th	Win & Pl
5	1	2	-	1	£18,772
	1/23 Fair	2m Mdn Hdl soft			£6,527

Looked a potentially smart novice hurdler last season but failed to deliver in the spring; won on hurdles debut at Fairyhouse and beaten a head in a Grade 2 at Navan but then managed only eighth at Aintree and a distant fourth at Punchestown when stepped up in class.

Flame Bearer (left) has Grade 1 victory in his sight at *Fairyhouse*

Foxy Girl (Fr)
5 b m Saint Des Saints - Far Burg (Sageburg)
Henry de Bromhead (Ire) — Robcour

PLACINGS: 2/218-   RPR **135+**h

Starts	1st	2nd	3rd	4th	Win & Pl
4	1	2	-	-	£21,487
12/22	Limk	2m Mdn Hdl 4yo sft-hvy £6,197

Lightly raced mare who got off the mark on her second run for current connections at Limerick last season having also finished second in a Listed hurdle in France; sent off just 13-2 for the mares' novice at the Cheltenham Festival but failed to settle and didn't get home.

Franco De Port (Fr)
8 b g Coastal Path - Ruth (Agent Bleu)
Willie Mullins (Ire) — Bruton Street V

PLACINGS: 52/F77240/34554533-8   RPR **161**c

Starts	1st	2nd	3rd	4th	Win & Pl
25	4	4	3	3	£295,554
12/20	Leop	2m1f Nov Gd1 Ch yield.................................. £40,000
11/20	Thur	2m2f Ch soft... £5,500
11/19	Gowr	2m Nov Hdl 4yo heavy.................................... £8,253
3/19	Autl	2m1½f Hdl 4yo heavy.................................... £19,459

Without a win since 2020 despite connections trying a host of plans, including several trips to France; has produced best form back at home, often running to a high level; nearly won the 2022 Thyestes but handicap mark not helped by close fourth in last season's Savills Chase.

French Dynamite (Fr)
8 b g Kentucky Dynamite - Matnie (Laveron)
Mouse Morris (Ire) — Robcour

PLACINGS: /2512/45161/3125244-   RPR **162**c

Starts	1st	2nd	3rd	4th	Win & Pl
20	6	4	1	4	£166,996
10/22	Thur	2m7f Hdl gd-yld... £7,933
3/22	Thur	2m2f Nov Gd3 Ch good................................ £14,874
11/21	Punc	2m3½f Ch yield.. £6,585
3/21	Leop	2m2½f Hdl yield... £8,955
2/20	Thur	2m4½f Nov Hdl gd-yld................................... £9,000
11/19	Thur	2m Mdn Hdl 4yo soft..................................... £5,857

Kicked off last season with a hurdles win at Thurles but couldn't add to it when back over fences; produced two best runs at Cheltenham, finishing second in the Paddy Power Gold Cup and fourth in the Ryanair Chase; took record to 0-9 at Grade 1 or Grade 2 level.

Frodon (Fr)

11 b g Nickname - Miss Country (Country Reel)

Paul Nicholls — P J Vogt

PLACINGS: 4/14151/1470/133539- — RPR **167+c**

Starts	1st	2nd	3rd	4th	Win & Pl
50	19	3	10	4	£1,162,151

158	11/22	Winc	3m1f Cls1 Gd3 132-158 Ch Hcap gd-fm	£41,608
	10/21	DRoy	3m Gd1 Ch soft	£65,848
	4/21	Sand	2m6½f Cls1 Gd2 Ch good	£23,919
	12/20	Kemp	3m Cls1 Gd1 Ch gd-sft	£116,178
164	10/20	Chel	3m1f Cls2 138-164 Ch Hcap good	£30,140
	1/20	Kemp	2m4½f Cls1 Gd2 Ch gd-sft	£34,170
	3/19	Chel	2m4½f Cls1 Gd1 Ch gd-sft	£196,945
	1/19	Chel	3m1½f Cls1 Gd2 Ch gd-sft	£56,536
164	12/18	Chel	2m4½f Cls1 Gd3 138-164 Ch Hcap good	£74,035
158	10/18	Aint	2m4f Cls1 Gd2 138-158 Ch Hcap good	£45,016
154	1/18	Chel	2m5f Cls1 Gd3 131-154 Ch Hcap heavy	£42,713
	2/17	Kemp	2m4½f Cls1 Nov Gd2 Ch good	£18,793
	2/17	Muss	2m4f Cls3 Nov Ch good	£7,798
149	12/16	Chel	2m5f Cls1 Gd3 132-158 Ch Hcap soft	£56,950
	11/16	Winc	2m4f Cls1 Nov Gd2 Ch good	£28,486
	9/16	Font	2m5f Cls4 Nov Ch good	£5,198
	9/16	NAbb	2m½f Cls3 Nov Ch good	£7,187
	2/16	Hayd	1m7½f Cls2 Hdl 4yo heavy	£9,747
	4/15	Autl	1m7f Hdl 3yo heavy	£20,465

Hugely popular chaser who famously won the 2019 Ryanair Chase and 2020 King George at his peak; had a fabulous record in top handicaps as a youngster and added another big prize in last season's Badger Beer Chase; struggled subsequently but back down to same mark.

Fugitif (Fr)

8 b g Ballingarry - Turiane (Arvico)

Richard Hobson — Carl Hinchy & Dr Emad Hussain

PLACINGS: /56713/1P1448/21225- — RPR **157c**

Starts	1st	2nd	3rd	4th	Win & Pl
19	4	3	2	2	£109,535

133	12/22	Chep	2m3½f Cls2 128-154 Ch Hcap soft	£18,211
131	1/22	Newc	2m½f Cls3 Nov 124-135 Ch Hcap soft	£8,169
120	11/21	Worc	2m½f Cls4 Nov 108-121 Ch Hcap gd-sft	£3,594
113	2/21	Uttx	2m Cls4 102-119 Hdl Hcap heavy	£3,769

Hugely progressive handicap chaser last season despite winning only once at Chepstow; finished second at Cheltenham three times either side of that, including in the Plate; tame fifth in Grade 1 company at Aintree after that (second poor run at that meeting in successive seasons).

Fun Fun Fun (Ire)

5 b m Martaline - Ocean Breeze (Presenting)

Willie Mullins (Ire) — Simon Munir & Isaac Souede

PLACINGS: 1104- — RPR **122+b**

Starts	1st	2nd	3rd	4th	Win & Pl
4	2	-	-	1	£59,011

	2/23	Leop	2m Gd2 NHF 4-7yo yield	£52,212
	10/22	Slig	2m2f NHF yld-sft	£5,206

Looked a future star when winning first two bumpers by wide margins, including a Grade 2 mares' bumper at Leopardstown; sent off just 5-1 for the Champion Bumper at Cheltenham but managed only 15th; beaten favourite back in mares' company at Punchestown.

Funambule Sivola (right): goes particularly well at Newbury, where he has three wins to his name

Funambule Sivola (Fr)

8 b g Noroit - Little Memories (Montjeu)

Venetia Williams — My Racing Manager Friends

PLACINGS: 12112/29112P/6451F5- — RPR **164+c**

Starts	1st	2nd	3rd	4th	Win & Pl
25	7	6	-	1	£278,170

	2/23	Newb	2m½f Cls1 Gd2 Ch good	£39,865
	2/22	Newb	2m½f Cls1 Gd2 Ch gd-sft	£34,170
152	1/22	Donc	2m½f Cls2 128-152 Ch Hcap good	£20,812
141	3/21	Asct	2m1f Cls2 Nov 129-141 Ch Hcap good	£16,243
133	2/21	Chep	2m Cls2 126-145 Ch Hcap soft	£11,930
124	12/20	Newb	2m½f Cls3 113-125 Ch Hcap soft	£7,018
112	11/20	Weth	1m7f Cls4 Nov 112-120 Ch Hcap gd-sft	£4,289

Has won the last two runnings of the Game Spirit Chase and also finished second in the 2022 Champion Chase; generally well below his best last season apart from when bouncing back at Newbury, finishing no better than fourth otherwise, always in small fields.

Fury Road (Ire)

9 b g Stowaway - Molly Duffy (Oscar)

Gordon Elliott (Ire) — Gigginstown House Stud

PLACINGS: 2P/P23152/31336F5-06 — RPR **162c**

Starts	1st	2nd	3rd	4th	Win & Pl
27	7	3	6	2	£301,792

	11/22	DRoy	2m3½f Gd2 Ch yield	£24,790
	12/21	Leop	3m Nov Gd1 Ch yield	£52,679
	11/20	Punc	2m5½f Gd2 Hdl heavy	£30,000
	12/19	Limk	2m7f Nov Gd2 Hdl heavy	£39,865
	11/19	Navn	2m4f Nov Gd3 Hdl soft	£22,590
	11/19	DRoy	2m6f Mdn Hdl yld-sft	£7,986
	2/19	Fair	2m NHF 5-7yo gd-yld	£5,550

Smart staying chaser who struggled in the face of some very stiff tasks last season; has dropped below Grade 1 level just twice since chase debut in 2021, winning a Grade 2 at Down Royal last term; third in the Savills Chase and Irish Gold Cup before form tailed off.

Ga Law (Fr)

7 b g Sinndar - Law (Lute Antique)

Jamie Snowden — The Footie Partnership

PLACINGS: 16/11132/31F5P- — RPR **160c**

Starts	1st	2nd	3rd	4th	Win & Pl
12	5	1	2	-	£151,446

142	11/22	Chel	2m4f Cls1 Gd3 130-156 Ch Hcap good	£90,032
	11/20	Winc	2m4f Cls1 Nov Gd2 Ch good	£15,217
128	10/20	Extr	2m3f Cls3 110-130 Ch Hcap gd-fm	£7,018
	9/20	Font	2m3½f Cls4 Ch good	£4,029
	10/19	Agtn	2m2f Hdl 3yo heavy	£6,054

Won last season's Paddy Power Gold Cup at Cheltenham having been dropped 8lb during 18-month layoff; might well have followed up on first run at 3m in the Sky Bet Chase but for final-fence fall; fair fifth in the Ryanair Chase but pulled up in the Aintree Bowl.

Gaelic Warrior (Ger)
5 b g Maxios - Game Of Legs (Hernando)
Willie Mullins (Ire)   Mrs S Ricci
PLACINGS: 6/332/11121-   RPR **158**+h

Starts	1st	2nd	3rd	4th	Win & Pl
9	4	2	2	-	£211,501

	4/23	Punc	3m Nov Gd1 Hdl yield............................£65,265
143	2/23	Leop	2m 118-143 Hdl Hcap yield......................£78,319
	1/23	Clon	2m¹/₂f Hdl heavy......................................£6,004
	12/22	Tram	2m Mdn Hdl soft...£4,958

Won four out of five races last season, with sole defeat when second behind Impaire Et Passe in the Ballymore at Cheltenham; had done well at 2m prior to that, including a valuable handicap win, but looked a proper stayer when easily winning a 3m Grade 1 at Punchestown on final run.

Gaillard Du Mesnil (Fr)
7 gr g Saint Des Saints - Athena Du Mesnil (Al Namix)
Willie Mullins (Ire)   Mrs J Donnelly
PLACINGS: 2/2112/133333/21313-   RPR **160**c

Starts	1st	2nd	3rd	4th	Win & Pl
21	6	7	7	-	£480,321

	3/23	Chel	3m6f Cls1 Nov Gd2 Am Ch soft...............£62,156
	12/22	Leop	3m Nov Gd1 Ch soft...............................£49,580
	4/21	Punc	2m4f Nov Gd1 Hdl yield..........................£52,679
	2/21	Leop	2m6f Nov Gd1 Hdl sft-hvy......................£65,848
	12/20	Leop	2m4f Mdn Hdl 4yo soft............................£6,000
	8/19	Sjdm	1m5f NHF 3yo gd-sft................................£4,279

Thorough stayer who made the most of second-season novice status last season to win a 3m Grade 1 over Christmas and the National Hunt Chase at Cheltenham; followed up with a fine third in the Grand National (also third in the Irish version in 2022).

Gala Marceau (Fr)
4 b f Galiway - Alma Marceau (Kendargent)
Willie Mullins (Ire)   Kenneth Alexander
PLACINGS: 1/12123-1   RPR **140**+h

Starts	1st	2nd	3rd	4th	Win & Pl
7	4	2	1	-	£286,099

	5/23	Autl	2m3¹/₂f Gd1 Hdl 4yo v soft..................£110,708
	2/23	Leop	2m Gd1 Hdl 4yo yield.............................£78,319
	4/22	Autl	1m7f List Hdl 3yo v soft.........................£30,252
	3/22	Comp	2m Hdl 3yo heavy..................................£20,168

Smart juvenile hurdler last season; finished behind Lossiemouth three times, including when second in the Triumph Hurdle, but came out on top when winning a Grade 1 at Leopardstown; added a second win at the top level in impressive fashion at Auteuil in May.

Galia Des Liteaux (Fr)
7 b m Saddler Maker - Serie Love (Agent Bleu)
Dan Skelton   Michael Ariss
PLACINGS: 1133/1P154-   RPR **153**+c

Starts	1st	2nd	3rd	4th	Win & Pl
8	3	-	2	1	£73,701

	1/23	Wwck	3m Cls1 Nov Gd2 Ch heavy....................£31,323
	11/22	Bang	2m1¹/₂f Nov List Ch heavy.....................£22,887
	12/21	Weth	2m3¹/₂f Cls4 Nov Hdl soft........................£4,085

Very useful novice chaser last season; won a

Gala Marceau: high-quality juvenile hurdler last season

THANK YOU TO ALL OUR SUPPORTERS WITHIN THE INDUSTRY AND FROM THE PUBLIC WHOSE GENEROSITY ENABLES US TO PROVIDE OUR SERVICES

Irish Injured Jockeys was set up in 2014 to increase awareness and raise vital funds to support our injured jockeys. Funds raised through Irish Injured Jockeys go to the injured riders who are most in need of support. Our aim is to make a difference to the lives and welfare of jockeys past and present, and their families by using funds donated by the public

www.irishinjuredjockeys.com

RACING POST

Listed mares' novice on chase debut and later added an open Grade 2 at Warwick; not up to Grade 1 company but far from disgraced when fifth behind The Real Whacker at Cheltenham and fourth behind Gerri Colombe at Aintree.

Galopin Des Champs (Fr)

7 bl g Timos - Manon Des Champs (Marchand De Sable)
Willie Mullins (Ire)   Mrs Audrey Turley
PLACINGS: 12P61/111F1/1112-   RPR **184**+c

Starts	1st	2nd	3rd	4th	Win & Pl
14	9	2	-	-	£804,100

	3/23	Chel	3m2½f Cls1 Gd1 Ch soft	£351,991
	2/23	Leop	3m Gd1 Ch yield	£123,894
	12/22	Punc	2m4f Gd1 Ch yield	£39,664
	4/22	Fair	2m4f Nov Gd1 Ch yield	£49,580
	2/22	Leop	2m5½f Nov Gd1 Ch yield	£74,370
	12/21	Leop	2m5f Ch yield	£9,219
	4/21	Punc	3m Nov Gd1 Hdl yield	£52,679
142	3/21	Chel	2m4½f Cls2 132-143 Cond Hdl Hcap gd-sft	£32,498
	5/20	Autl	2m2f Hdl 4yo v soft	£16,475

Brilliant winner of last season's Cheltenham Gold Cup, beating Bravemansgame by seven lengths, to make amends for a famous final-fence fall at the meeting in 2022; below par second at Punchestown but has won all six other completed chases, including the Irish Gold Cup.

Galvin (Ire)

9 b g Gold Well - Burren Moonshine (Moonax)
Gordon Elliott (Ire)   R A Bartlett
PLACINGS: 2/11111/1214/61462U-   RPR **167**+c

Starts	1st	2nd	3rd	4th	Win & Pl
26	13	5	-	3	£346,915

	10/22	Punc	3m Gd3 Ch good	£14,130
	12/21	Leop	3m Gd1 Ch good	£92,188
	10/21	Punc	3m Gd3 Ch good	£14,487
	3/21	Chel	3m6f Cls1 Nov Gd2 Ch gd-sft	£52,753
	10/20	Chel	3m1½f Cls2 Nov Ch good	£12,558
	10/20	Tipp	2m4f Nov Gd3 Ch good	£13,750
	8/20	Klny	2m5f Nov Ch yield	£6,250
	7/20	Klny	2m5f Ch yield	£6,250
	2/19	Ayr	2m Cls4 Nov Hdl soft	£4,094
	1/19	Navn	2m Nov Hdl yield	£8,879
	8/18	Prth	2m Cls4 Mdn Hdl good	£4,549
	7/18	Limk	2m NHF 4-7yo gd-yld	£5,996
	7/18	Rosc	2m NHF 4-7yo good	£5,451

Beat A Plus Tard to win the Savills Chase in 2021 but has struggled at the top level since then; looked regressive last term until running a big race on cross-country debut when second behind Delta Work at the Cheltenham Festival; unseated at the first in the Grand National.

Gentleman De Mee (Fr)

7 b g Saint Des Saints - Koeur De Mee (Video Rock)
Willie Mullins (Ire)   John P McManus
PLACINGS: 22/10/752111/U4614-   RPR **170**+c

Starts	1st	2nd	3rd	4th	Win & Pl
15	5	3	-	2	£212,476

	2/23	Leop	2m1f Gd1 Ch yield	£78,319
	4/22	Aint	2m Cls1 Nov Gd1 Ch gd-sft	£67,524
	3/22	Navn	2m Nov Gd3 Ch yield	£18,097
	2/22	Thur	2m½f Ch good	£5,702
	2/21	Naas	1m7½f Mdn Hdl soft	£6,321

Largely out of sorts last season but belatedly built on high-class novice form (had beaten Edwardstone in a Grade 1 at Aintree) when thrashing Blue Lord at Leopardstown for a second top-flight win; missed the Champion Chase through injury and disappointed at Punchestown.

Gentlemansgame

7 gr g Gentlewave - Grainne Ni Maille (Terimon)
Mouse Morris (Ire)   Robcour
PLACINGS: 1123/2071/31-   RPR **154**+c

Starts	1st	2nd	3rd	4th	Win & Pl
9	3	2	2	-	£82,727

	12/22	Leop	2m5f Ch soft	£8,676
	3/22	Thur	2m7f Hdl good	£5,950
	1/21	Cork	2m Mdn Hdl 4-5yo sft-hvy	£6,321

Impressive winner on chase debut at Leopardstown's Christmas meeting last season but missed the rest of the campaign; had been a smart staying hurdler, twice finishing second in Grade 1 novice hurdles in 2021 and progressing again in a light campaign the following season.

Gericault Roque (Fr)

7 b g Montmartre - Nijinska Delaroque (Lute Antique)
David Pipe   Prof Caroline Tisdall & Bryan Drew
PLACINGS: 4/2131/32222/53-   RPR **145**c

Starts	1st	2nd	3rd	4th	Win & Pl
11	2	5	3	-	£93,949

	3/21	Sand	2m Cls4 100-117 Cond Hdl Hcap gd-sft	£3,769
117	1/21	Plum	2m Cls4 Mdn Hdl soft	£3,769

Lightly raced chaser who hasn't won over fences in six runs but has gone close in some of the biggest staying handicaps; finished second four times in 2021-22, including in the Ultima at Cheltenham; fine third in last season's Coral Gold Cup but missed the rest of the campaign.

Gerri Colombe (Fr)

7 b g Saddler Maker - Ruse De Guerre (Cadoudal)
Gordon Elliott (Ire)   Robcour
PLACINGS: 1/11/11/11121-   RPR **166**+c

Starts	1st	2nd	3rd	4th	Win & Pl
9	8	1	-	-	£232,264

	4/23	Aint	3m1f Cls1 Nov Gd1 Ch gd-sft	£67,843
	2/23	Sand	2m4f Cls1 Nov Gd1 Ch gd-sft	£45,560
	12/22	Limk	2m3½f Nov Gd1 Ch sft-hvy	£49,580
	11/22	Fair	2m5f Ch soft	£5,454
	1/22	Thur	2m7f Nov Hdl yield	£7,189
	12/21	DRoy	2m4f Mdn Hdl soft	£6,848
	2/21	Naas	1m7½f NHF 4-7yo soft	£6,058
	1/21	Fair	2m NHF 5-7yo heavy	£5,268

Exciting young chaser who has won eight out of nine races under rules, with sole defeat coming when failing by a nose to reel in The Real Whacker in last season's Brown Advisory at Cheltenham; landed three Grade 1 novice chases either side of that and won brilliantly at Aintree on final run.

Gesskille (Fr)
7 b g Network - Nashkille (Roi De Rome)
Oliver Greenall & Josh Guerriero   The Nevers Racing Partnership
PLACINGS: F2/134P11/212269-P71   RPR **146+c**

Starts	1st	2nd	3rd	4th	Win & Pl
23	7	6	3	1	£232,115
9/23	Autl	2m6f List Ch v soft			£48,850
6/22	Autl	2m6f List Ch 5-6yo v soft			£32,269
4/22	Kemp	2m4¹/₂f Cls5 Am Hunt Ch good			£2,567
3/22	Ludl	3m Cls4 Am Hunt Ch soft			£3,811
6/21	Toul	2m1¹/₂f Hdl 5yo soft			£9,000
6/20	Diep	2m1¹/₂f Ch 4yo soft			£8,705
9/19	Claf	2m1f Hdl 3yo v soft			£8,649

French recruit who flourished over the Grand National fences last season, finishing second in the Grand Sefton and the Becher; disappointing ninth in the Topham later in the campaign; yet to show same form over regulation fences, though did win two hunter chases in 2022.

Gin Coco (Fr)
7 b g Cokoriko - Qlementine (Video Rock)
Harry Fry   David's Partnership
PLACINGS: 22/1/2120-   RPR **142+h**

Starts	1st	2nd	3rd	4th	Win & Pl
7	2	4	-	-	£44,084
10/22	NAbb	2m1f Cls4 Nov Hdl 4-6yo good			£4,520
3/22	Font	2m1¹/₂f Cls4 Mdn Hdl good			£5,827

Lightly raced hurdler who continued to show plenty of promise in a light campaign last season, notably when second in the Greatwood at Cheltenham; had also finished second in a big 2m handicap at Punchestown but disappointed when well backed for the County.

Giovinco (Ire)
6 b g Walk In The Park - Whyalla (Bandari)
Lucinda Russell   The Young Ones
PLACINGS: 5F/1111-   RPR **146+h**

Starts	1st	2nd	3rd	4th	Win & Pl
3	3	-	-	-	£22,275
4/23	Prth	3m Cls1 Nov List gd-sft			£13,099
3/23	Carl	2m3¹/₂f Cls4 Nov Hdl heavy			£4,629
3/23	Ayr	2m4¹/₂f Cls4 Nov Hdl good			£4,547

Point-to-point winner who began under rules only last March but quickly reeled off a hat-trick; took a huge leap forward when winning a Listed novice hurdle at Perth by 12 lengths; should make a fine chaser but could stick to hurdles for a while yet.

Givega (Fr)
7 b g Authorized - Sivega (Robin Des Champs)
Gary Moore   Ashley Head
PLACINGS: 1/11P1P-   RPR **135+h**

Starts	1st	2nd	3rd	4th	Win & Pl
5	3	-	-	-	£15,248
2/23	Sand	2m Cls4 Nov Hdl gd-sft			£5,446
12/22	Font	2m1¹/₂f Cls4 Nov Hdl gd-sft			£4,901
11/22	Ling	2m Cls4 Nov Hdl soft			£4,901

Held in very high regard and went some way to justifying the faith with three easy wins in novice hurdles last season; twice pulled up when favourite in much stronger company, including in the Imperial Cup at Sandown, and subsequently found to have bled from the nose both times.

Good Land (Fr)
7 b g Blue Bresil - Unique Star (Khalkevi)
Barry Connell (Ire)   Barry Connell
PLACINGS: 2/1U114-   RPR **148h**

Starts	1st	2nd	3rd	4th	Win & Pl
6	3	1	-	1	£99,317
2/23	Leop	2m6f Nov Gd1 Hdl yield			£78,319
12/22	Leop	2m4f Mdn Hdl soft			£7,437
10/22	Wxfd	2m¹/₂f NHF heavy			£4,958

Quickly developed into a smart novice hurdler last season and won a 2m6f Grade 1 at Leopardstown on just his second completed run over hurdles (had unseated at the first on debut); disappointing fourth in the Ballymore, with jockey blaming soft ground; set to go novice chasing.

Good Risk At All (Fr)
7 ch g No Risk At All - Sissi Land (Grey Risk)
Sam Thomas   Walters Plant Hire
PLACINGS: 211/22216/1670-   RPR **143+h**

Starts	1st	2nd	3rd	4th	Win & Pl
12	4	-	-	-	£79,667
137	10/22	Carl	2m4f Cls2 122-146 Hdl Hcap heavy		£17,690
127	2/22	Asct	2m3¹/₂f Cls2 121-144 Hdl Hcap soft		£26,164
	2/21	Newb	2m¹/₂f Cls1 List NHF 4-6yo gd-sft		£11,390
	11/20	Chel	2m¹/₂f Cls1 List NHF 4-6yo soft		£10,251

Looked a future star when winning Listed bumpers at Cheltenham and Newbury but has delivered only sporadically in two light campaigns over hurdles; hacked up at Carlisle first time out last term to add to valuable Ascot win but came up short in top handicaps.

Good Time Jonny (Ire)
8 b g Shirocco - Shaylejon (Old Vic)
Tony Martin (Ire)   A Shiels, Donal Gavigan & Niall Reilly
PLACINGS: 4/95F316119/P403014-   RPR **148+h**

Starts	1st	2nd	3rd	4th	Win & Pl
22	5	1	3	3	£144,371
142	3/23	Chel	3m Cls1 Gd3 121-147 Hdl Hcap soft		£56,270
129	2/22	Leop	3m 116-142 Hdl Hcap yield		£49,580
120	12/21	Leop	2m4f Nov 105-126 Hdl Hcap yld-sft		£13,170
111	10/21	Gowr	2m4f 107-128 Hdl Hcap good		£8,429
	1/20	Muss	1m7¹/₂f Cls4 NHF 4-6yo good		£3,249

Has won valuable 3m handicap hurdles in each of the last two seasons, bouncing back to form by winning last season's Pertemps Final at Cheltenham; had done little in between other than a distant third to qualify at Leopardstown; fair fourth at Aintree on final run.

Goshen (Fr)

7 b g Authorized - Hyde (Poliglote)
Gary Moore Steven Packkham

PLACINGS: U/018/547311/312352- RPR **159**h

Starts	1st	2nd	3rd	4th	Win & Pl
19	7	2	3	1	£221,100
11/22	Asct	2m3½f Cls1 Gd2 Hdl good			£56,950
2/22	Winc	1m7f Cls1 Gd2 Hdl soft			£39,865
2/22	Sand	2m Cls1 List Hdl gd-sft			£17,085
2/21	Winc	1m7½f Cls1 Gd2 Hdl heavy			£21,628
1/20	Asct	1m7½f Cls3 Hdl 4yo heavy			£7,018
12/19	Sand	2m Cls2 Hdl 3yo soft			£12,512
11/19	Font	2m1½f Cls4 Hdl 3yo soft			£4,094

Still most famous for agonising final-flight exit in the 2020 Triumph Hurdle but has since confirmed himself a smart hurdler, winning three times at Grade 2 level; didn't take to fences last season but won the Ascot Hurdle and was second in the Long Walk; must go right-handed.

Gowel Road (Ire)

7 b/br g Flemensfirth - Hollygrove Samba (Accordion)
Nigel Twiston Davies Options O Syndicate

PLACINGS: 24110/61327/21- RPR **145**+c

Starts	1st	2nd	3rd	4th	Win & Pl
12	4	3	1	1	£69,374
146	10/22	Asct	2m3f Cls3 Nov 146-157 Ch Hcap gd-sft		£9,614
134	11/21	Chel	2m5f Cls3 113-136 Hdl Hcap good		£13,070
	2/21	Newb	2m½f Cls3 Nov Hdl gd-sft		£5,913
122	1/21	Newb	2m1½f Cls4 110-122 Hdl Hcap heavy		£3,769

Useful three-time hurdles winner who looked to be going the right way in two runs over fences early last season only to miss the rest of the campaign through injury; beaten favourite first time out but got off the mark at Ascot,

albeit when left clear two out (might have won anyway).

Grangeclare West (Ire)

7 b g Presenting - Hayabusa (Sir Harry Lewis)
Willie Mullins (Ire) Cheveley Park Stud

PLACINGS: 1/1/1561- RPR **147**+h

Starts	1st	2nd	3rd	4th	Win & Pl
5	3	-	-	-	£26,244
4/23	Punc	2m4f Hdl yield			£10,442
11/22	Navn	2m4f Mdn Hdl soft			£7,437
5/21	Punc	2m1½f NHF 4-7yo soft			£5,268

£430,000 purchase who didn't quite match lofty expectations in novice hurdles last season; twice came up short at Grade 1 level having been sent off favourite on the first occasion; won well back in calmer waters at Punchestown; could do better over fences.

Greaneteen (Fr)

9 b g Great Pretender - Manson Teene (Mansonnien)
Paul Nicholls Chris Giles

PLACINGS: 4/12341/41251/12333- RPR **170**+c

Starts	1st	2nd	3rd	4th	Win & Pl
24	10	3	5	3	£552,804
168	11/22	Extr	2m1½f Cls1 Gd2 148-168 Ch Hcap good		£47,552
	4/22	Sand	1m7½f Cls1 Gd1 Ch good		£92,192
	12/21	Sand	1m7½f Cls1 Gd1 Ch gd-sft		£85,425
	4/21	Sand	1m7½f Cls1 Gd1 Ch good		£65,493
151	11/20	Extr	2m1½f Cls1 Gd2 138-158 Ch Hcap good		£32,329
	2/20	Fknm	2m½f Cls3 Nov Ch soft		£8,058
138	2/20	Muss	2m Cls3 124-140 Ch Hcap gd-sft		£13,256
132	12/19	Asct	2m1f Cls3 Nov 119-132 Ch Hcap heavy		£10,007
	1/19	Font	2m1½f Cls4 Nov Hdl gd-sft		£4,094
	1/19	Extr	2m2½f Cls4 Mdn Hdl gd-sft		£4,549

Three-time Grade 1 winner, with all those wins

coming at Sandown; began last season with a good win in the Haldon Gold Cup but no match for Edwardstone when chasing a Tingle Creek repeat; well below par subsequently, including when beaten at 1-2 in the Game Spirit.

Grey Dawning (Ire)
6 gr g Flemensfirth - Lady Wagtail (Milan)
Dan Skelton   Robert Kirkland
PLACINGS: 11/2111F-   RPR **143+**h

Starts	1st	2nd	3rd	4th	Win & Pl
7	5	1	-	-	£54,891
123	1/23 Wwck	2m5f Cls1 Nov Gd2 Hdl heavy			£31,470
	12/22 Kemp	2m5f Cls3 118-137 Hdl Hcap soft			£11,110
	12/22 Extr	2m½f Cls4 Nov Hdl 4-6yo gd-sft			£4,629
	3/22 Weth	2m Cls5 NHF 4-6yo heavy			£2,722
	12/21 Weth	2m Cls5 NHF 4-6yo soft			£2,451

Very useful novice hurdler; won three times to add to two bumper victories, culminating in a smooth victory in a Grade 2 at Warwick; expected to appreciate step up to 3m but fell five out in the Sefton before stamina could be tested.

Grey Diamond (Fr)
9 b g Gris De Gris - Diamond Of Diana (Kapgarde)
Gordon Elliott (Ire)   Walters Plant Hire
PLACINGS: 31233/3215/247/3F17-   RPR **148+**c

Starts	1st	2nd	3rd	4th	Win & Pl
24	8	3	5	3	£57,060
135	3/23 Hayd	2m½f Cls3 124-135 Ch Hcap soft			£8,450
128	3/21 Sand	1m7½f Cls3 Nov 128-147 Ch Hcap good			£7,190
120	9/19 Prth	2m Cls4 100-120 Hdl Hcap heavy			£5,588
	4/19 Chep	2m Cls5 Mdn Hdl good			£3,119
	5/18 Ffos	2m Cls5 NHF 4-6yo good			£2,599

Interesting new recruit for Gordon Elliott after producing a career-best effort for Sam Thomas on his penultimate run last season, winning a 2m handicap chase at Haydock; better than bare form when seventh in the Red Rum at Aintree after a bad mistake at the last.

Gust Of Wind (Fr)
4 br g Great Pretender - Rafale Pearl (Verbier)
Willie Mullins (Ire)   Hollywood Syndicate & Barnane Stud
PLACINGS: 1543-   RPR **137**h

Starts	1st	2nd	3rd	4th	Win & Pl
4	1	-	1	1	£34,092
	9/22 Autl	2m2f Hdl 3yo v soft			£20,874

Didn't add to hurdles debut win in France following move to Willie Mullins last season but was very highly tried; did best when fourth (best of the geldings) in the Triumph Hurdle; failed to build on that when only third in a Grade 2 at Fairyhouse.

Gowel Road: had the makings of a smart chaser early last season before injury intervened

GUIDE TO THE JUMPS 2023-24

Ha D'Or (Fr)
6 b g Nidor - Rosewort (Network)
Willie Mullins (Ire)   Mrs S Ricci
PLACINGS: 135/2132/21425F-   RPR **148+**c

Starts	1st	2nd	3rd	4th	Win & Pl
13	3	4	2	1	£53,099
	12/22 Fair	2m5f Nov Ch yld-sft			£10,908
	1/22 Fair	2m Mdn Hdl gd-yld			£6,197
	7/20 Seno	1m3½f NHF 3yo soft			£4,534

Useful novice chaser last season; won well first time out at Fairyhouse and finished a good second in a Grade 3 at Navan; out of his depth in the Arkle at Cheltenham but was just 11-10 at Punchestown on handicap debut when falling around halfway.

Haddex Des Obeaux (Fr)
6 b g
Gary Moore
PLACINGS: 31501/21/U211-   RPR **154**c

Starts	1st	2nd	3rd	4th	Win & Pl
11	5	2	1	-	£67,893
136	1/23 Wwck	2m Cls2 122-147 Ch Hcap heavy			£20,812
130	12/22 Donc	2m½f Cls3 Nov 119-138 Ch Hcap good			£6,535
120	10/21 Font	2m3f Cls3 120-132 Hdl Hcap soft			£5,228
	4/21 Autl	2m1½f Hdl 4yo v soft			£19,304
	9/20 Chat	1m5f NHF 3yo soft			£5,720

Exciting youngster who improved rapidly when sent chasing last season; had got off the mark in Britain on second run over hurdles before missing a year; progressed with every run last term and signed off with a 19-length win in a four-runner 2m handicap at Warwick; raised 10lb.

Halka Du Tabert (Fr)
6 b m Balko - Naska (Grand Tresor)
Gordon Elliott (Ire)   Kenneth Alexander
PLACINGS: 1/11337-   RPR **132**h

Starts	1st	2nd	3rd	4th	Win & Pl
5	2	-	2	-	£25,101
	12/22 Naas	2m Mdn Hdl soft			£6,197
	11/22 Naas	2m NHF yld-sft			£5,454

Very useful mare who finished third in the mares' novice hurdle at the Cheltenham Festival; had won a bumper and maiden hurdle before a close third in a strong Grade 3 novice; disappointed at Fairyhouse on final run; likely to go novice chasing.

Hansard (Ire)
5 b g The Gurkha - Quiet Down (Quiet American)
Gary Moore   Noel Fehily Racing Syndicates
PLACINGS: 4361/1154-   RPR **145**h

Starts	1st	2nd	3rd	4th	Win & Pl
8	3	-	1	2	£22,471
	1/23 Plum	2m Cls4 Nov Hdl soft			£4,225
	12/22 Hntg	2m Cls4 Nov Hdl good			£4,901
	4/22 Baln	1m7½f NHF 4yo gd-yld			£5,206

Useful novice hurdler last season; won twice in

modest company only to run no sort of race when favourite for a Grade 2 at Kempton; bounced back with a huge run at 40-1 in a Grade 1 at Aintree, travelling very strongly before finishing a close fourth.

Happygolucky (Ire)

9 br g Jeremy - Mydadsabishop (Bishop Of Cashel)
Kim Bailey   Lady Dulverton

PLACINGS: 2/1334/12121/309-   RPR **157**+c

Starts	1st	2nd	3rd	4th	Win & Pl
12	4	2	3	1	£90,735
149	4/21 Aint	3m1f Cls1 Gd3 128-154 Ch Hcap gd-sft			£31,538
	12/20 Chel	3m1½f Cls2 Nov Ch gd-sft			£12,974
	10/20 Strf	2m5f Cls4 Ch gd-sft			£4,289
	10/19 Strf	2m6f Cls4 Mdn Hdl soft			£4,549

Smart novice chaser in 2020-21 (second in the Ultima before winning at Aintree) but then missed 18 months; showed he retains his ability with a four-length third behind L'Homme Presse in the Rehearsal Chase last term but disappointed in two further runs at Cheltenham.

Harper's Brook (Ire)

7 b g Ask - Un Jour D Ete (Dano-Mast)
Ben Pauling   The Megsons

PLACINGS: 13/14F21/215P2-   RPR **140**+c

Starts	1st	2nd	3rd	4th	Win & Pl
11	3	2	1	1	£36,455
130	11/22 Bang	2m4½f Cls3 Nov 127-138 Ch Hcap heavy			£7,080
	4/22 Ffos	2m4f Cls4 Nov Hdl good			£5,655
	10/21 Carl	2m4f Cls4 Nov Hdl soft			£4,085

Useful and progressive novice chaser last season

despite managing only a sole win at Bangor; twice disappointed at Cheltenham, including when pulled up in the Ultima, but bounced back when unlucky not to win a good novice handicap at Sandown (pulled himself up on the run-in).

Haut En Couleurs (Fr)

6 b g Saint Des Saints - Sanouva (Muhtathir)
Willie Mullins (Ire)   Mrs J Donnelly

PLACINGS: 13/31F6/54F254-8   RPR **163**c

Starts	1st	2nd	3rd	4th	Win & Pl
13	2	1	2	2	£70,120
	12/21 Leop	2m1f Ch gd-yld			£9,219
	10/20 Autl	2m2f Hdl 3yo heavy			£18,305

Hasn't lived up to expectations since a winning chase debut in 2021 but was set to land a Grade 2 at Thurles last season when falling at the last; struggled in Grade 1 races and gradually dropped in class, running well in handicaps when fifth at Cheltenham and fourth in the Topham.

Heltenham (Fr)

6 b g Masked Marvel - Souris Blanche (Saint Des Saints)
Dan Skelton   N W Lake

PLACINGS: 012032/22111F-   RPR **142**+c

Starts	1st	2nd	3rd	4th	Win & Pl
12	4	4	1	-	£58,798
123	3/23 Newb	2m4f Cls2 123-140 Ch Hcap soft			£20,812
116	2/23 Ffos	2m3½f Cls4 Nov 94-120 Ch Hcap gd-sft			£8,344
109	12/22 Newc	2m4f Cls4 105-115 Ch Hcap soft			£10,562
	7/21 Gran	1m7½f NHF 4-5yo soft			£4,464

Big improver when sent chasing last season

Hewick: thoroughly likeable chaser who can always be relied upon to step up to the occasion

having begun handicapping off a very low base; won three times and comfortably handled a sharp rise in class when completing the hat-trick at Newbury; favourite for the Silver Trophy at Cheltenham on final run but fell early.

Hercule Du Seuil (Fr)
6 br g Saddler Maker - Cibelle Du Seuil (Saint Des Saints)
Willie Mullins (Ire) John P McManus
PLACINGS: 2/8/11P1-2111 RPR **157+**c

Starts	1st	2nd	3rd	4th	Win & Pl
10	6	2	-	-	£81,017
8/23	Gway	2m2f Nov Gd1 Ch gd-yld			£20,885
7/23	Klny	2m1f Nov Ch gd-yld			£8,354
5/23	Baln	2m1f Ch good			£5,743
4/23	Fair	2m Nov Gd2 Hdl yield			£20,885
11/22	Navn	2m Nov Gd3 Hdl yield			£14,130
10/22	Tipp	2m Mdn Hdl gd-yld			£4,958

Prolific youngster who won three out of four novice hurdles last season and moved to the same record over fences in tremendous fashion at Galway this summer; bit to prove on winter ground having been pulled up on soft in last year's Royal Bond and subsequently given a break.

Hermes Allen (Fr)
6 b g Poliglote - Une Destine (Assessor)
Paul Nicholls Sir A Ferguson G Mason J Hales & J Diver
PLACINGS: 31/11163- RPR **150+**h

Starts	1st	2nd	3rd	4th	Win & Pl
5	3	-	1	-	£79,135
12/22	Newb	2m4½f Cls1 Nov Gd1 Hdl soft			£34,170
11/22	Chel	2m5f Cls1 Nov Gd2 Hdl good			£28,475
10/22	Strf	2m6f Cls4 Mdn Hdl good			£4,085

Disappointed in the spring but had looked an outstanding winner of the Challow Hurdle, completing a hat-trick from Cheltenham Festival winner You Wear It Well (pair clear); sixth in the Ballymore and only slightly better when third at Aintree (favourite both times).

Hewick (Ire)
8 b g Virtual - Ballyburn Rose (Oscar)
John Joseph Hanlon (Ire) T J McDonald
PLACINGS: 124P2121P1/21U1F1-40 RPR **168+**c

Starts	1st	2nd	3rd	4th	Win & Pl
33	9	6	4	3	£470,313
	4/23	Sand	2m6½f Cls1 Gd2 Ch gd-sft		£46,364
	10/22	Fars	2m5f Gd1 Hdl yield		£111,111
155	7/22	Gway	2m6½f 143-160 Ch Hcap good		£133,866
149	4/22	Sand	3m5f Cls1 Gd3 128-154 Ch Hcap good		£90,299
142	10/21	Sedg	3m5f Cls2 116-142 Ch Hcap good		£14,308
118	9/21	List	3m 107-132 Hdl Hcap good		£8,429
	6/21	Clon	2m7f Ch good		£5,795
102	9/20	Navn	2m6f 80-102 Hdl Hcap good		£5,000
94	9/20	Kbgn	3m1f 80-95 Hdl Hcap yield		£4,500

High-class staying chaser who has won a string of big races over the last 18 months, even as far afield as last year's American Grand National; running a big race when falling two out in the Cheltenham Gold Cup last spring; preference for good ground might limit opportunities.

Hiddenvalley Lake (Ire)
6 ch g Sholokhov - Coming Home (Exit To Nowhere)
Henry de Bromhead (Ire) Robcour
PLACINGS: C/1129- RPR **142**h

Starts	1st	2nd	3rd	4th	Win & Pl
4	2	1	-	-	£28,195
12/22	Cork	3m Nov Gd3 Hdl yld-sft			£14,874
11/22	Naas	2m3f Mdn Hdl yld-sft			£7,437

£200,000 purchase who looked a future star early last season but didn't quite go on as expected; hacked up in a Grade 3 at Cork but beaten at 8-13 in the same grade at Clonmel; still sent off in single figures for the Albert Bartlett at Cheltenham but managed only ninth.

High Class Hero
6 ch g Sulamani - Mil Ft Une Nui Flo (Turgeon)
Willie Mullins (Ire) Sullivan Bloodstock & Neill Hughes & P Cro
PLACINGS: 2/P1/111 RPR **132+**h

Starts	1st	2nd	3rd	4th	Win & Pl
3	3	-	-	-	£24,539
9/23	List	2m4f Nov Hdl yld-sft			£9,659
8/23	Gway	2m5f Mdn Hdl gd-yld			£8,876
6/23	List	2m4f NHF gd-yld			£6,004

Given plenty of time after moving to Willie Mullins following a point-to-point win in 2021 and made a bright start this summer; won a bumper at Listowel before switching to hurdles to win a 2m5f maiden at Galway; looks a strong stayer and should get at least 3m.

Highstakesplayer (Ire)
7 b g Ocovango - Elivette (Arvico)
Tom Lacey Jerry Hinds & Ashley Head
PLACINGS: 325/7843112/11- RPR **132+**c

Starts	1st	2nd	3rd	4th	Win & Pl
12	4	2	2	1	£32,667
121	11/22	Hrfd	2m5f Cls4 100-121 Ch Hcap gd-sft		£8,605
114	10/22	Hrfd	2m5f Cls4 Nov 105-121 Ch Hcap good		£8,169
108	3/22	Tntn	2m3f Cls5 79-108 Hdl Hcap soft		£3,431
101	3/22	Sthl	2m4½f Cls5 79-107 Hdl Hcap gd-sft		£6,208

Missed much of last season through injury but had looked a potentially smart chaser when winning first two races over fences; had progressed from a very low base over hurdles and built on that again when twice winning by wide margins at Hereford; still feasibly handicapped.

Hitman (Fr)
7 b g Falco - Tercah Girl (Martaline)
Paul Nicholls Mason, Hogarth, Ferguson & Done
PLACINGS: 1/12F13/2232/21P236- RPR **165**c

Starts	1st	2nd	3rd	4th	Win & Pl
18	4	7	3	-	£260,883
11/22	Hayd	2m5½f Cls2 Ch soft			£26,015
3/21	Newb	2m4f Cls3 Nov Ch good			£7,798
11/20	Ffos	2m Cls3 Ch soft			£7,791
1/20	Pau	2m1½f Hdl 4yo v soft			£12,203

Very smart chaser but has become a source of

155

frustration, finishing second or third seven times in the last two seasons; beaten at odds-on in last season's Denman Chase and subsequently dropped back in trip, finishing third in the Ryanair Chase only to flop at Aintree.

Hollow Games (Ire)

7 b g Beat Hollow - I'm Grand (Raise A Grand)
Gordon Elliott (Ire)   Bective Stud

PLACINGS: 1/11/11333/514P4-3   RPR **143** +c

Starts	1st	2nd	3rd	4th	Win & Pl
13	5	-	4	2	£94,499

11/22	Navn	2m1f Ch yield	£7,685
11/21	Navn	2m4f Nov Gd3 Hdl good	£14,487
10/21	DRoy	2m6½f Mdn Hdl soft	£6,848
12/20	Leop	2m NHF 4-7yo soft	£5,000
11/20	Punc	2m NHF 4yo heavy	£5,000

Lightly raced chaser who has quickly made up into a very useful handicapper, finishing third in this summer's Galway Plate in just his fifth chase having also made the frame in a big handicap at Punchestown; did well in similar races over hurdles, finishing third in the Martin Pipe in 2022.

Home By The Lee (Ire)

8 b g Fame And Glory - Going For Home (Presenting)
Joseph O'Brien (Ire)   Sean O'Driscoll

PLACINGS: /113P10/0P226/0115P-   RPR **163** h

Starts	1st	2nd	3rd	4th	Win & Pl
22	8	3	1	-	£187,740

12/22	Leop	3m Gd1 Hdl soft	£74,370
11/22	Navn	2m4f Gd2 Hdl yield	£18,097
2/21	Naas	2m4½f Nov 118-139 Ch Hcap soft	£21,071
11/20	Cork	2m4f Nov Gd3 Ch soft	£17,500
10/20	Limk	2m6f Ch soft	£7,750
1/20	Fair	2m4f Mdn Hdl yield	£6,511
6/19	Rosc	2m NHF 4yo good	£6,659
5/19	Klny	2m1f NHF 4yo good	£5,827

139

Progressed into a high-class staying hurdler last season; had come up short back over hurdles two seasons ago after losing his way over fences but won the Lismullen Hurdle and Christmas Hurdle last term; beaten less than four lengths when fifth in the Stayers' Hurdle.

Howlingmadmurdock (Ire)

6 b g Soldier Of Fortune - Bell Storm (Glacial Storm)
Tom Lacey   Valueracingclub.co.uk

PLACINGS: 1/1215-   RPR **141** h

Starts	1st	2nd	3rd	4th	Win & Pl
5	3	1	-	-	£17,463

3/23	Sand	2m4f Cls4 Nov 94-119 Hdl Hcap soft	£5,281
12/22	Plum	2m Cls4 Nov Hdl soft	£4,901
2/22	Font	2m1½f Cls5 NHF 4-6yo soft	£2,614

118

Useful and progressive novice hurdler last season; won twice in Class 4 company, most notably a novice handicap at Sandown; coped well with a sharp rise in trip and grade when fifth in the Sefton at Aintree.

Howlingmadmurdock (nearest): talented novice hurdler last season

RACING POST

Hugos New Horse (Fr)
6 b g *Coastal Path - Pour Le Meilleur (Video Rock)*
Paul Nicholls   The Stewart Family

PLACINGS: 19/2111131-   RPR **133+**h

Starts	1st	2nd	3rd	4th	Win & Pl
9	6	1	1	-	£46,008
	4/23	Ayr	2m4½f Cls3 Nov Hdl gd-sft		£8,168
	2/23	MRas	2m4½f Cls3 Nov Hdl 4-7yo gd-sft		£7,624
	1/23	Extr	2m½f Cls4 Nov Hdl heavy		£3,961
117	12/22	Sand	2m Cls4 Nov 95-117 Hdl Hcap soft		£6,154
	11/22	Winc	1m7f Cls3 Nov Hdl 4-6yo gd-fm		£7,624
	10/21	Worc	2m Cls5 NHF 4-6yo soft		£1,906

Prolific novice hurdler last season who won five out of seven races, albeit never above Class 3 level; solid third in the EBF Final at Sandown and got back to winning ways in good style at Ayr.

Hunters Yarn (Ire)
6 b g *Fame And Glory - Full Of Birds (Epervier Bleu)*
Willie Mullins (Ire)   Simon Munir & Isaac Souede

PLACINGS: 31/411/31102-   RPR **143+**

Starts	1st	2nd	3rd	4th	Win & Pl
10	5	1	2	1	£52,016
	2/23	Navn	2m Nov List Hdl gd-yld		£14,358
	1/23	Naas	2m Mdn Hdl soft...................................		£7,832
	4/22	Fair	2m NHF 4-7yo yield................................		£9,916
	3/22	Limk	2m NHF 5-7yo sft-hvy		£5,454
	3/21	Thur	2m½f NHF 4yo yield		£5,268

Useful novice hurdler last season; won twice to add to three bumper victories, most notably in a Listed novice at Navan; didn't build on that in the spring, failing to land a blow when 11-2 for the Martin Pipe at Cheltenham and a beaten favourite in a Grade 2 at Fairyhouse.

I Am Maximus (Fr)
7 b g *Authorized - Polysheba (Poliglote)*
Willie Mullins (Ire)   John P McManus

PLACINGS: 1/3124/22441-   RPR **160+**c

Starts	1st	2nd	3rd	4th	Win & Pl
10	3	3	1	3	£285,080
149	4/23	Fair	3m5f 134-160 Ch Hcap soft......................		£238,938
	12/21	Newb	2m½f Cls4 Mdn Hdl gd-sft		£4,085
	10/20	Chel	2m½f Cls2 NHF 4-6yo soft......................		£8,758

Won last season's Irish Grand National as a maiden over fences, grinding out an attritional race having run in snatches and needed early reminders; had been progressive in top novice company, most recently finishing fourth in the Brown Advisory on first run over 3m.

I Like To Move It
6 b g *Trans Island - Nobratinetta (Celtic Swing)*
Nigel Twiston-Davies   Anne-Marie & Jamie Shepperd

PLACINGS: 1129/111520/16165-   RPR **164+**h

Starts	1st	2nd	3rd	4th	Win & Pl
15	7	2	-	-	£211,754
	2/23	Winc	1m7f Cls1 Gd2 Hdl good.........................		£41,608
142	11/22	Chel	2m½f Cls1 Gd3 124-142 Hdl Hcap good......		£56,270
	11/21	Chel	2m½f Cls1 Nov Gd2 Hdl good.................		£30,890
	10/21	Chel	2m½f Cls2 Hdl 4yo good........................		£20,812
	10/21	Worc	2m Cls4 Nov Hdl 4-6yo gd-sft..................		£4,629
	12/20	Winc	1m7½f Cls5 NHF 3yo soft......................		£2,274
	11/20	Aint	2m1f Cls4 NHF 3yo gd-sft......................		£3,249

Second best two-mile hurdler in Britain last season on Racing Post Ratings; did brilliantly to win the Greatwood under 12st and romped home in the Kingwell, both on good ground; twice disappointed on soft and jumping fell apart in the Aintree Hurdle on final run.

I Will Be Baie (Fr)
5 gr g *Crillon - Passion Du Berlais (Poliglote)*
Willie Mullins (Ire)   Roaringwater Syndicate

PLACINGS: 1/2d12   RPR **121+**b

Starts	1st	2nd	3rd	4th	Win & Pl
3	1	2	-	-	£12,743
	8/23	Gway	2m2f NHF gd-yld		£8,876

Bought for £150,000 after winning sole point-to-point in 2022 and made a promising start in bumpers this summer; demoted to second after being first past the post on debut at Punchestown and made amends with a comfortable win at Galway.

Iberico Lord (Fr)
5 b g *Cokoriko - Valcelita (Voix Du Nord)*
Nicky Henderson   John P McManus

PLACINGS: 16F12-   RPR **128**h

Starts	1st	2nd	3rd	4th	Win & Pl
5	2	1	-	-	£33,799
	4/23	Strf	2m½f Cls4 Nov Hdl heavy		£3,812
	5/22	Le L	1m7f NHF 4yo soft................................		£5,672

Good chasing type who disappointed initially last season but came good in the spring following wind surgery; got off the mark over hurdles with a narrow win at Stratford and stepped up significantly with a half-length second in a valuable novice handicap at Sandown.

RACING POST

Now in its 13th year, the *Racing Post Annual* is firmly established as the perfect Christmas gift for any horseracing fan.

This exciting review of 2023 from the Racing Post, the nation's voice of horse racing, has 208 colour pages packed with the best stories of the racing year and is beautifully illustrated with stunning images.

Racing Post's top writers look back on the best of the Flat and jumps seasons, the big names both equine and human, the moments to treasure and unusual stories of the year; plus there's a look forward at the top prospects for 2024. With a glittering line-up, this large-format, magazine-style publication is a must for every horse racing fan.

NEW SHOP WEBSITE LIVE NOW!
www.racingpost.com/shop

RACING POST

Iceo (Fr)
5 b g *Coastal Path - Rocroi (Robin Des Champs)*
Paul Nicholls — Chris Giles
PLACINGS: 1144/214- — RPR **143** +h

Starts	1st	2nd	3rd	4th	Win & Pl
7	3	1	-	3	£91,341
132	3/23 Sand	2m Cls1 Gd3 121-143 Hdl Hcap heavy............			£56,270
	12/21 Kemp	2m Cls2 Hdl 3yo soft.....................................			£10,406
	8/21 Diep	2m1f Hdl 3yo soft..			£9,000

Very lightly raced hurdler who won last season's Imperial Cup; hadn't built on runaway British debut win in two further runs in 2022 but followed up a promising return last term with a hugely impressive victory at Sandown; failed to stay 2m4f when favourite back there on final run.

Il Etait Temps (Fr)
5 gr g *Jukebox Jury - Une Des Sources (Dom Alco)*
Willie Mullins (Ire) — Hollywood Syndicate & Barnane Stud
PLACINGS: 5/235/412152- — RPR **157** +h

Starts	1st	2nd	3rd	4th	Win & Pl
10	2	3	1	1	£144,490
	2/23 Leop	2m Nov Gd1 Hdl yield............................			£78,319
	11/22 Thur	2m Mdn Hdl yld-sft..............................			£4,958

Very highly tried since joining Willie Mullins and finally landed a Grade 1 at Leopardstown last season when exploiting Facile Vega's below-par run; well beaten six times at the top level otherwise and fifth in the Triumph and Supreme at the last two Cheltenham Festivals.

GUIDE TO THE JUMPS 2023-24

Il Ridoto (Fr)
6 b g Kapgarde - L'Exploratrice (Trempolino)
Paul Nicholls Giles, Hogarth, Mason & McGoff

PLACINGS: 6611F2/31P383/4416P- RPR **154+c**

Starts	1st	2nd	3rd	4th	Win & Pl
17	4	1	3	2	£135,206
138	1/23	Chel	2m4½f Cls1 Gd3 128-154 Ch Hcap soft		£56,270
131	11/21	Newb	2m½f Cls2 130-145 Ch Hcap gd-sft		£20,812
	2/21	Pau	2m1½f Hdl 4yo heavy		£12,321
	1/21	Pau	2m1½f Hdl 4yo v soft		£12,732

Did well in top handicap chases last season and won at Cheltenham in January having twice made the frame in similar races earlier in the campaign, including the Paddy Power Gold Cup; raised 8lb and only sixth in the Plate before being pulled up in the Topham.

Impaire Et Passe (Fr)
5 b g Diamond Boy - Brune Ecossaise (Le Fou)
Willie Mullins (Ire) Simon Munir & Isaac Souede

PLACINGS: 1/1111- RPR **162+h**

Starts	1st	2nd	3rd	4th	Win & Pl
5	5	-	-	-	£171,489
	4/23	Punc	2m3½f Nov Gd1 Hdl yield		£65,265
	3/23	Chel	2m5f Cls1 Nov Gd1 Hdl soft		£75,965
	1/23	Punc	2m Nov Gd2 Hdl heavy		£19,058
	12/22	Naas	2m3f Mdn Hdl 4yo soft		£5,950
	3/22	Nanc	1m4½f NHF 4-5yo soft		£5,252

Last season's highest-rated novice hurdler on the strength of a hugely impressive win in the Ballymore at Cheltenham (below); twice won well over shorter trips at Punchestown either side of that; connections likely to consider a Champion Hurdle campaign but also has the look of a chaser.

161

Impervious (Ire)

7 b m Shantou - Blodge (Kalanisi)
Colm Murphy (Ire) — John P McManus

PLACINGS: 111565/11111-   RPR **162**+c

Starts	1st	2nd	3rd	4th	Win & Pl
11	8	-	-	-	£193,237
4/23	Punc	2m5f Gd2 Ch yield			£41,770
3/23	Chel	2m4½f Cls1 Gd2 Ch soft			£67,582
1/23	Punc	2m3½f Nov Gd3 Ch heavy			£19,071
12/22	Cork	2m½f Nov Gd2 Ch yld-sft			£21,071
10/22	Wxfd	2m Ch heavy			£5,702
10/21	DRoy	2m1f Nov Gd3 Hdl soft			£17,121
9/21	List	2m4f Nov Hdl gd-yld			£8,955
8/21	Cork	2m3f Mdn Hdl gd-yld			£7,638

Outstanding mare who went from strength to strength in winning all five chases last season; beat geldings in a Grade 3 novice before stepping into open mares' company to win at Cheltenham and Punchestown; could even be a Gold Cup horse.

Impose Toi (Fr)

5 b g It's Gino - Saraska D'Airy (Ungaro)
Nicky Henderson — John P McManus

PLACINGS: 11/212-1   RPR **128**+h

Starts	1st	2nd	3rd	4th	Win & Pl
6	4	2	-	-	£24,304
5/23	Ludl	2m5f Cls4 Nov Hdl good			£4,524
3/23	Extr	2m½f Cls4 Mdn Hdl good			£4,935
4/22	Le L	1m4f NHF 4yo soft			£6,303
3/22	Saum	2m NHF 4yo gd-sft			£4,202

Dual French bumper winner who could yet prove an exciting recruit for JP McManus despite a slightly underwhelming campaign over hurdles; won twice at very short odds in weak races and beaten when facing only slightly stiffer tasks; imposing horse with size and scope for fences.

Indeevar Bleu (Fr)

5 b g Blue Bresil - Ardissone (Martaline)
Olly Murphy — Mrs Diana L Whateley

PLACINGS: 1-   RPR **125**+b

Starts	1st	2nd	3rd	4th	Win & Pl
1	1	-	-	-	£2,722
3/23	Weth	2m Cls5 NHF 4-6yo soft			£2,722

Made a huge impression when winning sole bumper last season, hacking up by 12 lengths at Wetherby in March; out of a Listed-placed half-sister to high-class hurdler/chaser Al Ferof; exciting prospect for novice hurdles.

Indiana Dream (Fr)

5 b g Cokoriko - Tamise (Sleeping Car)
Willie Mullins (Ire) — John P McManus

PLACINGS: 1/1-   RPR **135**+h

Starts	1st	2nd	3rd	4th	Win & Pl
2	2	-	-	-	£13,198
1/23	Fair	2m4f Mdn Hdl soft			£6,265
2/22	Fntb	1m7f NHF 4yo v soft			£6,933

Ran only once last season but made a big impression when running away with a maiden hurdle at Fairyhouse by 15 lengths on New Year's Day over 2m4f, shaping like a strong

stayer; had been bought by JP McManus after also winning his sole bumper run in France.

Indiana Jones (Fr)
7 b g Blue Bresil - Matnie (Laveron)
Mouse Morris (Ire) Robcour
PLACINGS: 143P/22FFF/83431143- RPR **152**c

Starts	1st	2nd	3rd	4th	Win & Pl
18	3	3	4	3	£71,077
	3/23	Navn	2m Nov Gd3 Ch gd-yld £19,058
	2/23	Punc	2m Nov Ch yield..................................£11,487
	11/20	Cork	2m Mdn Hdl 4yo soft.............................£6,000

Took a long time to get the hang of fences (fell three times in a row in 2021-22) but progressed well as a second-season novice last term; won at Punchestown and Navan (2m Grade 3) and far from disgraced when third behind El Fabiolo on Grade 1 bow.

Inneston (Fr)
5 b g Doctor Dino - Robbe (Video Rock)
Gary Moore O S Harris
PLACINGS: 1/331221- RPR **129**h

Starts	1st	2nd	3rd	4th	Win & Pl
7	3	2	2	-	£41,080
	4/23	NAbb	2m1f Cls4 Nov Hdl soft...........................£4,955
111	2/23	Sand	2m4f Cls4 Nov 109-120 Hdl Hcap gd-sft.........£5,281
	10/21	Mans	1m3½f NHF 3yo gd-sft...........................£6,696

Useful novice hurdler last season; gained second win on final run at Newton Abbot but produced best form in novice handicaps, notably when second in the EBF Final at Sandown; had won at that track previously and finished second in another good race at Newbury.

Instit (Fr)
5 b m Saint Des Saints - Bonne Maman (Coastal Path)
Willie Mullins (Ire) Bruton Street
PLACINGS: 12/24421312-6 RPR **150**+c

Starts	1st	2nd	3rd	4th	Win & Pl
11	3	4	1	2	£72,713
	4/23	Fair	2m5½f Nov List Ch soft..........................£15,664
	2/23	Fair	2m5f Ch yield.....................................£7,310
	12/21	Pau	2m1½f Hdl 3yo heavy...........................£13,964

Progressive young mare who went chasing as a four-year-old last season and came of age during the spring; easily beat Allegorie De Vassy at Fairyhouse and finished in front of that rival again when second behind Impervious at Punchestown.

Inthepocket
6 b g Blue Bresil - Egretta Island (Heron Island)
Henry De Bromhead (Ire) John P McManus
PLACINGS: 1/11221- RPR **150**+h

Starts	1st	2nd	3rd	4th	Win & Pl
5	3	1	-	1	£112,196
	4/23	Aint	2m½f Cls1 Nov Gd1 Hdl gd-sft.................£56,270
	12/22	Naas	2m4f Nov Gd2 Hdl soft..........................£18,097
	10/22	Wxfd	2m Mdn Hdl heavy................................£5,454

Smart novice hurdler last season and took advantage of a more straightforward Grade 1 opportunity at Aintree after twice running well in defeat at that level; had finished fourth in the Supreme at Cheltenham; has won from 2m-2m4f; likely to go novice chasing.

Inthewaterside (Fr)
5 b g Jeu St. Eloi - Vared (Denham Red)
Paul Nicholls McNeill Family & G C Stevens
PLACINGS: 11- RPR **125**+b

Starts	1st	2nd	3rd	4th	Win & Pl
2	2	-	-	-	£7,624
	2/23	Sand	2m Cls3 NHF 4-5yo gd-sft........................£5,446
	12/22	Extr	2m1½f Cls5 NHF 4-6yo gd-sft....................£2,178

Looked a smart prospect when winning both bumpers last season; very green when getting off the mark at Exeter but looked much more professional when hacking up at Sandown; held in very high regard by trainer and already earmarked for the Challow Hurdle.

Into Overdrive
8 b g Court Cave - Lady Brig (Overbury)
Mark Walford Mrs Wendy Hamilton
PLACINGS: 2/441/5364111/121P- RPR **152**+c

Starts	1st	2nd	3rd	4th	Win & Pl
	26	6	1	1	2	£89,038
142	12/22	Weth	3m Cls1 Gd3 142-159 Ch gd-sft..............£28,475
132	10/22	Weth	2m3½f Cls1 Gd3 128-151 Ch Hcap gd-sft....£22,780
123	4/22	Prth	3m Cls3 Nov 104-123 Ch Hcap gd-sft..........£6,317
118	3/22	Hexm	2m4f Cls4 93-118 Ch Hcap gd-sft..............£5,119
112	3/22	Carl	2m5f Cls4 Nov 103-118 Ch Hcap gd-sft........£5,446
	3/21	Carl	2m3½f Cls4 Nov Hdl gd-sft......................£3,159

Hugely progressive during the last two seasons and made it five wins in six races when landing last season's Rowland Meyrick, with only defeat a close second behind L'Homme Presse in the Rehearsal; pulled up in the Ultima at Cheltenham on only subsequent run.

Impervious: unbeaten in five starts over fences last season

RACING POST

Irish Point (Fr)
5 gr g Joshua Tree - Burkina (Fragrant Mix)
Gordon Elliott (Ire)   Robcour

PLACINGS: 321/122411-   RPR **149**+h

Starts	1st	2nd	3rd	4th	Win & Pl
9	4	3	1	1	£140,206

4/23	Aint	2m4f Cls1 Nov Gd1 Hdl gd-sft	£56,270
3/23	Naas	1m7½f Nov Gd3 Hdl soft	£14,850
11/22	Cork	2m Mdn Hdl 4yo soft	£5,950
11/21	StCl	1m4½f Gd1 NHF 3yo heavy	£22,321

Smart novice hurdler last season who ran mainly at Grade 1 level and finally struck at Aintree, returning to the form that brought a head second to Marine Nationale in the Royal Bond; slightly disappointing in between but helped by confidence-boosting Grade 3 win at Naas.

Iroko (Fr)
5 b g Cokoriko - Boscraie (Martaline)
Oliver Greenall & Josh Guerriero   John P McManus

PLACINGS: 4244/1113-   RPR **146**h

Starts	1st	2nd	3rd	4th	Win & Pl
8	3	1	1	3	£81,426

138	3/23	Chel	2m4½f Cls2 126-145 Cond Hdl Hcap soft	£39,023
128	1/23	Weth	2m3½f Cls3 116-142 Hdl Hcap soft	£8,265
121	11/22	Weth	2m3½f Cls3 112-132 Hdl Hcap good	£5,609

Hugely progressive hurdler last season who completed a hat-trick of handicap victories by landing the Martin Pipe at Cheltenham; underlined quality and proved stamina for 3m when a fine third in the Sefton at Aintree; set to go novice chasing.

GUIDE TO THE JUMPS 2023-24

It's For Me (Fr)
5 ch g Jeu St Eloi - Ugoline (Dom Alco)
Willie Mullins (Ire)　　　　　　　Simon Munir & Isaac Souede
PLACINGS: 1/155-　　　　　　　　　　　　　RPR **130**b

Starts	1st	2nd	3rd	4th	Win & Pl
3	1	-	-	-	£9,396

1/23 Navn 2m NHF soft £5,482

Very useful bumper performer last season; won well at Navan on rules debut to go into the Champion Bumper at Cheltenham as a 6-1 shot and ran creditably in fifth; well below that level when beaten much further in the same position at Punchestown.

Iwilldoit
10 b g Flying Legend - Lyricist's Dream (Dreams End)
Sam Thomas　　　　　　　　　　　　　Diamond Racing
PLACINGS: 61612/91/6273/11/15-　　　　　　RPR **160**+c

Starts	1st	2nd	3rd	4th	Win & Pl
19	6	2	2	2	£186,310

147	1/23	Wwck	3m5f Cls1 Gd3 125-151 Ch Hcap heavy	£56,950
140	12/21	Chep	3m6½f Cls1 Gd3 140-166 Ch Hcap soft	£85,827
130	12/21	Chep	2m7½f Cls2 124-150 Ch Hcap gd-sft	£13,008
126	12/19	Kels	2m6½f Cls3 Nov 105-126 Ch Hcap soft	£11,826
113	3/19	Catt	3m1½f Cls4 107-122 Hdl Hcap soft	£4,159
103	1/19	Bang	2m7f Cls4 101-111 Hdl Hcap gd-sft	£4,094

Has a remarkable record in top staying handicaps despite very limited appearances; won the Welsh National in 2021 and the Classic Chase last term after more than a year out; didn't qualify for the Grand National (too inexperienced), instead finishing fifth under 12st in the Midlands National.

James Du Berlais (Fr)
7 ch g Muhtathir - King's Daughter (King's Theatre)
Willie Mullins (Ire)　　　　　　　Simon Munir & Isaac Souede
PLACINGS: 212/1212129/2/16643-　　　　　　RPR **155**+c

Starts	1st	2nd	3rd	4th	Win & Pl
20	5	6	1	1	£346,531

	1/23	Fair	2m5f Ch soft	£7,310
	10/20	Autl	2m3½f Gd3 Hdl 4yo heavy	£36,038
	7/20	Autl	2m3½f Gd3 Hdl 4yo v soft	£36,038
0	5/20	Autl	2m2f List Hdl 4yo v soft	£34,322
0	11/19	Autl	2m2f List Hdl 3yo heavy	£47,027

Classy French recruit who has finished second in three Grade 1 hurdles, including over 3m at Punchestown in 2021; missed the following campaign and didn't reach the same level over fences last season when often let down by jumping, albeit with all defeats in Grade 1 company.

Iroko in the Cheltenham winner's enclosure after landing the Martin Pipe handicap hurdle

Janidil (Fr)
9 b g Indian Daffodil - Janidouce (Kaldounevees)
Willie Mullins (Ire)　　　　　　　　　　　John P McManus
PLACINGS: 15/13F1/22532F/P17F-　　　　　　RPR **168**c

Starts	1st	2nd	3rd	4th	Win & Pl
22	6	5	2	1	£324,669

	2/23	Gowr	2m4f Gd2 Ch sft-hvy	£19,580
	4/21	Fair	2m4f Nov Gd1 Ch yield	£42,143
	11/20	Naas	2m3f Ch sft-hvy	£6,250
135	12/19	Fair	2m 118-144 Hdl Hcap yld-sft	£53,153
125	11/19	DRoy	2m½f 116-139 Hdl Hcap soft	£26,577
	10/19	Tipp	2m Mdn Hdl yield	£5,857

Has just come up short in Grade 1 chases (0-7 since novice win at that level in 2021) but did better when dropped slightly in class last term; won the Red Mills Trial Chase and looked set for another Grade 2 victory when falling at the last at Fairyhouse.

Jazzy Matty (Fr)
4 ch g Doctor Dino - Robbe (Video Rock)
Gordon Elliott (Ire)　　　　　　　　Caldwell Construction
PLACINGS: 5215410-　　　　　　　　　　　　RPR **126**+h

Starts	1st	2nd	3rd	4th	Win & Pl
7	2	1	-	1	£55,171

| 125 | 3/23 | Chel | 2m½f Cls1 Gd3 119-142 Hdl 4yo Hcap soft ... | £45,016 |
| | 12/22 | Fair | 2m Mdn Hdl 3yo yld-sft .... | £5,206 |

Narrow winner of last season's Fred Winter Hurdle at Cheltenham, putting stamina and experience to good use on handicap debut; had won one of five previous races, coming up short in better company; half-brother to Delta Work who should stay further.

Jet Powered (Ire)
6 b g Jet Away - Cloghoge Lady (Presenting)
Nicky Henderson　　　　　　　　　　Mrs J Donnelly
PLACINGS: 1/15-　　　　　　　　　　　　　　RPR **129**+h

Starts	1st	2nd	3rd	4th	Win & Pl
2	1	-	-	-	£6,885

| | 11/22 | Newb | 2m½f Cls3 Mdn Hdl good .... | £6,535 |

Bought for 350,000gns after winning sole point-to-point in 2021 but first season under rules fell well short of expectations; won well in a maiden hurdle first time out at Newbury but was only fifth when 2-7 there next time; future chaser and could head straight into that sphere.

Jetoile (Ire)
8 b g Jeremy - Accordingtoherself (Accordion)
Ryan Potter　　　　　　　　　　　　　Ms J Bennett
PLACINGS: 5/3F/311202/2532411-　　　　　　RPR **144**+c

Starts	1st	2nd	3rd	4th	Win & Pl
13	4	4	2	1	£55,334

137	4/23	Chep	2m3½f Cls3 119-137 Ch Hcap gd-sft	£6,337
132	3/23	Chep	2m3½f Cls3 Nov 126-136 Ch Hcap soft	£8,335
	12/21	Leic	2m4½f Cls4 Nov Hdl soft	£4,357
	11/21	Chep	2m3½f Cls4 Mdn Hdl gd-sft	£4,085

Made belated and rapid progress last spring

RACING POST

when twice winning well at Chepstow; had taken an age to build on Tolworth second in 2022 but got off the mark at the sixth attempt over fences from a smart subsequent winner and followed up in an open handicap; raised another 9lb.

Johnnywho (Ire)
6 br g Califet - Howaya Pet (Montelimar)
Jonjo O'Neill   John P McManus
PLACINGS: 1/1-   **RPR 120+b**

Starts	1st	2nd	3rd	4th	Win & Pl
1	1	-	-	-	£2,639
	3/23	Tntn	2m¹/₂f Cls5 Mdn NHF 4-6yo heavy		£2,640

Given plenty of time after a wide-margin win in sole point-to-point in 2021 (Hermes Allen third) and made a successful debut under rules in a Taunton bumper last spring; came clear on the bridle on heavy ground despite being weak in the betting; fine novice hurdle prospect.

Jonbon (Fr)
7 b g Walk In The Park - Star Face (Saint Des Saints)
Nicky Henderson   John P McManus
PLACINGS: 11/11121/111211-   **RPR 170+c**

Starts	1st	2nd	3rd	4th	Win & Pl
12	10	2	-	-	£437,390
4/23	Sand	1m7¹/₂f Cls1 Gd1 Ch gd-sft			£91,120
4/23	Aint	2m Cls1 Nov Gd1 Ch gd-sft			£69,644
2/23	Wwck	2m Cls1 Nov Gd1 Ch gd-sft			£31,323
12/22	Sand	1m7¹/₂f Cls1 Nov Gd1 Ch gd-sft			£45,560
11/22	Wwck	2m Cls3 Nov Ch soft			£9,531
4/22	Aint	2m¹/₂f Cls1 Nov Gd1 Hdl gd-sft			£56,319
1/22	Hayd	1m7¹/₂f Cls2 Gd2 Hdl soft			£28,475
12/21	Asct	1m7¹/₂f Cls1 Nov Gd2 Hdl gd-sft			£28,475
11/21	Newb	2m¹/₂f Cls3 Mdn Hdl gd-sft			£5,991
11/21	Newb	2m¹/₂f Cls3 NHF 4-6yo gd-sft			£4,520

Top-class novice chaser last season and even proved himself in Grade 1 open company when beating Champion Chase runner-up Captain Guinness in the Celebration Chase at Sandown; suffered sole defeat behind El Fabiolo in the Arkle, with five wins coming at 8-13 or shorter.

Journey With Me (Ire)
7 ch g Mahler - Kilbarry Demon (Bob's Return)
Henry De Bromhead (Ire)   Robcour
PLACINGS: 11/11F/7F121F-   **RPR 155+c**

Starts	1st	2nd	3rd	4th	Win & Pl
10	5	1	-	-	£50,461
3/23	Naas	2m4f Nov Gd3 Ch soft			£14,881
12/22	Naas	2m4f Ch yld-sft			£6,445
2/22	Naas	2m3f Nov Hdl soft			£9,916
12/21	Leop	2m4f Mdn Hdl yld-sft			£7,902
3/21	Gowr	2m2f NHF 4-7yo heavy			£5,268

Talented gelding who has been let down by jumping issues and fell for the third time in seven races when favourite for a 3m Grade 1 novice chase at Punchestown; has won five out of six when completing below that level, with sole defeat coming narrowly behind Impervious.

Junta Marvel (Fr)
5 b m Masked Marvel - Junta Des Champs (Robin Des Champs)
Willie Mullins (Ire)   The Turner Family
PLACINGS: 11-   **RPR 117+b**

Starts	1st	2nd	3rd	4th	Win & Pl
2	2	-	-	-	£29,761
4/23	Punc	2m¹/₂f Gd3 NHF 4-7yo yield			£23,496
3/23	Limk	2m3f NHF soft			£6,265

Won both bumpers last season, including a Grade 3 mares' race at Punchestown; was more impressive on better ground having looked only workmanlike in winning at Limerick, scoring with plenty to spare; good prospect for mares' novice hurdles.

Kateira
6 b m Kayf Tara - Raitera (Astarabad)
Dan Skelton   Little Lodge Farm & Dan Skelton
PLACINGS: 15/1112-   **RPR 138h**

Starts	1st	2nd	3rd	4th	Win & Pl
6	4	1	-	-	£40,774
2/23	MRas	2m¹/₂f Cls3 Nov Hdl good			£6,535
1/23	Hntg	2m4¹/₂f Cls4 Nov Hdl gd-sft			£4,357
11/22	Uttx	2m Cls4 Nov Hdl soft			£4,901
2/22	Hntg	2m Cls5 NHF 4-6yo soft			£2,451

Lightly raced mare who won three novice hurdles last season before a fine second in a Grade 1 at Aintree; kept to moderate company prior to that, winning her last two by wide margins at odds-on, but coped well with a sharp rise in class when second behind Irish Point.

Kilbeg King (Ire)
8 b g Doyen - Prayuwin Drummer (Presenting)
Anthony Honeyball   M R Chapman, E Jones & H Kingston
PLACINGS: 2/11/16121-   **RPR 139h**

Starts	1st	2nd	3rd	4th	Win & Pl
6	4	1	-	-	£42,790
126	4/23	Punc	2m7¹/₂f 119-142 Hdl Hcap gd-yld		£26,106
	2/23	Font	2m5¹/₂f Cls4 Nov Hdl good		£4,901
	11/22	Ffos	2m4f Cls4 Mdn Hdl soft		£4,901
	3/21	Uttx	2m Cls5 NHF 4-6yo gd-sft		£2,274

Missed 18 months after winning sole bumper but made up for lost time with an excellent novice hurdle campaign last term; only sixth in the Challow Hurdle on second run but flourished when switched to handicaps and signed off with a terrific win at Punchestown.

Kilcruit (Ire)
8 b g Stowaway - Not Broke Yet (Broken Hearted)
Willie Mullins (Ire)   Miss M A Masterson
PLACINGS: 2/112/12313/41351-00   **RPR 166+c**

Starts	1st	2nd	3rd	4th	Win & Pl
16	6	3	3	1	£220,697
148	4/23	Punc	2m5f Nov 125-148 Ch Hcap yield		£52,212
	11/22	Punc	2m3¹/₂f Ch yield		£6,445
	1/22	Punc	2m Mdn Hdl yield		£5,950
	4/21	Punc	2m¹/₂f Gd1 NHF 4-7yo yield		£52,679
	2/21	Leop	2m Gd2 NHF 4-7yo sft-hvy		£52,679
	12/20	Navn	2m NHF 4-7yo soft		£4,500

Has taken an age to build on bumper potential

(second in the 2021 Champion Bumper) but finally got it right when hacking up in a novice handicap chase at Punchestown last spring; had cut little ice in Grade 1 novices and now 0-4 at the top level over obstacles.

Kitty's Light
7 b g Nathaniel - Daraiyna (Refuse To Bend)

Christian Williams   R J Bedford & All Stars Sports Racing

PLACINGS: 2/22P47223/66873111-   RPR **153+**c

Starts	1st	2nd	3rd	4th	Win & Pl
28	7	6	4	1	£435,071

140	4/23	Sand	3m4½f Cls1 Gd3 134-160 Ch Hcap gd-sft £90,032
140	4/23	Ayr	4m Cls1 Gd3 128-154 Ch Hcap good............ £112,540
132	2/23	Newc	4m1½f Cls2 116-142 Ch Hcap gd-sft............ £41,624
135	3/21	Kels	3m2f Cls2 125-142 Ch Hcap gd-sft.............. £18,159
123	10/20	Extr	3m Cls3 119-132 Ch Hcap gd-fm................. £9,747
117	9/20	Wwck	3m Cls4 Nov 97-117 Ch Hcap good............ £4,289
109	8/20	Sthl	2m4½f Cls4 Nov 97-118 Ch Hcap good........ £3,964

Classy staying handicapper who pulled off a remarkable treble last season when winning the Eider Chase, Scottish National and bet365 Gold Cup; had also enjoyed a fine spring in 2022 without winning before plummeting in the handicap during a quieter winter.

Klassical Dream (Fr)
9 b g Dream Well - Klassical Way (Septieme Ciel)

Willie Mullins (Ire)   Mrs Joanne Coleman

PLACINGS: 111/135/1145/12291-3   RPR **168**h

Starts	1st	2nd	3rd	4th	Win & Pl
21	8	3	4	2	£860,789

4/23	Punc	2m7½f Gd1 Hdl gd-yld................. £156,637
4/22	Punc	2m7½f Gd1 Hdl gd-yld................. £136,345
12/21	Leop	3m Gd1 Hdl soft........................... £52,679
4/21	Punc	3m Gd1 Hdl yield......................... £131,696
4/19	Punc	2m½f Nov Gd1 Hdl yield................ £53,153
3/19	Chel	2m½f Cls1 Nov Gd1 Hdl soft........... £70,338
2/19	Leop	2m Nov Gd1 Hdl good................... £66,441
12/18	Leop	2m Mdn Hdl 4yo gd-yld.................. £8,177

Has won the last three runnings of the Champion Stayers Hurdle at Punchestown, taking Grade 1 tally to seven (three as a novice in 2019) with narrow win in April; close second in last season's Hatton's Grace but disappointed for the second time in the Stayers' Hurdle at Cheltenham.

Knappers Hill (Ire)
7 b g Valirann - Brogella (King's Theatre)

Paul Nicholls   P K Barber & P J Vogt

PLACINGS: 111/1136011/114231-   RPR **154**h

Starts	1st	2nd	3rd	4th	Win & Pl
16	10	3	2	1	£261,260

	4/23	Sand	2m5½f Cls1 Gd2 Hdl soft................. £45,560
	11/22	Winc	1m7f Cls1 Gd2 Hdl good................. £41,608
141	10/22	Chep	2m3½f Cls2 120-145 Hdl Hcap good.. £39,023
134	4/22	Sand	2m Cls2 Nov 108-136 Hdl Hcap good. £51,040
	4/22	NAbb	2m1f Cls4 Nov Hdl good.................. £5,010
	11/21	Winc	1m7f Cls3 Nov Hdl 4-6yo good......... £6,535
	10/21	Chep	2m Cls4 Nov Hdl good................... £4,738
	4/21	Aint	2m1f Cls1 Gd2 NHF 4-6yo gd-sft..... £19,132
	12/20	Asct	1m7½f Cls1 List NHF 4-6yo soft....... £9,682
	10/20	Chep	2m Cls4 NHF 4-6yo good................. £3,249

Smart hurdler who won three times last season, including two Grade 2 races; made it four wins in a row at the time when landing the Elite Hurdle but didn't quite kick on in similar races until finding a good opening when just beating Goshen at Sandown; set to go novice chasing.

Knowsley Road (Ire)
6 b g Flemensfirth - Rowanville Lady (Milan)

Paul Nicholls   Charles Pelham & Henry Pelham

PLACINGS: 221/1136-   RPR **136**h

Starts	1st	2nd	3rd	4th	Win & Pl
6	3	1	1	-	£18,946

12/22	Chep	2m3½f Cls4 Nov Hdl gd-sft................. £4,520
11/22	Chep	2m3½f Cls4 Mdn Hdl gd-sft............... £4,901
3/22	Chep	2m Cls5 NHF 4-6yo gd-sft................. £2,614

Useful novice hurdler last season; won first two races at Chepstow to add to bumper win at the same track; fair third at Warwick when stepped up to Grade 2 level but only sixth when favourite on handicap debut at Newbury; likely to go novice chasing.

L'Homme Presse (Fr)
8 b g Diamond Boy - Romance Turgot (Bateau Rouge)

Venetia Williams   DFA Racing (Pink & Edwards)

PLACINGS: 52/16/111113/1U-   RPR **175+**c

Starts	1st	2nd	3rd	4th	Win & Pl
12	7	1	1	-	£267,031

164	11/22	Newc	2m7½f Cls1 Gd3 138-164 Ch Hcap gd-sft....... £39,865
	3/22	Chel	3m½f Cls1 Nov Gd1 Ch soft............................. £98,558
	2/22	Sand	2m4f Cls1 Nov Gd1 Ch gd-sft......................... £46,096
	1/22	Chel	2m4½f Cls1 Nov Gd2 Ch soft.......................... £31,323
	12/21	Asct	2m5f Cls2 Ch gd-sft...................................... £20,812
128	12/21	Extr	2m3f Cls3 119-138 Ch Hcap gd-sft................. £8,605
	4/21	Chep	2m Cls4 Nov Hdl good................................... £3,159

Missed the second half of last season through injury but had already graduated from novice ranks to the top tier; won the Brown Advisory in 2022 and built on that by defying a big weight in the Rehearsal Chase; would have been a clear second in the King George but for final-fence exit.

Lac De Constance (Fr)
7 gr g Martaline - Kendova (Kendor)

Dan Skelton   Andrew L Cohen

PLACINGS: 35/111/1U246-   RPR **146+**c

Starts	1st	2nd	3rd	4th	Win & Pl
10	4	1	1	1	£41,610

11/22	Kemp	2m2f Cls3 Nov Ch soft................................ £9,803
3/22	Wwck	2m Cls4 Nov Gd1 Ch gd-sft....................... £4,085
2/22	Extr	2m1½f Cls1 Nov List Hdl sft..................... £16,134
12/21	Extr	2m1½f Cls4 Mdn Hdl soft............................ £4,085

Looked a potential star early last term before season unravelled; won by 20 lengths on chase debut to follow unbeaten novice hurdle campaign; unseated when favourite for a Grade 2 at Kempton and then second at odds-on before two tame efforts in handicap company.

RACING POST

Langer Dan (Ire)
7 b g Ocovango - What A Fashion (Milan)
Dan Skelton — Colm Donlon
PLACINGS: 1226/95412/6B1/3781- — RPR **147**h

Starts	1st	2nd	3rd	4th	Win & Pl
17	5	3	1	1	£170,320
141	3/23	Chel	2m5f Cls1 Gd3 134-151 Hdl Hcap soft		£56,270
137	4/22	Aint	2m4f Cls1 Gd3 130-148 Hdl Hcap gd-sft		£42,203
130	3/21	Sand	2m Cls1 Gd3 121-146 Hdl Hcap soft		£28,230
	11/19	Weth	2m Cls1 List Hdl 3yo soft		£14,238
	10/19	Ludl	2m Cls4 Mdn Hdl 3yo good		£5,263

Has an outstanding record in big handicap hurdles and added a Cheltenham Festival victory to his CV when landing last season's Coral Cup *(pictured in the winner's enclosure below)*; also won the Imperial Cup in 2021 and at Aintree's Grand National meeting in 2022; has largely been kept away from Graded races.

Le Milos
8 b g Shirocco - Banjaxed Girl (King's Theatre)
Dan Skelton — The Jolly Good Partnership
PLACINGS: 13040/313/2114/1120- — RPR **157**+c

Starts	1st	2nd	3rd	4th	Win & Pl
24	7	2	3	3	£245,031
146	11/22	Newb	3m2f Cls1 Gd3 134-160 Ch Hcap good		£142,375
142	11/22	Bang	3m Cls2 123-147 Ch Hcap heavy		£20,931
139	2/22	Sand	3m Cls2 128-145 Ch Hcap gd-sft		£26,164
130	1/22	Extr	3m Cls3 104-130 Ch Hcap heavy		£11,219
122	2/21	Font	2m3½f Cls4 Nov 105-122 Ch Hcap heavy		£4,289
	9/19	Kels	2m5f Cls4 Nov Hdl good		£3,899
118	3/19	Sand	2m Cls3 108-127 Hdl 4yo Hcap soft		£6,498

Progressive staying chaser who was winning for the fourth time in five races when landing last season's Coral Gold Cup at Newbury; subsequently laid out for the Grand National but looked a patent non-stayer having made a promising forward move.

RACING POST

The highly popular Racing Post calendars feature stunning racing photos taken by the Racing Post's award-winning photographers.

Each calendar features one month to view and includes the most up-to-date race meeting information in the UK and Ireland at the time of publication, and highlights the key races each month.

Racing Post's *Unforgettable Moments Wall Calendar 2024* features stunning and evocative racing photos from the Racing Post archives and will stir up memories from racing's history for all fans of the sport.

NEW SHOP WEBSITE LIVE NOW!
www.racingpost.com/shop

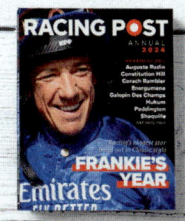   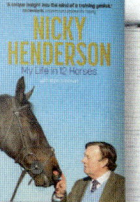   

RACING POST

Lecky Watson (Ire)

5 ch g Valirann - Anno Whyte (Stowaway)
Willie Mullins (Ire) — Slaneyville Syndicate
PLACINGS: 2/1d245- — RPR **134+**b

Starts	1st	2nd	3rd	4th	Win & Pl
5	-	3	-	1	£25,365

Failed to win a bumper in five attempts but ran a huge race when fourth in last season's Champion Bumper at Cheltenham, relishing a stiffer stamina test; had finished second three times, including when demoted from first on debut; should make a good staying novice hurdler.

Letsbeclearaboutit (Ire)

8 b g Flemensfirth - Clarification (Westerner)
Gavin Cromwell (Ire) — Alymer Stud
PLACINGS: 11221/242144- — RPR **147+**h

Starts	1st	2nd	3rd	4th	Win & Pl
11	4	4	-	3	£64,040

1/23	Punc	3m½f Mdn Hdl heavy		£6,265
4/21	Fair	7m NHF 4-7yo yield		£6,321
11/20	Punc	2m1f NHF 4 7yo sft-hvy		£5,000
10/20	Tipp	2m NHF 5-7yo sft-hvy		£4,500

Very useful staying novice hurdler last season having missed previous 18 months through injury; won only a maiden hurdle but was highly tried otherwise, doing best when a close fourth in the Albert Bartlett at Cheltenham; not at the same level down in trip when fourth at Aintree.

Lifetime Ambition (Ire)

8 br g Kapgarde - Jeanquiri (Mansonnien)
Jessica Harrington (Ire) — Linda Mulcahy & Mary Wolridge
PLACINGS: 1/1142721/242343U-04 — RPR **153**c

Starts	1st	2nd	3rd	4th	Win & Pl
25	4	7	3	8	£108,393

3/22	Limk	3m½f Nov Gd3 Ch gd-yld		£14,130
10/21	DRoy	2m3½f Ch soft		£5,795
4/21	Punc	2m4½f Hdl yield		£10,536
3/21	Limk	2m3f Mdn Hdl heavy		£7,375

Very useful staying chaser who finished a fine second in last season's Troytown but rarely got his conditions otherwise; trained for the Grand National after finishing fourth in the Grand Sefton first time out but unseated his rider on the first circuit after being badly hampered.

Limerick Lace (Ire)

6 b m Walk In The Park - Sway (Califet)
Gavin Cromwell (Ire) — John P McManus
PLACINGS: 10/621f/9521123- — RPR **146+**c

Starts	1st	2nd	3rd	4th	Win & Pl
13	4	3	1	-	£55,546

135	2/23	Naas	2m4f Nov 112-135 Ch Hcap yield	£23,496
	1/23	DRoy	2m Nov Ch soft	£9,659
	1/22	Punc	2m4½f Mdn Hdl soft	£6,197
	3/21	Punc	2m1½f NHF 4yo heavy	£4,214

Very useful young mare who took well to fences last season, most notably winning a 2m4f novice handicap at Naas; good second behind Journey With Me in a Grade 3 back there but failed to build on that when third in a Listed mares' novice at Fairyhouse.

Longhouse Poet (Ire)

9 b g Yeats - Moscow Madame (Moscow Society)
Martin Brassil (Ire) — Sean & Bernardine Mulryan
PLACINGS: 38/6231/7176/P16U1U- — RPR **132**h

Starts	1st	2nd	3rd	4th	Win & Pl
20	6	2	3	-	£141,257

	3/23	DRoy	3m2f Ch soft	£8,093
	12/22	Limk	2m4f Hdl sft-hvy	£6,941
145	1/22	Gowr	3m1f 135-162 Ch Hcap soft	£49,580
	12/20	Punc	3m1f Ch heavy	£6,250
	12/19	Navn	2m4f Mdn Hdl soft	£7,188
	5/19	Punc	2m2f NHF 5-7yo gd-yld	£8,324

Smart staying chaser who landed his biggest win in the Thyestes in 2022; finished sixth in the Grand National that year and laid out for the same race when winning twice last term; started over hurdles and switched back to fences after the weights only to unseat early at Aintree.

Lookaway (Ire)

6 ch g Ask - Burrack's Choice (Westerner)
Neil King — Peter Beadles
PLACINGS: 111/346-11 — RPR **129+**h

Starts	1st	2nd	3rd	4th	Win & Pl
7	4	-	1	1	£42,561

5/23	Uttx	2m4f Cls4 Nov Hdl good	£4,524
5/23	Uttx	2m Cls4 Mdn Hdl gd-sft	£4,357
4/22	Aint	2m1f Cls1 Gd2 NHF 4-6yo gd-sft	£28,135
2/22	Newb	2m½f Cls4 NHF 4-6yo soft	£2,723

Looked a fine prospect when winning both bumper races in 2022, including a Grade 2 at Aintree, but disappointed in three novice hurdles last season; did better when winning twice at Uttoxeter in May, albeit in moderate company, and retains novice status.

Lossiemouth (Fr)

4 gr f Great Pretender - Mariner's Light (Gentlewave)
Willie Mullins (Ire) — Mrs S Ricci
PLACINGS: 1/11211- — RPR **143+**h

Starts	1st	2nd	3rd	4th	Win & Pl
6	5	1	-	-	£225,739

4/23	Punc	2m Gd1 Hdl 4yo gd-yld	£65,265
3/23	Chel	2m1f Cls1 Gd1 Hdl 4yo soft	£78,333
12/22	Leop	2m Gd2 Hdl 3yo soft	£22,311
12/22	Fair	2m Gd3 Hdl 3yo soft	£13,634
4/22	Autl	1m7f Hdl 3yo v soft	£20,975

Last season's dominant juvenile hurdler, winning four out of five including the Triumph Hurdle; unlucky in running when suffering sole defeat at Leopardstown but bounced back when a warm favourite at Cheltenham and followed up at Punchestown; likely type for the Mares' Hurdle.

Lossiemouth caps a superb season with Grade 1 victory at the Punchestown festival

Love Envoi (Ire)

7 b m Westerner - Love Divided (King's Ride)
Harry Fry   Noel Fehily Racing Syndicates Love Envoi
PLACINGS: 1/111112/1126-   RPR **153**h

Starts	1st	2nd	3rd	4th	Win & Pl
11	8	2	-	-	£205,926
139	1/23 Sand	2m4f Cls1 List Hdl soft.................................£14,405				
	12/22 Sand	2m Cls2 117-143 Hdl Hcap soft £31,218				
	3/22 Chel	2m1f Cls1 Nov Gd2 Hdl soft £59,084				
	2/22 Sand	2m4f Cls1 Nov Gd2 Hdl heavy £28,475				
	1/22 Ling	2m Cls2 Nov Hdl heavy................................£15,609				
	12/21 Wwck	2m5f Cls4 Nov Hdl heavy..............................£4,629				
	12/21 Leic	2m4½f Cls4 Mdn Hdl gd-sft £4,085				
	3/21 Wwck	2m4f NHF 5yo yield..£4,214				

High-class mare who nearly ruined Honeysuckle's farewell party when second in the Mares' Hurdle at the Cheltenham Festival; had won the mares' novice at that meeting in 2022 before twice winning well at Sandown last term; sixth when favourite for a Grade 1 at Punchestown.

Luccia

5 ch m The Gurkha - Earth Amber (Hurricane Run)
Nicky Henderson   Pump & Plant Services
PLACINGS: 11/1143-   RPR **142+**h

Starts	1st	2nd	3rd	4th	Win & Pl
6	4	-	1	1	£66,124
	2/23 Extr	2m1½f Cls1 Nov List Hdl good...........................£17,832				
	11/22 Newb	2m½f Cls1 Nov List Hdl good...........................£14,860				
	3/22 Sand	2m Cls1 List NHF 4-6yo soft...............................£14,807				
	1/22 Wwck	2m Cls5 NHF 4-6yo soft..£2,451				

Smart mare who won her first four races under rules (three Listed races) before making the frame at Cheltenham and Aintree last spring;

Magical Zoe (Ire)

5 b m Shantou - Fedaia (Anabaa)
Henry De Bromhead (Ire)   Patrick & Scott Bryceland
PLACINGS: 1/1125-   RPR **138+**h

Starts	1st	2nd	3rd	4th	Win & Pl
5	3	1	-	-	£51,298
	11/22 DRoy	2m1f Nov Gd3 Hdl soft....................................£16,113				
	9/22 Wxfd	2m Mdn Hdl 4yo gd-yld..................................£6,197				
	3/22 Cork	2m NHF 4-7yo good..£4,958				

Lightly raced mare who won twice early last season before a big run when second after a long absence in the mares' novice hurdle at the Cheltenham Festival, doing best of those held up; well below par when fifth at Fairyhouse on final run; fine long-term prospect for fences.

Mahler Mission (Ire)

7 b g Mahler - Finnow Turkle (Turtle Island)
John McConnell (Ire)   Colm Herron & Rockview Racing Syndicate
PLACINGS: 2/321171/2312F-   RPR **154**c

Starts	1st	2nd	3rd	4th	Win & Pl
11	4	3	2	-	£61,787
	1/23 Navn	3m Ch sft-hvy...£6,788				
	4/22 Prth	3m Cls1 Nov List Hdl gd-sft £13,160				
	1/22 Donc	3m½f Cls1 Nov Gd2 Hdl good......................£17,165				
	1/22 Sedg	2m4f Cls4 Mdn Hdl gd-sft...............................£5,651				

Progressive novice chaser last season who might well have won the National Hunt Chase

at Cheltenham but for falling two out when four lengths clear; had got off the mark at the third attempt at Navan before a close second to Churchstonewarrior in a Grade 2 there.

Major Dundee (Ire)
8 b g Scorpion - Be My Granny (Needle Gun)
Alan King   Exors Of The Late Trevor Hemmings
PLACINGS: 10F6/22810/1123/031-   RPR **141+**c

Starts	1st	2nd	3rd	4th	Win & Pl
16	5	3	2	4	£128,082
129	3/23	Uttx	4m2f Cls1 Gd3 129-155 Ch Hcap soft................£84,405
126	12/21	Bang	3m Cls3 115-127 Ch Hcap soft.........................£5,936
123	11/21	Fknm	2m5f Cls3 Nov 123-131 Ch Hcap good...............£7,407
	3/21	Chep	2m7½f Cls4 Nov Hdl good..............................£3,769
	5/19	Sthl	1m5½f Cls5 Mdn NHF 4-6yo good.....................£2,274

Lightly raced staying chaser who showed stamina in abundance to win last season's Midlands Grand National; had also run well on only previous run beyond 3m when third in the 2022 Scottish National; has the Grand National as his aim but needs to rise in the weights.

Makin' Yourmindup
6 b g Kayf Tara - Subtility (With Approval)
Paul Nicholls   Owners Group
PLACINGS: 362/11214-   RPR **134+**h

Starts	1st	2nd	3rd	4th	Win & Pl
7	3	2	-	1	£44,799
	2/23	Hayd	3m½f Cls1 Nov Gd2 Hdl gd-sft.......................£28,475
	12/22	Chep	2m7½f Cls4 Nov Hdl gd-sft............................£4,520
	10/22	Chep	2m3½f Cls4 Nov Hdl gd-sft............................£4,901

Useful staying novice hurdler last season, most notably winning a 3m Grade 2 at Haydock when gamely prevailing by a head; reportedly found ground too quick at Perth when below par on final run, though had won three times on similar good to soft; likely to go novice chasing.

Malystic
9 b g Malinas - Mystic Glen (Vettori)
Peter Niven   Clova Syndicate And P D Niven
PLACINGS: 22/2112/U2/42P11401-   RPR **157+**c

Starts	1st	2nd	3rd	4th	Win & Pl
21	7	7	-	2	£116,351
147	4/23	Ayr	2m1½f Cls1 Gd3 121-147 Ch Hcap good................£22,780
145	1/23	Donc	2m7½f Cls2 124-145 Ch Hcap good...................£26,405
142	12/22	Weth	1m7f Cls2 127-146 Ch Hcap soft....................£13,615
140	12/20	Newc	2m1½f Cls3 Nov 122-141 Ch Hcap soft...............£7,018
	11/20	Weth	1m7f Cls4 Nov Ch soft................................£4,679
	12/19	Muss	1m7½f Cls4 Mdn Hdl 4-6yo gd-sft.....................£3,899
	2/19	Newc	2m½f Cls5 NHF 4-6yo slow............................£2,274
	11/18	Newc	2m Cls5 NHF 4-6yo good..............................£2,274

Flourished in good 2m handicap chases last season; won three times, most notably when bouncing back from a Grand Annual flop to score under 12st in a premier handicap at Ayr;

last of four but far from disgraced when stepping out of handicap company in the Game Spirit.

Manothepeople (Ire)
8 b g Mahler - Midnight Insanity (Insan)
Fergal O'Brien   The Fob Racing Partnership
PLACINGS: 1/54311/112P-   RPR **134**c

Starts	1st	2nd	3rd	4th	Win & Pl
9	4	1	1	1	£29,947
122	12/22	Chep	2m7½f Cls3 Nov 117-137 Ch Hcap gd-sft............£6,535
114	10/22	Chep	3m2f Cls4 Nov 102-118 Ch Hcap good...............£7,624
108	3/22	Donc	3m½f Cls4 Nov 100-115 Ch Hcap good...............£6,208
102	2/22	Hntg	3m1f Cls5 79-105 Hdl Hcap soft.....................£3,758

Lightly raced and progressive stayer; won last two races over hurdles in early 2022 and continued to improve over fences last season, winning twice more before a fair second at Newbury; faded in the straight and pulled up when 9-1 for the Scottish National.

Marble Sands (Fr)
7 gr g Martaline - Sans Rien (Poliglote)
Fergal O'Brien   DI Adams, JA Adams & G McPherson
PLACINGS: 5152/2322/115156-   RPR **139**h

Starts	1st	2nd	3rd	4th	Win & Pl
14		4	4	1	£64,402
	2/23	Hntg	2m3½f Cls1 Nov List Hdl good.......................£17,618
	11/22	Leic	2m4½f Cls3 Nov Hdl gd-sft............................£6,535
	10/22	Hrfd	2m3½f Cls4 Mdn Hdl good.............................£4,901
	10/20	Asct	1m7½f Cls4 NHF 4-6yo good...........................£3,899

Did well in the face of several stiff tasks as a second-season novice hurdler last season; won all three races below Grade 1 level, most notably a Listed novice at Huntingdon; good fifth in the Ballymore at Cheltenham at 150-1 and stayed the 3m trip when a closer sixth in the Sefton.

Marie's Rock (Ire)
8 b/br m Milan - By The Hour (Flemensfirth)
Nicky Henderson   Middleham Park Racing
PLACINGS: 111/73/371P11/1172-   RPR **156+**h

Starts	1st	2nd	3rd	4th	Win & Pl
15	8	1	2		£285,601
	1/23	Chel	2m4½f Cls1 Gd2 Hdl soft.............................£39,865
	4/22	Punc	2m3f Gd1 Hdl soft..................................£61,975
	3/22	Chel	2m4f Cls1 Gd1 Hdl gd-sft...........................£67,524
	2/22	Wwck	2m5f Cls1 List Hdl gd-sft...........................£17,085
131	12/21	Kemp	2m5f Cls3 122-139 Hdl Hcap soft...................£10,892
	12/19	Tntn	2m1½f Cls1 Nov List Hdl good........................£12,529
	12/19	Hayd	1m7½f Cls2 Hdl soft.................................£12,660
	5/19	Ffos	2m Cls5 NHF 4-6yo good..............................£2,599

Top-class mare who landed a Grade 1 double at Cheltenham and Punchestown in 2022 and was a force against the boys last term; seventh in the Mares' Hurdle at Cheltenham but won well in the Relkeel Hurdle and was second behind Sire Du Berlais at Aintree on first try at 3m.

Marine Nationale (Ire)

6 b g French Navy - Power Of Future (Definite Article)
Barry Connell (Ire)   Barry Connell
PLACINGS: 11111-   RPR **158+**h

Starts	1st	2nd	3rd	4th	Win & Pl
5	5	-	-	-	£134,964

3/23	Chel	2m½f Cls1 Nov Gd1 Hdl soft	£75,965
12/22	Fair	2m Nov Gd1 Hdl soft	£42,143
10/22	Punc	2m Mdn Hdl good	£6,197
8/22	Klny	2m½f NHF gd-yld	£5,702
5/22	Punc	2m NHF good	£4,958

Brilliant unbeaten gelding who won two bumpers and three novice hurdles last season, including the Supreme at Cheltenham; put away for the winter after winning the Royal Bond by a head and looked much improved when comfortably beating Facile Vega; likely to go chasing.

Maskada (Fr)

7 b m Masked Marvel - Mandina (Saint Des Saints)
Henry De Bromhead (Ire)   M K Mariga
PLACINGS: 153122/32313F/4F101-   RPR **155+**c

Starts	1st	2nd	3rd	4th	Win & Pl
24	6	3	6	2	£160,331
142					
132					
120					
115					

3/23	Chel	2m Cls3 Gd3 139-155 Ch Hcap soft	£70,338
12/22	Limk	2m3f 119-145 Ch Hcap heavy	£22,311
1/22	Leic	2m Cls List Ch gd-sft	£18,509
1/21	Newb	2m½f Cls2 108-133 Hdl Hcap heavy	£9,747
11/20	Hrfd	2m Cls4 102-120 Hdl Hcap gd-sft	£3,769
12/19	Wwck	2m Cls4 Mdn Hdl 3yo soft	£4,549

Listed winner for Stuart Edmunds in Britain but much improved last season after £80,000 purchase to move to Henry de Bromhead; disappointed at Leopardstown when favourite to follow up victory at Limerick but made amends in the Grand Annual at Cheltenham.

Maximilian (Ger)

7 ch g Adlerflug - Maxima (Platini)
Donald McCain   Owners Group
PLACINGS: 111/11312-   RPR **149**h

Starts	1st	2nd	3rd	4th	Win & Pl
7	5	1	1	-	£68,371

1/23	Donc	3m½f Cls1 Nov Gd2 Hdl good	£22,780
11/22	Bang	2m7f Cls3 Nov Hdl sft	£8,168
10/22	Carl	2m4f Cls4 Nov Hdl gd-sft	£4,629
3/22	Carl	2m1f Cls4 NHF 4-6yo sft	£2,723
2/22	Carl	2m1f Cls5 NHF 4-6yo soft	£2,451

Smart novice hurdler last season who won three times and finished second in the Sefton at Aintree (might have won but for final-flight error); had claimed the scalp of Stay Away Fay in a Grade 2 at Doncaster on first run after wind surgery, relishing step up to 3m.

Maxxum (Ire)

6 b g Westerner - Anshan Bay (Anshan)
Gordon Elliott (Ire)   Patrick Rabbitt
PLACINGS: 76416/5421100-1   RPR **152+**h

Starts	1st	2nd	3rd	4th	Win & Pl
13	4	1	-	2	£44,290

5/23	Tipp	3m Ch gd-yld	£6,004
120 12/22	Leop	3m 115-141 Hdl Hcap soft	£24,790
103 11/22	Navn	2m6f 88-116 Hdl Hcap yield	£5,702
3/22	Clon	2m2½f Mdn Hdl soft	£4,958

Massive improver when sent to Gordon Elliott last season, climbing 39lb in the handicap in just three runs, including a 16-length win in a Pertemps qualifier at Leopardstown; disappointed twice subsequently, including at Cheltenham, but won well on chase debut in May.

McFabulous (Ire)

9 b g Milan - Rossavon (Beneficial)
Paul Nicholls   Giraffa Racing
PLACINGS: 1/13128/2431/P112PP-   RPR **155+**c

Starts	1st	2nd	3rd	4th	Win & Pl
23	10	4	2	2	£288,256
132					

11/22	Newb	2m7½f Cls1 Nov Gd2 Ch good	£28,475
11/22	Extr	2m3f Cls3 Nov Ch good	£9,671
4/22	Sand	2m5½f Cls1 Gd2 Hdl good	£45,560
1/21	Kemp	2m5f Cls1 Nov Gd2 Hdl soft	£17,085
10/20	Chep	2m Cls1 Nov Gd2 Hdl good	£17,085
3/20	Kemp	2m5f Nov Cls3 123-134 Hdl 4-7yo Hcap gd-sft	£39,389
2/20	MRas	2m Cls1 Nov Hdl 4-7yo gd-sft	£6,498
4/19	Aint	2m1f Cls1 Gd2 NHF 4-6yo soft	£25,322
3/19	Newb	2m½f Cls5 NHF 4-6yo soft	£2,599
10/18	Chep	2m Cls4 NHF 4-6yo gd-sft	£3,899

Looked a talented novice chaser early last season but later beset by physical problems; won a Grade 2 at Newbury to add to two victories over hurdles at that level; finished lame in second when favourite for a Grade 1 and twice pulled up when suffering from an irregular heartbeat.

Meet And Greet (Ire)

7 b g Mustameet - Lady Conn (Whitmore's Conn)
Oliver McKiernan (Ire)   Keep The Faith Bloodstock
PLACINGS: 294215/8312/3034247-   RPR **158+**h

Starts	1st	2nd	3rd	4th	Win & Pl
17	2	4	3	3	£63,135

2/22	Naas	1m7½f Mdn Hdl soft	£6,197
3/21	Leop	2m NHF 5-7yo gd-yld	£5,268

Has won just once over hurdles but has developed into a smart stayer with some big runs in defeat; came closest last season when second to Blazing Khal in the Boyne Hurdle and twice made the frame at Grade 1 level, notably when a close third behind Home By The Lee.

RACING POST

Midnight River
8 ch g Midnight Legend - Well Connected (Presenting)
Dan Skelton   Frank McAleavy
PLACINGS: /12141F/F71P3/13101-   RPR **160**+c

Starts	1st	2nd	3rd	4th	Win & Pl
18	7	1	4	2	£173,639

151	4/23	Aint	3m1f Cls1 Gd3 132-158 Ch Hcap gd-sft £56,270
145	1/23	Chel	2m4½f Cls1 Gd3 129-155 Ch Hcap soft £56,950
137	10/22	Strf	2m3½f Cls3 116-137 Ch Hcap good £7,080
135	12/21	Weth	2m3½f Cls3 Nov 128-141 Ch Hcap soft £5,882
	2/21	Asct	2m3½f Cls2 Nov Hdl soft £10,989
	11/20	Leic	2m4½f Cls4 Nov Hdl soft £5,913
	10/20	Uttx	2m4f Cls4 Mdn Hdl gd-sft £3,769

Big improver in good handicap chases; finished third in the Paddy Power Gold Cup before winning valuable races on New Year's Day at Cheltenham and Grand National day at Aintree; appreciated step up to 3m for final win and has the Coral Gold Cup as an early target.

Might I (Ire)
7 b g Fame And Glory - Our Honey (Old Vic)
Harry Fry   Brian & Sandy Lambert
PLACINGS: 15/1232/824-5   RPR **147**+h

Starts	1st	2nd	3rd	4th	Win & Pl
10	2	3	1	1	£52,246

	10/21	NAbb	2m2½f Cls4 Nov Hdl heavy £4,085
	12/20	Wwck	2m Cls5 NHF 4-6yo soft £2,274

Very useful novice hurdler in 2021-22, finishing second in a Grade 1 at Aintree; well fancied for some top handicaps last season, failing to stay 3m at Haydock but doing better down in trip when a neck second at Cheltenham and fourth back there in the Martin Pipe.

Millers Bank
9 b g Passing Glance - It Doesn't Matter (Karinga Bay)
Alex Hales   Millers Bank Partnership
PLACINGS: 98113/1UU21/5U2265P-   RPR **159**c

Starts	1st	2nd	3rd	4th	Win & Pl
21	6	4	1	-	£165,888

	4/22	Aint	2m4f Cls1 Nov Gd1 Ch gd-sft £68,721
	10/21	Hntg	2m4f Cls3 Nov Ch good £8,169
137	3/21	Newb	2m1½f Cls3 122-140 Hdl Hcap good £7,507
133	1/21	Kemp	2m Cls3 120-141 Hdl Hcap soft £5,913
	12/19	MRas	2m1½f Cls4 Nov Hdl gd-sft £4,549
	11/19	Bang	2m1½f Cls4 Nov Hdl heavy £4,094

Won a Grade 1 novice chase at Aintree in 2022 but couldn't kick on to the next level last season; good second in the Peterborough Chase behind Pic D'Orhy before coming up well short in three Grade 1 races; quickly dropped back to a realistic handicap mark.

Minella Cocooner (Ire)
7 b g Flemensfirth - Askanna (Old Vic)
Willie Mullins (Ire)   David Bobbett
PLACINGS: 2/12112/22-   RPR **149**+c

Starts	1st	2nd	3rd	4th	Win & Pl
7	3	4	-	-	£140,409

	2/22	Leop	2m6f Gd1 Hdl yield £74,370
	12/21	Navn	2m4f Mdn Hdl gd-yld £6,321
	6/21	Kbgn	2m NHF 4-7yo good £5,268

High-class novice hurdler in 2021-22, winning a Grade 1 at Leopardstown and twice finishing second behind The Nice Guy, including in the Albert Bartlett at Cheltenham; ran just once last season, suffering a setback after finishing second on chase debut behind Classic Getaway.

GUIDE TO THE JUMPS 2023-24

Minella Crooner (Ire)
7 b g Shantou - Laren (Monsun)
Gordon Elliott (Ire) KTDA Racing, Nick Courtney & Cillian Moran

PLACINGS: 1/11212/P2132P- RPR **147**c

Starts	1st	2nd	3rd	4th	Win & Pl
11	4	4	1	-	£62,478

12/22	Fair	2m5f Ch yield	£6,445
1/22	Punc	3m Mdn Hdl soft	£6,197
11/21	Punc	2m NHF 4-7yo yield	£5,795
10/21	Slig	2m2f NHF 4-7yo yield	£5,268

Didn't quite match very useful novice hurdle form (runner-up in a Grade 1 at Leopardstown) when sent chasing last season; still did well to win a good beginners' chase and finish second twice in stronger company; pulled up when second favourite for the National Hunt Chase.

Minella Drama (Ire)
8 b g Flemensfirth - Midsummer Drama (King's Theatre)
Donald McCain Green Day Racing

PLACINGS: 211217/125142/43113- RPR **161**c

Starts	1st	2nd	3rd	4th	Win & Pl
17	7	5	2	2	£166,088

150	2/23	Kels	2m5½f Cls2 132-150 Ch Hcap good	£13,008
145	1/23	Muss	2m4½f Cls2 119-145 Ch Hcap soft	£15,609
	1/22	Hayd	2m4f Cls1 Nov Gd2 Ch soft	£30,137
143	10/21	Uttx	2m Cls3 Nov 132-143 Ch Hcap gd-sft	£5,882
	2/21	MRas	2m4½f Cls1 Nov List Hdl soft	£10,402
	12/20	Bang	2m½f Cls4 Nov Hdl heavy	£3,769
	11/20	Sedg	2m1f Cls4 Nov Hdl good	£3,769

Steadily progressive chaser who won small-field handicaps at Musselburgh and Kelso under 12st last season; coped well with sharp rise in class for first open Grade 1 in the Marsh Chase at Aintree, finishing a solid third behind Pic D'Orhy.

Minella Indo (Ire)
10 b g Beat Hollow - Carrigeen Lily (Supreme Leader)
Henry De Bromhead (Ire) Barry Maloney

PLACINGS: 1212/11F41/3P22/P1P- RPR **160+**c

Starts	1st	2nd	3rd	4th	Win & Pl
20	7	5	3	1	£697,467

1/23	Tram	2m6f Gd3 Ch heavy	£16,969
3/21	Chel	3m2½f Cls1 Gd1 Ch gd-sft	£263,766
11/20	Navn	3m Gd2 Ch good	£30,000
10/20	Wxfd	2m7f Gd3 Ch soft	£13,750
1/20	Navn	3m Ch sft-hvy	£7,262
5/19	Punc	3m Nov Gd1 Hdl yield	£53,153
3/19	Chel	3m Cls1 Nov Gd1 Hdl gd-sft	£73,506

Brilliant winner of the Cheltenham Gold Cup in 2021 and finished second in the race the following season; purposely given a very light campaign last term in a bid to peak at Cheltenham again but was pulled up after winning sole prep run at Tramore.

Mirazur West (Ire)
5 br g Westerner - Mirazur (Good Thyne)
Willie Mullins (Ire) John P McManus

PLACINGS: F1- RPR **122+**b

Starts	1st	2nd	3rd	4th	Win & Pl
1	1	-	-	-	£5,221

3/23	Naas	2m½f NHF yld-sft	£5,221

Full-brother to Ferny Hollow who made an impressive start when easily making all in a bumper at Naas last season; had also looked set to win sole point-to-point until falling at the last; looks a good prospect for novice hurdles.

Mister Coffey (Fr)
8 b g Authorized - Mamitador (Anabaa)
Nicky Henderson Lady Bamford & Alice Bamford

PLACINGS: /12/1374/32220/7238 RPR **147**c

Starts	1st	2nd	3rd	4th	Win & Pl
16	3	6	3	1	£109,953

128	11/20	Sand	2m Cls3 117-130 Hdl Hcap soft	£9,747
	12/19	Newb	2m½f Cls4 Hdl soft	£4,484
	4/19	Hntg	2m Cls5 NHF 4-6yo good	£2,274

Yet to win over fences after two seasons but has run some huge races in that time and finished second five times; placed at the Cheltenham Festival for the second successive year when third in last season's National Hunt Chase; even led at the last in the Grand National before fading.

Mister Policeman (Fr)
5 ch g Triple Threat - Manhattan Princess (Pivotal)
Willie Mullins (Ire) Mrs S Ricci

PLACINGS: 41/1- RPR **150+**h

Starts	1st	2nd	3rd	4th	Win & Pl
3	2	-	-	1	£18,380

4/23	Cork	2m Hdl yield	£9,137
3/22	Fntb	2m2f Hdl 4yo v soft	£7,731

Exciting French recruit who won over hurdles at Fontainebleau in March 2022 and made a successful Irish debut at Cork's Easter festival last season; raced over 2m that day but should reportedly get further.

Monbeg Genius (Ire)
7 b g Shantou - Ella Watson (Supreme Leader)
Jonjo O'Neill Barrowman Racing

PLACINGS: 2/1431/41113- RPR **152+**c

Starts	1st	2nd	3rd	4th	Win & Pl
9	5	1	2	2	£54,392

132	2/23	Chep	2m7½f Cls3 Nov 114-132 Ch Hcap gd-sft	£9,506
127	1/23	Chep	2m7½f Cls3 Nov 123-132 Ch Hcap soft	£9,823
122	12/22	Newc	2m7½f Cls4 99-122 Ch Hcap gd-sft	£8,483
	3/22	Chep	2m7½f Cls4 Nov Hdl good	£6,498
	10/21	Ffos	2m4f Cls4 Mdn Hdl soft	£4,085

Very useful and progressive novice chaser last season; won three times at around 3m, the last two in novice handicaps at Chepstow; sent off

Minella Drama: consistent performer over fences who won two of his five starts last season

Monbeg Park (Ire)

6 b g Walk In The Park - Cyclone's Sister (Stowaway)
Sean Thomas Doyle (Ire)   Donnchadh Doyle
PLACINGS: 121/3213P21d1-   RPR **147** +h

Starts	1st	2nd	3rd	4th	Win & Pl
10	3	4	2	-	£49,274
4/23	Punc	2m Nov Hdl yield...			£10,442
11/22	Punc	2m5½/f Mdn Hdl yield.....................................			£6,941
4/22	Cork	2m3f NHF 4-6yo sft-hvy................................			£5,454

favourite for the Ultima at Cheltenham and ran a fine race in third behind subsequent Grand National and Grade 1 winners.

Useful and progressive novice hurdler last season; bounced back from sole flop when pulled up in Grade 1 company by finishing second in two good handicaps before winning back in calmer waters at Punchestown; likely to go novice chasing.

Monkfish (Ire)

9 ch g Stowaway - Martovic (Old Vic)
Willie Mullins (Ire)   Mrs S Ricci
PLACINGS: P/1/22111/1111/2/29-   RPR **154**h

Starts	1st	2nd	3rd	4th	Win & Pl
12	7	4	-	-	£305,413
3/21	Chel	3m½/f Cls1 Nov Gd1 Ch gd-sft.......................			£75,164
2/21	Leop	2m5½/f Nov Gd1 Ch soft.................................			£65,848
12/20	Leop	3m Nov Gd1 Ch yield.....................................			£40,000
11/20	Fair	2m5f Ch soft..			£6,250
3/20	Chel	3m Cls1 Nov Gd1 Hdl soft.............................			£73,506
1/20	Thur	2m6½/f Nov Hdl yield.....................................			£7,262
12/19	Fair	2m7f Mdn Hdl heavy.....................................			£5,847

Outstanding novice chaser in 2020-21, landing a Grade 1 hat-trick and second Cheltenham Festival win in the Brown Advisory; missed two years through injury and kept to hurdles in just two runs last spring, finishing a promising second at Fairyhouse only to flop at Punchestown.

Monmiral (Fr)

6 bl g Saint Des Saints - Achere (Mont Basile)
Paul Nicholls   Sir A Ferguson G Mason J Hales & L Hales
PLACINGS: 1/1111/542/2247-   RPR **153**c

Starts	1st	2nd	3rd	4th	Win & Pl
12	5	3	-	2	£191,318
4/21	Aint	2m1f Cls1 Gd1 Hdl 4yo gd-sft.......................			£42,203
2/21	Hayd	1m7½/f Cls2 Hdl 4yo soft...............................			£9,747
12/20	Donc	2m½/f Cls1 Gd2 Hdl 3yo gd-sft.....................			£28,468
11/20	Extr	2m1f Cls4 Hdl 3yo soft..................................			£3,769
3/20	Autl	1m7f Hdl 3yo heavy......................................			£21,153

Looked a future star when winning a Grade 1 juvenile hurdle at Aintree in 2021 but hasn't won since, albeit in two light campaigns; highly tried over fences last term, finishing second behind Jonbon and The Real Whacker before a fourth at Grade 1 level; retains novice status.

Monty's Star (Ire)

6 b g Walk In The Park - Tempest Belle (Glacial Storm)
Henry De Bromhead (Ire)   Barry Maloney
PLACINGS: 224/21P-   RPR **137** +h

Starts	1st	2nd	3rd	4th	Win & Pl
4	1	1	-	1	£20,712
2/23	Clon	3m Nov Gd3 Hdl soft......................................			£18,274

Half-brother to Grade 1 winner and Gold Cup fourth Monalee who did well in a light campaign in novice hurdles last season; got off the mark by winning a Grade 3 at Clonmel over an odds-on stablemate; pulled up in the Albert Bartlett on final run; could do better over fences.

Moroder (Ire)

9 b g Morozov - Another Tonto (Definite Article)

Seamus Mullins — Mrs Ann Leftley

PLACINGS: 423/P212/61111/P012- RPR **145c**

Starts	1st	2nd	3rd	4th	Win & Pl
19	7	5	2	1	£118,441

131	3/23	Donc	3m2f Cls2 131-141 Ch Hcap good	£36,421
127	3/22	Extr	3m6½f Cls3 112-131 Ch Hcap gd-sft	£11,219
121	2/22	Extr	3m Cls3 Nov 121-132 Ch Hcap soft	£8,257
117	1/22	Extr	3m Cls3 Nov 117-135 Ch Hcap gd-sft	£9,388
113	12/21	Plum	3m1½f Cls4 102-115 Ch Hcap good	£4,139
115	2/21	Fknm	2m7½f Cls4 Nov 115-121 Hdl Hcap soft	£5,326
	3/19	Uttx	2m Cls5 NHF 4-6yo heavy	£2,859

Prolific chaser who developed into a very useful staying handicapper last spring; won his last four races as a novice in 2021-22 and resumed upward curve when winning the Grimthorpe at Doncaster; ran another big race when second in the bet365 Gold Cup on final run.

Mr Incredible (Ire)

7 b g Westerner - Bartlemy Bell (Kalanisi)

Willie Mullins (Ire) — Paul Byrne & J Carthy

PLACINGS: 221/12RP/B23U- RPR **150c**

Starts	1st	2nd	3rd	4th	Win & Pl
10	2	3	1	-	£57,638

11/21	Naas	2m3f Ch yield	£6,585
1/21	Naas	2m3f Mdn Hdl heavy	£7,902

Lightly raced chaser who did well in top staying handicaps last season having lost his way as a novice after a promising start; got back on track when second in the Classic Chase and then came third in the Kim Muir; midfield when unseated on the second circuit in the Grand National.

Mucho Mas (Ire)

7 b g Fame And Glory - Ceart Go Leor (Montelimar)

Ben Pauling — Ms J A Wakefield

PLACINGS: 1P/617302/2211- RPR **134+c**

Starts	1st	2nd	3rd	4th	Win & Pl
12	4	3	1	-	£37,835

125	3/23	Sand	3m Cls3 117-132 Ch Hcap soft	£10,406
120	12/22	Ling	2m7½f Cls4 Nov 105-120 Ch Hcap heavy	£7,733
	12/21	Donc	2m3½f Cls3 Nov Hdl gd-sft	£5,991
	12/20	Winc	1m7½f Cls5 NHF 4-6yo soft	£2,274

Progressive novice chaser last season, flourishing when stepped up to around 3m; finished second on first two runs over fences but then won at Lingfield and followed up in a deeper handicap chase at Sandown; raised just 4lb and open to further improvement.

Paul Nicholls with Monmiral, who looks an interesting proposition for novice chases

My Drogo

8 b g Milan - My Petra (Midnight Legend)

Dan Skelton — Mr & Mrs R Kelvin-Hughes

PLACINGS: 21111/F1/ RPR **156h**

Starts	1st	2nd	3rd	4th	Win & Pl
7	5	1	-	-	£101,416

12/21	Chel	2m4½f Cls2 Nov Ch gd-sft	£13,008
4/21	Aint	2m4f Cls1 Nov Gd1 Hdl gd-sft	£42,239
3/21	Kels	2m2f Cls1 Nov Gd2 Hdl gd-sft	£22,780
12/20	Asct	1m7½f Cls1 Nov Gd2 Hdl soft	£14,305
11/20	Newb	2m½f Cls3 Mdn Hdl good	£6,498

Off for nearly two years with a tendon injury but had been a hugely exciting prospect prior to layoff; Britain's leading novice hurdler three seasons ago and looked to be heading to similar heights as a novice chaser when winning easily at Cheltenham in December 2021.

Mystical Power (Ire)

4 b g Galileo - Annie Power (Shirocco)

Willie Mullins (Ire) — John P McManus, Mrs John Magnier & Mrs S Ricci

PLACINGS: 11 RPR **126+h**

Starts	1st	2nd	3rd	4th	Win & Pl
2	2	-	-	-	£16,185

7/23	Gway	2m½f Nov Hdl 4yo soft	£10,965
5/23	Baln	2m½f NHF 4yo good	£5,221

First foal of superstar hurdler Annie Power; won sole bumper at Ballinrobe in May before quickly being sent over hurdles at Galway this summer, winning easily despite jumping moderately and failing to settle; should be open to lots of improvement.

Nassalam (Fr)

6 ch g Dream Well - Ramina (Shirocco)

Gary Moore — John & Yvonne Stone

PLACINGS: 211220/11221/56307- RPR **148c**

Starts	1st	2nd	3rd	4th	Win & Pl
16	5	5	1	-	£95,208

144	2/22	Font	2m3½f Cls3 Nov 121-144 Ch Hcap soft	£6,535
	11/21	Newb	2m4f Cls1 Nov Gd2 Ch gd-sft	£32,483
140	10/21	Asct	2m3f Cls3 Nov 130-140 Ch Hcap soft	£6,535
	12/20	Font	2m1½f Cls4 Hdl 3yo soft	£3,769
	11/20	Font	2m1½f Cls4 Hdl 3yo heavy	£3,861

Won three times as a novice chaser in 2021-22 but came up short in top handicaps last season; did best when a close third at Cheltenham in January having also finished sixth at the track in the Paddy Power Gold Cup; creeping down the weights but might need more help.

Nemean Lion (Ger)

6 b g Golden Horn - Ninfea (Selkirk)

Kerry Lee — Will Roseff

PLACINGS: 1231- RPR **138+h**

Starts	1st	2nd	3rd	4th	Win & Pl
4	2	1	1	-	£46,212

3/23	Kels	2m2f Cls1 Nov Gd2 Hdl gd-sft	£28,475
11/22	Hrfd	2m Cls4 Mdn Hdl gd-sft	£4,901

Talented but fragile gelding who did well in

novice hurdles last season after two years out with injury; had finished second in a Group 2 in France on final Flat run and reached a similar level, winning twice including a Grade 2 at Kelso and finishing third in the Tolworth; needs soft ground.

Nick Rockett (Ire)
6 b g Walk In The Park - Eireann Rose (Flemensfirth)
Willie Mullins (Ire) — Stewart & Sadie Andrew

PLACINGS: 1/4111-   RPR **148+**h

Starts	1st	2nd	3rd	4th	Win & Pl
4	3	-	-	1	£33,246
4/23	Fair	2m4½f Nov Gd2 Hdl yield			£20,585
3/23	Naas	2m3f Mdn Hdl soft			£6,527
2/23	Thur	1m7½f NHF gd-yld			£5,482

Point-to-point winner who made a bright start under rules last season, landing a bumper and adding both hurdle races; particularly impressive when stepped up to a 2m4f Grade 2 at Fairyhouse, scoring by 15 lengths; should stay further.

Night And Day
6 b m Sea The Moon - Distinctive Look (Danehill)
Willie Mullins (Ire) — Simon Munir & Isaac Souede

PLACINGS: 9/1P5-P   RPR **136+**h

Starts	1st	2nd	3rd	4th	Win & Pl
5	1	-	-	-	£5,752
1/23	Clon	2m1½f Mdn Hdl heavy			£5,221

Created a big impression when winning a maiden hurdle by 22 lengths first time out and was among Cheltenham Festival favourites until reputation took a knock in the spring; at least did better when fifth at Punchestown before being struck into on last run in May.

No Looking Back (Ire)
5 gr g Kingston Hill - Holy Vow (Luso)
Oliver McKiernan (Ire) — Keep The Faith Bloodstock

PLACINGS: 14/11203-   RPR **148+**h

Starts	1st	2nd	3rd	4th	Win & Pl
7	3	1		1	£46,121
12/22	Limk	2m Gd2 Hdl 4yo heavy			£18,097
12/22	Thur	2m Mdn Hdl 4yo yield			£4,958
3/22	Thur	1m7½f NHF 4yo good			£4,958

Bred to improve over fences but made a good fist of hurdling last season; won his first two races, including a four-year-old Grade 2 at Limerick, before finishing second to Irish Point at Naas; disappointed at Aintree but bounced back when third to Facile Vega at Punchestown.

No Ordinary Joe (Ire)
7 b g Getaway - Shadow Dearg (Beneficial)
Nicky Henderson — John P McManus

PLACINGS: 14/113P/1927-   RPR **144**h

Starts	1st	2nd	3rd	4th	Win & Pl
10	4	1	1	1	£51,120
134					
12/22	Kemp	2m Cls3 116-140 Hdl Hcap soft			£11,110
5/21	Worc	2m4f Cls4 Nov Hdl gd-sft			£3,159
5/21	Sthl	2m4½f Cls4 Nov Hdl good			£3,159
11/20	Sand	2m Cls4 NHF 4-6yo soft			£3,249

Well fancied for a string of big handicap hurdles since winning two novices in 2021 and has produced a mixed bag of efforts; did at least win at Kempton last season before a good second in the Martin Pipe at Cheltenham; reverted to type when a beaten favourite at Aintree.

Nick Rockett: made smooth progress over hurdles last season

Racing Post diaries are a great gift idea for any fan of the sport.

Bound in simulated leather, the Racing Post diaries are the perfect office accessories for every horse racing fan.

Each diary includes all the UK and Irish racing fixtures at the time of publication – jumps, Flat and the all-weather as well as major sporting fixtures, a wealth of racing statistics, principal race dates and details of the racecourses in Britain and Ireland.

The A4 desk diary also includes the principal races and bloodstock sales dates in a week-to-view format along with a racecourse guide, plus a marker-ribbon and gilt edging.

NEW SHOP WEBSITE LIVE NOW!
www.racingpost.com/shop

Noble Yeats (Ire)

8 b g Yeats - That's Moyne (Flemensfirth)
Emmet Mullins (Ire) — Robert Waley-Cohen

PLACINGS: 61/1469P291/P11344-7 — RPR **171** +c

Starts 19	1st 6	2nd 1	3rd 2	4th 3	Win & Pl £719,733

	12/22	Aint	3m1f Cls1 Gd2 Ch gd-sft.................................£45,229
	10/22	Wxfd	2m7f List Ch heavy £12,395
147	4/22	Aint	4m2½f Cls1 Gd3 142-161 Ch Hcap gd-sft....£500,000
	10/21	Gway	2m2½f Ch soft..£6,585
	3/21	Navn	2m6f Mdn Hdl yld-sft.......................................£6,321
	1/21	Thur	2m3½f NHF 5-7yo sft-hvy................................£5,268

Famously won the Grand National as a novice in 2022; stepped up on that form last season, finishing fourth in the Cheltenham Gold Cup and filling the same spot under a big weight back in the National, though undone by growing tendency to get too far behind in races.

Not So Sleepy

11 ch g Beat Hollow - Papillon De Bronze (Marju)
Hughie Morrison — Lady Blyth

PLACINGS: 5/110P/U157/155/355- — RPR **155** h

Starts 17	1st 5	2nd -	3rd 1	4th 1	Win & Pl £262,601

	11/21	Newc	2m Cls1 Gd1 Hdl gd-sft..................................£44,545
142	12/20	Asct	1m7½f Cls1 Gd3 128-148 Hdl Hcap heavy......£56,950
127	12/19	Asct	1m7½f Cls1 Gd3 127-150 Hdl Hcap heavy......£85,425
122	11/19	Asct	1m7½f Cls2 122-143 Hdl Hcap soft.................£18,768
	2/19	Winc	1m7½f Cls4 Nov Hdl good £4,224

Dual-purpose veteran who has run well in many top hurdle races in recent seasons, finishing fifth at huge odds in the last two runnings of the Champion Hurdle; dead-heated in the 2021 Fighting Fifth but only third in that race last term before failing to stay 3m in the Long Walk.

Nube Negra gets last season off to the perfect start by winning the Shloer Chase at Cheltenham

Notlongtillmay

7 b g Malinas - Tara Croft (Kayf Tara)
Laura Morgan   Alan Rogers

PLACINGS: 2341/1112-   RPR **155**c

Starts	1st	2nd	3rd	4th	Win & Pl
8	4	2	1	1	£69,081

134	2/23	Muss	2m4½f Cls3 Nov 119-138 Ch Hcap gd-sft £10,630
124	1/23	Muss	2m4½f Cls3 Nov 115-134 Ch Hcap soft............. £6,428
120	11/22	Weth	1m7f Cls3 Nov 120-131 Ch Hcap good............. £6,862
	1/22	Font	2m1½f Cls4 Nov Hdl good £5,991

Lightly raced and progressive chaser who proved a revelation when second at 40-1 in the Turners Novices' Chase at Cheltenham last season; had run just twice over hurdles and then won first three chases at a much lower level, twice by wide margins at Musselburgh.

Nube Negra (Spa)

9 br g Dink - Manly Dream (Highest Honor)
Dan Skelton   T Spraggett

PLACINGS: 36/1122/12/3143/12P-   RPR **162**+c

Starts	1st	2nd	3rd	4th	Win & Pl
22	7	5	4	1	£336,728

11/22	Chel	2m Cls1 Gd2 Ch good £56,950
11/21	Chel	2m Cls1 Gd2 Ch good £42,203
12/20	Kemp	2m Cls1 Gd2 Ch soft £46,364
10/19	Fknm	2m½f Cls3 Nov Ch good £8,058
10/19	Wwck	2m Cls4 Ch good £5,198
1/18	Donc	2m½f Cls4 Nov Hdl soft £4,094
11/17	MRas	2m½f Cls4 Hdl 3yo gd-sft..................................... £3,899

Second in the Champion Chase in a breakthrough 2020-21 campaign but hasn't quite built on that; has twice won the Shloer Chase, albeit at 1-10 in a three-runner race last term; well beaten by Editeur Du Gite at Kempton after that and pulled up in the Champion Chase.

Nusret

4 b c Golden Horn - Serres (Daylami)
Joseph O'Brien (Ire)   Jayne McGivern

PLACINGS: 133134-   RPR **135**h

Starts	1st	2nd	3rd	4th	Win & Pl
6	2	-	3	1	£73,473

2/23	Kemp	2m Cls1 Gd2 Hdl 4yo good £45,560
11/22	Punc	2m½f Hdl 3yo yield £6,941

Very useful juvenile hurdler last season; came up short against the best Irish youngsters but was well placed to raid a Grade 2 at Kempton; subsequently made the frame in Grade 1 races at Aintree and Punchestown.

O'Toole (Ire)

7 ch g Mahler - On Galley Head (Zaffaran)
Stuart Crawford (Ire)   Simon Munir & Isaac Souede

PLACINGS: 1/2143/12-   RPR **145**c

Starts	1st	2nd	3rd	4th	Win & Pl
7	3	2	1	-	£52,172

130	1/23	Newc	2m4f Cls3 117-130 Ch Hcap soft £8,377
	12/21	DRoy	2m1f Mdn Auct Hdl soft...................................... £10,536
	2/21	Fair	2m NHF 5-7yo soft... £5,268

Very lightly raced gelding who was second in a Grade 1 bumper at Punchestown in April 2021 and showed promise in just two runs over fences last season; won a handicap chase at Newcastle on chase debut before a fair second in a 3m Grade 2 at Wetherby.

Our Power (Ire)

8 b g Power - Scripture (Sadler's Wells)
Sam Thomas   Walters Plant Hire & Potter Group

PLACINGS: 31/634PP/51F135/110-   RPR **151**c

Starts	1st	2nd	3rd	4th	Win & Pl
24	7	1	4	3	£221,533

141	2/23	Kemp	3m Cls1 Gd3 131-161 Ch Hcap good............... £85,425
136	10/22	Asct	3m Cls1 Gd3 131-148 Ch Hcap good............... £56,950
134	1/22	Hntg	2m4f Cls3 Nov 115-134 Ch Hcap good............. £8,483
129	12/21	Winc	2m4f Cls3 Nov 121-132 Ch Hcap good............. £8,169
130	3/20	Kemp	2m5f Cls2 127-136 Hdl Hcap gd-sft................. £21,896
	12/18	Newb	2m½f Cls4 Hdl 3yo soft... £4,809
	11/18	MRas	2m½f Cls4 Nov Hdl 3yo good............................. £4,549

Progressive chaser who flourished in a quiet campaign last season, winning valuable 3m handicaps at Ascot and Kempton punctuated by a four-month break; failed to stay after a bold show in the Grand National; should have more to come in good staying handicaps.

Outlaw Peter (Ire)

7 b g Mustameet - My Katie (Classic Cliche)
Paul Nicholls   The Stewart Family, Dench, Ferguson & Mason

PLACINGS: 2/1434/121P2119-1   RPR **136**+h

Starts	1st	2nd	3rd	4th	Win & Pl
14	6	3	1	2	£66,458

130	9/23	NAbb	2m5f Cls3 Nov Ch heavy £6,535
	3/23	Kemp	2m5f Cls2 117-134 Hdl Hcap soft....................... £20,812
	3/23	Winc	2m5½f Cls4 Nov Hdl good £4,085
	11/22	Extr	2m5½f Cls3 Nov Hdl good £8,482
	5/22	Kemp	2m5f Cls4 Mdn Hdl good £4,357
	10/21	Worc	2m Cls5 Mdn NHF 4-6yo gd-sft........................... £1,906

Made the most of second-season novice status over hurdles last season, winning four times; gained biggest win in a handicap at Kempton in March and didn't quite get home when running better than bare form at Aintree over 3m next time; likely to go novice chasing.

Paint The Dream

9 b g Brian Boru - Vineuil (Muhtathir)
Fergal O'Brien   David Brace

PLACINGS: /22313/104414/34133-   RPR **164**+c

Starts	1st	2nd	3rd	4th	Win & Pl
28	5	5	6	5	£157,352

154	11/22	Newb	2m4f Cls2 137-154 Ch Hcap good £26,015
147	3/22	Newb	2m4f Cls1 Gd3 128-148 Ch Hcap soft............... £28,475
147	10/21	Chep	2m3½f Cls2 133-158 Ch Hcap good................. £20,812
137	12/20	Newb	2m6½f Cls3 Nov 131-148 Ch Hcap soft............ £10,267
120	4/19	Prth	2m4f Cls4 Nov 102-120 Hdl Hcap good............ £4,265

Stormed to two wide-margin wins at Newbury in 2022, adding a victory at last season's Coral Gold Cup meeting to the Greatwood Gold Cup; only third in that race last term, with higher mark seemingly beyond him, though handicapper quick to bring him back to realistic level.

RACING POST

Paisley Park (Ire)
11 b g Oscar - Presenting Shares (Presenting)
Emma Lavelle — Andrew Gemmell

PLACINGS: 17/213P/33313/52137- RPR **164**+h

Starts	1st	2nd	3rd	4th	Win & Pl
27	11	5	6	-	£678,096

12/22	Kemp	3m½f Cls1 Gd1 Hdl soft	£45,560
1/22	Chel	3m Cls1 Gd2 Hdl good	£39,389
12/20	Asct	3m½f Cls1 Gd1 Hdl heavy	£45,560
1/20	Chel	3m Cls1 Gd2 Hdl soft	£33,762
11/19	Newb	3m Cls1 Gd2 Hdl gd-sft	£28,810
3/19	Chel	3m Cls1 Gd1 Hdl gd-sft	£182,878
1/19	Chel	3m Cls1 Gd2 Hdl gd-sft	£33,762
12/18	Asct	3m½f Cls1 Gd1 Hdl soft	£56,950
147 11/18	Hayd	3m½f Cls1 Gd3 125-147 Hdl Hcap good	£56,950
140 10/18	Aint	2m4f Cls2 116-140 Hdl Hcap good	£17,204
12/17	Hrfd	2m3½f Cls4 Nov Hdl soft	£4,549

Legendary stayer who won the Stayers' Hurdle in 2019 and has continued to race at a high level ever since; won his third Long Walk Hurdle last season before finishing third when going for a fourth Cleeve Hurdle; seventh in the Stayers' having been third in previous two runnings.

Pembroke
6 b g Blue Bresil - Moyliscar (Terimon)
Dan Skelton — Jon & Julia Aisbitt

PLACINGS: 2F1/711205- RPR **139**h

Starts	1st	2nd	3rd	4th	Win & Pl
7	3	1	-	-	£24,536

12/22	Ludl	2m Cls4 Nov Hdl 4-6yo gd-sft	£4,929
11/22	Weth	2m Cls4 Nov Hdl heavy	£4,085
3/22	Hntg	2m Cls5 NHF 4-6yo soft	£2,178

Useful novice hurdler last season; twice won well in modest company before finishing second when favourite for a Grade 2 at Cheltenham; disappointed when favourite again in the County Hurdle but did better back in novice company when fifth in a Grade 1 at Aintree.

GUIDE TO THE JUMPS 2023-24

Pic D'Orhy (Fr)
8 b g Turgeon - Rose Candy (Rali Abi)
Paul Nicholls   Mrs Johnny De La Hey
PLACINGS: /2F424/1F131P/11121-   RPR **168** +c

Starts	1st	2nd	3rd	4th	Win & Pl
27	11	6	1	2	£632,604

	4/23	Aint	2m4f Cls1 Gd1 Ch soft................................	£140,608
	1/23	Kemp	2m4¹/₂f Cls1 Gd2 Ch soft.............................	£45,774
	12/22	Hntg	2m4f Cls1 Gd2 Ch good..............................	£42,713
	10/22	NAbb	2m5f Cls2 Ch good.....................................	£11,707
	2/22	Kemp	2m4¹/₂f Cls1 Nov Gd2 Ch gd-sft.................	£34,170
	12/21	Asct	2m3f Cls1 Nov Gd2 Ch gd-sft...................	£29,614
147	10/21	Ffos	2m5f Cls3 Nov 132-147 Ch Hcap good.......	£9,581
146	10/21	Newb	2m¹/₂f Cls1 Gd3 130-153 Hdl Hcap good.....	£87,219
	9/18	Autl	2m2f Hdl 3yo v soft.....................................	£25,487
	4/18	Autl	1m7f Hdl 3yo v soft....................................	£23,363
	3/18	Autl	1m7f Hdl 3yo heavy..................................	£22,088

Smart chaser who rewarded pragmatic campaigning by winning four out of five races last season; skipped Cheltenham to wait for easier Grade 1 opening at Aintree and beat Fakir D'Oudairies; had won twice at Grade 2 level before being outclassed by Shishkin at Ascot.

Pied Piper
5 ch g New Approach - Pure Fantasy (Fastnet Rock)
Gordon Elliott (Ire)   Caldwell Construction
PLACINGS: 1131d/115426-   RPR **161** h

Starts	1st	2nd	3rd	4th	Win & Pl
10	4	2	1	1	£157,375

11/22	DRoy	2m1f Gd2 Hdl yld-sft...................................	£24,790
10/22	Chel	2m¹/₂f Cls2 Hdl 4yo good............................	£20,812
1/22	Chel	2m1f Cls1 Gd2 Hdl 4yo good.....................	£34,170
12/21	Punc	1m7¹/₂f Mdn Hdl 3yo heavy......................	£6,321

Very smart hurdler who ran a stormer when beaten a head under top weight in last season's County Hurdle at Cheltenham (strong traveller and relished that end-to-end gallop); had also won twice at that track in 2022 but has been found wanting in Grade 1 races.

Pink Legend
9 b m Midnight Legend - Red And White (Red Ransom)
Venetia Williams   Francis Mahon
PLACINGS: 221/1P61F22/6341311-   RPR **147** +c

Starts	1st	2nd	3rd	4th	Win & Pl
32	9	7	3	5	£210,356

	4/23	Prth	3m Cls1 List Ch gd-sft.................................	£18,596
	4/23	Chel	2m¹/₂f Cls3 114-142 Ch Hcap good............	£13,203
	2/23	Extr	3m Cls1 List Ch good..................................	£19,318
	1/22	Hntg	2m4f Cls1 List Ch gd-sft..............................	£42,713
129	11/21	Asct	2m5f Cls2 127-142 Ch Hcap good............	£13,008
127	4/21	Chel	2m4¹/₂f Cls1 Nov List 106-130 Ch Hcap good	£15,377
	11/20	Bang	2m4¹/₂f Cls4 Ch soft...................................	£4,874
119	12/19	Sthl	1m7¹/₂f Cls3 116-123 Hdl Hcap heavy.......	£5,894
	3/19	Catt	2m7¹/₂f Cls4 Nov Hdl soft..........................	£4,484

Best of the British in the Mares' Chase at Cheltenham in each of the last two years despite going off at 33-1 both times; followed fine third behind Impervious last term by winning a handicap back at Cheltenham and then landing a fourth Listed race at Perth.

Premier Magic (Ire)
10 b g Court Cave - Burn (Selkirk)
Bradley Gibbs   Julian Sherriff
PLACINGS: P/21/111/311P1/111-1   RPR **147** +c

Starts	1st	2nd	3rd	4th	Win & Pl
5	3	-	1		£34,969

5/23	Chel	3m2¹/₂f Cls4 Am Hunt Ch good..................	£5,133
3/23	Chel	3m2¹/₂f Cls2 Am Hunt Ch soft....................	£24,445
2/21	Leic	2m6¹/₂f Cls5 Nov Am Hunt Ch heavy........	£2,989

66-1 winner of last season's Festival Hunters' Chase at Cheltenham, finally bringing his point-to-point form to the racecourse; had been pulled up in the race in 2022 yet won his last eight points dating back to March 2020; followed up with another win at Cheltenham in May.

Proschema (Ire)
8 ch g Declaration Of War - Notable (Zafonic)
Dan Skelton   Empire State Racing Partnership
PLACINGS: 14/2P51/152F/371P4P-   RPR **153** +h

Starts	1st	2nd	3rd	4th	Win & Pl
17	4	2	2	2	£76,957

	10/22	Weth	3m Cls1 Gd2 Hdl gd-sft...............................	£28,475
140	5/21	Aint	2m4f Cls2 119-141 Hdl Hcap good............	£8,169
129	4/21	Chel	2m4¹/₂f Cls2 114-140 Hdl Hcap good........	£8,195
	2/21	Newc	2m¹/₂f Cls4 NHF std-slw.............................	£4,549
	1/21	Newc	2m¹/₂f Cls4 NHF std-slw.............................	£4,679
	11/19	Weth	2m Cls3 Nov Hdl soft..................................	£6,173

Won a 3m Grade 2 hurdle by ten lengths at Wetherby early last season but failed to build on that promise; pulled up when 5-2 for Newbury's Long Distance Hurdle next time and again at Aintree on final run after an underwhelming fourth at Fontwell.

Protektorat (Fr)
8 b g Saint Des Saints - Protektion (Protektor)
Dan Skelton   Sir A Ferguson, G Mason, J Hales & L Hales
PLACINGS: 2130/11221/2134/145-   RPR **174** +c

Starts	1st	2nd	3rd	4th	Win & Pl
21	6	6	2	2	£411,643

11/22	Hayd	3m1¹/₂f Cls1 Gd1 Ch soft............................	£113,870
12/21	Aint	3m1f Cls1 Gd2 Ch soft.................................	£44,775
4/21	Aint	2m4f Cls1 Nov Gd1 Ch gd-sft....................	£42,285
11/20	Aint	2m4f Cls2 Nov Ch gd-sft.............................	£12,820
10/20	Carl	2m Cls3 Ch gd-sft..	£7,018
1/20	Chel	2m4¹/₂f Cls1 Nov List Hdl soft....................	£14,238

High-class staying chaser who has finished third and fifth in the last two runnings of the Cheltenham Gold Cup; tends to be very lightly raced through the winter and not fully wound up when a beaten favourite in last season's Cotswold Chase after winning a weak Betfair Chase.

Pic D'Orhy: high-class operator over fences and winner of four of his five races last season

183

RACING POST

Punctuation
6 b g Dansili - Key Point (Galileo)
Fergal O'Brien   Grant Leon
PLACINGS: 46/5911/114P1-   RPR **139+**h

Starts	1st	2nd	3rd	4th	Win & Pl
11	5	-	-	2	£51,766
129	4/23	Aint	2m½f Cls2 124-134 Am Hdl Hcap soft		£25,720
121	12/22	Chel	2m1f Cls3 114-137 Hdl Hcap good		£11,110
115	11/22	Uttx	2m4f Cls4 114-118 Hdl Hcap soft		£4,684
106	3/22	Newb	2m½f Cls4 Nov 104-118 Hdl Hcap soft		£3,431
95	1/22	Wwck	2m Cls4 Nov 84-110 Hdl Hcap soft		£4,575

Prolific and progressive hurdler who made it five wins in his last seven races when resuming upward curve at Aintree's Grand National meeting; had won four successive handicaps in 2022 before disappointing at Cheltenham but bounced back on second run after wind surgery.

Qualimata (Fr)
4
Gordon Elliott (Ire)
PLACINGS: 1   RPR **91**p

Starts	1st	2nd	3rd	4th	Win & Pl
1	5	-	-	-	
	4/23	Fpp	3m soft		

Most expensive horse sold at a blockbuster Punchestown Goffs Sale in April when fetching a whopping €500,000 to go into training with Gordon Elliott; had won sole point-to-point at Fairyhouse by 30 lengths.

Queens Brook (Ire)
8 b m Shirocco - Awesome Miracle (Supreme Leader)
Gordon Elliott (Ire)   Bective Stud
PLACINGS: /113/123/2122/31213-   RPR **149**h

Starts	1st	2nd	3rd	4th	Win & Pl
14	5	5	4	-	£121,639
	2/23	Punc	2m4½f Gd3 Hdl yield		£15,142
	11/22	Punc	2m2f List Hdl yield		£12,395
	11/21	Fair	2m4f Hdl yield		£8,165
	10/20	Fair	2m Mdn Hdl yield		£6,500
	2/20	Gowr	2m1f NHF 4-7yo heavy		£5,500

High-class mare who has been placed in the last two runnings of the Mares' Hurdle at Cheltenham (also third in the 2020 Champion Bumper there); gained two biggest career victories last season when landing Grade 3 and Listed mares' hurdles.

GUIDE TO THE JUMPS 2023-24

Quel Destin (Fr)
8 ch g Muhtathir - High Destiny (High Yield)
Paul Nicholls   Martin Broughton & Friends
PLACINGS: 115/18512/2P/3P1323-   RPR **139**c

Starts 24	1st 9	2nd 4	3rd 3	4th 1	Win & Pl £229,122
	1/23	Ling	2m Cls3 Ch gd-sft..£7,922
	2/20	Sand	2m Cls1 List Hdl heavy....................................£17,286
	10/19	Chel	2m½f Cls2 Hdl 4yo heavy.............................£25,024
	2/19	Hayd	1m7½f Cls2 Hdl 4yo gd-sft.............................£12,996
	12/18	Chep	2m Cls1 Gd1 Hdl 3yo soft.............................£37,018
	12/18	Donc	2m½f Cls1 Gd2 Hdl 3yo good £28,135
	11/18	Chel	2m½f Cls1 Gd2 Hdl 3yo good £18,006
	10/18	Kemp	2m Cls3 Hdl 3yo good....................................£6,498
	5/18	Autl	1m7f Hdl 3yo heavy......................................£19,115

Former smart hurdler (Grade 1 winner as a juvenile) who rediscovered his form in novice chases last season after nearly two years out through injury; finished a neck second in a premier novice handicap at Sandown and third in a similar race at the same track on final run.

Quilixios
6 b g Maxios - Quilita (Lomitas)
Henry de Bromhead (Ire)   Cheveley Park Stud
PLACINGS: 1/1111/7223/   RPR **153**h

Starts 9	1st 5	2nd 2	3rd 1	4th -	Win & Pl £164,311
	3/21	Chel	2m1f Cls1 Gd1 Hdl 4yo gd-sft.......................£52,753
	2/21	Leop	2m Gd1 Hdl 4yo sft-hvy..................................£65,848
	10/20	DRoy	2m½f Hdl 3yo soft..£5,750
	10/20	Punc	2m Hdl 3yo yield...£6,750
	3/20	Comp	2m Hdl 3yo heavy...£20,339

Won the Triumph Hurdle at Cheltenham in 2021, making it five out of five over hurdles at the time, but career has stuttered since; failed to win the following season, albeit running well in defeat, and missed last term through injury; has the size and scope to make a chaser.

Rare Edition (Ire)
6 b g Califet - Quaspia (Fragrant Mix)
Charlie Longsdon   Pay The Bill Syndicate
PLACINGS: 421/1112P0-   RPR **144**+h

Starts 7	1st 4	2nd 1	3rd -	4th -	Win & Pl £31,352
	12/22	Kemp	2m Cls2 Nov Hdl soft....................................£11,447
	11/22	Donc	2m½f Cls4 Nov Hdl good..............................£4,901
	10/22	Worc	2m Cls3 Nov Hdl 4-6yo good......................£5,446
	4/22	Sthl	2m Cls5 NHF 4-6yo good.............................£2,614

Looked a very smart prospect when winning first three races over hurdles last season, most impressively when beating Rubaud at Kempton, but regressed subsequently; beaten at odds-on at Huntingdon and looked out of his depth at Cheltenham and Aintree.

Quel Destin (left): regained his form last season when sent over fences for the first time

Readin Tommy Wrong (Ire)
5 b g Authorized - Roque De Cyborg (High Chaparral)
Willie Mullins (Ire)   Simon Munir & Isaac Souede
PLACINGS: 2/11   RPR **125**+b

Starts 2	1st 2	2nd -	3rd -	4th -	Win & Pl £11,486
	5/23	Tipp	2m NHF gd-yld..£6,004
	5/23	Baln	2m½f NHF gd-yld..£5,482

Made a bright start this spring when easily winning both bumpers; made a stylish winning debut at Ballinrobe in May and hacked up under a penalty at Tipperary soon after; good prospect for novice hurdles.

Redemption Day
6 b g Blue Bresil - Cutielilou (Astarabad)
Willie Mullins (Ire)   Tim O'Driscoll
PLACINGS: 10/2-   RPR **140**b

Starts 3	1st 1	2nd 1	3rd -	4th -	Win & Pl £22,287
	12/21	Leop	2m NHF 4-7yo soft..£6,321

Missed last season through injury but had been a high-class bumper performer in 2021-22; fluffed his lines when 7-1 for the Champion Bumper at Cheltenham after winning at Leopardstown but did much better when second behind Facile Vega at Punchestown.

Remastered
10 ch g Network - Cathodine Cayras (Martaline)
David Pipe   Brocade Racing
PLACINGS: 33/1115/3F249/121PP-   RPR **156**+c

Starts 27	1st 7	2nd 6	3rd 3	4th 1	Win & Pl £164,303
146	12/22	Kemp	3m Cls2 119-146 Ch Hcap soft...................£26,015
132	11/22	Aint	3m½f Cls2 120-139 Hdl Hcap gd-sft............£15,609
	2/21	Asct	3m Cls1 Nov Gd2 Ch soft.............................£16,819
	12/20	Weth	3m Cls4 Nov Ch heavy..................................£4,289
	11/20	Carl	2m4f Cls3 Nov Ch heavy................................£7,018
	11/18	Ffos	2m Cls4 Nov Hdl heavy..................................£4,159
	2/18	Chep	2m Cls5 NHF 4-6yo heavy.............................£2,274

Talented but fragile stayer who has had persistent breathing problems during his career but underlined his quality early last season; won twice either side of a fine second in the Coral Gold Cup at Newbury (had also held every chance when falling four out in that race in 2022).

Richmond Lake (Ire)
7 b g Westerner - Chic Milan (Milan)
Donald McCain   Exors Of The Late Trevor Hemmings
PLACINGS: 8P/541312F0/61211-   RPR **148**+c

Starts 12	1st 5	2nd 2	3rd 1	4th -	Win & Pl £67,182
140	4/23	Ayr	2m4½f Cls2 128-150 Ch Hcap gd-sft..........£26,164
135	3/23	Hayd	2m4f Cls3 Nov 120-137 Ch Hcap soft...........£8,265
128	1/23	Weth	1m7f Cls3 126-138 Ch Hcap soft...................£8,383
	12/21	Sedg	2m4f Cls4 Nov Hdl soft..................................£4,085
	11/21	Bang	2m½f Cls4 Mdn Auct Hdl soft.........................£4,139

Progressive novice chaser last season, winning

three of his last four races; kept to small-field handicaps in that time and passed his toughest test when winning over 2m4f at Ayr on final run; should stay 3m.

Risk Belle (Fr)
4 b f No Risk At All - Belle Du Berry (Network)
Willie Mullins (Ire) — John P McManus
PLACINGS: 1/154F316- — RPR **128**h

Starts	1st	2nd	3rd	4th	Win & Pl
8	3	-	1	1	£88,971
127	4/23 Fair	2m1½f 114-138 Hdl Hcap yield			£52,212
	5/22 Autl	1m7f Hdl 3yo v soft			£18,151
	3/22 Nant	2m1½f Hdl 3yo soft			£7,261

Battle-hardened juvenile filly last season who won twice in France and found her feet in Ireland once sent handicapping; finished a close third in the Fred Winter at Cheltenham and then beat her elders at Fairyhouse; only sixth when favourite to score again at Punchestown.

Riviere D'Etel (Fr)
6 gr m Martaline - Angesse (Indian River)
Gordon Elliott (Ire) — Bective Stud
PLACINGS: 2137/1112253/24FP- — RPR **152**+c

Starts	1st	2nd	3rd	4th	Win & Pl
15	4	4	2	1	£119,562
	12/21 Navn	2m1f Nov Gd3 Ch yield			£17,121
	11/21 Punc	2m1f Nov Gd2 Ch yield			£18,438
	10/21 Fair	2m Ch good			£5,795
	12/20 Punc	2m Mdn Hdl 3yo heavy			£6,000

Very useful novice chaser two seasons ago but hasn't won since 2021; ran right up to her best when second to Captain Guinness first time

out last term; fell three out when shaping well in the Mares' Chase at Cheltenham and twice disappointed either side of that.

Rock My Way (Ire)
5 b g Getaway - Far Rock (Old Vic)
Syd Hosie — Nick Case, Syd Hosie, John Romans

PLACINGS: P3/121P9- — RPR **139+**h

Starts	1st	2nd	3rd	4th	Win & Pl
4	1	1	-	-	£33,335
	1/23 Chel	2m4½f Cls1 Nov Gd2 Hdl soft			£28,475

Made a rapid impact in novice hurdles last season, winning a Grade 2 at Cheltenham on just his second run; well below par in two subsequent runs at the same track; had begun the season by winning a point-to-point and likely to go novice chasing.

Royale Pagaille (Fr)
9 b g Blue Bresil - Royale Cazoumaille (Villez)
Venetia Williams — Mrs S Ricci

PLACINGS: 2/23/1116/21255/26F- — RPR **164+**c

Starts	1st	2nd	3rd	4th	Win & Pl
24	5	6	2	-	£318,250
163	1/22 Hayd	3m1½f Cls2 143-163 Ch Hcap soft			£42,713
156	1/21 Hayd	3m1½f Cls1 Gd2 136-156 Ch Hcap heavy			£27,036
140	12/20 Kemp	3m Cls2 129-147 Ch Hcap soft			£25,024
	12/20 Hayd	2m5½f Cls2 Nov Ch heavy			£12,021
	1/18 Pau	2m1½f Hdl 4yo heavy			£13,593

High-class chaser who has twice won the Peter Marsh Chase under big weights; has come up short in top company (656 in the last three Cheltenham Gold Cups) but dropped in the handicap last season and was among the favourites for the Irish Grand National when falling at halfway.

Rubaud (Fr)
5 b g Air Chief Marshal - Fulgence (Cardoun)
Paul Nicholls — Chris Giles & Brendan McManus

PLACINGS: 8/112011- — RPR **144+**h

Starts	1st	2nd	3rd	4th	Win & Pl
7	4	1	-	-	£91,947
135	4/23 Ayr	2m Cls1 Gd2 130-150 Hdl Hcap good			£42,713
	2/23 Kemp	2m Cls1 Gd2 Hdl good			£34,170
	12/22 Tntn	2m½f Cls4 Nov Hdl good			£4,901
	11/22 Tntn	2m½f Cls4 Mdn Hdl good			£4,901

Prolific and progressive novice hurdler last season, winning four times; bounced back from sole disappointment in the Betfair Hurdle to win a soft Grade 2 at Kempton; stepped up on that form on final run when making all for a decisive victory in the Scottish Champion Hurdle.

Sail Away: smart novice chaser last season after lengthy break from action

GUIDE TO THE JUMPS 2023-24

Run Wild Fred (Ire)
9 ch g Shantou - Talkin Madam (Talkin Man)
Gordon Elliott (Ire) — Gigginstown House Stud

PLACINGS: 1/3455222/2122FF/23- — RPR **146**c

Starts	1st	2nd	3rd	4th	Win & Pl
23	5	7	4	1	£231,810
145	11/21 Navn	3m 124-149 Ch Hcap good			£42,143
	2/20 Punc	3m Nov Gd3 Hdl heavy			£17,500
	12/19 Navn	2m4f Mdn Hdl soft			£7,188
	3/19 Limk	2m NHF 5-7yo good			£6,382
	1/19 Fair	2m NHF 5-7yo good			£5,827

Missed most of last season through injury but has proved himself a smart staying chaser despite a poor strike-rate; deservedly landed a valuable handicap chase in the 2021 Troytown having finished second in the Thyestes and Irish Grand National that year.

Sail Away (Fr)
7 gr g Martaline - Baraka Du Berlais (Bonnet Rouge)
Dan Skelton — Mr & Mrs J D Cotton

PLACINGS: 0/125P/9/262/3121- — RPR **150+**c

Starts	1st	2nd	3rd	4th	Win & Pl
13	3	4	1	-	£78,579
136	4/23 Ayr	3m Cls2 Nov 116-142 Ch Hcap good			£26,015
135	5/22 Wwck	3m Cls3 Nov 116-135 Ch Hcap good			£5,882
	5/19 Comp	2m Hdl 3yo v soft			£19,459

Lightly raced chaser who shrugged off a long absence with two fine runs last spring, winning a novice handicap at Ayr's Scottish National meeting but then missing intended summer targets; likes good ground and could be one for a major staying handicap when conditions suit.

Saint Felicien (Fr)
6 br g Saint Des Saints - In Race (Sageburg)
Gordon Elliott (Ire) — Robcour

PLACINGS: 1/12P/ — RPR **153**h

Starts	1st	2nd	3rd	4th	Win & Pl
4	2	1	-	-	£30,965
	11/21 Gowr	2m Nov Hdl 4yo yield			£7,112
	3/21 Autl	2m1½f Hdl 4yo v soft			£19,304

Lightly raced and highly rated French recruit who hasn't run since being sent off favourite for the 2022 Coral Cup on just his fourth run only to be pulled up; had made a winning Irish debut at Gowran before a solid second behind Darasso when stepped up in class at Naas.

Saint Roi (Fr)
8 br g Coastal Path - Sainte Vigne (Saint Des Saints)
Willie Mullins (Ire) — John P McManus

PLACINGS: 1/1244/343/4321U324- — RPR **158**c

Starts	1st	2nd	3rd	4th	Win & Pl
19	4	2	5	5	£293,600
	12/22 Leop	2m1f Nov Gd1 Ch yield			£49,580
	10/20 Tipp	2m Gd3 Hdl good			£17,500
137	3/20 Chel	2m1f Cls1 Gd3 133-150 Hdl Hcap soft			£56,270
	1/20 Tram	2m Mdn Hdl soft			£5,760

Has won just once since October 2020 (also

won the County Hurdle that year) but has been very highly tried in that time, with 12 out of 14 runs at Grade 1 level; finally struck at the top level in a novice chase last season but found wanting again in the very best company.

Saint Sam (Fr)
6 b g Saint Des Saints - Ladeka (Linda's Lad)
Willie Mullins (Ire)   Edward Ware
PLACINGS: 2422/513U/615201-11F   RPR **158**c

Starts	1st	2nd	3rd	4th	Win & Pl
20	7	4	1	1	£128,028

8/23	Gway	2m6½f Ch yield £13,053
5/23	Klny	2m4f Gd3 Ch good £14,881
4/23	Tram	2m5½f Ch soft £6,788
12/22	Punc	2m3½f Hdl sft-hvy £8,676
1/22	Fair	2m1f Ch soft £8,165
7/20	Claf	2m1f Hdl 3yo soft £10,983
6/20	Diep	2m1f Hdl 3yo soft £8,258

Came up short in Grade 1 novice chases after winning on debut in January 2022 but has looked a much better specimen on a second crack at fences this year; won at Tramore in April after marking time over hurdles and added two more victories this summer, impressively at Galway.

Sam Brown
11 b g Black Sam Bellamy - Cream Cracker (Sir Harry Lewis)
Anthony Honeyball   T C Frost
PLACINGS: /11P/3/732P1/35P5FF-   RPR **160**c

Starts	1st	2nd	3rd	4th	Win & Pl
19	6	2	3	1	£131,129

147	4/22	Aint	3m1f Cls3 Gd3 130-155 Ch Hcap gd-sft £56,319
	1/20	Hayd	2m4f Cls1 Nov Gd2 Ch heavy £18,793
	1/20	Ling	2m7½f Cls4 Nov Ch heavy £4,289
	12/17	Plum	2m4½f Cls4 Nov Hdl soft £3,249
	3/17	Newb	2m½f Cls5 NHF 4-6yo soft £2,599
	2/17	Winc	1m7½f Cls6 NHF 4-6yo heavy £1,949

Enjoyed his finest hour when winning on Grand National day at Aintree in 2022 and might well have added another major spring handicap last term but for falling two out at Punchestown; had struggled when forced into Graded company by higher mark in between.

Samarrive (Fr)
6 b g Coastal Path - Sambirane (Apeldoorn)
Paul Nicholls   Mrs Johnny De La Hey
PLACINGS: 11/71P91/F333-   RPR **145+**h

Starts	1st	2nd	3rd	4th	Win & Pl
11	4	-	3	-	£70,875

137	4/22	Sand	2m4f Cls2 121-141 Hdl Hcap good £18,211
130	12/21	Sand	2m Cls1 List 123-149 Hdl Hcap good £28,475
	4/21	Kemp	2m Cls4 Nov Hdl good £3,159
	12/20	Ange	2m1f Hdl 3yo heavy £8,258

Dual Sandown handicap hurdle winner who made a highly promising chase debut at Ascot last season but didn't go on; fell two out that day when running a big race against Gowel Road but was well beaten at odds-on next time; did better in two runs back over hurdles after a break.

Sandor Clegane (Ire)
6 b g Fame And Glory - Betty Roe (Vinnie Roe)
Paul Nolan (Ire)   Mrs K Browne & Mrs Anne Coffey
PLACINGS: 122/721331-   RPR **150**h

Starts	1st	2nd	3rd	4th	Win & Pl
9	3	3	2	-	£104,402

4/23	Punc	2m4f Hdl yield £39,159
11/22	Punc	2m5½f Mdn Auct Hdl yld-sft £9,916
12/21	Punc	2m NHF 4-7yo yield £7,902

Useful staying novice hurdler last season who twice finished third at Grade 1 level, most notably when relishing step up to 3m in the Albert Bartlett at Cheltenham; won a valuable series final at Punchestown having qualified with a maiden win at the same track; likely to go novice chasing.

Sceau Royal (Fr)
11 b g Doctor Dino - Sandside (Marchand De Sable)
Alan King   Simon Munir & Isaac Souede
PLACINGS: F153/1136232/124326-   RPR **158**c

Starts	1st	2nd	3rd	4th	Win & Pl
50	17	11	7	4	£711,818

	10/22	Kemp	2m Cls1 List Hdl good £28,475
	11/21	Winc	1m7f Cls1 Gd2 Hdl good £34,170
	10/21	Kemp	2m Cls1 List Hdl good £22,780
	2/21	Newb	2m½f Cls1 Gd2 Ch gd-sft £25,628
	11/20	Winc	1m7½f Cls1 Gd2 Hdl good £27,336
150	10/20	Ffos	2m Cls2 134-154 Hdl Hcap gd-sft £25,024
	11/18	Chel	2m Cls1 Gd2 Ch good £42,203
	1/18	Donc	2m½f Cls1 Nov Gd2 Ch soft £19,933
	12/17	Sand	1m7½f Cls1 Nov Gd1 Ch gd-sft £29,810
	11/17	Wwck	2m Cls3 Nov Ch 4-5yo gd-sft £9,384
	10/17	Wwck	2m Cls4 Nov Ch good £5,198
149	11/16	Winc	1m7½f Cls1 Gd2 133-149 Hdl Hcap good £35,772
	10/16	Chel	2m½f Cls2 Hdl 4yo good £21,977
	1/16	Hntg	2m Cls2 Hdl 4yo soft £12,512
	12/15	Chel	2m1f Cls2 Hdl 3yo soft £12,628
	11/15	Wwck	2m Cls4 Hdl 3yo gd-sft £3,249
	3/15	Bord	2m½f Hdl 3yo v soft £7,814

High-class hurdler and chaser over many seasons, with seven Graded victories stretching back to 2016; not quite at his best last term and failed to add to Listed hurdle win at Kempton in October; third in a Grade 1 chase at Leopardstown on sole run over fences.

Seddon (Ire)
10 b g Stowaway - Andreas Benefit (Beneficial)
John McConnell (Ire)   Galaxy Horse Racing Syndicate
PLACINGS: /515721/328F231111-2   RPR **154+**c

Starts	1st	2nd	3rd	4th	Win & Pl
30	9	5	6	-	£203,511

134	4/23	Punc	2m3f 122-148 Hdl Hcap gd-yld £52,212
143	3/23	Chel	2m4½f Cls1 Gd3 133-157 Ch Hcap soft £67,524
123	12/22	Leop	2m5f 98-123 Ch Hcap soft £9,916
129	10/22	Chel	2m4f Cls3 114-141 Hdl Hcap good £11,654
128	4/22	NAbb	2m5f Cls3 122-134 Ch Hcap good £6,535
128	11/21	Ling	2m3½f Cls3 106-130 Hdl Hcap gd-sft £4,956
132	8/20	Ctml	2m5f Cls3 Nov 123-132 Ch Hcap gd-sft £6,303
	11/18	Strf	2m½f Cls3 Nov Hdl 4-6yo good £8,058
	2/18	Muss	1m7½f Cls4 NHF 4-6yo soft £3,249

Lost his way in Britain but went from strength to strength following move to John McConnell last season; won his last four races, including the Plate at Cheltenham; also took advantage of

RACING POST

Firsts, Lasts & Onlys: Horse Racing: A Truly Wonderful Collection of Horse Racing Trivia is filled with improbable facts and mind-boggling trivia that will test and tease every horse racing enthusiast.

Try these questions for size: How did the word 'thoroughbred' come into existence, and what is a dam sire? Which Grand National-winning horse opened supermarkets after he retired and was sent requests for autographs? Which BBC sports commentator often had bad luck around the time of the National? Which classic race almost came to be known as the Bunbury?

The perfect gift for every horse racing fan, this is a book you can pick up while waiting for the stewards' inquiry for the 3.15 at Newmarket and learn something new, weird or fascinating. Often all three.

NEW SHOP WEBSITE LIVE NOW!
www.racingpost.com/shop

   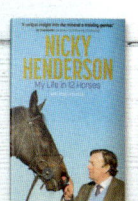  

RACING POST

lower hurdles mark, winning at Cheltenham in October and Punchestown in April.

Seeyouinmydreams
5 b m Telescope - Sierra (Anabaa)
Paul Nicholls   Mason, Hogarth, Ferguson, Done, McGoff

PLACINGS: 110-   RPR **120**+B

Starts	1st	2nd	3rd	4th	Win & Pl
2	1	-	-	-	£3,812
	3/23	Newb	2m¹/₂f Cls4 NHF 4-6yo good		£3,812

Bought for 235,000gns after easily winning sole point-to-point in early 2022 and made a big impression on debut under rules when scoring just as impressively in a Newbury bumper; raced much too freely when below par in a Grade 2 mares' bumper at Aintree.

Shakem Up'Arry (Ire)
9 b g Flemensfirth - Nun Better (Presenting)
Ren Pauling   Harry Redknapp

PLACINGS: 20/14280/U1323/1534   RPR **144**c

Starts	1st	2nd	3rd	4th	Win & Pl
19	3	4	4	2	£76,783
134	12/22	Extr	2m3f Cls3 117-137 Ch Hcap gd-sft		£10,130
131	12/21	Hayd	2m¹/₂f Cls3 121-131 Ch Hcap soft		£7,624
	11/20	Ffos	2m Cls4 Nov Hdl soft		£3,769

Useful handicap chaser who made the frame at Cheltenham and Aintree last spring; had won well at Exeter first time out and stepped up on that when third in the Plate behind Seddon; didn't quite last home over 3m1f when fourth on final run having led between the last two.

Shanbally Kid (Ire)
6 b g Presenting - Kalanisi's Lady (Kalanisi)
Willie Mullins (Ire)   Gigginstown House Stud

PLACINGS: 01/418-   RPR **136**+h

Starts	1st	2nd	3rd	4th	Win & Pl
5	2	-	-	1	£12,363
	1/23	Navn	2m4f Mdn Hdl soft		£6,527
	4/22	Clon	2m¹/₂f NHF 4-7yo yield		£4,958

Bought for £190,000 after winning a Clonmel bumper for Richard O'Brien and proved useful in just three runs over hurdles last season; won a Navan maiden at the second attempt over 2m4f before finishing eighth in the Albert Bartlett, perhaps not staying 3m.

Shannon Royale (Ire)
5 b g Walk In The Park - Shannon Rose (Topanoora)
Gordon Elliott (Ire)   Robcour

PLACINGS: 2/91-   RPR **126**+B

Starts	1st	2nd	3rd	4th	Win & Pl
2	1	-	-	-	£5,221
	4/23	Clon	2m¹/₂f NHF heavy		£5,221

Bought for £300,000 after finishing second in sole point-to-point in early 2022; fluffed his lines on debut under rules last season but got things right at the second attempt when making all to win well in a bumper at Clonmel.

Sharjah (Fr)
10 b g Doctor Dino - Saaryeh (Royal Academy)
Willie Mullins (Ire)   Mrs S Ricci

PLACINGS: 62/132/211/232424-21   RPR **161**h

Starts	1st	2nd	3rd	4th	Win & Pl
31	10	7	4	4	£904,767
	8/23	Gway	2m2f Ch yield		£8,876
	12/21	Leop	2m Gd1 Hdl yld-sft		£79,018
	11/21	Punc	2m Gd1 Hdl gd-yld		£52,679
	12/20	Leop	2m Gd1 Hdl soft		£50,000
	12/19	Leop	2m Gd1 Hdl yield		£66,441
	12/18	Leop	2m Gd1 Hdl gd-yld		£65,265
	11/18	Punc	2m Gd1 Hdl good		£52,212
146	8/18	Gway	2m 135-146 Hdl Hcap soft		£156,637
	11/17	Gowr	2m Nov Hdl 4yo heavy		£8,161
	9/17	Gowr	2m Mdn Hdl 4yo heavy		£6,844

Six-time Grade 1 winner who also finished second in back-to-back Champion Hurdles in 2020 and 2021; not quite at his best last season but still a fine fourth in the County Hurdle when seeking to exploit reduced handicap mark and second in the Aintree Hurdle in the spring.

Shishkin (Ire)
9 b g Sholokhov - Labarynth (Exit To Nowhere)
Nicky Henderson   Mrs J Donnelly

PLACINGS: F111/11111/11P/3121-   RPR **178**+c

Starts	1st	2nd	3rd	4th	Win & Pl
17	13	1	1	-	£736,802
	4/23	Aint	3m1f Cls1 Gd1 Ch gd-sft		£146,925
	2/23	Asct	2m5f Cls1 Gd1 Ch gd-sft		£100,132
	1/22	Asct	2m1f Cls1 Gd1 Ch gd-sft		£85,425
	12/21	Kemp	2m Cls1 Gd2 Ch soft		£56,950
	4/21	Aint	2m Cls1 Nov Gd1 Ch gd-sft		£42,701
	3/21	Chel	2m Cls1 Nov Gd1 Ch soft		£73,854
	1/21	Donc	2m¹/₂f Cls1 Nov Gd2 Ch soft		£14,682
	12/20	Kemp	2m Cls1 Nov Gd2 Ch soft		£18,224
	11/20	Kemp	2m2f Cls4 Ch good		£4,394
	3/20	Chel	2m¹/₂f Cls1 Nov Gd1 Hdl soft		£70,338
	2/20	Hntg	2m3¹/₂f Cls1 Nov List Hdl gd-sft		£17,286
	1/20	Newb	2m¹/₂f Cls4 Nov Hdl heavy		£4,549
	3/19	Kemp	2m Cls5 Mdn NHF 4-6yo gd-sft		£3,119

Has lost his aura of invincibility since winning his first 11 races under rules but still won two Grade 1 chases when stepped up in trip last season; most impressive in the Ascot Chase and finished strongly on first run at 3m to add the Aintree Bowl from Ahoy Senor.

Sir Gerhard (Ire)
8 b g Jeremy - Faanan Aldaar (Authorized)
Willie Mullins (Ire)   Cheveley Park Stud

PLACINGS: 1/111/3111/3192P-   RPR **155**+c

Starts	1st	2nd	3rd	4th	Win & Pl
12	7	1	2	-	£247,294
	1/23	Gowr	2m Ch sft-hvy		£6,788
	3/22	Chel	2m5f Cls1 Nov Gd1 Hdl soft		£76,030
	2/22	Leop	2m Nov Gd1 Hdl yld-sft		£74,370
	12/21	Leop	2m Mdn Hdl soft		£7,902
	3/21	Chel	2m¹/₂f Cls1 Gd1 NHF 4-6yo gd-sft		£31,652
	12/20	Navn	2m List NHF 4-7yo sft-hvy		£11,250
	10/20	DRoy	2m¹/₂f NHF 4-7yo soft		£5,000

Dual Cheltenham Festival winner whose bubble

190

burst when ninth in the Brown Advisory last term after a condensed season (just one prior run over fences); at least did better when a close second to Flame Bearer at Fairyhouse but pulled up after being struck into at Punchestown.

Sire Du Berlais (Fr)
11 b g Paliglote - Royale Athenia (Garde Royale)
Gordon Elliott (Ire) — John P McManus

PLACINGS: /132/2P401/455P4113- — RPR **166h**

Starts	1st	2nd	3rd	4th	Win & Pl
31	7	3	4	6	£736,037

4/23	Aint	3m¹/₂f Cls1 Gd1 Hdl gd-sft	£140,419
3/23	Chel	3m Cls1 Gd1 Hdl soft	£197,696
4/22	Aint	3m¹/₂f Cls1 Gd1 Hdl gd-sft	£140,325
11/20	Navn	2m4f Gd2 Hdl sft-hvy	£17,500
152 3/20	Chel	3m Cls1 Gd3 131-152 Hdl Hcap soft	£56,270
145 3/19	Chel	3m Cls1 Gd3 134-148 Hdl Hcap gd-sft	£56,270
5/16	Comp	2m1f Hdl 4yo v soft	£7,765

Remarkable 33-1 winner of last season's Stayers' Hurdle *(below)*, taking his form to new heights at the age of 11; rarely at his best through the winter but tends to come good in the spring, boasting a terrific Cheltenham Festival record and also winning at Aintree for the last two years.

So Scottish (Fr)
6 b g Martaline - Mer D'Arabie (Ballingarry)
Emmet Mullins (Ire) — John P McManus

PLACINGS: 3/14956/70211127U- — RPR **144+c**

Starts	1st	2nd	3rd	4th	Win & Pl
14	3	2	1	1	£60,617

10/22	Carl	2m4f Cls3 Nov Ch good	£7,407
10/22	Tipp	2m3¹/₂f Nov Ch gd-yld	£7,189
9/22	Kbgn	2m Mdn Hdl good	£4,958

Lightly raced chaser who shaped with huge promise last autumn; won at the seventh attempt over hurdles and immediately added his first two chases; finished a good second on handicap chase debut at Ascot but came up short at Cheltenham and Punchestown.

RACING POST

Solo (Fr)
7 b g Kapgarde - Flameche (Balko)
Paul Nicholls   Mrs Johnny De La Hey
PLACINGS: 8/45040/22367/1221P-   RPR **152+c**

Starts	1st	2nd	3rd	4th	Win & Pl
19	4	5	1	2	£122,357

	2/23	Kemp	2m4½f Cls1 Nov Gd2 Ch good	£34,170
135	11/22	Sand	2m4f Cls3 Nov 120-135 Ch Hcap soft	£8,169
	2/20	Kemp	2m Cls1 Gd2 Hdl 4yo gd-sft	£17,085
	11/19	Autl	2m1½f Hdl 3yo heavy	£19,459

Got back on track last season having taken an age to build on impressive British debut in 2020; won at the fifth attempt over fences first time out last term and continued to progress in novice company, winning a Grade 2 at Kempton; pulled up when raised in class at Sandown.

Sonigino (Fr)
6 b g It's Gino - Soniador (Legolas)
Paul Nicholls   Sir A Ferguson G Mason J Hales & L Hales
PLACINGS: 4/1135455/11813-   RPR **140+h**

Starts	1st	2nd	3rd	4th	Win & Pl
13	5	-	2	2	£73,616

131	2/23	Hntg	2m3½f Cls2 116-142 Hdl Hcap good	£15,609
123	10/22	Chep	2m Cls3 119-127 Hdl Hcap gd-sft	£5,664
119	10/22	Chep	2m Cls3 119-131 Hdl Hcap good	£8,387
	6/21	Autl	2m1½f Hdl 4yo heavy	£18,893
	5/21	Mlns	2m1½f Hdl 4yo v soft	£9,036

Progressive handicap hurdler last season; had disappointed on first season in Britain (dual hurdles winner in France) but then won three times and finished a fine third when up in class at Aintree's Grand National meeting; likely to go novice chasing.

Spanish Harlem (Fr)
5 ch g Spanish Moon - Souverainete (Doctor Dino)
Willie Mullins (Ire)   Dr S P Fitzgerald
PLACINGS: 1322P-   RPR **130h**

Starts	1st	2nd	3rd	4th	Win & Pl
5	1	2	1	-	£23,464

6/22	Autl	2m1½f Hdl 4yo heavy	£17,782

Yet to make much dent in huge €360,000 purchase price after winning at Auteuil last June; still ran solid races to finish second or third in three novice hurdles; well fancied on handicap debut in the Martin Pipe at Cheltenham only to be pulled up.

Springwell Bay
6 b g Kayf Tara - Winning Counsel (Leading Counsel)
Jonjo O'Neill   Mrs Gay Smith
PLACINGS: 21/13116-   RPR **139+h**

Starts	1st	2nd	3rd	4th	Win & Pl
7	4	1	1	-	£48,058

3/23	Weth	2m3½f Cls4 Nov Hdl soft	£4,901
2/23	Asct	2m3½f Cls2 Nov Hdl good	£13,008
10/22	Carl	2m1f Cls4 Nov Hdl 4-6yo good	£4,629
11/21	MRas	2m½f Cls5 NHF 4-6yo good	£1,906

Fine chasing type who won three novice hurdles last season to add to sole bumper victory, most notably when impressing at Ascot; beaten on both runs in Graded company, finding 2m1f inadequate at Cheltenham before a fair sixth at Aintree; likely to go novice chasing.

Stage Star (Ire)
7 b g Fame And Glory - Sparky May (Midnight Legend)
Paul Nicholls   Owners Group
PLACINGS: 123/111PP/121115-   RPR **159+c**

Starts	1st	2nd	3rd	4th	Win & Pl
14	8	2	1	-	£201,195

	3/23	Chel	2m4f Cls1 Nov Gd1 Ch soft	£98,473
	1/23	Chel	2m4½f Cls2 Nov 120-142 Ch Hcap soft	£15,609
	1/23	Plum	2m3½f Cls3 Nov Ch soft	£10,075
142	11/22	Wwck	2m Cls3 Nov Ch gd-sft	£9,242
	12/21	Newb	2m4½f Cls1 Nov Gd1 Hdl soft	£34,331
	11/21	Newb	2m4½f Cls3 Nov Hdl gd-sft	£5,991
	10/21	Chep	2m3½f Cls4 Mdn Hdl good	£4,085
	10/20	Chep	2m Cls5 Am NHF 4-6yo soft	£2,274

Won the Turners Novices' Chase at the Cheltenham Festival last season under a fine front-running ride; had also won the Challow Hurdle in 2021 before progressing at a lower level over fences, winning a novice handicap at Cheltenham on his previous run; below-par fifth at Aintree.

State Man (Fr)
6 ch g Doctor Dino - Arret Station (Johann Quatz)
Willie Mullins (Ire)   Mrs J Donnelly
PLACINGS: 2/F11/111121-   RPR **168+h**

Starts	1st	2nd	3rd	4th	Win & Pl
10	7	2	-	-	£617,840

	4/23	Punc	2m Gd1 Hdl yield	£156,637
	2/23	Leop	2m Gd1 Hdl yield	£99,115
	12/22	Leop	2m Gd1 Hdl soft	£74,370
	11/22	Punc	2m½f Gd1 Hdl yield	£59,496
	4/22	Punc	2m3½f Nov Gd1 Hdl gd-yld	£61,975
141	3/22	Chel	2m1f Cls1 Gd3 134-152 Hdl Hcap gd-sft	£56,270
	2/22	Limk	2m Mdn Hdl soft	£4,958

Dominated the two-mile hurdling scene in Ireland last season, winning four times at Grade 1 level; put in his place by Constitution Hill in the Champion Hurdle but finished best of the rest and got back to winning ways with a clearcut win over Vauban at Punchestown.

Stattler (Ire)
8 br g Stowaway - Our Honey (Old Vic)
Willie Mullins (Ire)   R A Bartlett
PLACINGS: 132/3134/3111/22P-   RPR **167+c**

Starts	1st	2nd	3rd	4th	Win & Pl
14	5	3	4	1	£167,042

3/22	Chel	3m6f Cls1 Nov Gd2 Am Ch gd-sft	£60,763
1/22	Naas	3m1f Nov Gd3 Ch gd-yld	£14,874
12/21	Fair	2m5f Ch yld-sft	£5,795
12/20	Leop	2m4f Mdn Hdl soft	£6,000
1/20	Fair	2m NHF 5-7yo heavy	£5,008

Won the National Hunt Chase in 2022 and did well in a light campaign last season despite not winning; ran Minella Indo to a neck over an inadequate trip at Thurles and chased home

GUIDE TO THE JUMPS **2023-24**

Galopin Des Champs in the Irish Gold Cup; never travelling in the Cheltenham Gold Cup.

Stay Away Fay (Ire)
6 b g Shantou - Augusta Bay (Oscar)
Paul Nicholls   Chris Giles & Dave Staddon
PLACINGS: 1/1214-   RPR **151+**h

Starts	1st	2nd	3rd	4th	Win & Pl
4	2	1	-	1	£96,347
	3/23	Chel	3m Cls1 Nov Gd1 Hdl soft............................£75,965
	11/22	Newb	2m4½f Cls3 Nov Hdl good............................£6,535

Strong stayer who gamely won what might prove a moderate running of the Albert Bartlett at Cheltenham last season, benefiting from a more positive ride than when second previously at Doncaster; beaten again when a close fourth in the Sefton at Aintree; set to go novice chasing.

Steal A March
8 b g Mount Nelson - Side Step (Norse Dancer)
Nicky Henderson   The King & The Queen
PLACINGS: 4414/36P12/2121-   RPR **133+**h

Starts	1st	2nd	3rd	4th	Win & Pl
13	4	3	1	3	£41,794
	12/22	Winc	2m½f Cls2 113-139 Hdl Hcap gd-sft.............£13,008
	6/22	Worc	2m7f Cls3 115-134 Hdl Hcap good................£6,219
	4/21	Extr	2m5½f Cls4 102-121 Hdl Hcap gd-fm............£3,159
	12/19	Hrfd	2m5½f Cls4 Nov Hdl heavy............................£3,769

Progressive staying hurdler who has finished first or second in his last five runs in that discipline, winning three times; won a Pertemps qualifier

on final run last season at Kempton only to miss the rest of the season; still a novice over fences, finishing second in only chase.

Stolen Silver (Fr)
8 gr g Lord Du Sud - Change Partner (Turtle Island)
Sam Thomas   Walters Plant Hire & Potter Group
PLACINGS: P/332P8/124341/U2P0-   RPR **157**c

Starts	1st	2nd	3rd	4th	Win & Pl
23	4	4	3	2	£120,290
	143	4/22	Chel	2m4½f Cls1 Gd2 140-154 Ch Hcap good.......£39,466
	136	10/21	MRas	2m1f Cls3 Nov 131-142 Ch Hcap good..........£7,080
		1/20	Hayd	1m7½f Cls1 Nov Gd2 Hdl heavy...................£17,085
		11/19	Ffos	2m Cls4 Nov Hdl soft......................................£3,769

Cheltenham specialist whose best three Racing Post Ratings have all been achieved at the track; won the Silver Trophy in 2022 and finished a close second in another valuable handicap on New Year's Day last term; well below par in two subsequent runs.

Straw Fan Jack
8 gr g Geordieland - Callerlilly (Double Trigger)
Sheila Lewis   Graham Wilson
PLACINGS: 12126/206P247/11444-   RPR **148**c

Starts	1st	2nd	3rd	4th	Win & Pl
21	4	4	-	5	£59,591
		10/22	Chel	2m Cls2 Nov Ch good.....................................£13,008
	128	10/22	Ffos	2m Cls3 Nov 121-129 Ch Hcap good..............£8,169
		12/20	Aint	2m1f Cls3 Nov Hdl soft..................................£5,913
		10/20	Hrfd	2m3½f Cls4 Nov Hdl gd-fm............................£3,769

Too highly tried last spring but still proved a

State Man: major force over hurdles in Ireland

useful novice chaser; won first two races over fences, including at Cheltenham, before a good fourth at Newbury; far from disgraced when fourth in the Arkle and got closer when filling the same spot in another Grade 1 at Aintree.

Strong Leader
6 b g Passing Glance - Strong Westerner (Westerner)
Olly Murphy   Welfordgolf Syndicate
PLACINGS: 1211192-   RPR **146**h

Starts	1st	2nd	3rd	4th	Win & Pl
7	4	2	-	-	£43,141

1/23	Sthl	2m Cls4 Nov Hdl good	£4,901
12/22	Aint	2m1f Cls3 Nov Hdl gd-sft	£6,372
11/22	Uttx	2m Cls4 Nov Hdl good	£4,901
5/22	Wwck	2m Cls5 NHF 4-6yo good	£2,178

Very useful novice hurdler last season; won first three races, albeit in moderate company, before facing a sharp rise in class in the spring; far from disgraced when ninth in the Supreme (best of the British runners) and stepped up on that when second behind Inthepocket at Aintree.

Stumptown (Ire)
6 br g Laverock - Active Fieldgale (Beneficial)
Gavin Cromwell (Ire)   Furze Bush Syndicate
PLACINGS: 2/104/637537112P-48   RPR **146**+c

Starts	1st	2nd	3rd	4th	Win & Pl
15	3	1	2	2	£44,472

125	2/23	Sand	3m Cls3 117-131 Ch Hcap good	£7,805
112	1/23	Thur	2m5½f 104-129 Ch Hcap yield	£8,354
	10/21	Limk	2m Mdn Hdl soft	£6,321

Progressive staying chaser who flourished when sent handicapping and stepped up in trip in second half of last season; hacked up at Thurles and Sandown before finishing a neck second when favourite for the Kim Muir at Cheltenham; pulled up in the Irish National.

Tahmuras (Fr)

6 b g Falco - Alinga's Lass (Whipper)

Paul Nicholls — Noel Fehily Racing Syndicates

PLACINGS: 121/11107- — RPR **144+h**

Starts	1st	2nd	3rd	4th	Win & Pl
7	4	1	-	-	£62,774

	1/23	Sand	2m Cls1 Nov Gd1 Hdl soft	£39,865
	11/22	Hayd	1m7½f Cls1 Nov List Hdl soft	£14,238
	11/22	Chep	2m Cls4 Mdn Hdl gd-sft	£4,901
	3/22	Winc	1m7f Cls5 Mdn NHF 4-6yo gd-sft	£1,906

Grand chasing type who did well to excel in novice hurdles last season, completing a hat-trick in the Tolworth Hurdle when conditions brought stamina to the fore; outpaced when down the field in Grade 1 company at Cheltenham and Aintree; should thrive over further when chasing.

Tea For Free (Ire)

8 b g Court Cave - Golan Gale (Golan)

Charlie Longsdon — Mrs Susan Monkland

PLACINGS: 14/35332/1111F- — RPR **143c**

Starts	1st	2nd	3rd	4th	Win & Pl
11	4	1	3	1	£31,727

131	12/22	Newb	2m6½f Cls3 Nov 121-134 Ch Hcap soft	£7,407
125	11/22	Uttx	3m2f Cls3 109-125 Ch Hcap good	£9,694
112	10/22	Uttx	3m Cls4 84-112 Ch Hcap good	£5,174
105	5/22	Hntg	2m7½f Cls5 Nov 79-107 Ch Hcap good	£3,812

Massive improver when sent chasing last season; began in a novice handicap off a mark of just 105 and won his first four races over fences to go up 33lb; joint-favourite for the Sky Bet Chase on sharp rise in class and running another big race when falling two out.

Teahupoo (Fr)

6 b g Masked Marvel - Droit D'Aimer (Sassanian)

Gordon Elliott (Ire) — Robcour

PLACINGS: 1112/1119/61134- — RPR **168+h**

Starts	1st	2nd	3rd	4th	Win & Pl
13	8	1	1	1	£224,032

	1/23	Gowr	3m½f Gd2 Hdl sft-hvy	£19,058
	12/22	Fair	2m3½f Gd1 Hdl soft	£59,496
	2/22	Gowr	2m Gd3 Hdl heavy	£14,874
	12/21	Limk	2m Gd2 Hdl 4yo heavy	£18,438
	11/21	Naas	2m Gd3 Hdl 4yo yield	£14,487
	2/21	Fair	2m Gd3 Hdl 4yo soft	£14,487
	1/21	Fair	2m Hdl 4yo heavy	£8,955
	10/20	Autl	2m2f Hdl 3yo heavy	£18,305

Top staying hurdler who landed a first Grade 1 in last season's Hatton's Grace Hurdle and proved just as effective over 3m; hacked up in the Boyne Hurdle and was a close second past the post in the Stayers' Hurdle at Cheltenham (demoted to third); best on soft ground.

The Big Doyen: twice a winner over hurdles during the summer

The Big Breakaway (Ire)

8 ch g Getaway - Princess Mairead (Blueprint)

Joe Tizzard — Eric Jones, Geoff Nicholas, John Romans

PLACINGS: 114/1223P/F23P/22PF- — RPR **157c**

Starts	1st	2nd	3rd	4th	Win & Pl
16	3	5	2	1	£118,419

	11/20	Chel	3m½f Cls2 Nov Ch soft	£12,628
	12/19	Newb	2m4½f Cls4 Nov Hdl 4-6yo soft	£4,484
	11/19	Chep	2m3½f Cls5 Mdn Hdl soft	£2,794

Fine second in last season's Welsh Grand National, finally looking like fulfilling early potential when stepping up to a marathon trip for the first time; still hasn't won since chase debut in 2020, though, and was pulled up in the Ultima before falling early in the Grand National.

The Big Doyen (Ire)

6 b g Doyen - An Bhean Rua (Fracas)

Peter Fahey (Ire) — Money For Jam Syndicate

PLACINGS: 116/21d259-11 — RPR **144+h**

Starts	1st	2nd	3rd	4th	Win & Pl
10	4	3	-	-	£34,632

	8/23	Gway	2m4½f Nov Hdl gd-yld	£11,487
	7/23	Tipp	2m4f Mdn Hdl gd-yld	£5,482
	11/21	Punc	2m NHF 4yo gd-yld	£5,795
	9/21	Rosc	1m7½f NHF 4yo good	£5,268

Dual bumper winner who has made the most of second-season novice status this summer, winning twice including a strong Listed heat at Galway; had run well in defeat last winter, finishing second three times including when demoted at Punchestown.

The Carpenter (Ire)

7 gr g Shantaram - Just Another Penny (Terimon)

Nicky Henderson — Owners Group

PLACINGS: 2/11-1 — RPR **139+h**

Starts	1st	2nd	3rd	4th	Win & Pl
4	3	1	-	-	£16,491

129	5/23	Uttx	2m4f Cls3 120-133 Hdl Hcap soft	£5,809
	3/23	Newb	2m4½f Cls4 Nov Hdl soft	£4,901
	2/23	Extr	2m2½f Cls4 Nov Hdl 4-7yo good	£4,085

Very lightly raced for his age and had been out for nearly two years until returning last season but soon made up for lost time; won both novice hurdles last term, most impressively by 11 lengths at Newbury, and completed a hat-trick on handicap debut at Uttoxeter in May.

The Goffer (Ire)

6 b g Yeats - Ballylough Lady (Mister Lord)

Gordon Elliott (Ire) — Allan Snow

PLACINGS: /7144104/412314P4-85 — RPR **155c**

Starts	1st	2nd	3rd	4th	Win & Pl
17	4	1	1	6	£136,746

138	2/23	Leop	2m5f 122-148 Ch Hcap yield	£78,319
	11/22	Thur	2m6f Ch yield	£6,445
	2/22	Thur	2m4½f Nov Gd3 Hdl soft	£14,874
	12/21	Navn	2m4f Mdn Hdl yield	£6,321

Very useful novice chaser last season, improving

RACING POST

for the switch to big handicaps; won at Leopardstown and did even better when fourth in a red-hot Ultima at Cheltenham; pulled up in the Irish National but saw out marathon trip well when fourth in the bet365 Gold Cup.

The Nice Guy (Ire)

8 b g Fame And Glory - Kilbarry Beauty (Saffron Walden)
Willie Mullins (Ire) — Malcolm C Denmark

PLACINGS: 1111/1- — RPR **156**h

Starts	1st	2nd	3rd	4th	Win & Pl
5	5	-	-	-	£160,207
4/22	Punc	3m Nov Gd1 Hdl gd-yld			£61,975
3/22	Chel	3m Cls1 Nov Gd1 Hdl gd-sft			£78,680
1/22	Naas	2m3f Mdn Hdl gd-yld			£7,437
12/21	Leop	2m NHF 4-7yo yld-sft			£6,848
11/21	Fair	2m NHF 4-7yo good			£5,268

Brilliant unbeaten gelding who missed last season through injury but had landed a Grade 1 double at Cheltenham and Punchestown in the spring of 2022; won the Albert Bartlett on just his second run over hurdles (also won two bumpers); likely to go novice chasing.

The Real Whacker (Ire)

7 b g Mahler - Credit Box (Witness Box)
Patrick Neville — Neville, Mann, Duffus & Dennis

PLACINGS: 612/0111- — RPR **163**+c

Starts	1st	2nd	3rd	4th	Win & Pl
7	4	1	-	-	£157,294
3/23	Chel	3m½f Cls1 Nov Gd1 Ch soft			£102,095
1/23	Chel	2m4½f Cls1 Nov Gd2 Ch soft			£31,323
11/22	Chel	3m½f Cls2 Nov Ch good			£13,194
12/21	Carl	3m1f Cls4 Mdn Hdl soft			£4,085

Enjoyed a fairytale campaign for his small yard

last season and made it three out of three over fences, all at Cheltenham, when winning the Brown Advisory from a top-class rival in Gerri Colombe; outstanding jumper and trainer convinced he's a Gold Cup horse.

The Two Amigos
11 b g Midnight Legend - As Was (Epalo)
Nicky Martin   Bradley Partnership
PLACINGS: 542/32238/F242/7317-   RPR **138+**c

Starts	1st	2nd	3rd	4th	Win & Pl
30	4	7	4	4	£205,918

127	12/22	Chep	3m6½f Cls1 Gd3 123-149 Ch Hcap soft	£85,425
134	1/19	Plum	3m4½f Cls3 108-134 Ch Hcap gd-sft	£19,018
124	12/18	Extr	3m6½f Cls3 105-127 Ch Hcap soft	£16,245
109	10/18	NAbb	3m2f Cls4 Nov 107-122 Ch Hcap heavy	£5,425

Veteran stayer who landed his biggest win in last season's Welsh National after finishing second in the race in 2021; had plummeted in the weights in between and still 14lb below peak mark having finished seventh on only subsequent run in the Midlands National.

The Yellow Clay (Ire)
4 b g Yeats - Winning Indian (Indian Danehill)
Gordon Elliott (Ire)   Bective Stud
PLACINGS: 11-   RPR **111+**b

Starts	1st	2nd	3rd	4th	Win & Pl
2	2	-	-	-	£24,278

| | 3/23 | Limk | 2m List NHF 4yo soft | £18,274 |
| | 3/23 | Leop | 2m NHF 4yo yield | £6,004 |

Useful bumper performer last season; won well on debut at Leopardstown and followed up at odds-on in a Listed four-year-old bumper at Limerick; good prospect for novice hurdles.

Theatre Glory (Ire)
6 b m Fame And Glory - Native Beauty (King's Theatre)
Nicky Henderson   Canter Banter Racing
PLACINGS: 113111/U3163-   RPR **146+**h

Starts	1st	2nd	3rd	4th	Win & Pl
11	6	-	3	-	£85,599

	2/23	Wwck	2m5f Cls1 List Hdl good	£17,085
	4/22	Chel	2m4½f Cls1 Nov List Hdl good	£14,238
129	3/22	Kels	2m Cls2 Nov 103-129 Hdl Hcap good	£26,015
	1/22	Wwck	2m3f Cls3 Nov Hdl gd-sft	£6,671
	11/21	Hntg	2m Cls4 Nov Hdl good	£4,085
	5/21	Worc	2m Cls5 Mdn NHF 4-6yo good	£1,906

Dual Listed-winning mare who hacked up in that grade at Warwick last term; twice ran well in stronger company when sixth in the Mares' Hurdle at Cheltenham and third in a Grade 2 at Sandown; could do better on quicker ground (six wins on good and good to soft).

Thedevilscoachman (Ire)
7 br g Elusive Pimpernel - Hagawi (Selkirk)
Noel Meade (Ire)   John P McManus
PLACINGS: 1/15117/321/1F11P-   RPR **152+**c

Starts	1st	2nd	3rd	4th	Win & Pl
14	8	1	1	-	£96,565

	3/23	Limk	3m½f Nov Gd3 Ch soft	£14,881
	1/23	Naas	3m1f Nov Gd3 Ch soft	£15,664
	10/22	Gway	2m6½f Ch sft-hvy	£8,429
	2/22	Navn	2m5f Gd2 Hdl heavy	£18,097
	2/21	Punc	2m½f Nov List Hdl soft	£14,487
	1/21	Navn	2m1½f Nov Hdl heavy	£8,429
	11/20	Cork	2m Mdn Hdl 4yo heavy	£6,000
	1/20	Naas	2m NHF 4yo gd-yld	£5,591

High-class staying hurdler who hasn't quite reached the same heights in two campaigns over fences but did win three times (twice at Grade 3 level) as a second-season novice last term; pulled up when just 7-1 for the Irish National on final run.

Third Time Lucki (Ire)
8 br g Arcadio - Definite Valley (Definite Article)
Fergal O'Brien   Mike & Eileen Newbould
PLACINGS: 21464/113123/463149-   RPR **155+**c

Starts	1st	2nd	3rd	4th	Win & Pl
23	9	2	4	5	£183,197

143	2/23	Sand	1m7½f Cls2 127-146 Ch Hcap gd-sft	£26,015
	1/22	Donc	2m½f Cls1 Nov Gd2 Ch good	£23,674
	11/21	Chel	2m Cls1 Nov Gd2 Ch good	£30,280
	10/21	Chel	2m Cls2 Nov Ch good	£13,008
	12/20	Kemp	2m Cls2 Nov Hdl gd-sft	£10,047
	10/20	Weth	2m Cls3 Nov Hdl gd-sft	£5,913
	10/20	Uttx	2m Cls4 Nov Hdl 4-6yo gd-sft	£3,769
	1/20	Hntg	2m Cls5 NHF 4-6yo soft	£2,274
	12/19	MRas	2m½f Cls5 Mdn NHF 4-6yo soft	£2,274

Found out in top company after winning three of his first four novice chases but did better in handicaps in second half of last season; exploited rapidly falling mark to win at Sandown and finished fourth in the Grand Annual; below-par favourite at Aintree on final run.

Thomas Darby (Ire)
10 b g Beneficial - Silaoce (Nikos)
Olly Murphy   Mrs Diana L Whateley
PLACINGS: 13/3303/414P4/23615-   RPR **149+**c

Starts	1st	2nd	3rd	4th	Win & Pl
24	6	4	7	3	£195,688

145	2/23	Ayr	3m Cls3 Nov 126-145 Ch Hcap soft	£7,393
	11/21	Newb	3m Cls1 Gd2 Hdl gd-sft	£34,170
151	1/20	Asct	2m3½f Cls1 Gd3 125-151 Hdl Hcap heavy	£28,475
	1/19	Tntn	2m½f Cls4 Nov Hdl gd-sft	£5,133
	10/18	Chel	2m½f Cls3 Mdn Hdl good	£9,285
	5/18	Hntg	2m Cls5 Am Mdn NHF 4-6yo good	£2,274

Best known for hurdling exploits (won the 2021 Long Distance Hurdle at Newbury) but has come up short in similar races since and switched back to fences for first time since 2019 when winning a novice handicap at Ayr in February; not up to Grade 1 level on only subsequent run.

The Two Amigos: posted a landmark performance when winning last season's Welsh Grand National

RACING POST

Three Card Brag (Ire)
6 b g Jet Away - Belon Breeze (Strong Gale)
Gordon Elliott (Ire)   McNeill Family & Patrick & Scott Bryceland

PLACINGS: 1/132156-   RPR **149+h**

Starts	1st	2nd	3rd	4th	Win & Pl
7	3	1	1	-	£35,595

1/23	Fair	2m3½f Nov Hdl sft-hvy	£6,004
10/22	Gway	2m½f Mdn Auct Hdl sft-hvy	£9,916
3/22	Wxfd	2m NHF 4-7yo heavy	£7,437

Useful novice hurdler last season; won twice either side of a close second to Inthepocket in a Grade 2 at Naas; fair fifth in the Albert Bartlett despite not staying 3m as well as pedigree had suggested; below-par sixth down in trip at Punchestown on final run.

Threeunderthrufive (Ire)
8 b g Shantou - Didinas (Kaldou Star)
Paul Nicholls   McNeill Family

PLACINGS: /11161/211116/3U684-   RPR **151c**

Starts	1st	2nd	3rd	4th	Win & Pl
18	9	2	1	1	£151,905

1/22	Wwck	3m Cls1 Nov Gd2 Ch soft	£31,691
12/21	Donc	3m Cls1 Nov Gd2 Ch gd-sft	£24,489
11/21	Chel	3m½f Cls2 Nov Ch good	£15,624
11/21	Extr	3m Cls2 Nov Ch gd-sft	£12,725
4/21	Prth	3m Cls1 Nov List Hdl gd-sft	£11,960
2/21	Muss	3m Cls2 Nov Hdl soft	£12,512
11/20	Ludl	2m5f Cls2 Hdl good	£9,747
10/20	Ling	2m3½f Cls4 Mdn Hdl soft	£3,769
1/20	Chep	2m Cls5 NHF 4-6yo heavy	£2,274

Won four times as a novice chaser two seasons ago, twice at Grade 2 level, but has had limitations exposed since despite running respectably in top staying handicaps last season; mark slowly falling and ran best race on last run when fourth in the Scottish National.

Thunder Rock (Ire)
7 b g Shirocco - La Belle Sauvage (Old Vic)
Olly Murphy   McNeill Family & Ian Dale

PLACINGS: 2/31/211191/113362-   RPR **155c**

Starts	1st	2nd	3rd	4th	Win & Pl
14	7	2	3	-	£91,433

142	11/22	Asct	2m3f Cls2 Nov 134-142 Ch Hcap gd-sft	£9,614
135	10/22	Uttx	2m Cls3 Nov 129-135 Ch Hcap good	£14,704
	4/22	Ayr	2m4½f Cls3 Nov Hdl gd-sft	£8,714
123	2/22	Hntg	2m3½f Cls2 123-145 Hdl Hcap soft	£15,833
	12/21	Muss	2m4f Cls4 Nov Hdl 4-6yo gd-sft	£4,629
	11/21	Weth	2m3½f Cls5 Hdl 4-6yo soft	£6,535
	2/21	Extr	2m1f Cls5 NHF 4-6yo heavy	£2,274

Very useful novice chaser last season; won first two starts in novice handicaps and ran several good races in stronger company while dropping to just 4lb above last winning mark; didn't seem to stay 3m when sixth in the Brown Advisory before a good second in a Grade 2 at Ayr.

Thyme Hill
9 b g Kayf Tara - Rosita Bay (Hernando)
Philip Hobbs & Johnson White   The Englands And Heywoods

PLACINGS: 1114/121/5225/12184-   RPR **157+c**

Starts	1st	2nd	3rd	4th	Win & Pl
19	8	5	1	2	£417,891

12/22	Kemp	3m Cls1 Nov Gd1 Ch soft	£59,620
11/22	Extr	3m Cls2 Nov Ch good	£13,664
4/21	Aint	3m½f Cls1 Gd1 Hdl gd-sft	£84,195
11/20	Newb	3m Cls1 Gd2 Hdl good	£28,475
12/19	Newb	2m4½f Cls1 Nov Gd1 Hdl soft	£25,929
11/19	Chel	2m5f Cls1 Nov Gd2 Hdl soft	£18,006
10/19	Chep	2m3½f Cls1 Nov Gd2 Hdl gd-sft	£19,933
10/18	Worc	2m Cls5 NHF 4-6yo good	£2,274

Dual Grade 1 winner over hurdles (also second in the 2022 Stayers' Hurdle) and managed a third top-level success last term despite a mixed campaign over fences; got things right when winning at Kempton but jumping fell apart at other times, notably at Cheltenham.

Tommy's Oscar (Ire)
8 b g Oscar - Glibin (Luso)
Ann Hamilton   Ian Hamilton

PLACINGS: 2613/2311118/125212-   RPR **156c**

Starts	1st	2nd	3rd	4th	Win & Pl
21	10	6	2	-	£196,879

	1/23	Donc	2m7½f Cls1 Nov Gd2 Ch good	£28,810
155	10/22	Carl	2m Cls3 Nov 138-155 Ch Hcap good	£6,862
	1/22	Hayd	1m7½f Cls2 Hdl soft	£42,713
150	1/22	Muss	1m7½f Cls2 124-150 Hdl Hcap gd-sft	£15,609
147	12/21	Donc	2m½f Cls2 121-147 Hdl Hcap gd-sft	£9,626
138	11/21	Hayd	2m3f Cls2 123-145 Hdl Hcap good	£26,015
132	3/21	Kels	2m Cls2 122-148 Hdl Hcap gd-sft	£15,432
124	1/21	Muss	1m7½f Cls3 104-130 Hdl Hcap soft	£6,238
	12/20	Newc	2m Cls4 Nov Hdl soft	£3,769
	12/20	Sedg	2m1f Cls4 Mdn Hdl gd-sft	£3,769

Developed into a very smart hurdler two seasons ago, winning Haydock's Champion Hurdle Trial; not quite as effective over fences last season but did land a Grade 2 novice chase at Doncaster; beaten in three-runner races conceding lumps of weight either side of that.

Torn And Frayed (Fr)
9 b g Califet - Chic Et Zen (Chichicastenango)
Nigel Twiston-Davies   Mrs Caroline Beresford-Wylie

PLACINGS: /25242/421213/322P1/-   RPR **140c**

Starts	1st	2nd	3rd	4th	Win & Pl
17	3	7	2	2	£89,414

131	1/22	Chel	2m4½f Cls1 Gd3 130-147 Ch Hcap good	£56,270
	3/21	Fknm	2m4f Cls4 Nov Hdl good	£3,268
122	2/21	Hrfd	2m3½f Cls4 103-122 Hdl Hcap soft	£3,671

Progressive novice chaser two seasons ago before missing last term through injury; got off the mark when winning a valuable 2m4f handicap chase at Cheltenham on latest run; had done well against smart novices before a rare flop on unsuitably heavy ground.

RACING POST

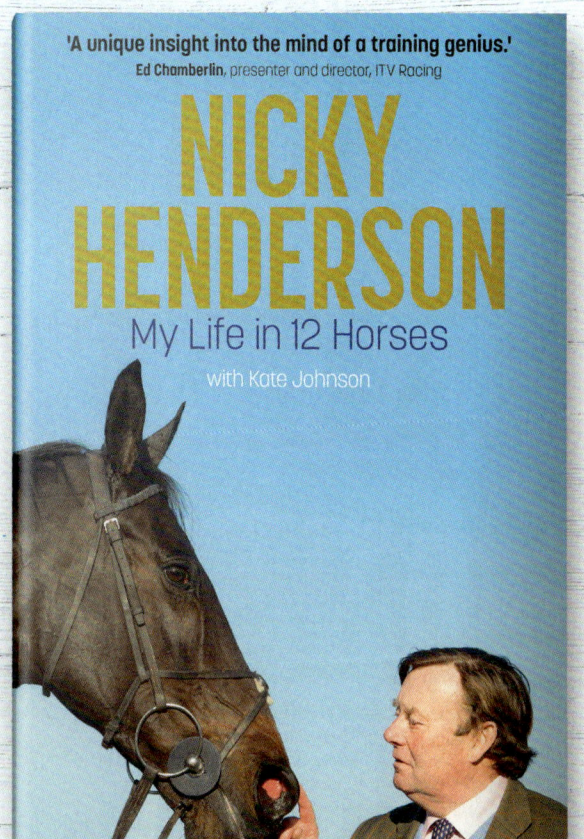

'A unique insight into the mind of a training genius.'
Ed Chamberlin
Presenter and director, ITV Racing

Nicky Henderson: My Life in 12 Horses schools us on life, sport, magic, courage, loss, hope and love. Beautifully written, this book is a revealing and intimate account of a master racehorse trainer's work.

Exclusive interviews and candid insights from Nicky, his jockeys including Sir AP McCoy OBE, Barry Geraghty and Mick Fitzgerald, owners and breeders who have worked with him for nearly 50 years, and the stable lads and lasses who develop profound bonds with the magnificent horses in their care, all take us to the heart of Nicky's intriguing world.

The extraordinary camaraderie at Seven Barrows and Nicky's unparalleled genius and intuitive skill in knowing his horses and training these fragile superstars to glory are described in unprecedented detail and create a thrilling chronicle of Nicky's 45-year love affair with jump racing.

'A beautiful portrait of the love between Nicky Henderson and his greatest horses. Intimate, revealing and unforgettable, with a long reach in racing but also far beyond.'
Paul Hayward
Five times Sports Writer of the Year

NEW SHOP WEBSITE LIVE NOW!
www.racingpost.com/shop

RACING POST

Tornado Flyer (Ire)
10 b g Flemensfirth - Mucho Macabi (Exceed And Excel)
Willie Mullins (Ire)   T F P Partnership
PLACINGS: 11P35/22543/51P/772-   RPR **167+c**

Starts	1st	2nd	3rd	4th	Win & Pl
22	6	3	3	2	£342,184
	12/21 Kemp	3m Cls1 Gd1 Ch soft			£143,045
	12/19 Navn	2m1f Nov Gd3 Ch soft			£19,932
	11/19 Naas	2m3f Ch sft-hvy			£7,720
	12/18 Punc	2m4f Mdn Hdl good			£7,087
	4/18 Punc	2m$^{1}/_{2}$f Gd1 NHF 4-7yo yield			£52,212
	1/18 Fair	2m NHF 5-7yo soft			£5,451

Surprise winner of the King George in 2021, relishing step up to 3m for only the second time having regularly come up short in top races over shorter; well below par in next three runs the following spring and ran only once subsequently when second in a Grade 2 at Clonmel.

Trelawne
7 b g Geordieland - Black Collar (Bob's Return)
Kim Bailey   The Real Partnership
PLACINGS: 13/11-   RPR **140+h**

Starts	1st	2nd	3rd	4th	Win & Pl
4	3		1	-	£40,372
130	3/23 Uttx	2m7$^{1}/_{2}$f Cls2 121-147 Hdl Hcap soft			£25,720
124	11/22 Ffos	2m6f Cls3 116-124 Hdl Hcap soft			£9,083
	2/22 Extr	2m2$^{1}/_{2}$f Cls4 Nov Hdl 4-7yo soft			£4,629

Very lightly raced staying hurdler who won both races last season to take record to 3-4 under rules; won well at Ffos Las first time out and comfortably followed up in another handicap at Uttoxeter; had a long break in between to wait for soft ground; likely to go novice chasing.

Tullyhill (Fr)
5 gr g Martaline - Ragtime (Le Havre)
Willie Mullins (Ire)   Cheveley Park Stud
PLACINGS: 112-   RPR **135+b**

Starts	1st	2nd	3rd	4th	Win & Pl
2	1	1	-		£22,035
	3/23 Gowr	2m2f NHF sft-hvy			£5,221

Bought for £220,000 after winning sole point-to-point and showed rich promise in two bumpers last season; won well at Gowran in March and finished a fine second behind A Dream To Share at Punchestown the following month; should make a good novice hurdler.

Twinjets (Ire)
6 b g Jet Away - Shenamar (Beneficial)
Milton Harris   C W Rodgers
PLACINGS: 11/16112P1-   RPR **135+h**

Starts	1st	2nd	3rd	4th	Win & Pl
8	5	1	-	-	£30,289
	4/23 Kemp	2m5f Cls4 Nov Hdl gd-sft			£4,357
	1/23 Plum	2m4$^{1}/_{2}$f Cls3 Nov Hdl 4-7yo soft			£7,080
	12/22 Leic	1m7$^{1}/_{2}$f Cls3 Mdn Hdl soft			£6,535
	5/22 Hayd	1m7$^{1}/_{2}$f Cls3 NHF 4-6yo gd-sft			£6,808
	4/22 Hrfd	2m Cls5 NHF 4-6yo good			£2,614

Point-to-point and dual bumper winner who was again prolific in novice hurdles last season, winning three times; second when odds-on for a novice handicap at Sandown and pulled up back there in the EBF Final but bounced back with a 13-length win at Kempton on final run.

Two For Gold (Ire)
10 b g Gold Well - Two Of Each (Shernazar)
Kim Bailey   May We Never Be Found Out Partnership
PLACINGS: 112/2P313U/112P/501-   RPR **160+c**

Starts	1st	2nd	3rd	4th	Win & Pl
24	11	3	2	2	£242,743
150	4/23 Asct	3m Cls2 124-150 Ch Hcap gd-sft			£15,609
	1/22 Ling	2m Ch heavy			£79,725
150	12/21 Donc	3m Cls2 124-150 Ch Hcap gd-sft			£11,707
149	2/21 Wwck	2m4f Cls2 129-155 Ch Hcap soft			£21,896
	1/20 Wwck	3m Cls1 Nov Gd2 Ch soft			£19,933
	12/19 Kels	2m7$^{1}/_{2}$f Cls3 Nov Ch soft			£12,116
132	11/19 Carl	2m4f Cls3 Nov 117-135 Ch Hcap soft			£8,123
	1/19 Bang	2m7f Cls4 Nov Hdl gd-sft			£4,094
	12/18 Weth	2m5$^{1}/_{2}$f Cls4 Nov Hdl soft			£4,224
	2/18 Donc	2m$^{1}/_{2}$f Cls5 NHF 4-6yo gd-sft			£2,599
	12/17 Sthl	1m7$^{1}/_{2}$f Cls5 Am NHF 4-6yo good			£2,599

Very useful chaser at his best in small fields, often bossing inferior rivals under big weights; won a 3m veterans' handicap off ceiling mark of 150 on final run last season having come fifth in the Grand Sefton (second try over National fences) and down the field in the Plate at Cheltenham.

Under Control (Fr)
4 ch f Doctor Dino - Delinda (Sea The Stars)
Nicky Henderson   John P McManus
PLACINGS: 11011-   RPR **130+h**

Starts	1st	2nd	3rd	4th	Win & Pl
5	4	-	-	-	£87,625
128	4/23 Sand	2m Cls2 Nov 113-129 Hdl Hcap soft			£51,440
121	4/23 Chel	2m1f Cls1 Gd3 98-124 Hdl 4yo Hcap good			£22,780
	3/23 Newb	2m$^{1}/_{2}$f Cls4 Hdl 4yo good			£4,901
	12/22 Fntb	2m3f Hdl 3yo v soft			£8,504

Prolific and progressive juvenile hurdler last season, winning four out of five races; bought by JP McManus after a winning debut in France; suffered sole defeat in the mares' novice at the Cheltenham Festival but made amends with wins at Cheltenham and Sandown in April.

Unexpected Party (Fr)
8 gr g Martaline - Reform Act (Lemon Drop Kid)
Dan Skelton O'Reilly Maclennan Tynan Carthy Shanahan
PLACINGS: 2/41221P/232353- RPR **151c**

Starts	1st	2nd	3rd	4th	Win & Pl
13	2	5	3	1	£58,726
130	1/22	Asct	2m3½f Cls2 125-143 Hdl Hcap soft		£15,609
109	10/21	Weth	2m5½f Cls4 Nov 84-110 Hdl Hcap gd-sft		£3,159

Useful and consistent novice chaser last season, with only poor run coming when given a good chance to break his duck at Leicester; finished fifth in the Turners at the Cheltenham Festival and third in a Grade 2 at Ayr on final run; retains novice status.

Vanillier (Fr)
8 gr g Martaline - Virgata (Turgeon)
Gavin Cromwell (Ire) Mrs H M Keaveney
PLACINGS: 21201/431333/636F22- RPR **154c**

Starts	1st	2nd	3rd	4th	Win & Pl
17	3	4	5	1	£329,936
	11/21	Punc	2m6½f Nov Gd2 Ch yield		£18,438
	3/21	Chel	3m Cls1 Nov Gd1 Hdl gd-sft		£55,127
	11/20	Naas	2m3f Mdn Hdl sft-hvy		£7,000

Ran a huge race to finish second in last season's Grand National, staying on from a long way back to underline stamina; has won just once since running away with the Albert Bartlett in 2021 but spent much of last season over inadequate trips before a close second in the Bobbyjo.

Vauban (Fr)
5 ch g Galiway - Waldfest (Hurricane Run)
Willie Mullins (Ire) Mrs S Ricci
PLACINGS: 211/12342- RPR **161h**

Starts	1st	2nd	3rd	4th	Win & Pl
8	3	3	1	1	£316,121
	4/22	Punc	2m Gd1 Hdl 4yo yield		£61,975
	3/22	Chel	2m1f Cls1 Gd1 Hdl 4yo gd-sft		£75,965
	2/22	Leop	2m Gd1 Hdl 4yo yield		£61,975

Future over jumps very much up in the air after a fine summer on the Flat but has proved his quality in the winter code too, winning the 2022 Triumph Hurdle and making the frame in four Grade 1 races last season; likely to run in the Melbourne Cup before potential hurdles return.

Wakool (Fr)
7 gr g Motivator - Symba's Dream (Vindication)
Nick Alexander Turcan, Borwick, Dunning & Elles
PLACINGS: 3322/1311123/172410- RPR **145h**

Starts	1st	2nd	3rd	4th	Win & Pl
21	7	4	5	2	£92,075
	2/23	Hayd	3m½f Cls1 Gd2 Hdl gd-sft		£34,170
133	10/22	Ayr	3m½f Cls3 117-140 Hdl Hcap gd-sft		£7,842
122	1/22	Ayr	3m½f Cls2 117-141 Hdl Hcap soft		£10,892
112	12/21	Muss	3m Cls3 110-134 Hdl Hcap gd-sft		£6,862
108	11/21	Muss	3m Cls4 93-118 Hdl Hcap gd-sft		£3,594
103	5/21	Prth	3m Cls4 88-113 Hdl Hcap soft		£3,594
100	1/20	Donc	2m½f Cls5 Nov 74-102 Hdl Hcap gd-sft		£2,794

Massive improver over the last couple of seasons, winning six times; started off a mark of 103 and ended up a Grade 2 winner when landing the Rendlesham last season; dropped lucky in a weak running of that race and well held in better staying handicaps otherwise.

West Balboa (Ire)
7 b m Yeats - Rostellan (Flemensfirth)
Dan Skelton Bullen-Smith & Faulks
PLACINGS: 2/12/211- RPR **143+h**

Starts	1st	2nd	3rd	4th	Win & Pl
5	3	2	-	-	£116,530
135	4/23	Aint	3m½f Cls1 Gd3 127-147 Hdl Hcap gd-sft		£42,203
130	1/23	Kemp	2m5f Cls2 121-147 Hdl Hcap soft		£53,150
	11/21	Wwck	2m5f Cls4 Nov Hdl gd-sft		£4,357

Progressive, lightly raced hurdler who flourished in good handicaps last season after an aborted novice campaign; missed nearly a year after coming second in the 2021 Challow but built on a solid return by winning the Lanzarote and followed up impressively over 3m at Aintree.

Western Diego (Ire)
6 b g Westerner - Ask Me Sister (Safety Catch)
Willie Mullins (Ire) Clipper Logistics Group
PLACINGS: 1/178- RPR **131+b**

Starts	1st	2nd	3rd	4th	Win & Pl
3	1	-	-	-	£5,221
	1/23	Naas	2m3f NHF soft		£5,221

Useful bumper performer last season; hacked up at Naas to book Champion Bumper spot and ran a remarkable race when seventh at Cheltenham, still leading a furlong out despite pulling hard only to be badly hampered; blew out at Punchestown on final run.

Weveallbeencaught (Ire)
6 b g Getaway - Curvacious (Anshan)
Nigel Twiston-Davies Jimmy & Susie Wenman, Edward & Jane James
PLACINGS: 11/3187P- RPR **136h**

Starts	1st	2nd	3rd	4th	Win & Pl
6	2	-	1	-	£18,984
	1/23	Chel	2m4½f Cls2 Mdn Hdl gd-sft		£10,562
	3/22	Newb	2m½f Cls5 NHF 4-6yo soft		£2,178

Found wanting when very highly tried last season but has won every race below Graded company comprising a point-to-point, bumper and maiden hurdle; beat subsequent Grade 2 winner Rock My Way at Cheltenham but no better than seventh in three Grade 1s.

Whistleinthedark (Ire)

8 b g Fame And Glory - Last Of Many (Lahib)
Laura Morgan   Racing On Together Club
PLACINGS: 324/2133/21111-   RPR **150+c**

Starts	1st	2nd	3rd	4th	Win & Pl
10	5	2	2	1	£50,522
138	4/23	Prth	2m4f Cls2 130-124 Ch Hcap gd-sft		£13,008
134	3/23	Kemp	2m2f Cls3 Nov 116-135 Ch Hcap gd-sft		£11,951
	2/23	Weth	2m5½f Cls3 Nov Ch good		£5,991
113	12/22	MRas	2m5½f Cls4 Nov 108-119 Ch Hcap gd-sft		£8,483
	12/21	Plum	2m4½f Cls4 Mdn Hdl gd-sft		£4,085

Big improver last season, winning all four chases while climbing 31lb in the handicap; found a soft opening when stepped up to Class 2 level at Perth on final run but had also won a deep novice handicap at Kempton previously; best at around 2m4f.

Willmount

5 b g Blue Bresil - Youngstar (Old Vic)
Nicky Henderson   O S Harris
PLACINGS: 1/11-   RPR **117+b**

Starts	1st	2nd	3rd	4th	Win & Pl
2	2	-	-	-	£5,148
	3/23	Donc	2m1½f Cls5 NHF 4-6yo good		£2,614
	1/23	Donc	2m1½f Cls5 Mdn NHF 4-6yo gd-sft		£2,535

Exciting recruit for Nicky Henderson having been bought for £340,000 by Neil Mulholland after winning sole point-to-point and then won two Doncaster bumpers for him; hacked up by 13 lengths on debut and followed up despite reportedly finding good ground quicker than ideal.

You Oughta Know (Ire)

5 b g Beat Hollow - Pont De Alma (Soldier Of Fortune)
Willie Mullins (Ire)   Luke McMahon
PLACINGS: 11   RPR **128+b**

Starts	1st	2nd	3rd	4th	Win & Pl
2	2	-	-	-	£14,097
	8/23	Gway	2m NHF good		£8,876
	5/23	Kbgn	2m NHF yield		£5,221

Impressive in winning both bumpers early this season; thrashed £400,000 gelding Croke Park by 11 lengths at Kilbeggan and beat four previous winners when following up at Galway; strong galloper who could go up in trip over hurdles.

You Wear It Well

6 b m Midnight Legend - Annie's Answer (Flemensfirth)
Jamie Snowden   Sir Chips Keswick
PLACINGS: 21/112115-   RPR **140+h**

Starts	1st	2nd	3rd	4th	Win & Pl
8	5	2	-	-	£117,175
	3/23	Chel	2m1f Cls1 Nov Gd2 Hdl soft		£59,084
	2/23	Sand	2m4f Cls1 Nov Gd2 Hdl soft		£28,475
	11/22	Hexm	2m Cls4 Nov 4-6yo soft		£4,901
	10/22	Worc	2m Cls4 Nov Hdl good		£4,901
	2/22	Catt	1m7½f Cls5 NHF 4-6yo soft		£2,451

Smart mare who won four times last season,

most notably when making all in the mares' novice hurdle at the Cheltenham Festival; strong stayer who had also won a 2m4f Grade 2 at Sandown; second against the boys in the Challow Hurdle but below par when fifth at Aintree.

Zambella (Fr)

8 b m Zambezi Sun - Visby (Irish Wells)
Nigel Twiston-Davies   Simon Munir & Isaac Souede
PLACINGS: 112F2/4112143/21124-   RPR **148+c**

Starts	1st	2nd	3rd	4th	Win & Pl
24	10	5	1	5	£258,642
	12/22	Donc	2m4½f Cls1 List Ch good		£42,203
	11/22	Carl	2m4f Cls1 List Ch soft		£18,794
	2/22	Uttx	2m Cls2 Ch soft		£14,503
	12/21	Donc	2m4½f Cls1 List Ch good		£33,762
	12/21	Aint	2m4f Cls1 List Ch soft		£16,346
	1/21	Leic	2m Cls1 List Ch soft		£14,682
	12/20	Wwck	2m4f Cls1 Nov List Ch soft		£11,746
	11/20	Bang	2m1½f Cls1 Nov List Ch soft		£14,238
	4/19	Comp	2m2f Hdl 4yo v soft		£19,459
	3/19	Fntb	2m2f Hdl 4yo v soft		£8,649

Useful and consistent mare who won two Listed mares' chases last term, taking tally at that level to six across the last three seasons; also finished fourth in the Mares' Chase at Cheltenham for the second successive year (second best of the British both times).

Zanahiyr (Ire)

6 ch g Nathaniel - Zariyna (Marju)
Gordon Elliott (Ire)   Bective Stud
PLACINGS: 1114/212223dF/7P5335-   RPR **161h**

Starts	1st	2nd	3rd	4th	Win & Pl
17	4	4	2	1	£241,835
	10/21	DRoy	2m1f Gd2 Hdl soft		£26,339
	12/20	Leop	2m Gd2 Hdl 3yo soft		£17,500
	11/20	Fair	2m Gd3 Hdl 3yo soft		£13,750
	10/20	Baln	2m2f Mdn Hdl 3yo soft		£5,000

Without a win since 2021 but has been third past the post in the last two runnings of the Champion Hurdle (disqualified in 2022 for a banned substance); largely disappointing otherwise last season, including when pulled up on only attempt at 3m.

Zanza (Ire)

9 b g Arcadio - What A Bleu (Pistolet Bleu)
Philip Hobbs & Johnson White   Louisville Syndicate Elite
PLACINGS: FP6/362PP8P/6217147-   RPR **165+c**

Starts	1st	2nd	3rd	4th	Win & Pl
32	7	3	1	2	£155,874
	2/23	Newb	2m7½f Cls1 Gd2 Ch good		£39,865
134	11/22	Newb	2m6½f Cls2 128-140 Ch Hcap good		£20,812
138	11/20	Newb	2m1½f Cls2 134-147 Ch Hcap good		£19,028
136	11/19	Newb	2m1½f Cls3 120-136 Cond Hdl Hcap gd-sft		£6,433
131	3/19	Newb	2m1½f Cls2 122-134 Hdl Hcap gd-sft		£9,747
	12/18	Tntn	2m3f Cls4 Nov Hdl gd-sft		£5,133
	11/18	Chep	2m Cls4 Nov Hdl soft		£4,094

Newbury specialist whose last five wins have come at that track, including a 12-length win in a handicap chase and 16-1 success in the Denman Chase last season; hasn't come close to that form elsewhere and found 15lb rise beyond him even back at his favourite course.

Zarak The Brave (Fr)
4 b g Zarak - Tempo Royale (Boris De Deauville)
Willie Mullins (Ire)   Simon Munir & Isaac Souede
PLACINGS: 122-31   RPR **151+**h

Starts	1st	2nd	3rd	4th	Win & Pl
5	2	2	1	-	£203,322
145	8/23	Gway	2m Gd3 135-146 Hdl Hcap gd-yld		£140,973
	11/22	Fair	2m Mdn Hdl 3yo soft		£4,958

Very useful juvenile hurdler last season and stepped up again with a successful handicap debut in the Galway Hurdle this summer; had missed a key chunk of the campaign, returning from five months out to finish second behind Lossiemouth at Punchestown and third at Auteuil.

Zenta (Fr)
4 b f Pastorius - Zenturie (Tiger Hill)
Willie Mullins (Ire)   John P McManus
PLACINGS: 1131-   RPR **138**h

Starts	1st	2nd	3rd	4th	Win & Pl
4	3	-	1	-	£115,378
	4/23	Aint	2m1f Cls1 Gd1 Hdl 4yo gd-sft		£61,897
	2/23	Fair	2m½f Gd3 Hdl 4yo yield		£14,358
	9/22	Autl	2m2f List Hdl 3yo v soft		£24,353

Smart juvenile hurdler last season who won three out of four races and was beaten only by two other Willie Mullins fillies in the Triumph Hurdle; achieved her own Grade 1 victory when edging home by a nose in a much weaker race at Aintree; should stay beyond 2m.

Willmount: the unbeaten recruit to Nicky Henderson's yard on parade at Seven Barrows

RACING POST

KEY HORSES LISTED BY TRAINER

Neil Alexander
Elvis Mail (Fr)
Wakool (Fr)

Kim Bailey
Broomfield Present (Ire)
Does He Know
Espoir De Romay (Fr)
First Flow (Ire)
Happygolucky (Ire)
Trelawne
Two For Gold (Ire)

Chris Barber
Famous Clermont (Fr)

Martin Brassil
An Epic Song (Fr)
Fastorslow (Fr)
Longhouse Poet (Ire)

Charles Byrnes
Blazing Khal (Ire)

Jennie Candlish
Cheddleton

David Christie
Ferns Lock

Barry Connell
Good Land (Fr)
Marine Nationale (Ire)

Stuart Crawford
O'Toole (Ire)

Gavin Cromwell
Final Orders
Flooring Porter (Ire)
Letsbeclearaboutit (Ire)
Limerick Lace (Ire)
Stumptown (Ire)
Vanillier (Fr)

Sam Curling
Angels Dawn (Ire)

Henry de Bromhead
A Plus Tard (Fr)
Ain't That A Shame (Ire)
Amirite (Ire)
Ascending (Ire)
Aspire Tower (Ire)
Bob Olinger (Ire)
Captain Guinness (Ire)
Coeur Sublime (Ire)
Dancing On My Own (Ire)
Eklat De Rire (Fr)
Envoi Allen (Fr)
Foxy Girl (Fr)
Hiddenvalley Lake (Ire)
Inthepocket
Journey With Me (Ire)
Magical Zoe (Ire)
Maskada (Fr)
Minella Indo (Ire)
Monty's Star (Ire)
Quilixios

Sean Thomas Doyle
Monbeg Park (Ire)

Gordon Elliott
Absolute Notions (Ire)
American Mike (Ire)
Andy Dufresne (Ire)
Better Days Ahead (Ire)

Brighterdaysahead (Fr)
Chemical Energy (Ire)
Coko Beach (Fr)
Conflated (Ire)
Cool Survivor (Ire)
Delta Work (Fr)
Doctor Bravo (Fr)
Down Memory Lane (Ire)
Favori De Champdou (Fr)
Fil Dor (Fr)
Fils D'Oudairies (Fr)
Firefox (Fr)
Found A Fifty (Fr)
Fury Road (Fr)
Galvin (Ire)
Gerri Colombe (Fr)
Halka Du Tabert (Fr)
Hollow Games (Ire)
Irish Point (Ire)
Jazzy Matty (Fr)
Maxxum (Ire)
Minella Crooner (Ire)
Pied Piper
Qualimata (Fr)
Queens Brook (Ire)
Riviere D'Etel (Fr)
Run Wild Fred (Ire)
Saint Felicien (Fr)
Shannon Royale (Ire)
Sire Du Berlais (Fr)
Teahupoo (Fr)
The Goffer (Ire)
The Yellow Clay (Ire)
Three Card Brag (Ire)
Zanahiyr (Fr)

Peter Fahey
The Big Doyen (Ire)

Pat Fahy
Dunvegan (Fr)

Lorna Fowler
Colonel Mustard (Fr)

Harry Fry
Altobelli (Ire)
Boothill (Ire)
Gin Coco (Fr)
Love Envoi (Ire)
Might I (Ire)

Bradley Gibbs
Premier Magic (Ire)

Paul John Gilligan
Buddy One (Ire)

Chris Gordon
Aucunrisque (Fr)

Harriet Graham & Gary Rutherford
Aye Right (Fre)

Warren Greatrex
Bill Baxter (Ire)

Oliver Greenall & Josh Guerriero
Gesskille (Fr)
Iroko (Fr)

Alex Hales
Millers Bank

Ann Hamilton
Tommy's Oscar (Ire)

John Joseph Hanlon
Hewick (Ire)

Jessica Harrington
Ashdale Bob (Ire)
Lifetime Ambition (Ire)

Milton Harris
Twinjets (Ire)

Nicky Henderson
Attacca (Ire)
Balco Coastal (Fr)
Bold Endeavour
Champ (Ire)
City Chief (Ire)
Constitution Hill
Doddiethegreat (Ire)
Dusart (Ire)
Fantastic Lady (Fr)
First Street
Iberico Lord (Fr)
Impose Toi (Fr)
Jet Powered (Ire)
Jonbon (Fr)
Luccia
Marie's Rock (Ire)
Mister Coffey (Fr)
No Ordinary Joe (Ire)
Shishkin (Ire)
Steal A March
The Carpenter (Ire)
Theatre Glory (Ire)
Under Control (Fr)
Willmount

Richard Hobson
Fugitif (Fr)

Anthony Honeyball
Kilbeg King (Ire)
Sam Brown

Syd Hosie
Rock My Way (Ire)

Nick Kent
Erne River (Ire)

John Kiely
A Dream To Share (Ire)

Alan King
Edwardstone
Major Dundee (Ire)
Sceau Royal (Fr)

Neil King
Lookaway (Ire)

Tom Lacey
Blow Your Wad (Ire)
Highstakesplayer (Ire)
Howlingmadmurdock (Ire)

Emma Lavelle
Paisley Park (Ire)

Kerry Lee
Nemean Lion (Ger)

Sheila Lewis
Straw Fan Jack

Charlie Longsdon
Rare Edition (Ire)
Tea For Free (Ire)

Tony Martin
Good Time Jonny (Ire)

Nicky Martin
The Two Amigos

Donald McCain
Maximilian (Ger)
Minella Drama (Ire)
Richmond Lake (Ire)

John McConnell
Fennor Cross (Ire)
Mahler Mission (Ire)
Seddon (Ire)

Oliver McKiernan
Meet And Greet (Ire)
No Looking Back (Ire)

Andrew McNamara
Enjoy The Dream

Noel Meade
Affordale Fury (Ire)
Flanking Manœuvre (Ire)
Thedevilscoachman (Ire)

Gary Moore
Authorised Speed (Fr)
Bo Zenith (Fr)
Botox Has (Fr)
Editeur Du Gite (Fr)
Givega (Fr)
Goshen (Fr)
Hansard (Ire)
Inneston (Fr)
Nassalam (Fr)

Laura Morgan
Notlongtillmay
Whistlethedark (Ire)

Mouse Morris
French Dynamite (Fr)
Gentlemansgame
Indiana Jones (Fr)

Hughie Morrison
Not So Sleepy

Emmet Mullins
Corbetts Cross (Ire)
Feronily (Ire)
Filey Bay (Fr)
Noble Yeats (Ire)
So Scottish (Fr)

Seamus Mullins
Moroder (Ire)

Willie Mullins
Allaho (Fr)
Allegorie De Vassy (Fr)
Appreciate It (Ire)
Ashroe Diamond (Ire)
Asterion Forlonge (Fr)
Aurora Vega (Ire)
Authorized Art (Fr)
Ballyburn (Ire)
Bialystok (Ire)
Blizzard Of Oz (Ire)
Blood Destiny (Fr)
Blue Lord (Fr)
Brandy Love (Ire)
Bronn (Ire)
Capodanno (Fr)
Captain Cody (Ire)
Champ Kiely (Ire)
Classic Getaway (Ire)
Dinoblue (Fr)

Dysart Dynamo (Ire)
Echoes In Rain (Ire)
El Fabiolo (Fr)
Embassy Gardens
Energumene (Fr)
Facile Vega (Ire)
Fact To File (Fr)
Ferny Hollow (Ire)
Flame Bearer (Ire)
Franco De Port (Fr)
Fun Fun Fun (Fr)
Gaelic Warrior (Ger)
Gaillard Du Mesnil (Fr)
Gala Marceau (Fr)
Galopin Des Champs (Fr)
Gentleman De Mee (Fr)
Grangeclare West (Ire)
Gust Of Wind (Fr)
Ha D'Or (Fr)
Haut En Couleurs (Fr)
Hercule Du Seuil (Fr)
High Class Hero
Hunters Yarn (Ire)
I Am Maximus (Fr)
I Will Be Baie (Fr)
Il Etait Temps (Fr)
Impaire Et Passe (Fr)
Indiana Dream (Fr)
Instit (Fr)
It's For Me (Fr)
James Du Berlais (Fr)
Janidil (Fr)
Junta Marvel (Fr)
Kilcruit (Ire)
Klassical Dream (Fr)
Lecky Watson (Ire)
Lossiemouth (Fr)
Minella Cocooner (Ire)
Mirazur West (Fr)
Mister Policeman (Fr)
Monkfish (Ire)
Mr Incredible (Ire)
Mystical Power (Ire)
Nick Rockett (Ire)
Night And Day
Readin Tommy Wrong (Ire)
Redemption Day
Risk Belle (Fr)
Saint Roi (Fr)
Saint Sam (Fr)
Shanbally Kid (Ire)
Sharjah (Fr)
Sir Gerhard (Ire)
Spanish Harlem (Fr)
State Man (Fr)
Stattler (Ire)
The Nice Guy (Ire)
Tornado Flyer (Ire)
Tullyhill (Fr)
Vauban (Fr)
Western Diego (Ire)
You Oughta Know (Ire)
Zarak The Brave (Fr)
Zenta (Fr)

Colm Murphy
Impervious (Fr)

Olly Murphy
Brewin'Upastorm (Ire)
Chasing Fire
Doctor Ken (Fr)

KEY HORSES LISTED BY TRAINER

Indeevar Bleu (Fr)
Strong Leader
Thomas Darby (Ire)
Thunder Rock (Ire)

Patrick Neville
The Real Whacker (Ire)

Paul Nicholls
Afadil (Fr)
Blueking D'Oroux (Fr)
Bravemansgame (Fr)
Captain Teague (Ire)
Complete Unknown (Ire)
Frodon (Fr)
Greaneteen (Fr)
Hermes Allen (Fr)
Hitman (Fr)
Hugos New Horse (Fr)
Iceo (Fr)
Il Ridoto (Fr)
Inthewaterside (Fr)
Knappers Hill (Ire)
Knowsley Road (Ire)
Makin'Yourmindup
McFabulous (Ire)
Monmiral (Fr)
Outlaw Peter (Ire)
Pic D'Orhy (Fr)
Quel Destin (Fr)
Rubaud (Fr)
Samarrive (Fr)
Seeyouinmydreams
Solo (Fr)

Sonigino (Fr)
Stage Star (Ire)
Stay Away Fay (Ire)
Tahmuras (Fr)
Threeunderthrufive (Ire)

Peter Niven
Malystic

Paul Nolan
Sandor Clegane (Ire)

Fergal O'Brien
Crambo
Dysart Enos (Ire)
Manothepeople (Ire)
Marble Sands (Fr)
Paint The Dream
Punctuation

Joseph O'Brien
Banbridge (Ire)
Busselton (Fr)
Comfort Zone (Ire)
Fakir D'Oudairies (Fr)
Home By The Lee (Ire)
Nusret

Jonjo O'Neill
Collectors Item (Ire)
Crebilly (Ire)
Johnnywho (Ire)
Monbeg Genius (Ire)
Springwell Bay

Ben Pauling
Harper's Brook (Ire)

Mucho Mas (Ire)
Shakem Up'Arry (Ire)

David Pipe
Gericault Roque (Fr)
Remastered

Ryan Potter
Jetoile (Ire)

Nicky Richards
Crystal Glory
Florida Dreams (Ire)

Lucinda Russell
Ahoy Senor (Ire)
Apple Away (Ire)
Corach Rambler (Ire)
Douglas Talking (Ire)
Giovinco (Ire)

Jeremy Scott
Dashel Drasher

Michael Scudamore
Do Your Job (Ire)

Dan Skelton
Ashtown Lad (Ire)
Ballygrifincottage (Ire)
Calico (Ger)
Faivoir (Fr)
Galia Des Liteaux (Fr)
Grey Dawning (Ire)
Heltenham (Fr)
Kateira
Lac De Constance (Fr)

Langer Dan (Ire)
Le Milos
Midnight River
My Drogo
Nube Negra (Spa)
Pembroke
Proschema (Ire)
Protektorat (Fr)
Sail Away (Fr)
Third Time Lucki (Ire)
Unexpected Party (Fr)
West Balboa (Ire)

Jamie Snowden
Colonel Harry (Ire)
Datsalrightgino (Ger)
Ga Law (Fr)
You Wear It Well

Jonathan Sweeney
Churchstonewarrior (Ire)

Sam Thomas
Al Dancer (Fr)
Good Risk At All (Fr)
Grey Diamond (Fr)
Iwilldoit
Our Power (Ire)
Stolen Silver (Fr)

Joe Tizzard
Amarillo Sky (Ire)
Eldorado Allen (Fr)
Elixir De Nutz (Fr)
The Big Breakaway (Ire)

Nigel Twiston-Davies
Beauport (Ire)
Broadway Boy (Ire)
Gowel Road (Ire)
I Like To Move It
Torn And Frayed (Fr)
Weveallbeencaught (Ire)
Zambella (Fr)

Mark Walford
Into Overdrive

Ted Walsh
Any Second Now (Ire)

Philip Hobbs & Johnson White
Camprond (Fr)
Thyme Hill
Zanza (Ire)

Christian Williams
Kitty's Light

Evan Williams
Annsam

Venetia Williams
Brave Seasca (Fr)
Cloudy Glen (Ire)
Easy As That (Ire)
Fanion D'Estruval (Fr)
Funambule Sivola (Fr)
L'Homme Presse (Fr)
Pink Legend
Royale Pagaille (Fr)

RACING POST

INDEX OF HORSES

A Dream To Share 111, 140, 200
A Plus Tard 111, 150
Abbeyhill 60
Absolute Notions 111
Afadil 70, 111
Affordale Fury 99, 111
Ahoy Senor 100, 111, 190
Ain't That A Shame 111
Al Dancer 112
Alien Storm 54
Allaho 112
Allegorie De Vassy 112, 163
Altobelli 19-20, 112
Amarillo Sky 113
American Mike 113
Amirite 113
Amrons Sage 26
An Epic Song 113
Andy Dufresne 113
Angels Dawn 113
Anno Power 20
Annsam 113
Any Biscuits 10
Any News 60-61
Any Second Now 114
Apple Away 36, 114
Appreciate It 114, 143
Ascending 114
Ascending Lark 10
Ashdale Bob 115
Ashroe Diamond 115
Ashtown Lad 115
Ask Lileen 36
Aspire Tower 115
Asterion Forlonge 115
Attacca 27, 115
Aucunrisque 115
Aurora Vega 116
Authorised Speed 116
Authorized Art 117
Aye Right 117
Azof Des Mottes 102
Baby Shally 36
Balco Coastal 117
Balkardy 84-85
Ballyburn 117
Ballydesmond 80
Ballygrifincottage 117
Baltray 45
Banbridge 117
Bavington Bob 102
Beat The Bat 20
Beau Balko 69
Beauport 118
Bella Civena 8
Bellas Bridge 80
Beny Nahar Road 71

Better Days Ahead 118
Bialystok 118
Big Fish 44-45
Bill Baxter 118-120
Blackjack Magic 35, 36
Blairgowrie 26
Blazing Khal 120, 173
Blenkinsop 102-103
Blizzard Of Oz 120, 125
Blood Destiny 120
Blow Your Wad 120, 121
Blue Lord 120, 128, 150
Blueking D'Oroux 70, 120
Bo Zenith 121
Bob Olinger 121
Dold Fndeavour 26, 121
Book Of Tales 55
Boom Boom 26
Boothill 17, 18, 121-122
Botox Has 122
Brandy Love 122
Brave Seasca 122
Bravemansgame 32, 64-66, 89, 100, 122, 142, 150
Brentford Hope 8
Bretney 103
Brewin'Upastorm 122, 123
Brief Times 62
Brighterdaysahead 122
Broadway Boy 123
Bronn 123
Brookie 35-36
Broomfield Present 124
Broomfields Cave 61
Bubble Dubi 104
Buddy One 124
Busselton 125
Byorderofthecourt 71
Calico 125
Call Me Lord 25
Call To Duty 44
Camprond 125
Can You Call 85
Capodanno 125
Captain Cody 125
Captain Guinness 35, 120, 125, 166, 186
Captain Morgs 26
Captain Teague 70, 126
Castle Robin 52
Celtic Fortune 61
Champ 25, 126
Champ Kiely 127
Chantry House 26, 27
Chasing Fire 127
Cheddleton 126, 127
Chemical Energy 127
Choccabloc 29

Churchstonewarrior 127, 145, 172
City Chief 26, 127
Classic Getaway 127-128, 174
Classic King 41-42
Cloudy Glen 128
Coeur Sublime 128
Coko Beach 128
Collectors Item 128
Colonel Harry 79, 108, 128
Colonel Mustard 128
Colonial Empire 104
Comfort Zone 128-130
Complete Unknown 66-67, 130
Conflated 130-131, 137
Constitution Hill 22-25, 26, 27, 29, 89, 90, 92, 98, 131, 192
Cool Survivor 131
Coquelicot 35, 36
Corach Rambler 100, 130, 131
Corbetts Cross 131
Country Lady 71
Court Master 62-63
Crambo 131
Crebilly 131
Credo 36
Credrojava 19, 21
Crest Of Fortune 36
Crest Of Glory 31, 32, 36
Crystal Glory 131-132
Dancing On My Own 132
Darasso 187
Dargiannini 8
Dartmoor Pirate 32
Dashel Drasher 132-133
Datsalrightgino 72, 74, 75, 80, 133
De Rasher Counter 41, 45
De Tellers Fortune 29
Delta Work 133, 150, 165
Dinoblue 133
Do Your Job 133
Doctor Bravo 133
Doctor Ken 133
Doddiethegreat 26, 133-134
Does He Know 134
Double Powerful 59
Doughmore Bay 42
Douglas Talking 134-135
Down Memory Lane 135
Doyen Star 86
Duc Du Rene 87
Dunvegan 135
Dusart 26, 135

Dysart Dynamo 135
Dysart Enos 135
East India Express 29
Easy As That 135
Echoes In Rain 136
Editeur Du Gite 136, 181
Edwardstone 98, 136, 150, 153
Eklat De Rire 137
El Fabiolo 25, 26, 98, 117, 135, 137, 163, 166
Eldorado Allen 137
Elixir De Nutz 137
Elvis Mail 137
Embassy Gardens 137
Emir Sacree 26
Energumene 35, 98, 125, 138
Enjoy The Dream 120, 138
Envoi Allen 138
Erne River 138
Espoir De Romay 138
Etalon 106
Everyonesacritic 87
Excelerator Express 62
Facile Vega 94, 113, 116, 138, 160, 173, 185
Fact To File 138-140
Faivoir 140
Fakir D'Oudaires 140, 183
Famous Clermont 141
Fanion D'Estruval 141
Fantastic Lady 142
Farland 71
Farnoge 71
Fastorslow 100, 131, 142
Favori De Champdou 142
Fennor Cross 94, 142
Ferns Lock 143
Ferny Hollow 143, 175
Feronily 108, 143
Fidelio Vallis 106
Fierce Warrior 29
Fil Dor 143
Filey Bay 143
Fils D'Oudairies 143
Final Orders 142, 143
Fire Flyer 71
Firefox 144
First Flow 144
First Street 27, 144
Flame Bearer 144, 191
Flanking Maneuver 145
Flash Collonges 67
Flooring Porter 145
Florencethemachine 71
Florida Dreams 145
Followango 87

206

INDEX OF HORSES

Fontana Ellissi 106, 107
Fortuna Ligna 36
Forward Plan 34
Found A Fifty 145
Foxy Girl 146
Franco De Port 146
French Dynamite 146
Frodon 66, 147
Fugitif 147
Fun Fun Fun 147
Funambule Sivola 147
Fury Road 147
Ga Law 75-76, 147
Gaelic Park 54
Gaelic Warrior 99, 100, 111, 142, 148
Gaillard Du Mesnil 148
Gala Marceau 148
Galia Des Liteaux 148-150
Galopin Des Champs 66, 89, 100, 121, 122, 142, 150, 193
Galvin 150
Geezer Rockstar 10, 20
General Medrano 42
Gentleman De Mee 120, 150
Gentleman Jacques 55
Gentleman's Relish 29
Gentlemansgame 150
Gericault Roque 150
Gerri Colombe 100, 117, 123, 130, 150, 197
Gesskille 151
Gidleigh Park 19
Gin Coco 17, 151
Giovinco 106, 151
Git Maker 76-78
Givega 151
Glimpse Of Gala 52, 54
Golden Son 70
Good Land 89-90, 151
Good Risk At All 151
Good Time Jonny 151
Goodtimecrew 20
Goshen 152, 167
Gowel Road 152, 188
Grangeclare West 152
Greaneteen 66, 152-153
Great Snow 20
Grey Dawning 153
Grey Diamond 153
Guetapan Collonges 51
Gust Of Wind 153
Ha D'Or 153
Haddex Des Obeaux 153
Halka Du Tabert 153
Hang In There 45
Hansard 90, 153-154
Happygolucky 154

Hardy Fella 42
Harper's Brook 154
Haut En Couleurs 154
Hawaii Du Mestivel 56-58
Hector Javilex 52, 53
Heltenham 154-155
Henri The Second 70
Henry Box Brown 87
Hercule Du Seuil 155
Hermes Allen 69, 155, 166
Hewick 142, 144, 154, 155
Hiddenvalley Lake 155
High Class Hero 155
Highstakesplayer 155
Hillcrest 132
Hipop Des Ongrais 104
Hitman 67, 155-156
Hollow Games 156
Home By The Lee 115, 156, 173
How Will I Know 21
Howlingmadmurdock 156-157
Hugos New Horse 69, 158
Hunters Yarn 158
Hurricane Highway 87
Hymac 20-21
I Am Maximus 158
I Like To Move It 158
I Will Be Baie 158
Iberico Lord 27, 158
Iceo 70, 160
Iceo Madrik 106-107
Ideal Des Bordes 29
Idy Wood 80
Ike Sport 60
Il Etait Temps 160
Il Ridoto 67, 161
Il Va De Soi 10
Immortal 29
Impaire Et Passe 89, 90-92, 94, 98, 99, 100, 127, 148, 161
Impervious 162, 163, 166, 183
Impose Toi 27, 162
Indeevar Bleu 162
Indiana Dream 162-163
Indiana Jones 163
Inneston 163
Inoui Machin 59-60
Instit 163
Inthepocket 94, 163, 194, 198
Inthewaterside 70, 163
Into Overdrive 163
Iolaos Du Mou 29
Irandando Has 71
Irish Point 92, 164

Iroko 164
Issuing Authority 29
It's For Me 165
Iwilldoit 165
James Du Berlais 165
Janidil 165
Jayapura 54
Jazzy Matty 165
Jet Powered 27, 165
Jetoile 165-166
Jetronic 70
Jingko Blue 29
Johnny Blue 29
Johnnywho 166
Jonbon 18, 25-26, 27, 98, 99, 125, 137, 166
Journey With Me 166, 170
Junta Marvel 166
Kabral Du Mathan 71
Kalanisi Star 58
Kateira 166
Kilbeg King 32-34, 36, 166
Kilcruit 166-167
King Alexander 25
Kintail 29
Kitesurfer 80
Kitty's Light 100, 167
Klassical Dream 100, 115, 167
Knappers Hill 69, 167
Knowsley Road 70, 167
Kym Eyre 85, 86
Lac De Constance 167
Lahinch Wave 59
Lallygag 69
Langer Dan 168
Larchmont Lass 71
L'Astroboy 84, 85
Le Milos 168
Leave Of Absence 108
Lecky Watson 170
Letsbeclearaboutit 170
L'Homme Presse 100, 122, 154, 163, 167
Liari 71
Libberty Hunter 86-87
Lifetime Ambition 170
Lime Avenue 70
Limerick Lace 170
Longhouse Poet 170
Lookaway 170
Lord Accord 56-57, 60
Lossiemouth 130, 138, 148, 170, 203
Love Envoi 14-17, 122, 171
Luccia 171
Lucky Place 29
Magical Zoe 171

Mahler Mission 145, 171-172
Major Dundee 172
Makin'yourmindup 70, 128, 172
Malystic 172
Manorbank 42-44
Manothepeople 172
Marble Sands 172
Marie's Rock 100, 172
Marine Nationale 89, 94, 95, 164, 173
Maskada 173
Matterhorn 70
Maximilian 173
Maxxum 173
McFabulous 173
Meatloaf 71
Meet And Greet 173
Metier 18
Midnight River 174
Might I 17-18, 174
Milkwood 58, 60
Mill Green 25
Millers Bank 174
Minella Blueway 87
Minella Cocooner 174
Minella Crooner 80, 175
Minella Drama 175
Minella Indo 175, 192
Minella Missile 87
Mint Condition 54-55
Mirazur West 175
Miss Applejack 54-55
Mister Coffey 26, 175
Mister Policeman 175
Mojo Ego 10
Monbeg Genius 175-176
Monbeg Park 176
Monjules 18, 21
Monkfish 176
Monks Meadow 45
Monmiral 176
Montecam 29
Monty's Star 176
Monviel 10, 11
Moonset 58-59
Moroder 177
Mr Freedom 108
Mr Incredible 177
Mucho Mas 177
My Drogo 177
My Silver Lining 40, 41
Mystical Power 177
Nassalam 177
Nemean Lion 108, 177
New Order 55
Nick Rockett 178
Night And Day 178

RACING POST

INDEX OF HORSES

No Looking Back 178
No Ordinary Joe 27, 178
Noble Yeats 180
Not So Sleepy 180
Notlongtillmay 181
Nube Negra 180, 181
Nusret 181
Obsessedwithyou 79
On The Blind Side 25
O'Toole 181
Our Power 181
Out Of Office 87
Outlaw Peter 70, 181
Pageant Material 86
Paint The Dream 181
Paisley Park 39-40, 182
Panjari 71
Park Hill Dancer 29
Park Princess 36
Park This One 79-80
Parramount 50
Passing Well 79
Pawapuri 96
Peaky Boy 52
Pembroke 96, 182
Pentire Head 71
Persian Time 26
Petit Tonnerre 108
Pic D'Orhy 66, 140, 174, 175, 183
Picks Lad 10, 11
Pied Piper 183
Pink Legend 183
Porter In The Park 40-41
Premier Magic 183
Proschema 183
Protektorat 183
Punctuation 184
Qualimata 184
Queen Annie 20
Queens Brook 184
Queens Gamble 10, 11, 135
Quel Destin 184, 185
Quilixios 185
Quoi De Neuf 86
Ragamuffin 60, 61

Rare Edition 48-50, 58, 185
Rare Middleton 70
Reach For The Moon 78
Readin Tommy Wrong 185
Realisation 52-54
Red Rookie 44-45
Redemption Day 185
Remastered 185
Richmond Lake 185-186
Risk Belle 186
Riviere D'Etel 186-187
Rock House 29
Rock My Way 187, 201
Roger Pol 80
Royale Pagaille 187
Rubaud 69, 185, 187
Run Wild Fred 187
Russian Ruler 26, 54
Sabrina 70
Sail Away 186, 187
Saint Felicien 187
Saint Roi 187-188
Saint Sam 188
Sainte Doctor 60
Salsada 108
Salvatore 10
Sam Brown 32, 35, 188
Samarrive 188
San Francisco 80
Sandor Clegane 188
Santos Blue 104-105
Scandisk Park 29
Sceau Royal 188
Scrum Diddly 10
Secret Reprieve 83-84
Seddon 188-190
Seelotmorebusiness 4-7
Seeyouinmydreams 71, 190
Shakem Up'Arry 190
Shanagh Bob 29
Shanbally Kid 190
Shannon Royale 190
Sharjah 89, 115, 190
Shishkin 25, 26, 27, 100, 111, 138, 183, 190
Shuil Ceoil 61

Silver Jet 20
Silver Thorn 45
Sir Gerhard 144, 190-191
Sire Du Berlais 99, 100, 133, 172, 191
Siroco Jo 10
So Scottish 191
Solo 66, 192
Somespring Special 34
Sonigino 69, 192
Southoftheborder 29
Spanish Harlem 192
Springwell Bay 192
Stage Star 66, 133, 192
State Man 98, 128, 192, 193
Stattler 192-193
Stay Away Fay 68, 69, 96-97, 111, 173, 193
Steal A March 193
Stolen Silver 193
Straw Fan Jack 193-194
Strong Leader 194
Strutter 29
Stumptown 194
Super Survivor 78-79
Tahmuras 69, 84, 195
Tarahumara 41
Tarras Wood 71
Tea For Free 50-51, 195
Teahupoo 100, 195
Testflight 105
Thames Water 71
The Big Breakaway 195
The Big Doyen 194, 195
The Carpenter 26, 195
The Goffer 55, 195-196
The Nice Guy 174, 196
The Real Whacker 100, 150, 176, 196-197
The Two Amigos 196, 197
The Two Harrys 8-10
The Yellow Clay 197
Theatre Glory 197
Thedevilscoachman 197
Third Time Lucki 197
Thomas Darby 197

Three Card Brag 198
Three Cliffs Bay 87
Threeunderthrufive 66, 198
Thunder Rock 198
Thyme Hill 198
Tightenourbelts 41, 42
Tinklers Hill 71
Tommy's Oscar 198
Torn And Frayed 198
Tornado Flyer 200
Torneo 80
Tour Ovalie 87
Trelawne 200
Tullyhill 111, 200
Twinjets 200
Two For Gold 200
Under Control 200
Unexpected Party 201
Vanillier 201
Vauban 192, 201
Wakool 201
Walking On Air 26, 27
Walkinthewoods 85, 86
Watergrange Jack 61-62
Well Dick 55
Well Vicky 105
Wendigo 80
West Balboa 201
Western Diego 201
Western Zephyr 55
Weveallbeencaught 201
Whistleinthedark 202
Willmount 202, 203
Wiseguy 26
Wrappedupinmay 70
You Oughta Know 202
You Wear It Well 72, 73-75, 79, 155, 202
Zambella 202
Zanahiyr 202
Zanza 202-203
Zarak The Brave 130, 203
Zenta 121, 203